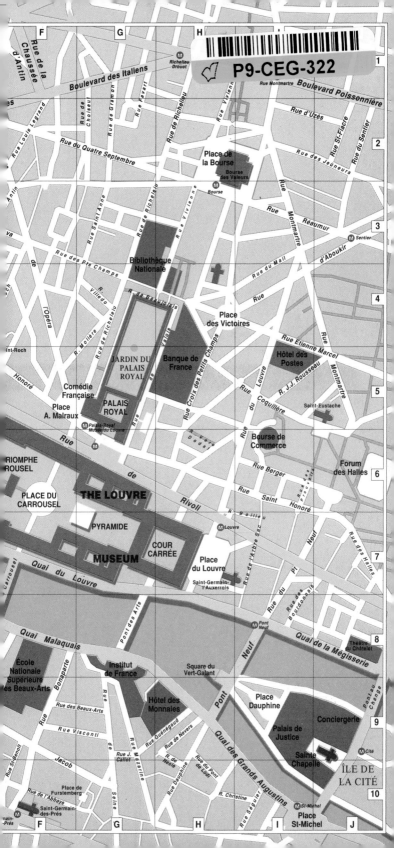

DAVID JACQUES LOUIS 1748-1825
LES SABINES ARRÊTANT LE COMBAT ENTRE
LES ROMAINS ET LES SABINS

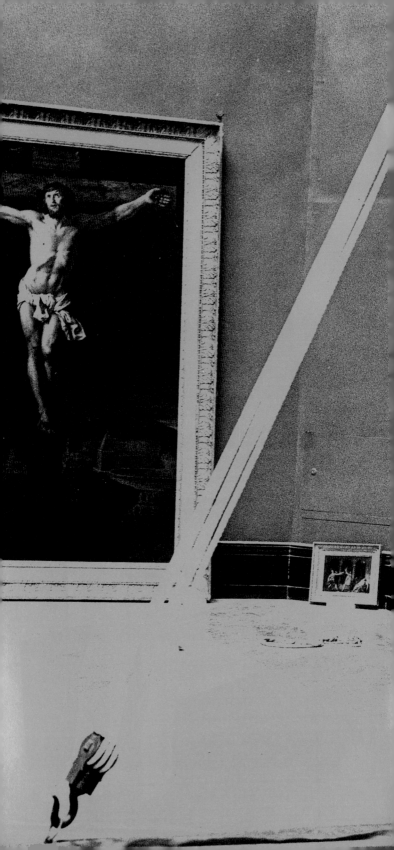

**NUMEROUS SPECIALISTS AND ACADEMICS
HAVE CONTRIBUTED TO THIS GUIDE:**

GUIDE TO THE LOUVRE
EDITORS: Elisabeth de Farcy and
Frédéric Morvan
Assisted by:
Maylis de Kerangal, Soraya Khalidy,
Frédérique Jubien, Clarisse Deniau,
Béatrice Méneux and, for the practical
information, Claire Forgeot, Philippe
Gallois, Odile George, Grégory Leroy
LAYOUT: Natacha Kotlarevsky
PRACTICAL INFORMATION LAYOUT:
François Chentrier and Olivier Brunot
PICTURE RESEARCH: Isabelle de Latour
ILLUSTRATIONS: Philippe Biard,
Jean-Michel Kacédan, Dominique
Duplantier, Laure Massin
PHOTOGRAPHY: Patrick Léger,
Patrick Horvais; Michel Chassat for the
Louvre Museum
COORDINATION:
ARCHITECTURE: Bruno Lenormand
MAPS: Vincent Brunot
NATURE: Philippe J. Dubois, Frédéric Bony
PHOTOGRAPHY: Éric Guillemot,
Patrick Léger

THE TEXTS FOR THIS GUIDE WERE WRITTEN
BY THE EDITORIAL DEPARTMENT OF GUIDES
GALLIMARD, WITH THE EXCEPTION OF THE
FOLLOWING SECTIONS:

NATURE (pages 15 to 24):
Pierre-Jean Trombetta and
Guilhem Lesaffre
HISTORY (pages 25 to 48), itinerary in
THE LOUVRE AND ITS HISTORY (pages 121 to
132) and **THE LOUVRE AS SEEN BY PAINTERS**
(pages 87 to 96): Geneviève Bresc
ARTS AND TRADITIONS and
BEHIND THE SCENES (pages 49 to 70):
Marc Plocki and Françoise Mardrus
THE LOUVRE THROUGH VISITORS'S EYES (pages
97 to 112): Jean Galard; texts
taken from Les Visiteurs du Louvre,
RMN, 1993, in collaboration with
Anne-Laure Charrier
ITINERARIES AROUND THE LOUVRE QUARTER
(pages 273 to 312): Vincent Bouvet
ITINERARIES FOR PRACTICAL INFORMATION
SECTION: Violaine Bouvet-Lanselle

RÉUNION DES MUSÉES NATIONAUX
EDITORIAL AND COMMERCIAL SERVICES
Jean-François Chougnet
Caroline Larroche
Anne de Margerie
Michel Richard

GUIDES GALLIMARD AND THE
RÉUNION DES MUSÉES NATIONAUX
WOULD LIKE TO THANK ALL THOSE
WHO CONTRIBUTED TO THIS GUIDE.

ENGLISH LANGUAGE EDITION CO-ORDINATED BY EVERYMAN'S LIBRARY, LONDON:
TRANSLATED BY SUSAN MACKERVOY, ANTHONY ROBERTS AND SIMON DALGLEISH.
EDITED AND TYPESET BY BOOK CREATION SERVICES, LONDON.
PRINTED IN FRANCE BY HERISSEY.

THE LOUVRE

KNOPF GUIDES

CONTENTS

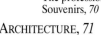

AROUND THE LOUVRE

1 Cour Napoléon 2 Cour Carrée 3 Carrousel 4 Jardin des Tuileries 5 Orangerie 6 Jeu de Paume 7 Place de la Concorde 8 Pont de la Concorde 9 Passerelle Solférino 10 Pont-Royal 11 Pont du Carrousel 12 Passerelle des Arts 13 Rue Royale 14 Église de la Madeleine

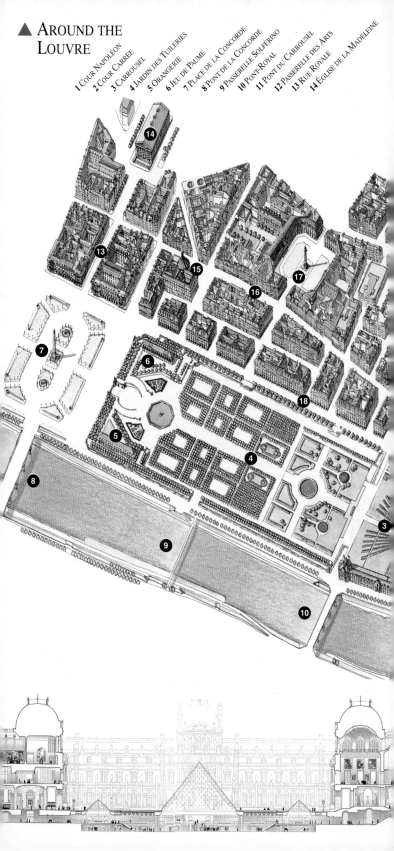

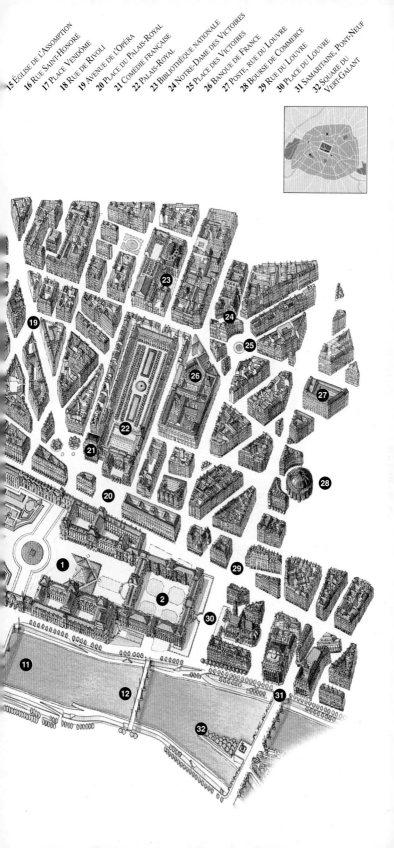

How to use this guide

The symbols at the top of each page refer to the different parts of the guide.

- ■ NATURE
- ● KEYS TO UNDERSTANDING
- ▲ ITINERARIES
- ◆ PRACTICAL INFORMATION

The itinerary map at the start of each section shows the numbered rooms referred to and the main stairways.

Each section is marked in a different color; the color-code chart is given on pages 114–15, and page 317.

The color-coding used here is the same as that used in the museum itself.

The mini map of the museum shows the location of a particular section and its position in relation to the Pyramid.

Information is given showing the relevant section (SULLY, DENON or RICHELIEU) and floor(s) for the different works.

The symbols alongside title or within the text itself provide cross-references to a theme place dealt with elsewhere in the guic

---

NOTE: The Louvre consists of five levels which have been translated throughout this guide as follows:

Entresol	=	Entresol
Mezzanine	=	Mezzanine
Rez-de-chaussée	=	Ground floor
Premier étage	=	First floor
Deuxième étage	=	Second floor

Owing to the current reorganization of the Louvre, due for completion in 1997, information on the various collections has been presented in two different forms: the sections that are now complete are shown on the white pages within the itinerary section. Those sections which are currently closed or undergoing changes are shown in the form of color spreads. Subsequent editions of this guide will include updated information as work proceeds.

NATURE

THE SITE

19th- and 20th-
century embankments
Medieval and modern
embankments
Alluvial silt
Ancient alluvial deposits
Coarse limestone

Escarpment

Remains of a 14th-century house, demolished when
city walls were built during the reign of Charles V

In this area of Paris, the bedrock
of coarse limestone and alluvial
gravel is overlaid with fertile silt deposits. As a result, it has
been continuously occupied from prehistoric times onward.
Below the area now covered by the Louvre and the Tuileries the
traces of human occupation can be found in layers extending
from the Neolithic age to modern times. From the layers came
the sparse evidence of our earliest ancestors' brief presence, the
remains of large medieval private houses, the city walls of Paris
and the tilers' workshops after which the 16th-century palace
was named. All these pages in the great book of the capital's
history were uncovered during work on the Grand Louvre.

TOPOGRAPHY OF THE SITE
The site of the Louvre is a continuation,
at the far western tip, of the hill of St-
Germain-l'Auxerrois. To the south is an
alluvial bank over 110 feet high which
dominates the surrounding landscape.
To the north, protected by this
bank, is a plain which slopes
down gently toward the
Rue St-Honoré.

ORNAMENTAL NAIL-CLEANER
This nail- and ear-cleaner made of bone in the
shape of a unicorn, dates from the 14th century.

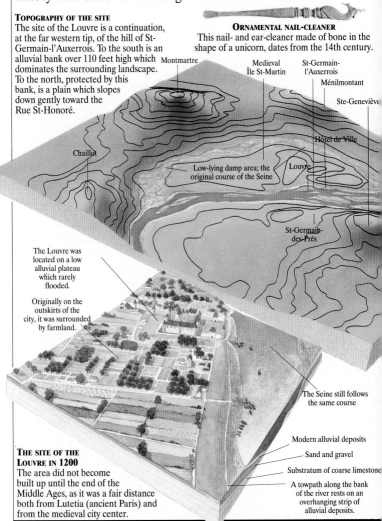

Montmartre

Medieval
Île St-Martin

St-Germain-
l'Auxerrois

Ménilmontant

Ste-Geneviève

Chaillot

Hôtel de Ville

Low-lying damp area; the
original course of the Seine

Louvre

The Louvre was
located on a low
alluvial plateau
which rarely
flooded.

St-Germain-
des-Prés

Originally on the
outskirts of the
city, it was surrounded
by farmland.

The Seine still follows
the same course

Modern alluvial deposits

Sand and gravel

Substratum of coarse limestone

A towpath along the bank
of the river rests on an
overhanging strip of
alluvial deposits.

THE SITE OF THE
LOUVRE IN 1200
The area did not become
built up until the end of the
Middle Ages, as it was a fair distance
both from Lutetia (ancient Paris) and
from the medieval city center.

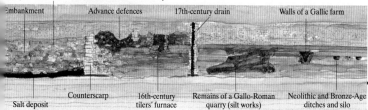

City walls of Charles V modified in the 16th century

Embankment   Advance defences   17th-century drain   Walls of a Gallic farm

Salt deposit   Counterscarp   16th-century tilers' furnace   Remains of a Gallo-Roman quarry (silt works)   Neolithic and Bronze-Age ditches and silo

CROSS-SECTION OF THE COUR DU CARROUSEL
Excavations brought a large number of objects to light, as well as the remains of buildings.

NEOLITHIC REMAINS
Neolithic and protohistoric pots.

SMALL GALLIC NECROPOLIS
The tombs dating from the end of the 1st century AD were partially destroyed by a Gallo-Roman quarry.

14TH-CENTURY JUGS
These vessels were made to hold liquids, particularly wine. The vase on the right has a remarkable tortoiseshell decoration.

LEAD-SMELTERS' WORKSHOP
This 14th-century workshop was devoted to lead smelting; below are the refining furnaces, above is the forge.

astille

Butte-aux-Cailles

Seine

Bièvre

GLASS
The shape and the white-colored decoration of this stemmed glass are typical of the 14th century.

16TH-CENTURY POTTERY
Everyday objects: dishes, bowls, small bottles and jugs.

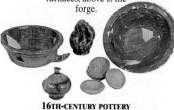

19TH-CENTURY PIPE BOWLS
One of five hundred pipe bowls discovered, this one depicts a soldier in the colonial army.

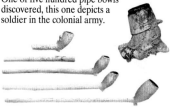

17TH- AND 18TH-CENTURY CLAY PIPES
More than 60 manufacturers and 50 different styles have been identified. Pipe bowls became larger as the price of tobacco fell.

TILERS AT THE TUILERIES
Around a dozen ovens have been discovered on this site, indicating that a large number of tilers' workshops were located here from the end of the 13th century to the 16th century. In the vault on the lefthand side a worker kept the fire burning. The heat was carried through two channels (*alandiers*) baking the tiles laid out in the heating chamber on the right.

17

■ MATERIALS OF THE LOUVRE

Pieces of classical sculpture arranged in front of the Louvre's Petite Galerie, as depicted by Hubert Robert ● 88.

The Louvre features a remarkable range of building materials, from the limestone of the building's main body, the brickwork contributed by the Industrial Revolution, to 20th-century concrete. Marble completes the picture; the Louvre offers an infinite variety of marbles, from the very whitest reserved for sculpture, to the most richly colored which decorate floors, walls and plinths. I.M. Pei's Louvre also holds its own, owing its combination of brilliance and sobriety to the use of Burgundian stone.

PARIS LIMESTONE
The stones used to build the medieval Louvre ▲ 122 came from quarries in the Paris basin; many bear marks made by the workers.

CONFLANS STONE
Percier and Fontaine used very fine limestone in the Salle des Cariatides ▲ 125, enabling the sculptor to produce this delicate ornamentation.

VERMICULATED STONE
The Île-de-France stone in the Cour du Sphinx ▲ 126 was worked in the 17th century. The quality of the stone itself is overshadowed by the random carved motif.

IMPERIAL MARBLE
Napoleon I's architects looked to antiquity and Italy for inspiration. They used the finest white Carrara marble which contrasts with the more veined French marble.

IMPERIAL BRICKWORK
Napoleon III's stables ▲ 132, which today provide a perfect setting for Italian sculpture, are constructed of vaulted brickwork with limestone supports.

MOLDED CONCRETE
Pei used two types of concrete: for the Hall Napoléon he used a fine white one; in the medieval Louvre he used a rough gray concrete imprinted with wooden planks.

This engraving shows the enormous stones used to build the pediment of the Colonnade in 1672.

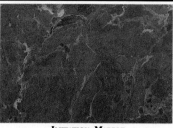

IMITATION MARBLE
Since 1935 the walls of Anne of Austria's apartments have been covered with stucco work which looks just like marble, providing a good backdrop for Roman sculptures ▲ 178.

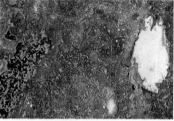

GRAY MARBLE
A gray marble with the traces of brown, red and white typical of Belgian quarries, can be seen in the Greek sculpture rooms of the Louvre ▲ 166.

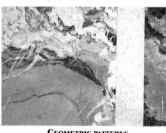

GEOMETRIC PATTERNS
Marbles lend themselves to the creation of ornamental floors like that in the Galerie Michel-Ange ▲ 195, which uses a variety of French marbles including some from Corsica.

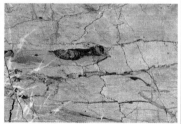

PLINTHS
In the 19th century a variety of colored marbles was used to make the plinths, including the serancolin marble shown here, as well as cracked and sea-green marbles.

GRAFFITI
Graffiti from 1862 can be seen on this close-up of the wall in the Rotonde d'Apollon ▲ 126. The delicate yellow marble is threaded with fine blue and gray veins.

EXPLOSION OF COLOR
The marble used to decorate the Musée Charles X ▲ 128 at the beginning of the 19th century is one of the most spectacular and colorful in the Louvre.

CHASSAGNE STONE
The stone of Chassagne (Burgundy), seen here with rose tints, goes perfectly with the marble sculptures of the Cour Marly ▲ 188, one of Louis XIV's favorite haunts.

BURGUNDY STONE
The newly opened Richelieu wing is faced in a very close-grained white stone which has been highly polished to produce a pleasing satin-smooth surface.

Thanks to progress in water treatment processes, the water of the Seine is now less polluted than it has been for many years. The present cloudy appearance of the water is due simply to suspended mineral particles. As a result of this significant improvement in water quality, aquatic plants have been reintroduced and over twenty species of fish have returned, even in the stretch of the river which runs through the city center. There is also the winter parade of seagulls with their circling flight, giving the city an unexpected seaside atmosphere.

Male

Female

Herring gull

Yellow-backed gull

GRAY WAGTAIL
The wagtail scurries along the quays, pecking away as it runs.

HERRING AND LESSER BLACK-BACKED GULLS
The herring gull can be seen throughout the year but is more common in winter. The black-backed gull is a seasonal visitor and can be spotted mainly in summer and autumn. Both species adapt well to town life.

KINGFISHER
A migrant bird that is generally seen in Paris in autumn and in spring.

MALE MALLARD
These ducks are quite tame but cautious, especially during the nesting season. Variations of plumage are common.

COOT
Only in winter can a few coots be seen on the river, driven there from frozen ponds near the capital.

Two centuries ago the Seine was used as a trading route, a washing-place and a watering-place for animals; it also had high levels of organic pollution.

DACE
This fish can tolerate poor-quality water better than other species.

GUDGEON
Gudgeon are very gregarious fish, swimming along the river bed in shoals.

ON THE RIVERBANKS
The riverside ▲ 306 supports plants well-suited to the conditions, both above and below water-level. Plants which thrive in damp conditions grow in the tiniest crevices.

PIKE
This powerful, well-armed predator feeds on other fish, crayfish or ducklings.

The pretty spikes of purple loosestrife can be seen from May to August.

Mosses and algae flourish close to outflows.

Young, hardy wall rocket manages to survive in cracks.

BREAM
With their flat, curved bodies adult bream stay in deep water during the day.

ROACH
Shoals of roach thread through the underwater vegetation.

Curled pondweed

The introduced aquatic vegetation attracts the fish.

Water milfoil

THE TUILERIES

ENGLISH OAK
An English (or pedunculate) oak, the
only example of its species in the Tuileries,
was planted to mark the bicentenary
of the French Revolution.

Through the changing seasons of
the year, the Tuileries gardens is inhabited by an astonishing
range of wildlife, often hidden from view. Insects, fish and birds
make up a complete animal population that flourishes in the
trees, among the flowers, on stones and in the water. Migrant
birds from distant lands can be found in the trees and sky above
the Tuileries. The plant kingdom is represented not only by trees
of various species but also by a range of wild plants which grow
up at random, and often fall victim to the gardeners' efforts.

Spring
plumage

Winter
plumage

STARLING
This bird walks across
the lawns of the
Tuileries in small
groups looking for
insect larvae.

TREECREEPER
This small climbing
bird with its bark-
colored plumage
often goes unnoticed
by visitors.

**LESSER SPOTTED
WOODPECKER**
Scarcely bigger than a
sparrow, this
woodpecker is seen
mainly in winter.

DUNNOCK
The dunnock with its
delicate slate-gray
coloring creeps under
the bushes, hidden
from view.

Lime leaf

Maple leaf

Horse chestnut leaf

The Tuileries ▲ *278* has a dense covering of nearly 3,000 trees belonging to around thirty species. Horse chestnuts and limes predominate, but maples, elms, and ornamental trees are also found in the gardens.

MAGPIE
From the end of the winter the magpie builds its nest of twigs high up in a chestnut or plane tree.

JAY
Despite its raucous screeching cries the jay is difficult to spot among the foliage.

WOODPIGEON
This pigeon can be identified by the white patch on its neck and its white wing patches.

CARP
Shoals of carp flourish in the two large ornamental lakes of the Tuileries; they are so successful that some must be removed from time to time to prevent overcrowding.

Male

Female

BLACKBIRD
One of the most common birds of the Tuileries. The male is identified by its ebony plumage, which contrasts with the brown and speckled tones of his mate.

ANIMALS OF THE LOUVRE

KESTREL
It is not unusual to see a kestrel
wheeling above the palace before
settling on a chimney or a roof.

Old buildings provide many opportunities for
nearby animals and birds. Crevices in walls,
carved motifs, cornices and roof trussings offer
homes to those species which have adapted to
man-made sites. The Louvre has its own habitual
residents. Birds are the most common of these,
but some unexpected mammals, like bats, have also settled here.
All seem unperturbed by the noise and movement of the
constant flow of tourists.

BLACK REDSTART
In the summer this
pretty little bird can
be seen hunting
around for insects on
the roofs.

HOUSE MARTIN
On its return from
Africa the house martin
seeks out its nest made
of mud hanging under a
cornice.

HOUSE SPARROW
The smallest of
cavities can provide a
home for this
opportunist little
sparrow.

PIPISTRELLE BAT
In the evening a few
of these small bats
can be seen flying
around the museum
buildings.

SWIFT
From the end of April to August,
swifts streak through the sky before
plunging into their nesting holes.

HISTORY

1066	1099		1180–1223	1226–70
Battle of	1st Crusade and		Reign of	Reign of
Hastings	capture of Jerusalem		Philippe Auguste	Louis IX

| 1000 | 1050 | | 1100 | 1150 | 1200 | 1250 | 13 |

	1187	1214
	Construction of	Bouvines
	St Thomas' church	
	at the Louvre	

The "Pietà of St-Germain-des-Prés", painted around 1500, features a rare depiction of the medieval Louvre. Here we see the fortress façade overlooking the Seine, viewed from the left bank.

THE BEGINNING TO CHARLES V

BEGINNINGS

Recent excavations have revealed traces of protohistoric habitation to the west of the Île de la Cité on the north bank of the Seine. A bank of clay has preserved the remains from the effect of floods ● *16*.

In the Gallo-Roman period this area on the outskirts of Lutetia was farmland. Ditches, various types of boundary and clay quarries have been discovered here. Today's Rue St-Honoré follows the course of the road which connected this district with the town to the east.

Under the reign of Philippe Auguste, Paris became the capital of France. Faced with the town's rapid growth and the increasing military resources required to defend it, the king ordered his citizens to build a town wall. In 1190 when the king left for the Crusades, the decision was taken to enclose the town with a strong rampart. On the river side it was to have a royal fortress which would function as an outpost of the palace in the city with the aim of countering potential invaders from the Seine; the Louvre was born. It was a flatland chateau with a circular keep placed at the center of a solid quadrangle of walls defended by towers. In 1214 in the Bouvines Philippe Auguste's army

THE MEDIEVAL LOUVRE

overcame a coalition of German, Flemish and English troops to defend the kingdom. The Louvre gradually lost its strategic function as a military bulwark and prison. The western suburbs of the city were growing, and Étienne Marcel, the merchants' provost and leader of the town council, set up a new system of defense after the Paris Rebellion of 1358, surrounding the first wall with a second defensive structure larger than the first. Charles V ordered the completion of the new barrier which was reinforced by a wide moat. The Louvre then became a richly decorated royal residence which housed the king's

magnificent library of manuscripts (1360–4). After Charles V's death the English conquerors installed the young Henry V in the Louvre and the Regent Bedford acquired the royal library.

As the French fought to regain the kingdom, violent battles took place around Charles V's city walls. Joan of Arc was wounded at the Porte St-Honoré.

1348		1453	1517	1572	1598
Great Plague		Fall of	Beginning of the	St Bartholomew's	Edict of
		Byzantium	Reformation	Day Massacre	Nantes

| 1350 | 1400 | 1450 | 1500 | 1550 | 1600 | 1650 |

1358	1380		1528	1546	1594
Paris Rebellion	Death of		Destruction	Pierre Lescot	Henri IV
	Charles V		of the Louvre's	converts the Old	enters
			Great Tower	Louvre.	Paris

FROM THE RENAISSANCE TO THE FRONDE

THE RENAISSANCE PALACE

The kings of the 15th century neglected Paris and the Louvre in favor of other residences, notably the chateaux of the Loire. François I thought Philippe Auguste's tower too austere and had it demolished in 1528; in 1540 he organized festivities in honor of Charles V. In 1546, he commissioned his architect Pierre Lescot to replace one section of the old medieval rampart with a new wing. Henri II (1547–59) completed this project, as well as beginning a second wing at right angles to the first and added the sturdy Royal Pavilion overlooking the Seine, intended for the king's own apartments. Jean Goujon added sculptural details to the exterior. After Henri II's death his widow Catherine de' Medici had the Tuileries Palace built overlooking an Italian-style garden. At the same time Charles IX undertook further building work to connect the Royal Pavilion with the Seine by a small gallery, itself joined by a long passage to the Tuileries Palace along the river, completed in 1566. A new fortified city wall was constructed even further to the west, surrounding the Tuileries Gardens and the St-Honoré quarter.

THE GREAT BUILDERS

Two kings were the force behind the conversion of the Louvre: François I (opposite) and Henri IV (below, on the medallion). Henri IV was the first to plan a palace-complex, joining the two existing buildings (the Louvre and the Tuileries) i█ █e whole. He █████ his artists and his works of art here, and had mulberry trees planted to provide silk.

HENRI IV'S GRAND PLAN

Henri IV's ceremonial entry into Paris in 1594 after the civil war, confirmed Paris as France's political and cultural center. He made the Louvre into a "royal city", creating a hall

Fresco in the Galerie des Cerfs in Fontai████ illustrating Henri IV's Grand Plan

to house his classical treasures and installing his artists in the Grande Galerie built alongside the Seine by his architects Androuet du Cerceau and Métezeau. He planned to create a vast complex of courts between the Louvre and the Tuileries, but did not have the time to carry out his projects. He was stabbed by Ravaillac in 1610 and died at the Louvre, leaving power in the hands of the regency. Louis XIII took up where his father had left off. The painter Nicolas Poussin came back from Rome to decorate the interior of the Grande Galerie, while the architect Mercier was commissioned to make the Cour Carrée four times larger, and to build the Pavillon de l'Horloge along with its adjoining wing. This scheme was supported by the powerful Cardinal Richelieu who lived in the residence bearing his name between 1627 and 1633. After this Richelieu built the Palais-Cardinal, which became the Palais-Royal after it was bequeathed to the king in 1642. Anne of Austria later lived here with the young Louis XIV during the Regency. They fled to St-Germain during the turmoils of the Fronde in 1650 and again in 1651.

		1661–1715 Reign of Louis XIV	1685 Revocation of the Edict of Nantes			1715–74 Reign of Louis XV
1650	1660	1670	1680	1690	1700	1710	1720

1656–8 Romanelli's decorations at the Louvre	1665 Bernini's project	1660–99 The Academies move to the Louvre	1699 The first Salon at the Louvre	1711 Watteau's *Embarkation for the Island of Cythera*

FROM LOUIS XIV TO THE REVOLUTION

THE LOUVRE UNDER LOUIS XIV

Once peace had been restored, the king moved into the Louvre, where large-scale improvements were being carried out. The queen mother's apartments were sumptuously decorated; Romanelli's frescos and Anguier's stuccos can still be seen today ▲ 126, while a theater, the Salle des Machines, was built in the Tuileries. Under the personal reign of Louis XIV (above right), the last remnants of the medieval building were destroyed, while improvements and additions continued. The architect Le Vau rebuilt the terrace of the Petite Galerie (now the Galerie d'Apollon), which was destroyed by fire in 1661, and completed the enlargement of the Cour Carrée. In 1665 the architect Bernini, chosen by competition, was invited to Paris where he made plans for an oriental façade. However this very ambitious project never saw the light of day. It was superseded by a plan devised by a group of architects

headed by Claude Perrault, who built the Colonnade (below). The great and powerful of the kingdom inhabited the area around the

Louvre: Mazarin lived in the Hôtel Tubeuf, renamed Palais Mazarin; the former queen of England, the king's aunt lived in the Palais-Royal; her daughter Henriette, who married Philippe, Louis XIV's brother and later Duc d'Orléans, established the Bourbon-d'Orléans branch of the family in this palace. As for Louis XIV, he bought the Palais Brion, an outbuilding of the Palais-Royal, as a home for his first official mistress, Louise de la Vallière, and used the Hôtel du Petit Bourbon, next to St-Germain-l'Auxerrois, as a theater and a furniture store. Louis XIV's choice of Versailles as his official residence marked the end of royal residency in Paris.

THE ARTISTS' AND PHILOSOPHERS' QUARTER

This quarter lived under the shadow of the court. Residences such as the Hôtels de Longueville and de Rambouillet, where the "Précieuses" met (destroyed in 1850), as well as more modest houses, were the last homes of famous figures such as Corneille, who died in 1684, Mignard (Rue de Richelieu) in 1695, Rigaud (Rue Louis-le-Grand) in 1743, La Fontaine and indeed Molière, who paced up and down these streets the day before his final performance. The king gave his favorite artists the use of studios in the entresol of the Louvre gallery, the Tuileries Palace and the pavilions in the gardens. After his death, authors, actors and creative artists of all kinds moved out to the surrounding district. Academies were established at the Louvre, bringing with them their books and collections. The Academy of Painting and Sculpture set up its annual exhibition there (the Salon). The Louvre quarter became a hotbed of intellectual and artistic activity taking over from the Marais district opposite the Faubourg St-Germain. Philosophers frequented the salons of Mme Geoffrin in Rue St-Honoré, and of Helvetius in Rue Ste-Anne.

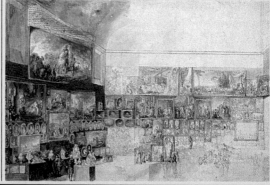

| 1730 | 1740 | 1751–80 Compilation of the *Encyclopédie* 1750 | 1760 | 1774–92 Reign of Louis XVI 1770 | July 14, 1789 Storming of the Bastille 1780 | August 10, 1792 Fall of the monarchy 1790 | 1800 |

1763 Port Royal destroyed by fire

1768–90 Plans for a museum at the Louvre

August 10, 1793 National museum opened at the Louvre

THE LOUVRE MUSEUM

The Louvre remained incomplete and abandoned, left to artists and courtiers. It became a subject of public debate in the age of Enlightenment, prompting demands for the palace to be completed and the royal collections to be opened to the public (these were soon exhibited in the Palais du Luxembourg). Gradually the plans for a Louvre museum took shape with the support of the Royal Directors of Buildings. The last of these, Angiviller, purchased paintings, commissioned statues of eminent figures and had pictures restored. The Revolution realized this plan and the museum, displaying mainly paintings by the old masters, was opened in the Grande Galerie on August 10, 1793, the anniversary of the monarchy's collapse. Works of art seized during military conquests were added to the collection and magnificent classical treasures were displayed in the former queen mother's apartments.

COMTE D'ANGIVILLER (1730–1809)

He was appointed Royal Director of Buildings in 1774, and was a member of both the Academy of Science and the Royal Academy of Painting and Sculpture. His major ambition was to open to the public a royal museum at the Louvre. In the portrait opposite he is shown proudly holding the plan of the Grande Galerie which was to house Louis XVI's museum.

THE TUILERIES, PALACE OF STATE

Louis XVI returned to the Tuileries in 1789 but was driven out again by the riot of August 10, 1792 (below). The Convention held session here before First Consul Bonaparte (right) made it his ceremonial palace. When he became Napoleon I, Emperor of France, he revived Henri IV's grand plan to combine the Louvre and the Tuileries. "Big is beautiful" he used to say and was delighted by the plan for an imperial city devised by his architects Percier and Fontaine. Yet the buildings completed by the fall of the Empire are few in number: part of the north wing (below) bordering the new Rue de Rivoli, a "Saint-Napoléon" chapel and the Arc de Triomphe, which

was built as a gateway to the Tuileries Gardens on the Carrousel in 1806.

1830
July
Revolution

1848
Revolution

1870
End of the
Second Empire

1871
Paris
Commune

1800   1820   1840   1860   1880   1900

1803
The Louvre:
Musée Napoléon

1826
Champollion
at the Egyptian
museum

1827
Naval
museum
established

1849–53
Restoration of
the Louvre, by
Félix Duban.

July 25, 1852
Visconti and Lefuel
begin work on New
Louvre.

May 23, 1871
Fire at the
Tuileries and
Palais-Royal

1882
Ruins of the
Tuileries
demolished

FROM THE RESTORATION TO THE GRAND LOUVRE

PALACE OF STATE AND GOVERNMENT

The Tuileries Palace was the residence of the head of state in Paris until 1870. The Louvre functioned partly as an administrative annexe. State openings of parliament took place in the Henri II wing until Napoleon III built a special chamber in his "New Louvre" (which now houses the museum ▲ 131). Charles X (below, presenting awards to artists at the Salon of 1827) installed the Conseil d'État (Council of State) in the ceremonial rooms of the Cour Carrée; it was moved to its current home at the Palais-Royal in 1871. The Ministry of Finance was located on the site of today's Hôtel Continental, Rue de Rivoli, before moving to the Rivoli wing of the Louvre from 1872 to 1989. The Ministry of Foreign Affairs was located in Rue des Capucines from 1820 until the Hôtel du Quai d'Orsay was built in 1853. The Ministry of Justice is located on the Place Vendôme. During the revolutionary era

An assembly held during the restoration in the State Room of the Henri II wing, where Greek bronzes are displayed today.

attacks and popular uprisings inevitably affected the government institutions. In 1820 the Duc de Berry was killed at the Opéra, then in the Square Louvois ▲ 298 (right). Ten years later, Charles X was overthrown in the July Revolution; the rebels attacked the Louvre, gained entry and vented their fury

on pictures of the king. In the disturbances of February 1848 the

Tuileries were attacked and pillaged and the Palais-Royal was burned down.

1914–18		1939–45	1958		1989
World War One		World War Two	Beginning of the Fifth Republic		Fall of the Berlin wall
1900	**1920**	**1940**	**1960**	**1980**	**2000**

| | 1930 | 1953 | | 1981 | 1989 | 1993 |
| | Naval museum moved to the Palais de Chaillot | Georges Braque is asked to produce a ceiling for the Royal Antechamber | | Plan for "Grand Louvre" | The Pyramide is opened | Richelieu wing is opened |

A HUGE DOUBLE PALACE: THE LOUVRE AND THE TUILERIES

The restored monarchy had been content to add only a few bays to the north wing of the Tuileries. Only with the Second Republic (1848–51) did major construction work begin again. Victor Hugo called upon the government of 1848 to make the Louvre a "Mecca for intellectuals", and the revolutionary government decided by decree to complete the palace which became one of France's largest building sites at a time when national building programs were leading the struggle against unemployment. Louis-Napoleon, the Prince-President, undertook to finance the project. When he became Emperor he decided to make it a showcase of his power. Baron Haussmann ordered the demolition of the run-down district between the Louvre and the Tuileries and built the Avenue de l'Opéra as a major axis connecting the new palace with the opera house; this project was carried out by Charles Garnier. Architects Visconti and then Lefuel built the "New Louvre", finally completing the old palace. (The architect Visconti is shown presenting his project to Napoleon III and the Empress Eugénie, right). The new buildings around the "Cour Napoléon" which were opened in 1857, glorified the regime with a prominent place given to decorative images of the Emperor and imperial allegories. In 1861, things took off again when architect Lefuel came up with the idea of an "imperial city". He destroyed one third of the Louvre gallery and the Pavillon Flore to make way for his new buildings; the large *guichets* (passages) and the Flore wing are the result of his scheme. When war broke out and the empire fell in 1870, the palace was a trapeze-shaped quadrangle at the center of the district. The Louvre and Tuileries complex was at its height, incorporating the redesigned Jardin des Tuileries. The 1871 fire reduced the Tuileries and part of the Palais-Royal to ashes.

THE "GRAND LOUVRE"

The Pyramide and alterations to the open spaces around the museum are merely the visible part of the "Grand Louvre" project which covers all the underground area beneath the Cour Napoléon and the Cour du Carrousel, as illustrated in the cut-away diagram (right). In the foreground, from left to right, are the Louvre amphitheater and school, the car park and the rooms of the Carrousel area. Behind this is the Carrousel shopping area, lit by an inverted pyramid.

THE MUSEUM TAKES OVER

Bit by bit the museum gradually took over the sites occupied by government bodies. The Union Centrale des Arts Décoratifs moved into the Marsan wing after it was rebuilt. The Louvre acquired the Flore wing in 1964. The departure of the Ministry of Finance in 1989 finally gave the Louvre control of the entire palace. Some sections have been transferred to other buildings – America, Asia, ethnography, and most recently the second half of the 19th century collection were moved to the Musée d'Orsay in 1986. Nonetheless the size of the Louvre's collections meant that a major reconstruction project was needed; the "Grand Louvre" scheme was devised in 1981 to meet these needs. Archeological excavations formed the first stage of the project, followed by the construction of an entrance hall crowned by I.M. Pei's glass pyramid, opened in 1989, and the opening of the Richelieu wing where the collections were rehoused in 1993. Completion of the work is scheduled for 1997.

▲ 1200: Philippe Auguste's château. ▼ 1380: Charles V's moat.

▲ 1572: The Valois palace and Tuileries. ▼ 1610: Henri IV's Grand Plan.

▲ 1643 Louis XIII has the Cour Carrée made four times larger.

The Louvre is eight hundred years old: in 1200 it was a fortress, today as the third millennium approaches it is the largest museum in the world. Kings and emperors, as well as presidents of the Republic, have all played a part in creating this immense architectural puzzle, a veritable encyclopedia of France's history, and a mirror of changing architectural fashions. This evolution is illustrated by ten models, here photographed from above, which are displayed in the room that the museum has set aside to display its history (the Hall Napoléon).

▲ 1715: the Colonnade and the Tuileries.   ▼ 1848: the Carrousel and the Rue de Rivoli.

▲ 1870: Napoleon III's Louvre completed.   ▼ 1980: before the Grand Louvre project.

▲ 1989: first stage of the Grand Louvre, the opening of the Pyramide.

● THE MEDIEVAL SUBURB

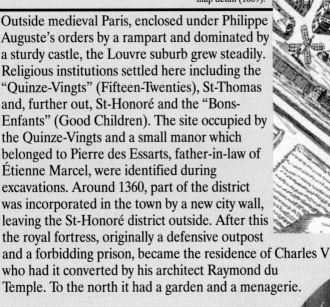

Outside medieval Paris, enclosed under Philippe
Auguste's orders by a rampart and dominated by
a sturdy castle, the Louvre suburb grew steadily.
Religious institutions settled here including the
"Quinze-Vingts" (Fifteen-Twenties), St-Thomas
and, further out, St-Honoré and the "Bons-
Enfants" (Good Children). The site occupied by
the Quinze-Vingts and a small manor which
belonged to Pierre des Essarts, father-in-law of
Étienne Marcel, were identified during
excavations. Around 1360, part of the district
was incorporated in the town by a new city wall,
leaving the St-Honoré district outside. After this
the royal fortress, originally a defensive outpost
and a forbidding prison, became the residence of Charles V
who had it converted by his architect Raymond du
Temple. To the north it had a garden and a menagerie.

FRESCO FRAGMENT
Fragments of secular
frescos were
discovered during
excavations. Originally
they decorated the
walls of a small
medieval manor (left, a
fragment of painted plaster).

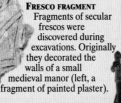

Excavations have revealed the size of the
fortifications. Above, the wide moat of
Charles V's city wall.

**THE LOUVRE
CHATEAU**
It can be
seen in the
background of
the *Retable of
the Paris
Parlement*
(above, ▲ 215).
The figures of
King Charles V
(left) and of the
queen (▲ 184)
became part of
the royal
collection in the
17th century after
the last medieval
buildings were
destroyed. They
may originally have
decorated the
palace gateway.

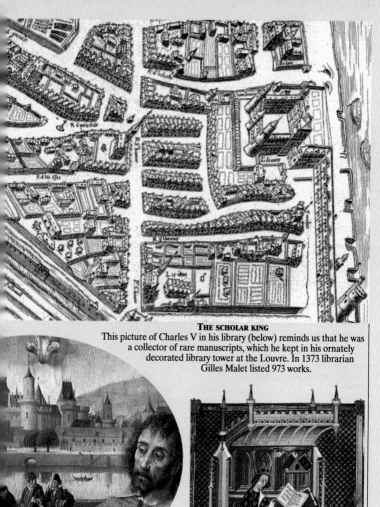

THE SCHOLAR KING

This picture of Charles V in his library (below) reminds us that he was a collector of rare manuscripts, which he kept in his ornately decorated library tower at the Louvre. In 1373 librarian Gilles Malet listed 973 works.

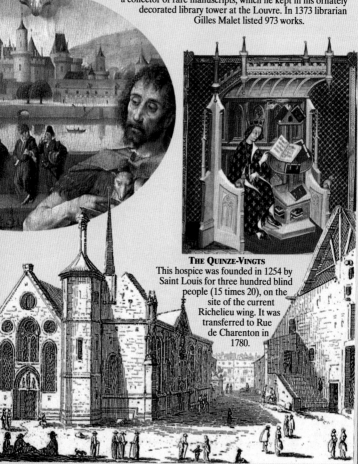

THE QUINZE-VINGTS

This hospice was founded in 1254 by Saint Louis for three hundred blind people (15 times 20), on the site of the current Richelieu wing. It was transferred to Rue de Charenton in 1780.

● THE LOUVRE UNDER THE VALOIS

The Valois stayed frequently at the Louvre. Intrigues, balls and marriages took place in the residence which Henri II had modernized to suit contemporary taste. It was here, on August 24 1572, the day after the King of Navarre married the king's sister, that the St Bartholomew's Day Massacre took place, announced by the bells of St-Germain-l'Auxerrois. During the turmoil of the Wars of Religion, the Louvre was a base for a weak regime until Henri III abandoned it after the "day of the barricades" (1588), and was also witness to the excesses of the Paris League.

THE LOUVRE: SCENE OF THE ST BARTHOLOMEW'S DAY MASSACRE
The terrible massacre of Protestants ordered by Charles IX took place under the windows of the chateau and even within its walls. Blood spattered the bedchamber of the young Marguerite de Valois, who had just married Henri de Navarre, the future Henri IV, himself a Protestant. The massacre took place after the assassination of Admiral de Coligny, who is commemorated by a 19th-century statue behind the Oratoire church ▲ 305.

THE TUILERIES
Catherine de' Medici had the garden designed by Bernard de Carnessequi, a Florentine landscape gardener, between 1563 and 1578. It was here in 1573 that a reception was held for the Polish ambassadors who had come to offer the crown to the future Henri III (opposite, right). In the background are avenues covered with bowers and vines bordering squares of lawn which offer a variety of attractions including a grotto ● 75, an echo and a maze.

THE TILER'S KILN

In the Tuileries gardens stood the grotto which ceramicist Bernard Palissy (1510–89 ▲ 205) decorated with lizards, snakes and rockeries. The famous researcher left behind a number of trial pieces which were discovered in a tiler's kiln during excavations in the Carrousel gardens ▲ 275.

"HIDEOUT" OF THE VALOIS

The pictures of the St Bartholomew's Day Massacre (left) may be unrealistic, but they evoke vividly the atmosphere of this large-scale carnage. Romantic versions of history were to present the Louvre as the Valois' hideout during these events. In the 19th century the window of the Petite Galerie (on the Seine side) was designated "Charles IX's Balcony": the king was supposed to have shot at Protestants with his crossbow from here. The legend is untrue since this part of the palace was completed under Henri IV.

THE PARIS LEAGUE

The Louvre was occupied by the Paris League after Henri III's departure (1588). It was here that the "torture of the Sixteen" took place, so-called after the sixteen men hanged in the great hall for having ordered the execution of President Brisson.

● THE REVOLUTION

THE KING'S RETURN TO PARIS
On July 17, 1789 the royal procession passed by the Louvre heading for the Hôtel de Ville. A few months later the people of Paris were to force the King to come and live in the Tuileries.

The Tuileries palace was Louis XVI's home after he was brought back from Versailles; after the fall of the monarchy it became a national palace, headquarters of the Convention and then of the Senate until the Bonapartist coup on November 9, 1799. The Revolution unfolded around this center of government, from the Prince of Lambesc's charge on July 14, 1789 to Bonaparte's cannons on the steps of St-Roch. Here too was the center of political debate: the Palais-Royal with its orators, the Club des Feuillants, the Assembly in the Salle du Manège and the "Fête de l'Être Suprême" (Festival of the Supreme Being).

THE FALL OF THE MONARCHY
On the morning of August 10, 1792, the King and his family fled to the Assembly in the Salle du Manège at the Tuileries. The monarchy was abolished and the royal family was taken to the Temple. Parisians, along with citizens of Marseilles who had come to the capital to overthrow the monarchy, attacked the Tuileries palace which was poorly defended by lightly armed Swiss guards. The rebels fired cannons before entering the hallway and the apartments inside, slaughtering the Swiss guards. These victims of the Revolution are commemorated by a grandiose pyramid in the garden.

THE PLACE DE LA CONCORDE
The guillotine was set up on the former Place Louis XV, renamed Place de la Révolution, in 1792. The emblems of royal power were also burned here (right). In its final decree, in 1795, the Convention renamed the square Place de la Concorde, to wipe out these tragic memories (1795) ▲ 280.

THE SALLE DU MANÈGE
The Republic was proclaimed on September 21, 1792 ▲ 285 in the former riding school of the Tuileries, built by Robert de Cotte (1720).

FESTIVAL OF THE SUPREME BEING
Designated by Robespierre to counter atheism by exalting Nature and the human soul, this festival took place on June 8, 1794. An optimistic vision of humanity was expressed in a grandiose national liturgy; the procession with the "Incorruptible" at its head passed before a circular platform set up in front of the palace.

THE CONVENTION
The former Salle des Machines in the Tuileries Palace ● 78 became the Salle de l'Assemblée and was redecorated by the Convention. It was here, on the last day of the Revolution, (May 20, 1795), that the head of deputy Ferraud was presented by the rebellious people to the President of the Convention, who admitted defeat.

The Musée Central des Arts opened at the Louvre on August 10, 1793. It was renamed Musée Napoléon in honor of Bonaparte in 1803. In addition to collections of paintings seized from the King, the churches and the émigrés, the Revolutionary army brought treasures from its conquests in Europe; paintings as well as magnificent classical statues were seized in Rome and Venice. The museum became a showcase of imperial power. The emperor, who lived at the Tuileries, made improvements and additions.

VICTORY CELEBRATIONS
The procession bringing the works of art seized in Italy was part of the victory celebrations commemorated on this magnificent Sèvres vase.

GLORIOUS PROCESSION WITH THE SPOILS OF WAR
The great classical marbles of the Vatican can be seen on these Sèvres vases, pulled on chariots ▲ *164*: the Apollo Belvedere, the *Cnidian Aphrodite* and the Laocoön (above, top, from left to right). The procession also honored the victorious soldiers in their ornate uniforms (left). The Laocoön was exhibited at the far end of the new museum of antiquities, and Napoleon came to see it lit up by torches, the predecessors of today's spotlights (above).

> **"ONLY WHAT IS BIG IS BEAUTIFUL;**
> SIZE AND SCALE CAN DISGUISE MANY FAILINGS."
>
> NAPOLEON I

THE ROTONDE D'APOLLON
The works seized in Europe were exhibited in the Rotonde d'Apollon in 1807 (above ▲ *126*), alongside the bust of Napoleon. Vivant Denon, the museum director, can be seen here guiding visitors.

IMPERIAL WEDDING
In April 1810, Napoleon married Marie-Louise of Austria (left). To reach the Salon Carré where the ceremony was to be held, the nuptial procession passed through the Grande Galerie ▲ *130* which displayed paintings from all over Europe.

MUSÉE NAPOLÉON
After it had presided over the new acquisitions, the huge bust of Napoleon (cast in bronze by Lorenzo Bartolini) was placed by the entrance to the museum. Today it can be seen in the rooms devoted to the history of the Louvre ▲ *122*.

41

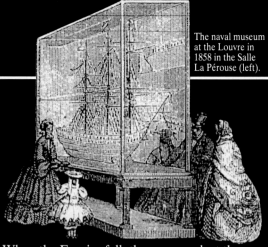

The naval museum at the Louvre in 1858 in the Salle La Pérouse (left).

When the Empire fell, the museum lost those pieces which were restored to France's allies. However it found a new lease of life, dedicating itself to the full range of artistic creation and exploring distant worlds. Champollion exhibited the masterpieces of ancient Egypt to brilliant effect and the discovery of the Assyrians followed in 1847. A series of new museums opened at the Louvre: of ethnography, América and China. As the collections grew, some sections had to be moved to other buildings.

THE MUSEUM OF ETHNOGRAPHY
The museum of ethnography (above, right) was established under the Second Republic to display oriental and African works in the Cour Carrée next to the naval museum. In 1878 these collections moved to the Musée du Trocadéro. The pre-Colombian antiquities of the American museum followed the same route.

NAVAL MUSEUM
The naval museum was created at the Louvre in 1827 under the name Musée Dauphin, to exhibit models of ships (but subsequently contained many ethnographic pieces). It was moved to the Palais de Chaillot in 1943.

MUSEUM OF LOST CIVILIZATIONS

Initially the collections of classical sculpture formed the nucleus of the Louvre's collection of antiquities; however, other areas gradually caught up. The Egyptian museum was established by Champollion under Charles X, in ornate rooms decorated by the architect Fontaine on the second story of the Cour Carrée (left, center). The Musée Charles X, as it was called, opened in 1827 ● *128*. In 1847 the Assyrian museum was created. Under the Second Empire it was transferred to the first story of the Colonnade, where the rich decorations of the palace of Khorsabad could be displayed, including the huge winged bulls ▲ *140*, arranged face to face and not in parallel as they should have been (opposite, below). In 1863, the Etruscans made their début at the Louvre, when the museum paid a vast sum for the collection of Marquis Campana, bankrupt former director of the Mont-de-Piété in Rome. The new museum of antiquities, named Musée Napoléon III, consisted mainly of ceramics ▲ *174* and jewelry, and was enriched by the proceeds of official archeological expeditions to Greece and the Eastern world. Gradually the museum opened up to the Far East and to Islam. Islamic arts have occupied a large area of the museum ever since ▲ *146*, while the Asian collections were transferred to the Musée Guimet in 1945.

● THE COMMUNE: 1871

MAY 1871
Barricades were set up in the
streets of Paris (Rue de Rivoli
to the right ▲ 287), to hold back
the advance of government
troops from Versailles.

The Second Empire had just collapsed. Artists elected
Gustave Courbet to the head of the Committee of Arts and he
took action to protect important works of art, while declaring
the Vendôme column to be a "monument devoid of all artistic
value . . . alien to the spirit of modern civilization and the union
of universal fraternity". The Commune, proclaimed on March
28, pulled it down on May 16. On May 23, government troops
entered Paris and *La Semaine Sanglante*
(Bloody Week) began. Communards
set fire to the Ministry of Finance,
the Tuileries, the Palais-Royal,
the Louvre library and the
headquarters of the
Beaux-Arts.

THE VENDÔME COLUMN:
A SYMBOL DESTROYED
It was rebuilt in 1873 at the expense of the
painter Gustave Courbet, leader of the
Committee of Arts (▲ 284).

THE TUILERIES
IN RUINS
The overall structure
of the palace stood
until 1882, when the
government took the
decision to erase all
memory of
discredited regimes
and demolished the
blackened ruins
(right). "The ruins
have neither beauty
nor grandeur, they
are merely ugly and
sad", argued Jules
Ferry, Minister for
Public Education,
who carried through
the vote for
demolition. The
stones of the building
were dispersed ▲ 276.

THE FIRE
On May 23, 1871, in
the middle of Bloody
Week, the
Communards
systematically set fire
to major institutions,
among them the
Tuileries. The Louvre
was saved from
burning thanks to its
curators, led by
Barbet de Jouy and to
the government
troops, but the
Tuileries fell victim to
the flames (right).

The masterpieces which had been evacuated during World War One were taken to safety once again in 1938. Their second exodus took place from August to December 1939, heading first for Chambord, and from there to nine other châteaux including Sources, Courtalain, Valençay, Brissac and Cheverny. As the Germans advanced, everything that could be transported was sent toward the southwest, to Loc-Dieu, and from there to Montal and the neighboring châteaux. The Resistance told the English of these sanctuaries and the BBC announced "The Mona Lisa is smiling", and "Van Dyck thanks Fragonard.".

PAUL JAMOT (1863–1939)
This brilliant Greek scholar joined the department of classical antiquities in 1902 but later turned to painting as his chief passion. He was entrusted with supervising the works evacuated from the Louvre to Toulouse during World War One. He painted the loaded lorries (left) and the crates piled up in the Augustine church at Toulouse (below).

A. Durandeau (1854–1941) was also fascinated by the contrast between the Gothic architecture and the crates: his interior view of the Jacobin church at Toulouse (above) dates from 1918.

"The Gioconda is smiling"
"Van Dyck thanks Fragonard"

On the Quai du Louvre

In 1939, the director of the museum, Henri Verne, and Jacques Jaujard (below), its general secretary, organized the evacuation of the works of art, assisted by the museum curators. The plan was in place even before the Munich agreements (1938) and some works had already left for Chambord. By September 1, 1939, two days before the declaration of war, all the works had left Paris.

Transportation in secret

Thousands of crates were ordered, each marked only with the package's department of origin. Most works were transported in crates, except for inlaid woods (too fragile) and sculptures that were too heavy to move. The Louvre had only one truck, so the vehicles of the Samaritaine store were requisitioned.

One of the museum entrances in the Flore wing is named after Jacques Jaujard.

A remarkable career

When Paul Jamot returned to Paris in 1919, he was appointed curator of the department of paintings. His energetic promotion of Impressionism and the painters of realism marked a turning point in the history of art between the two wars.

Trials and tribulations of moving

The *Raft of the Medusa*, too fragile to be packed in a crate, was evacuated in a scenery transporter belonging to the Comédie Française. From Chambord works were transferred to other locations under the supervision of curators.

● ORIGIN OF THE NAME "LOUVRE"

MÉDOR
"Médor, the faithful dog of the Louvre" stationed himself on the grave of his master, a victim of the 1830 Revolution buried in the shadow of the Louvre.

The name "Louvre" or *Lupara* in Latin, appeared relatively late at the end of the 12th century, and was used at first to designate the surrounding district. A great deal of effort has been expended to discover the word's origin and many interpretations have been proposed based on distortions of the word or similar words. These include: leper-house, Saxon fortress, kennels for wolf-hunting, watchtower, red place and place planted with small oak trees. The enigma must remain unsolved, but there are a number of fascinating expressions which originated at the Louvre and the Tuileries palace.

THE SALON
The Academy of Painting and Sculpture exhibited its members' works at the Palais-Royal (1672), then in the Grande Galerie of the Louvre (1699). After 1725 it used the Salon Carré. From this point on the exhibition became known as the "Salon", and the critics were called *salonniers*.

THE "GUICHETS" OF THE LOUVRE
A *guichet* is a hole or opening in a doorway, especially in the gateway to a town. The word is still used of any passageway through the Louvre (one of the *guichets* of the Cour Carrée, right).

COURT SIDE AND GARDEN SIDE
From 1770 to 1782 the Comédie Française used the Salle des Machines in the Tuileries as a theater. The stage was between the Tuileries gardens on one side, and the court in front of the palace on the other, hence the French habit of referring to stage left and stage right as "court side" and "garden side".

ARTS AND TRADITIONS

THE LOUVRE
ON PAPER

In the 18th century stalls selling paintings and prints took over the archways (*guichets*) of the Cour Carrée, which became a popular place to stroll.

Paper as the vehicle of knowledge and memory, as a source of income and an instrument of power, has always played a major role in the life of the Louvre and its surrounding district – the Bibliothèque Nationale is just minutes away. The Louvre became the official center of intellectual life because of the Academies, and it housed the Ministry of Foreign Affairs archives for a time at the beginning of the 18th century. The Royal Press was founded in the galleries of the Louvre in 1640 and grew steadily up to the Revolution. Under the influence of the royal collections, and with the presence of dozens of artists living at the Louvre, paper became important in the form of engravings. The printing press has been central to the life of the Louvre quarter for the last two centuries since freedom of the press was established in 1789.

THE ROYAL PRESS
The quantity and variety of characters used made this the most important typographic workshop in Europe in the 18th century. On the eve of the Revolution the Royal Press was operating some twenty presses and employed over a hundred workers. Rétif de la Bretonne worked here as a printer from 1761 to 1764. Today's Imprimerie Nationale (National Printing Office) is its direct descendant.

THE IMPERIAL LIBRARY
This was established in the north wing of the Louvre built in 1857.

THE SECONDHAND BOOKSELLERS
The stalls between Pont Royal and Pont Henri IV are the descendants of the 18th-century print dealers.

> **"THIS EXPENSIVE AND IDIOTIC CRAZE FOR PAINTINGS AND DRAWINGS, WHICH ARE BOUGHT AT RIDICULOUS PRICES, IS QUITE UNBELIEVABLE. NO OTHER LUXURY, EXCEPT DIAMONDS AND CHINA, IS MORE TRIVIAL AND INCREDIBLE."** L.-S. MERCIER

PRINT DEALERS
In his *Tableaux de Paris*, Louis-Sébastien Mercier protests against the invasion of the Louvre and its quarter by a horde of small traders. Foremost among these were the print sellers who plied their trade under the arches of the Cour Carrée (below).

THE BIBLIOTHÈQUE NATIONALE
Paper still plays a vital role today, as is confirmed by the transfer of France's Bibliothèque Nationale (left, the former Print Room) to the larger Tolbiac site. This will leave the historic building in Rue de Richelieu free to house the future Centre National des Arts, bringing together collections and specialist archives in the field of art history.

The Louvre's location between the
Seine and the Tuileries Gardens and the
appeal of its buildings and its
collections, have made it a natural
setting for festivities and celebrations.
This tradition was established under the
last of the Valois dynasty and the
Bourbons who celebrated births and
marriages here; it continued under the
Empire and the Restoration,
culminating with Napoleon III. The Louvre was the centerpiece
of the "Grands Travaux" in the 1980's and is once again the
scene of many important official events.

FESTIVITIES AT THE LOUVRE

THE CARROUSEL OF 1662
An equestrian display, carnival and tournament combined, the Carrousel of 1662 took over the Cour des Tuileries for two days ▲ *276*. The procession consisted of five equestrian quadrilles, with riders dressed in costumes designed by Henri Gissey. Louis XIV at the head of the quadrille of Romans, is surrounded by thirteen hundred courtiers dressed as dancers and acrobats. Leading court figures headed the quadrilles of Persians, Turks, Indians and Americans.

NAPOLEON'S MARRIAGE
In April 1810 Napoleon was married for the second time, to Marie-Louise, Archduchess of Austria. The reception was held at the Louvre. After crossing the court the procession, preceded by pages and chamberlains, paraded through the museum's Grande Galerie ▲ *130*.

LADIES' SUPPER AT THE TUILERIES
A banquet for ladies was held in 1836 in the Salle des Spectacles at the Tuileries, on the site of the Salle de la Convention ● *39*.

THE ARRIVAL OF MOHAMMED EFENDI
The procession of the Grand Turk's ambassador made a great impression on Parisians in 1721. Accompanied by royal troops on horseback he crossed the Tuileries Gardens on his way to the palace to meet the young Louis XIV.

● FASHION

THE FIRST COUTURIERS
Founded in 1891 at 3, Rue de la Paix ▲ *284*, Paquin was one of the most famous couture houses (right, fashion workers leaving the workshops).

Since the 18th century the Louvre has been the Mecca of Parisian couture. Under the Directoire the dandies and fashion victims of their day strutted about at the Palais-Royal, starting one of the first fashion crazes. Dressmakers attached to the palace and the court prospered in the Saint-Honoré quarter. The oldest and most famous fashion names are linked with this district: Rose Bertin, Revillon, Paquin, Worth, Lanvin and Coco Chanel. This tradition continued in the 20th century with the establishment of the Musée de la Mode in 1982, fashion parades in the Cour Carrée since 1982 and the Carrousel du Louvre, which became the center of world fashion when it opened in 1993.

LE NORMAND › PROSPER LE DUC › & COMPAGNIE ,
Succeſſeurs de Monſieur B U F F A U L T ,
MARCHANDS DE TOUTES SORTES D'ÉTOFFES DE SOIE, D'OR ET D'ARGENT, ET MEUBLES,
R U E S A I N T H O N O R É ,

THE ROYAL TRADE
The first modern boutiques came into being in the palace arcades; the oldest of these is at the Palais-Royal ▲ *299*. During the Directoire the fashion-conscious (left) found their most exquisite materials and loveliest finery here.

THE FIRST LADY OF COUTURE
Rose Bertin founded her couture house in 1774 at 26, rue Saint-Honoré ▲ *282*, in a shop with glass windows, a novelty for the time. Her vanity was only equaled by her fame, and she was the first to impose her own taste on her clients, who included Queen Marie-Antoinette. In 1784 she moved to 96, Rue de Richelieu, remaining loyal to the Palais-Royal district.

54

Jeanne Lanvin created her couture house in 1885, in Rue du Marché-Saint-Honoré ▲ 287, but left in 1889 for Rue Boissy-d'Anglas.

Coco Chanel in 1932.

THE CARROUSEL FASHION SHOWS
The Paris fashion shows have had a number of homes including the Palais des Congrès, the Palais de Chaillot and the Musée d'Art Moderne before settling in the Louvre's Cour Carrée in 1982. Then, however, the minister of culture Jack Lang, decided to give them the Carrousel (above).

● Walks around the Louvre

The renovation of the Tuileries Gardens is currently being completed as part of the Grand Louvre project.

Renovation work on the Louvre's façades over the last decade or so has brought to light the rich sculptural decoration of the Cour Carrée, the Cour Napoléon, and the Rue de Rivoli side. The Pyramide designed by architect I.M. Pei with its ornamental lakes and fountains has become a favorite meeting place. Bordered by the Seine to the south and close to the Pont-Neuf and the Pont des Arts footbridge, with the Palais-Royal Gardens to the north and the Tuileries Gardens to the west, the Louvre palace is a magnetic attraction, drawing in curious visitors and those who just want to take a stroll.

THE TUILERIES ORNAMENTAL LAKE
As in the Luxembourg Gardens the ornamental lake forms a crossroads, enticing passers-by to pause and enjoy the spectacle of the water fountains and the children's play area.

THE TERRASSE DES FEUILLANTS
This avenue backing on to the Rue de Rivoli (which was built under the First Empire), is a transitional area halfway between the city and the garden. For a long time it was here that changing fashions in politics and in clothes could be observed.

THE PALAIS-ROYAL

Unlike the Tuileries Gardens which are open to the city, the Palais-Royal garden is enclosed, as though protected from its urban surroundings by a series of courtyards and buildings. To the south there is the Comédie Française and the Conseil d'État, while solid terraced buildings stand on the other sides, mostly dating from the Ancien Régime. The Palais-Royal garden is national property, open to the public throughout the year. To the stroller it offers serene shady avenues and a number of shops and restaurants to explore under the 180 arches of its arcades as well as the curious sight of the columns by contemporary artist Daniel Buren, which have been installed in the main courtyard ▲ 296.

The Palais Royal was fashionable from the 18th century onward. Its attraction lay not only in the variety of entertainments on offer, but also in the prostitution which flourished here, protected by a law forbidding police officers from entering the area.

● CAFÉS AND RESTAURANTS

The Boeuf à la Mode,
Rue de Valois,
around 1830.

The cafés and restaurants recently opened in the Louvre and the Carrousel are not mere concessions to fashion but a response to needs expressed by the public and museum visitors. Some want to come and savor a gastronomic experience in a prestigious location; others simply want to enjoy a pleasant break during a visit to the museum's collections. In catering for these needs the Louvre is carrying on one of the district's strong traditions: it was here that the first restaurants and cafés were opened at the end of the 18th century as places for meetings and discussion during the Revolutionary era.

THE RESTAURANTS

The first restaurants opened in the 18th century on Rue de Richelieu and at the Palais-Royal: for example the Frères Provençaux, pictured here in the year 1846 (right). Le Grand Louvre, the restaurant under the Pyramide at the heart of the museum, offers a splendid menu combining traditional and avant-garde cuisine, while Restaurama, near the inverted pyramid, offers a wide range of dishes from different countries.

THE CAFÉS

The café tradition established at the Palais-Royal and in the Tuileries Gardens under the Revolution (below, the Café des Aveugles) has not died out. The museum now has two new cafés; the Marly, opposite the Pyramide, and the Café Richelieu.

BEHIND THE SCENES

Internal service routes (over a mile long) are used to supply all museum departments. The central surveillance office controls the security of the works of art, the building and its visitors around the clock.

The Louvre is like a theater in that it stages a spectacle for visitors to see, but the actors are the works of art. In this performance, however, there is no room for improvisation even though it is the same every day. It is organized according to rules, traditions and rituals, time-honored customs and procedures. On both sides of the curtain, in the public areas and in the wings, nothing is left to chance. The world of the Louvre combines celebrity and anonymity, light and shadow. A secret hidden world exists behind the displays, keeping the museum alive. This unseen side of the Louvre, the off-stage life which is vital for the performance, is astonishingly wide-ranging and diverse.

OF MASTERPIECES AND MEN

Large numbers of people are needed to find, acquire, store, catalog, restore, study, compare, communicate, manage, supervise, receive, present, maintain, air-condition, light, repair and feed. In order to carry out its twin tasks of research and receiving the public, the Louvre museum employs nearly 1,500 staff, active in forty different specialist areas.

THE LABORATOIRE DES MUSÉES DE FRANCE

The research laboratory of the French Museum Service in the basement of the Louvre, carries out all the chemical, physical

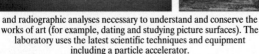

and radiographic analyses necessary to understand and conserve the works of art (for example, dating and studying picture surfaces). The laboratory uses the latest scientific techniques and equipment including a particle accelerator.

THE RESERVE COLLECTION

As part of the Grand Louvre project the museum was given new store rooms, even larger and more functional than the old ones. Works are kept in reserve temporarily, for storage or conservation, arranged on sliding racks or in rows, as shown here. The museum's curators, responsible for the inventory of the Louvre's collections, do much of their work here.

THE BIBLIOTHÈQUE DES MUSÉES DE FRANCE

The library of the French Museum Service open to curators and researchers only, is located in the south wing of the Cour Carrée. The library specializes in art history but also houses the archives of the French Museum Service.

● THE DEPARTMENT OF GRAPHIC ARTS

Over 126,000 works on paper make up the collection of this department, little known to the general public. Because of their fragility and the danger of exposing them to light for too long, the miniatures, engravings, drawings, watercolors, pastels and artists' sketchbooks are not exhibited. They can be seen on request in the consultation and documentation rooms located in the Flore wing. The department regularly organizes exhibitions and has spaces in the painting displays where drawings, pastels and sketches are shown in rotation.

A MAJOR COLLECTION
The Department of Graphic Arts and the Edmond de Rothschild collection together constitute the largest collection of drawings in Europe. The collection is particularly rich in works of the 16th-, 17th-, 18th- and 19th-century Italian and French schools, especially those of the great masters like Leonardo da Vinci (*Drapery for a Seated Figure*, right) ▲ *262*. The collection is the product of a traditional acquisition policy going back to the Ancien Régime and minor artists are less well represented than the major ones.

THE LOVE OF PEACE
This beautiful red chalk drawing by Edme Bouchardon is a study for a caryatid on the equestrian statue of Louis XV which stood on the site of the Place de la Concorde (▲ *280*). It was commissioned in 1748, dedicated fifteen years later, and finally destroyed in 1792.

Rembrandt's *Man's Head with Turban* and Rubens' *Young Woman Kneeling*.

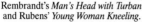

THE RANGE OF TECHNIQUES AND MATERIALS

This drawing entitled *View of Arco Valley in the Tirol* by Albrecht Dürer (above) demonstrates a variety of techniques: blue, brown, gray, ocher and green watercolors, black ink, brushwork and white highlights. The same is true of Leonardo da Vinci's drapery drawing (left-hand page), which has brushwork, white highlights and gray tempera on a primed canvas. The drawing by Rubens (below, left) is done in white pencil, black charcoal and red chalk. Rembrandt's drawing shows brown ink, brown wash, pen and white highlights; Raphael's uses charcoal, white highlights and metal point on beige paper; finally Claude Lorrain's uses graphite, sepia wash and China ink.

Self-portrait at Easel (left), pastel by Chardin; *Portrait of Mustapha* (above), by Géricault; (above this), *Shepherd by a Lake* by Claude Lorrain; *Woman's Head* (top left) by Raphael.

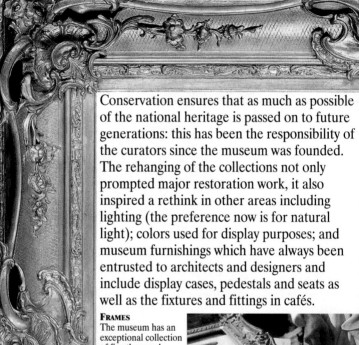

Conservation ensures that as much as possible of the national heritage is passed on to future generations: this has been the responsibility of the curators since the museum was founded. The rehanging of the collections not only prompted major restoration work, it also inspired a rethink in other areas including lighting (the preference now is for natural light); colors used for display purposes; and museum furnishings which have always been entrusted to architects and designers and include display cases, pedestals and seats as well as the fixtures and fittings in cafés.

FRAMES

The museum has an exceptional collection of five thousand antique frames although paintings rarely have their original frames. In the 17th and 18th centuries great care was lavished on frames as works of art, providing sumptuous settings for the royal paintings. This tradition continued with varying degrees of success after the Revolution, with the influx of works to the central museum of art. Only in the 20th century, however, has the style of the frame been matched to the date and style of each painting.

The new display of the painting collections gave curators the opportunity to bring out their reserves of antique frames, to have them

restored, even to have new ones made, and to complete the collection through acquisitions.

THE MAGIC OF NATURAL LIGHT

Top lighting, the most suitable for exhibiting paintings, ensures an even distribution of light. This type of lighting has been adopted in the new painting displays designed by Italo Rota (Cour Carrée) and by I.M. Pei (Richelieu wing). In both cases a system of adjustable (Rota), or fixed (Pei) screens is used to filter the intensity of the light which can damage works of art, while at the same time giving views of the sky.

COLOR

The new spaces in the Richelieu wing provided curators and architects with an opportunity to study the colors best suited to the collections in each department (right and top of the page).

All the furniture in the Richelieu wing was designed by Jean-Michel Wilmotte, from some five hundred display cases to seats for the public and chairs for security guards.

The École du Louvre was created in 1882 to train curators; today its lectures are also open to the public. In addition to its library and photographic collection, it now has a modern auditorium in the Carrousel.

Once work had finished on the Grande Galerie, Henri IV allowed artists and craftsmen to move into the new building. This tradition of taking in artists continued with the Academies under Louis XIV, the Salon exhibitions after 1699 and then the more or less authorized proliferation of artists' studios in the abandoned palace up to the time of the Revolution. This tradition of fostering knowledge, teaching and the living arts continues through activities organized and encouraged within the Louvre: visits, workshops, conferences, copying and the École du Louvre.

THE ACADEMIES
After Louis XIV authorized the Academies to establish their headquarters at the Louvre they took over the palace: they included the Académie Française, the Académie des Inscriptions et Belles-Lettres, the Académie de Peinture et de Sculpture, the Académie d'Architecture and the Académie des Sciences. The royal apartments were divided up and the mezzanines were adapted to house studios and to accommodate the Academies' protégés.

An academician is received into the Académie Française around 1700 (engraving by Poilly after Delamonce, above).

"WE MADE COPIES AT THE LOUVRE BOTH TO STUDY THE MASTERS AND TO LIVE WITH THEM, AND ALSO BECAUSE THE GOVERNMENT WOULD BUY THE COPIES" HENRI MATISSE

COPYISTS

For some it is a source of income, for others a means of study and apprenticeship: the tradition of copying great works of art is still alive although it has gradually become regulated by the museum.

Permits are now granted only for a

limited period, and on condition that certain technical conditions are observed. The Louvre's most famous copyists include Turner, Delacroix, Degas, Cézanne, Vuillard, Matisse and Picasso.

Dominique Vivant Denon was director of the Musée Napoléon from 1802 to 1815. This allegorical portrait of him (left) painted by Benjamin Zix deals with only one aspect of the curator's work.

Some forty different types of specialist staff work in the Louvre. They include curators, technical and artistic specialists, engineers and architects, reception and surveillance staff, security and emergency teams, warehouse staff, archivists, cleaners, administrators, sales assistants, cashiers, cooks and waiters, who all do their job with the same respect for the buildings, the works of art and the visitors. The large team of curators, which was first established under the Revolution, is divided among the seven departments of the Louvre. There are sixty-five curators in all and between them they are responsible for 420,000 works of fine and applied art, of which at least 13,000 are permanently exhibited in the museum displays.

Firemen's drill on the roof of the Cour Carrée.

The glass walls of the Pyramide being cleaned by abseiling specialists.

Heavy equipment in operation during the hanging of large-format French paintings.

The security guards in uniforms designed by Balenciaga attend to the safety of the works on display and inform and guide visitors.

Moving large-scale paintings is a masterpiece of organization in itself . . .

Madame Récamier by David gets a final touch of the duster before being hung in the new display of French painting.

. . . often requiring the use of large specialist teams.

On Tuesdays, when it is closed, the museum is given over to cleaning staff, electricians, painters, photographers and curators.

Sophisticated equipment specially adapted to the building, like this electricians' scaffolding (right), is used for restoring, repainting, repairing and replacing the museum's fittings.

Upholsterers, framers, restorers – many skilled specialists are needed in order to ensure that the museum fulfils its role.

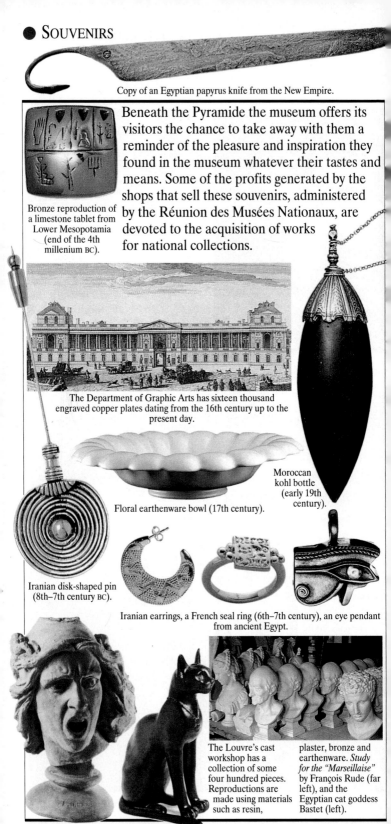

Copy of an Egyptian papyrus knife from the New Empire.

Bronze reproduction of a limestone tablet from Lower Mesopotamia (end of the 4th millenium BC).

Beneath the Pyramide the museum offers its visitors the chance to take away with them a reminder of the pleasure and inspiration they found in the museum whatever their tastes and means. Some of the profits generated by the shops that sell these souvenirs, administered by the Réunion des Musées Nationaux, are devoted to the acquisition of works for national collections.

The Department of Graphic Arts has sixteen thousand engraved copper plates dating from the 16th century up to the present day.

Floral earthenware bowl (17th century).

Moroccan kohl bottle (early 19th century).

Iranian disk-shaped pin (8th–7th century BC).

Iranian earrings, a French seal ring (6th–7th century), an eye pendant from ancient Egypt.

The Louvre's cast workshop has a collection of some four hundred pieces. Reproductions are made using materials such as resin, plaster, bronze and earthenware. *Study for the "Marseillaise"* by François Rude (far left), and the Egyptian cat goddess Bastet (left).

ARCHITECTURE

Recent work on the Grand Louvre provided an opportunity to undertake extensive archeological excavations in both the Cour Carrée and the Cour Napoléon.

The fortress built by Philippe Auguste around 1200 to the west of the capital outside the city walls was not just a stronghold. Indeed the Great Tower which housed the treasury and also served as a prison was a symbol of royal supremacy over all the kingdom. A circular keep surrounded by a quadrangle of walls set with towers, was the perfect model of a "philippian" fortress and was imitated throughout Europe. It was not until the 14th century under Charles V that the Louvre became a royal residence. This educated monarch had the austere fortress converted into an elegant residence.

MEDIEVAL REMAINS

The medieval Louvre ▲ 122 had already been excavated in the 19th century, but it was not until 1989 that the moats of this period were opened to the public (a). The lower hall (b) is the only part of the medieval building which survives today; it is called Salle Saint Louis ▲ 124 because its decoration dates from this king's reign.

a

b

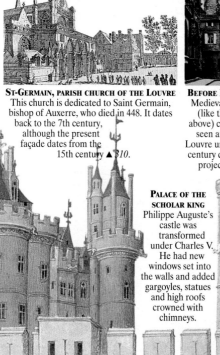

GOTHIC REVIVAL
The 19th-century painter Hoffbauer attempted to visualize Charles V's Louvre. The result was a Romantic vision of an idealized fortress (above).

ST-GERMAIN, PARISH CHURCH OF THE LOUVRE
This church is dedicated to Saint Germain, bishop of Auxerre, who died in 448. It dates back to the 7th century, although the present façade dates from the 15th century ▲ 310.

BEFORE HAUSSMANN
Medieval buildings (like the house, above) could still be seen around the Louvre until the 19th-century construction projects ▲ 310.

PALACE OF THE SCHOLAR KING
Philippe Auguste's castle was transformed under Charles V. He had new windows set into the walls and added gargoyles, statues and high roofs crowned with chimneys.

CLASSICAL SCULPTURE
Caryatids (columns in the form of female figures) by Jean Goujon (around 1550).

François I was used to an itinerant court life, staying in the châteaux of the Loire, Blois and Chambord, and later in castles of the Paris region (St-Germain, Villers-Cotterêts and Fontainebleau). However, in 1527 he decided to build a palace in his capital city. The Great Tower was pulled down in 1528 and then Charles V's west wing was demolished to make way for a new residence in the contemporary style. The Louvre became a favorite royal palace and the setting for court celebrations under the Valois dynasty. Henri II and his sons, including Charles IX, continued the work on the palace which they entrusted to architect Pierre Lescot. Catherine de' Medici decided to have Philibert Delorme build a palace outside the city walls with a garden in the Florentine style. This was to become the Tuileries, a few hundred yards away from the old Louvre but separate from it.

Court façade of Lescot's wing with decorations by Jean Goujon.

POMP AND CIRCUMSTANCE

The new palace of the king of France was intended principally as a setting for demonstrations of royal power. It was with this purpose in mind that Pierre Lescot built a new wing over the medieval foundations (right), with a large ceremonial room in the first story (the Salle des Cariatides, ▲ *125*). The room had a raised section for the throne and a gallery for musicians. The wide richly decorated staircase connecting it with the guards' room was completed under Henri II.

PHILIBERT DELORME
The architectural theorist
who designed the Tuileries.

THE TUILERIES PALACE
Philibert Delorme had planned a huge quadrangle but was only
able to complete one section of it, dominated
by a pavilion, in collaboration with Jean
Bullant (below).

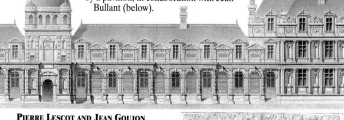

PIERRE LESCOT AND JEAN GOUJON
The architect and sculptor worked together
on the Louvre, collaborating on the façade of
the Cour Carrée and allegorical reliefs (below
and bottom of page). They also worked
together on the loggia of the Fontaine des
Innocents (which has now been converted into
a public convenience at the Halles, below).

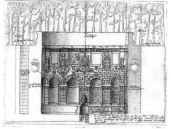

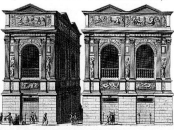

A FLORENTINE GARDEN
The main attraction of Catherine de' Medici's
Tuileries Palace seems to have been its
Italian-style garden. Here Bernard Palissy
▲ 205 created a grotto covered with imitation
rockwork, shells and animals, all made of
terracotta (similar to the
grotto in this drawing).

The Louvre as we know it today is the product of Henri IV's imagination and energies; his reign (1589–1610) was a time of intensive construction work at the palace. He completed a façade on the Cour Carrée (and dreamed of making this court four time larger), finished the Petite Galerie and carried out Charles IX's plan to join the Louvre and the Tuileries with an immense gallery along the Seine (which he would have liked to match with a second gallery to the north). Classicism, a new architectural style, developed during work on these projects. Alternating vertical pavilions and horizontal wings, simple forms tempered by elegant decorations, columns in the French style with fleur-de-lys ornamentation, curved and triangular pediments and carved monograms of the reigning monarch, were all to become typical of French Classical architecture. Louis XIII and his architect Le Mercier continued Henri IV's work, extending the west wing of the Cour Carrée and building the Pavillon de l'Horloge.

PALACE BY THE RIVERSIDE
Clearly visible in this painting (above) are the Pavillon du Roi and the Renaissance façade with a medieval tower, as well as the Petite Galerie overlooking a garden and the beginnings of the Grande Galerie. The Grande Galerie (top of the page) was built by two architects: Métezeau (the town end) and Androuet (the Tuileries end). At its western end is the riverside pavilion now called the Flore pavilion, forming the southern tip of the Tuileries Palace.

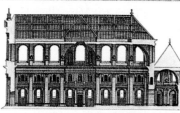

THE PAVILLON DE L'HORLOGE
This square pavilion built by Le Mercier between 1624 and 1640 was to serve as a model for Napoleon III ● 82.

JESUIT ARCHITECTURE
The first stone of the Oratoire, a chapel in the Jesuit style, was laid by Louis XIII in 1621. Clément Métezeau and then Le Mercier were the architects ▲ 305.

THE CARDINAL'S PALACE
Cardinal Richelieu's magnificent palace, the future Palais-Royal ▲ 294 was the perfect example of a private residence.

THE PONT-NEUF.
The first stone was laid by Henri III in 1578 and Henri IV opened the bridge in 1607.

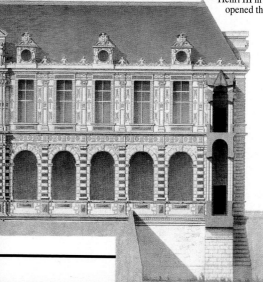

THE PETITE GALERIE
It was started under Charles IX and another story was added by Louis Métezeau. The upper story housed the Galerie des Rois, decorated with portraits of the kings and queens of France. The alternating arcades and openings matched Pierre Lescot's architecture but the style of decoration was new: pilasters with rustic or vermiculated bosses and ornamentation of fleurs-de-lys and royal initials.

PALACE OF THE SUN KING

The young Louis XIV wanted to demonstrate his power so undertook substantial improvements to the Louvre before leaving Paris for Versailles. He finished the Cour Carrée and the Tuileries palace with a garden designed by Le Nôtre and a theater (the Salle des Spectacles). He created apartments in the Tuileries and built a façade (the Colonnade) on the town side. This masterpiece was part of a program of improvements to the town, which included adding a number of royal squares.

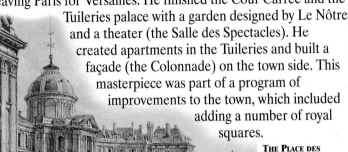

THE PLACE DES QUATRE-NATIONS
Le Vau's college (later the Institut de France) lies opposite the Louvre on the left bank.

THE ROYAL SQUARES

Henri IV created the triangular Place Dauphine and the square Place Royale (now Place des Vosges); Louis XIV created the almost circular Place des Victoires (above, right) and Place Vendôme (above). Jules Hardouin-Mansart built the latter (formerly Place Louis-le-Grand) in 1699. It is surrounded by private residences, all with identical façades.

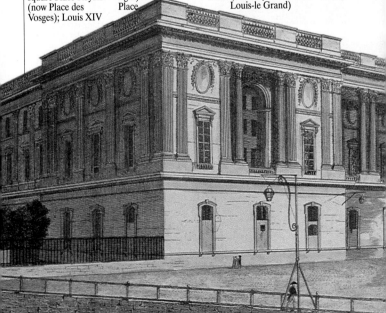

A GARDEN IN THE FRENCH STYLE
Le Nôtre, the king's gardener (1613–1700) created the gardens at Vaux, Versailles and Chantilly. His design for the Tuileries was strictly geometrical, set with ornamental lakes and arranged around a central axis, a key feature of Parisian town planning.

BAROQUE VERSUS CLASSICISM
The conflict between Italian Baroque style and French Classicism is a major landmark in French architectural history. Bernini, the architect who designed the colonnade at St Peter's in Rome, was invited to France by Louis XIV but left again without completing his project for the Louvre: he produced only a bust and an equestrian statue of the king, a copy of which has since stood in the Cour Napoléon ▲ 274. The winner was Claude Perrault, a doctor and engineer who led a small committee including Le Vau and Lebrun, a leading royal painter ▲ 224. Their design drew on a project by François Mansart. The monumental façade with columns on two levels, was to acquire exemplary status; it was used as a model for Louis XV's Place de la Concorde and for the Hôtel de la Monnaie (the Mint).

ITALIAN AND FRENCH DESIGNS
...val entries in the competition for the Louvre façade came from Bernini (top), Pietro da Cortona (two designs above) and Lebrun, Le Vau and Perrault, whose entry was the eventual winner.

● NEOCLASSICISM

The Place Louis XV, later renamed Place de la Révolution and finally Place de la Concorde (on the map, opposite) was completed in 1772.

The final flourish of French Classicism: the façade of the church of St-Roch (1738–9).

The key event at the Louvre in the period between 1750 and 1850 was the establishment of the museum in 1793. Major architectural work was abandoned since political instability meant that the reigning powers had no time to plan large projects let alone to complete them. Neoclassicism was to find political expression in the Republic and the Empire as well as in architecture. The ideas of the Enlightenment gave rise to town planning projects: new squares were created (Place de la Concorde), main roads were constructed (Rue de Rivoli), and public monuments and buildings were completed.

LA MONNAIE (THE MINT)
This building was completed in 1775, echoing the colonnade of the Louvre. Its style of decoration is neoclassical ▲ 306.

BIRTH OF THE PARISIAN APARTMENT BLOCK
The Palais-Royal buildings completed by Victor Louis in 1784 mark the birth of the Parisian apartment block (a) ▲ 296. Percier and Fontaine picked up on the idea in 1802 for the Rue de Rivoli (b) ▲ 286, as did Jules de Joly for no. 4, Rue d'Aboukir, around 1820 (c) ▲ 300.

(a) ELEVATION CROSS-SE

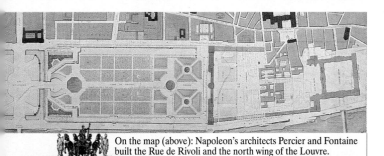

On the map (above): Napoleon's architects Percier and Fontaine built the Rue de Rivoli and the north wing of the Louvre.

IMPERIAL ARCH
The triumphal arch on the Carrousel by Percier and Fontaine marked the entrance to the Tuileries palace. It is typically neoclassical in the most literal sense of the term, being an imitation of an arch from classical antiquity, the arch of Septimius Severus in Rome.

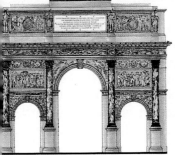

MUSÉE DES ARTS
First conceived under Louis XVI, the museum was finally opened under the Revolution. The project gave rise to several designs. On the left, an entrance designed by Wailly; below, another design for the Grande Galerie.

MUSÉE NAPOLÉON
Percier and Fontaine designed the corridors and staircases for the museum. The entrance had a staircase and a vestibule, of which only the latter survives ▲ *128*; the large south and north staircases of the colonnade (above) also feature huge columns and vaults richly decorated with sculptures, stucco-work and paintings. The palace-museum became a backdrop for imperial ceremonies.

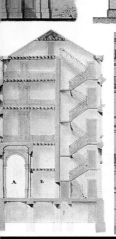

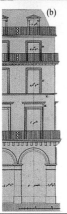

(b)

(c)

THE LOUVRE UNDER NAPOLEON III

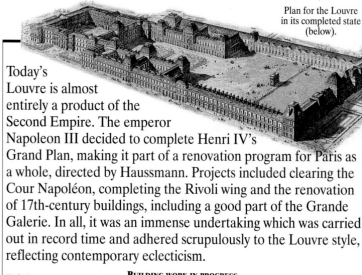

Plan for the Louvre
in its completed state
(below).

Today's Louvre is almost entirely a product of the Second Empire. The emperor Napoleon III decided to complete Henri IV's Grand Plan, making it part of a renovation program for Paris as a whole, directed by Haussmann. Projects included clearing the Cour Napoléon, completing the Rivoli wing and the renovation of 17th-century buildings, including a good part of the Grande Galerie. In all, it was an immense undertaking which was carried out in record time and adhered scrupulously to the Louvre style, reflecting contemporary eclecticism.

BUILDING WORK IN PROGRESS

This photograph shows the façade of the Cour Napoléon just before it was given its facing by Lefuel. On either side is the scaffolding for the new buildings which were to form the court as we know it today, composed of alternating wings and pavilions as in the 17th century.

HISTORICISM

Napoleon III's architects Lefuel and Visconti made a point of copying the Louvre's traditional style which was in keeping with the historical eclecticism of their own century, drawing both on medieval sources (Viollet-le-Duc) and on the Renaissance style which preceded French Classicism. The Denon pavilion (right) is the best example of this: it follows the structure of the Pavillon de l'Horloge which Le Mercier built two centuries earlier; the façades of the wings themselves show a similar structure of arcades and columns.

CARVED RELIEFS
The style of the Denon wing matches that of earlier centuries, but the ornamentation is thoroughly contemporary, featuring a locomotive on the pediment.

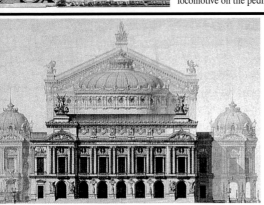

NAPOLEON III STYLE
When Empress Eugénie asked: "But what style is that? It's not Louis XIV, nor Louis XV, nor Louis XVI!", Charles Garnier architect of the Opéra (left) is supposed to have replied: "Madame, the style is Napoleon III. So how can you complain?"

THE "GUICHETS"
Although the Louvre formed an enclosed whole, the *guichets* (archways) ● *48* made it accessible to traffic.

PAVILLON DENON

83

● THE GRAND LOUVRE

A preliminary sketch: this strong architectural statement was to form the basis of the final design.

The Louvre's final transformation took place under President François Mitterrand's Grand Louvre scheme (1981–95). Architect Ieoh Ming Pei was entrusted with the architectural redevelopment of the Louvre which is scheduled for completion on the eve of the 21st century with the restoration of the Tuileries Gardens. The palace with its eight hundred years of rich architectural history now has at its center a symbol both of permanence and of contemporary creativity: the Pyramide which marks the museum entrance. The Pyramide was highly controversial at first; now it is considered a shining example of how to introduce new buildings into a historical context.

A RADICAL RECONSTRUCTION

The renovation of the Louvre observed two basic principles: to respect the old buildings and show them to their best advantage while at the same time making a resolutely contemporary contribution, free of pastiche, in the Richelieu wing and the underground areas, the Hall Napoléon and the Carrousel gallery.

The Pyramide is just a tiny, visible part of Pei's work which encompasses all the underground areas of the Cour Napoléon and the Carrousel, including the reserves, the laboratory, shopping center and car park. These same principles governed the design and lighting of museum rooms (above, an openwork ceiling).

THE SECOND PHASE
In 1993 the Richelieu wing was opened in the former Ministry of Finance buildings as was the Carrousel gallery further toward the Tuileries Gardens. This marked the completion of the project's second stage. The first phase culminated in the opening of the Pyramide in 1989 (above, left). The shopping center has an inverted pyramid which echoes the museum's entrance (above, center) and large escalators leading to the rooms of the Richelieu wing (right).

IEOH MING PEI
This American architect of Chinese origin had previously been given the job of redeveloping Washington's National Gallery.

FORM AND FUNCTION
This geometrical shape was chosen not only for its timeless character but also for technical reasons; the glass Pyramide helps provide light and space to the Hall Napoléon, the vast crossroads and reception area for the public.

THE 20TH CENTURY
The large, distinctive buildings of the Samaritaine department store ▲ *308*, from 1910 and 1930, stand out in the Louvre district as does the Georges-Pompidou center (Beaubourg), which was built in the 1970's.

The inverted pyramid (left and below, while under construction) is held together by a system of cables, as is the Pyramide which points skyward.

A LEITMOTIF
Attentive observers will note that the square with its diagonals marked, the basic single form of which the Pyramide is constructed, is featured on all surfaces, even on ceilings and elevators.

● A TECHNOLOGICAL CHALLENGE

The Pyramide is an extraordinary technical achievement: 70 ft high on a base of some 100 ft square, it is made of 793 glass diamonds and triangles fitted together with pinpoint accuracy and mounted on an aluminium framework supported by 93½ tons of girders and stainless steel joints. The French company Saint-Gobain developed an entirely new kind of glass for it which is both lightweight and strong, transparent but with minimum reflectivity. The same attention to technological detail governed the design of the many staircases, elevators, windows and ceilings.

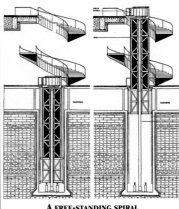

A FREE-STANDING SPIRAL
Alongside the simple, austere materials used in the Hall Napoléon (white Burgundy stone, glass, concrete glistening with crystals), the architect allowed himself a more personal touch in the staircase which surrounds the hydraulic elevator.

A UNIQUE TYPE OF GLASS
The iron oxide was removed to make this glass perfectly clear; it was drawn vertically for perfect smoothness and then polished in the traditional way in England.

THE CABLE CONSTRUCTION
The connecting joints on the Pyramide (above, a drawing by Pei) were cast by Eiffel Constructions, using the lost wax casting technique, rarely employed on an industrial scale.

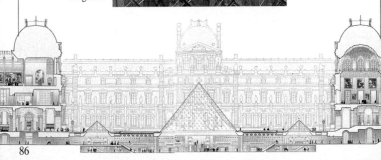

The Louvre
as seen by painters

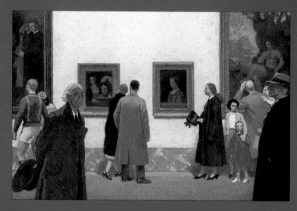

HUBERT ROBERT, CURATOR:
THE GRANDE GALERIE

The artist Hubert Robert (1733–1808) was entrusted with the royal painting collections intended for the future museum between 1784 and 1792. Between 1795 and 1802 he was put in charge of the nation's paintings in the newly renovated Grande Galerie ▲ *130*, and showed himself to be an imaginative curator. He lived at the Louvre in close contact with the buildings and works; here he painted and drew images of the museum's daily life, as well as visionary plans for its future development. To begin with his depiction of the reality (1): in 1794–6 the Grande Galerie was a long dark corridor, lit from the side by high windows. Paintings were tightly packed on the picture rails, while exhibits in the middle of the gallery were few in number and widely spaced out (including Giambologna's *Mercury* and a large Sèvres vase). In 1796 the gallery closed: the floors were renovated, the walls were painted green and statues were installed (some of these had been looted on military campaigns. In 1798 the new museum was ready to open its doors to the public (2). Such was the quiet, unremarkable day-to-day reality – a strong contrast to Hubert Robert's imaginary visions. He idealized the Louvre as a temple of art, imagining a wide gallery partitioned by columns (4). He dreamed of setting the masterpieces of classical antiquity alongside paintings of the great monuments in this gallery and his dream was indeed to become reality under Napoleon. The painter exhibited his plan for lighting the gallery in the Salon of 1796 (3): roof lights flood the gallery with light and the bays are separated by elegant pillars.

"Plan for lighting the museum gallery through the roof, and for dividing it up without removing the view along the length of the building."

Hubert Robert (1796)

Hubert Robert exhibited this *Imaginary View of the Grande Galerie in Ruins* at the Salon of 1796, as a counterpart to his plans for improving the Grande Galerie. He projects the viewer into the distant future when this glorious plan will itself, like the Roman monuments, be no more than a picturesque and melancholy ruin. The picture is a reflection on the passing of time, on the cycle of lost civilizations. It is also a homage to antiquity; the *Apollo Belvedere* stands intact with a bust of Raphael at its feet. On the ground is Michaelangelo's *Dying Slave* ▲ 195.

In addition to the Grande Galerie and the Salon Carré, painters have always been attracted by the apartments of Anne of Austria which housed the Musée des Antiques from 1799 onward. They relished the red walls, the long view opening in the distance through the riverside window with the midday light flooding in, the brilliant marble floors and the imposing pedestals ▲ 126. In earlier years visitors like this solitary lady (2) had to look upward to see the great marbles. Madeleine Goblot (19th century) (1) emphasized the profusion of statues and busts, the confusion of pillars and plinths, depicted in dim light. Around 1885 Guillaume Larrue (1851–1935) painted the Salle de la Colonnade (4) which was devoted to the large Egyptian monuments. He played on the opposition of the hieratic pink Sphinx of

"THERE WERE ASSYRIAN KINGS . . . EGYPTIAN BAS-RELIEFS PAINTED IN BRIGHT COLORS, MONUMENTAL KINGS, REAL SPHINXES, A WORLD AS IN A DREAM."

SIGMUND FREUD (1885)

Tanis (now in the Crypte du Sphinx, ▲ 148) and the worldly elegance of the visitors, in order to emphasize the contrast between this time-defying masterpiece and the transient fashions of the day, between the strong lines of the stone and the frail silhouettes of the living people. In 1946 the Musée d'Art Moderne acquired a number of small reportage paintings by Paul Hugues (1891–1972) depicting scenes during the reinstallation of collections after World War Two ● 46. Sarcophagi, packing crates and works of art (3) are here piled up in a passageway in the Musée Charles X ▲ 128.

T he Salon Carré
▲ *130* was
intended as the Holy
of Holies of high art,
an arena for painting
of all periods and all
countries, like the
Galleria degli Uffizi
in Florence.
However, up to 1914
paintings of all
formats were packed
in together with no
concern for
chronological or
even geographical
order. Many artists
painted it, some
conferring on the
room a hushed,
intimate atmosphere.
Through the black-
framed door of the
Salle Duchâtel (1
and 3) part of the
*Wedding Feast at
Cana*, a huge
painting by Paolo
Veronese ▲ *266*, can
be seen against the
far wall on the Seine
side. Alexandre Brun
(1853–1941) also
painted the Salon
with some accuracy
(2), showing that the
works were still hung
closely together in
his day. However he
does not show the
gold and stucco work
on the ceiling,
commissioned by

Duban during the
Second Republic.
High black plinths
and walls of a shade
variously described
as purple or
chocolate contribute
to a particularly
somber atmosphere.
High barriers with
brightly polished
brass protect the
works behind a row
of red seats. The
room has two
entrances, one from
the Salle Duchâtel
devoted to the early
masters, and the
other from the
Grande Galerie
where the majority
of paintings were
carefully ordered
according to school
and date. The entire
space is given over to
paintings: even the
windows looking
over the Seine are
filled. The room is
lit only by the roof
light. The doorways
are low, allowing for
two paintings to be
hung over the lintel
(Hyacinthe Rigaud's
Portrait of Bossuet
and Jacob Jordaens'
Jupiter and Antiope
can be seen here).
Cut-off corners in
the room allow large-

format works to be fitted in: Leonardo da Vinci's *The Virgin and Child with Saint Anne* ▲ 262 is seen below a large Guercino, for example. The far wall offers a typical example of the way paintings used to be hung. The higher section of the wall is used for large paintings (Jean Jouvenet's *Descent from the Cross*, Philippe de Champaigne's *Portrait of Richelieu*, and Valentin de Boulogne's *Concert*); the lower section features symmetrical arrangements of similar works, such as Raphael's *The Virgin and Child with Saint John the Baptist*, known as *La Belle Jardinière* ▲ 262, with oval landscapes by Claude Lorrain on either side, as well as Andrea da Solario's *Virgin with the Green Cushion* and a picture by Bernardino Luini.

1	
	2
3	

LOUIS BÉROUD

Although Louis Béroud (1852–1930) did produce ordinary paintings of the Louvre (above), from time to time he gave free rein to his imagination. Here (right) he imagines Rubens being welcomed in the room of the *History of Marie de' Medici* series arranged by Gaston Redon in 1900 (shown in its brand new state in top painting). In a joyous confusion all the figures descend from their frames to pay homage to their creator ▲ *250*. In another picture (bottom), the most famous paintings of the Salon Carré where the masterpieces are hung, leave the walls to join in Veronese's *Wedding Feast at Cana* and Rubens' *Hélène Fourment*, the *Mona Lisa*, Titian's *Man with a Glove*, and other figures by Raphael and Correggio all invite themselves to the feast.

THE LOUVRE THROUGH VISITORS' EYES

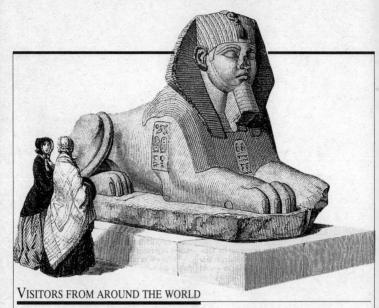

VISITORS FROM AROUND THE WORLD

*F*ree entry to all, collections consisting entirely of original works from all over the world and an administration which held steady through times of political instability: these were some of the qualities which made the 19th-century Louvre an exemplary institution in the eyes of visitors from England, China and Spain.

Tcheng Ki Tong (1851–1907), a Chinese general and diplomat was sent to France in 1877 to become secretary of the Chinese embassy in Paris. After holding the post of military attaché in various European capitals he returned to Paris in 1883 and wrote a number of humorous works about the French in their own language.

❝What is called a museum in Europe is a sort of large building which houses masterpieces of the arts and sciences, or simply objects which can tell us about the life, customs and ideas of different peoples.

Among all collections of this type, the Louvre is one of the finest. It contains treasures collected from nearly all corners of the civilized world and allows us to review at a glance the history of nations and their various destinies. It is an admirable institution and I regret that we have nothing like it in China. Of course we too have wonderfully rich collections, but they relate to China alone and are not concerned with the arts of other countries. Furthermore they belong to individuals, the ordinary people have no access to them; unlike the lucky Parisians they cannot go and see them every day and learn from them free of charge.❞

TCHENG KI TONG, *PARISIANS DESCRIBED BY A CHINESE*, PARIS, 1891

Mirza Aboul Taleb Khan was born in 1751 of a Persian father exiled to India. In 1799 he moved to Europe and lived in London for two years. He spent three weeks in Paris in 1802 before returning to Calcutta.

❝The Louvre is a very large and very lofty building: the entire ground floor is filled with statues and other objects, whose beauty I was entirely unable to judge. On the first floor there is a magnificent room, more than three hundred feet square and over fifty feet high, lit from above using mirrors placed at an angle: this method has the double advantage of increasing the intensity of light while keeping out snow and rain as effectively as a slate-covered roof. Several thousand magnificent paintings are displayed across the entire expanse of the walls. The collection is immense, its value incalculable: some of the paintings are 70 ft long and 30 ft high. After seeing the building and the treasures it holds I considered what I had seen in London and Dublin and realized that these two cities have mere trifles by comparison with these wonders. The museum is funded by the public who are admitted without charge: the aim is to encourage a taste for the fine arts, to keep a shrine for them in France's capital and to give the government a popular appeal. **"**

MIRZA ABOUL TALEB KHAN, *VOYAGES OF THE PERSIAN PRINCE MIRZA ABOUL TALEB KHAN IN ASIA, AFRICA, AND EUROPE*, PUB. CHARLES MALO, PARIS, 1819

VISITORS OF ALL CLASSES

*O*rdinary people crowded into the museum *from its first years onward. Under the Consulate and the Empire foreign visitors noted the presence of "rough commoners" and the poorest citizens of Paris among the Louvre's public. People of all social classes and conditions rubbed shoulders at the Louvre. The only condition was that they should be "decently dressed", except for old and invalid soldiers who sauntered about in tattered uniforms.*

Norbert Truquin, who came from the Somme, described himself as a proletarian and related his life's adventures as a series of experiences scarred by exploitation and inequality. At the time of the 1848 revolution he was living in Paris. In 1850 he left for Argentina and then Paraguay, where he wrote his memoirs.

"After arriving in Paris I has spent the whole time visiting the sights of the capital. Sometimes in the evening I bought the petit *Lazari* for a few centimes. I was able to visit the main buildings, museums and public gardens but this was because I was wearing a frock coat: people wearing overalls were not allowed in which meant that many young people grew old without knowing Paris.

In the museums it was the paintings that interested me most. I would try to guess at their subjects and often pestered other visitors with questions. Some turned away in

disdain; others by contrast responded to my request for explanations with good grace. At this time I began to observe the people there. I noticed that those with a full beard and a straight nose rarely refused me information whereas I could get nothing out of those with flat or beak-shaped noses. **"**

NORBERT TRUQUIN, *MEMOIRS AND ADVENTURES OF A PROLETARIAN IN 1848*, PUB. MASPERO, PARIS, 1977

One Saturday in July 1850 a wedding party decided to go to the Louvre because it was raining and to fill in the time before dinner. It was the wedding party of Coupeau and Gervaise, characters in the novel "L'Assommoir" by Emile Zola (1840–1902).

❝M. Madinier politely asked if he could lead the procession. The Louvre was very big and they might get lost there; furthermore he knew all the best places because he had often come with an artist, a very intelligent young man, whose drawings were bought by a large cardboard box company to adorn their products. Downstairs, when the party reached the Assyrian museum, a little shiver passed through it. Goodness! it wasn't exactly warm down here, the place would make a magnificent cellar. And slowly the couples advanced, chins lifted, eyelids fluttering, between the stone pillars the silent gods of black marble with their hieratic rigidity, the colossal beasts, half-cat and half-woman, with cadaverous faces, thin noses and bulging lips. They found all this quite unpleasant. Stone carving nowadays was a jolly sight better than that . . .

Then the wedding party set off down a long gallery which contained the Italian and Flemish schools. Yet more paintings, nothing but paintings of saints, of men and women with faces they couldn't understand, landscapes with nothing but black, animals which had yellowed with age, a chaos of people and things in a violent din of colors which was starting to give them a terrible headache. M. Madinier was no longer speaking and slowly led the procession which followed in an orderly manner, necks twisted and eyes in the air. Whole centuries of art passed before their stupefied ignorance, the exquisite dryness of the early masters, the splendors of the Venetians, the luxuriantly and beautiful light-filled world of the Dutch. What interested them more was the copyists with their easels set up among the crowd, painting away unabashed; an old lady struck them particularly, standing at the top of a large ladder, moving her brush through the soft sky of a huge canvas. Gradually however, the rumor must have spread about that a wedding party was visiting the Louvre. The painters hastened towards them grinning from ear to ear;

curious onlookers took advance seats on the benches to see the procession pass in comfort while the attendants with pursed lips held back their witty remarks. And the wedding party, weary already and less polite, dragged their studded slippers and tapped their heels on the echoing floors with the stamping of a herd let loose, unleashed amidst the bare, contemplative neatness of the museum rooms.**

ÉMILE ZOLA, *L'ASSOMMOIR* (1877), VOLUME 2 IN THE *ROUGON-MACQUART* SERIES, PUB. GALLIMARD, PARIS, 1961

Alfred de Musset (1810–57) considered that knowledge and explanations were by no means necessary to appreciate masterpieces: a naive sensibility was, to his mind, far better. Proof was supplied by a beautiful young peasant woman who happened to pass by.

**I am definitely one of those people who goes to the museum without a guidebook. . . . Yes it occurred to me that when you visit, for example, the old gallery at the Louvre, you might as well fold your arms behind your back. What can any explanation teach you?

Stubbornly convinced of this I rubbed my hands, deprived of their guide book. I paused by a railing just below a patriotic painting. I don't know what particular subject it depicted but a large crowd had gathered there and was gaping at it.

"Well," I said to myself, "what a typical holiday crowd," but suddenly I noticed in the middle of these gawping nonentities, the sullen, indifferent head of a beautiful young peasant woman whose uncle was nudging her in admiration of the picture, while she was looking the other way!

She was wearing a lace bonnet and a pair of earrings as big as six-franc pieces; she had a pensive, stupid air, eyes gazing into thin air; she heard nothing and took no interest in anything her uncle called upon her to admire.

"Truly," I said to myself, "I am a fool if I don't follow this girl and see what captures her interest." I fancied I saw in her whole being the appearance of naive sensibility. I set off on her heels . . .

In this manner we went round the Salle Carrée, the uncle crying out in admiration, the young girl stifling her yawns; all of which led me to think that I was probably wasting my time, that the girl was a complete fool and as nothing interested her, I had better leave.

And so I moved away and, chancing upon Henri, threw myself into a furious debate, denouncing everything as worthless . . .

A few paces away I caught sight of my beautiful peasant girl. Her large black eyes were fixed on a canvas quite high up; an expression of deep sensibility and a faint smile convinced me that I had not been wrong about her after all.

But what painting was she looking at? What had caught her attention? I took a few steps forwards and saw clearly that it was *The Flood* by Schnetz. What satisfaction I felt! . . . It is clear that this young girl knows nothing about it and here she is gazing at a masterpiece (for I must confess that this is my opinion of the work) . . . And what did I say then? What do we all say, all we demented artists who dare to claim that we are misunderstood? . . . Condemn and praise, argue and intrigue as you will, one day all of it will fall before the weak, ignorant gaze of a young girl.**

ALFRED DE MUSSET, *FANTASTIC REVIEWS*, LE TEMPS, MAY 9, 1831, IN *COMPLETE WORKS*, PUB. LE SEUIL, PARIS, 1966

The working public came on Sundays: traders, factory workers and clerks. So did Eugène Delacroix with his old servant, and Charles Baudelaire (1821–67), who bumped into them in the Assyrian museum.

❝One day, a Sunday, I spotted Delacroix at the Louvre accompanied by the old servant who has cared for him for thirty years. This elegant, refined, erudite man did not consider it beneath him to show and explain the mysteries of Assyrian sculpture to the excellent woman who listened to him with simple earnestness.❞

CHARLES BAUDELAIRE, *THE WORK AND LIFE OF DELACROIX* (1863),
IN *ESTHETIC CURIOSITIES*, BORDAS, PUB. CLASSIQUES GARNIER, PARIS, 1990

Jeanne Baudot, a pupil of Renoir, often worked at the Louvre in the last years of the century. Her book of reminiscences was published in 1949 after the Louvre had become "less accessible"; no doubt she was referring to the introduction of entrance charges in 1922. Here she records to great effect how the museum, open to all comers, was brimming with life.

❝During the time when we were working at the Louvre, the museum was brimming with life – it has been robbed of this by the new regulations which made it less accessible, less democratic. I knew it when it was open to anyone. The only condition was to be suitably dressed.

Sometimes tramps would thread their way through the crowds, warming themselves by the stoves or sitting on the benches. If they were unfortunate enough to doze off and fall over a frightened guard would rush over, glancing at the pictures for fear of an accident or theft and recovering only once the cause of the panic had fled. Nearly every day, always at the same time, a particular man would appear for his daily constitutional, walking straight ahead without pausing before any of the masterpieces. You could also see lovers, waiting in vain for their Dulcinea: others, happier, in couples, reminiscent of the *Embarcation for the Isle of Cythera*. And finally, a bourgeois Eros set marriages in motion through introductions made here!❞

JEANNE BAUDOT, *RENOIR, HIS FRIENDS AND HIS MODELS*,
PUB. ÉDITIONS LITTÉRAIRES DE FRANCE, PARIS, 1949

APPRENTICESHIP IN ART

*M*any *artists came to copy at the Louvre, in order to study the masters. It was through drawing Classical works that Auguste Rodin (1840–1917) fell in love with sculpture. Alberto Giacometti (1901–66) came to the Louvre every Sunday during his first years in Paris. Henri Matisse (1869–1954) frequently spoke about the copies he made at the Louvre: "I studied in the studios in the morning and copied at the Louvre in the afternoon. This lasted for ten years." He started at the École des Beaux-Arts in 1892, in Gustave Moreau's studio. Paul Cézanne (1839–1906) reverted to a more sensible opinion after having wanted, like many others, to "burn down the Louvre".*

❝I used to come here so often then, when I was only about fifteen years old. Initially I wanted passionately to be a painter. I was fascinated by color. I often went upstairs to see the Titians and Rembrandts. But alas! I didn't have enough money to buy canvas and tubes of color. To copy the Classical works, by contrast, I only needed paper and pencils. So I was forced to work only in the rooms downstairs and I soon fell so passionately in love with sculpture that I no longer thought of anything else.❞

AUGUSTE RODIN, *ART: CONVERSATIONS COLLECTED BY PAUL GSELL* (1911)
PUB. GRASSET, PARIS, 1986

❝I have nearly the whole of the Louvre in my head: room by room, painting by painting . . . I copied a great deal . . . Nearly all the works, going all the way back . . . By trying to copy you get to see the thing better. I questioned each work in turn, intensely and at length.❞

ALBERTO GIACOMETTI, IN *PIERRE SCHNEIDER*,
DIALOGUES OF THE LOUVRE (1972), PUB. ADAM BIRO, PARIS, 1991

❝Moreau took an interest in my work. He was an educated man, who encouraged his pupils to look at all types of painting while other teachers could only think of a single period or style – their own, that is, contemporary academicism, a mish-mash of all the conventions. We made copies at the Louvre, both to study the masters and to live with them, and also because the government would buy the copies. However for the government the copies had to be executed with minute exactness, faithful to the letter of the work rather than its spirit. It was because of this that the works most favored by the buying committee were those done by the mothers, wives and daughters of museum attendants. Our copies were only accepted through charity or sometimes when Roger Marx pleaded our cause. I would have liked to make literal copies like the attendants' mothers, wives and daughters, but I was incapable of doing so.❞

HENRI MATISSE, "CONVERSATION WITH TÉRIADE", *ART NEWS ANNUAL* (1952),
IN *WRITINGS AND REMARKS ON ART*, PUB. HERMANN, PARIS, 1972

❝I want to be a true classicist, to become classical again through nature, through feeling. Before my ideas were confused. Life! Life! This was the only word I could utter. I wanted to burn down the Louvre, poor cretin that I was! You have to go to the Louvre through nature, and return to nature through the Louvre.❞

PAUL CÉZANNE, QUOTED BY JOACHIM GASQUET, *PAUL CÉZANNE* (1921),
AS CITED IN *CONVERSATIONS WITH CÉZANNE*, PUB. MACULA, PARIS, 1978

A FOREST OF EASELS

Alongside the artists who worked at the Louvre on commission – some of them only ever worked as copyists – and those who studied the masters, there was a whole community of copyists who set up their easels there too. These were the students, especially female students (hardly any art schools in the 19th century admitted women) and elderly toilers who were a favorite subject for caricaturists. Edmond Duranty, in his novella "The Painter Louis Martin", described the Louvre as "a forest of easels and ladders". This is the Louvre that Jeanne Baudot (1877–1957), Renoir's pupil, knew at the very end of the last century.

❝At the Louvre, Renoir had me copy the right-hand group in Poussin's *Rape of the Sabine Women*. I wasn't yet twenty years old and I was worried at the prospect of painting in public. Renoir reassured me, saying that if the daubers bothered me he would come to my defence. He didn't have to intervene. My whole attitude let my colleagues know that I had come there purely to work . . . .

At the same time Matisse was copying Chardin's *The Furrow*; Flandrin was copying Ingres' *Odalisque* and Marquet, Poussin's *Arcadian Shepherds* . . . .

Another year I found Matisse and his friends at the Louvre, Matisse was copying Philippe de Champaigne's *The Dead Christ* in the hope of selling it to the committee to feed his large family. He was working conscientiously and unremittingly, and so well that looking at his copy you would have thought Philippe de Champaigne had just finished working at it. But the committee was inexorable, demanding a reproduction which was identical to the original, with the patina of age; Matisse, in order to achieve this, did not hesitate to cover his copy with "brown sauce" as he called it, two days before it was to be sold, to take off its freshness . . . .

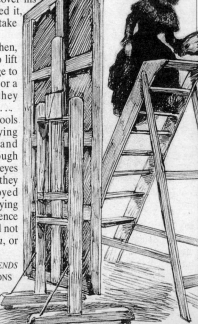

Ah! it was good to be at the Louvre then, with the Old Masters who seemed to lift you up to the Infinite. What a privilege to hear the modern painters – a Renoir, or a Degas – speaking of the shock they always felt before their predecessors! . . . .

Daubers of all countries and all schools came to learn their trade by copying paintings. Others still, old men and women, painted unceasingly, although their hands were trembling and their eyes worn out. Like shipwrecked sailors they clung to the art which had destroyed them! Many of them were still copying the same work, knowing from experience that it would be bought. A vicar could not fail to be charmed by Murillo's *Virgin*, or an American by the *Mona Lisa*.❞

JEANNE BAUDOT, *RENOIR, HIS FRIENDS AND HIS MODELS*, PUB. ÉDITIONS LITTÉRAIRES DE FRANCE, PARIS, 1949

It was in Paris that Henry James (1843–1916), the English writer of American origin, put the final touches to his novel "The American". After this he settled in London where he wrote most of his works. "The American" contains several descriptions of the Louvre.

❝As the little copyist proceeded with her work, she sent every now and then a responsive glance toward her admirer. The cultivation of the fine arts appeared to necessitate, to her mind, a great deal of by-play, a great deal of standing off with folded arms and head drooping from side to side, stroking of a dimpled chin with a dimpled hand, sighing and frowning and tapping of the foot, fumbling in disordered tresses for wandering hair-pins. These performances were accompanied by a restless glance, which lingered longer than elsewhere upon the gentleman we have described. At last he rose abruptly, put on his hat and approached the young lady. He placed himself before her picture and looked at it for some moments, during which she pretended to be quite unconscious of his inspection. Then, addressing her with the single word which constituted the strength of his French vocabulary, and holding up one finger in a manner which appeared to him to illuminate his meaning, 'Combien?' he abruptly demanded.❞

HENRY JAMES, *THE AMERICAN*, 1877, PUB. HERON BOOKS, LONDON 1976

Women painters, however, even the young ones, were not always regarded with goodwill. In 1844, Jules Fleury (1821–89) who later used the name Champfleury, described them as a "calamity".

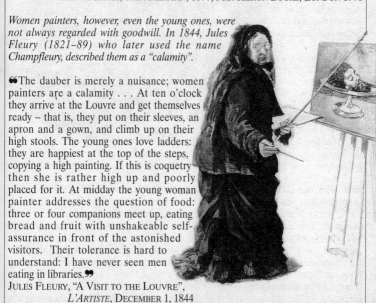

❝The dauber is merely a nuisance; women painters are a calamity . . . At ten o'clock they arrive at the Louvre and get themselves ready – that is, they put on their sleeves, an apron and a gown, and climb up on their high stools. The young ones love ladders: they are happiest at the top of the steps, copying a high painting. If this is coquetry then she is rather high up and poorly placed for it. At midday the young woman painter addresses the question of food: three or four companions meet up, eating bread and fruit with unshakeable self-assurance in front of the astonished visitors. Their tolerance is hard to understand: I have never seen men eating in libraries.❞

JULES FLEURY, "A VISIT TO THE LOUVRE",
L'ARTISTE, DECEMBER 1, 1844

With Edmond de Goncourt (1822–96) and Jules de Goncourt (1830–70), we rediscover the same copyists, only poorer . . . and seen through the eyes of a more bitter narrator. "Manette Solomon", one of the novels co-written by the brothers, describes the artistic scene under the Second Empire.

❝At the Louvre in the afternoon, he hardly worked any more. His mind, his eyes were quickly tired of looking at the colors and the design of the old canvases he was copying; and his attention soon wandered from the paintings to the baroque world of the copyists, men and women, who inhabited the galleries. He indulged his scorn on all these living ironies, thrown to the feet of masterpieces by hunger, poverty, need and the relentless pursuit of a false vocation; a population of paupers, so funny you could cry at them, picking up the crumbs of art from the feet of the gods! The old women with their grey ringlets, bent over copies of Bouchers – all pink and nude – looking like Alecto illuminating Anacreon; ladies with an orange complexion, in dresses without sleeves, a grey apron across their chest, perched, glasses on the bridge of the nose, at the top of ladders draped with green serge to preserve the modesty of their thin legs; the unfortunate china painters with their haggard eyes, squinting through a magnifying glass to copy Titian's *Entombment of Christ*, small old men in small black tunics, their long hair parted in the middle, each one like some fifty-year old baby Jesus preserved in brandy – all this world with its pitiable comedy, amused Anatole and made him laugh delightfully inside.❞

EDMOND AND JULES DE GONCOURT, *MANETTE SALOMON* (1867),
PUB. UNION GÉNÉRALE D'ÉDITIONS, PARIS, 1979

A DREAM WORLD

*I*t is a common desire to have access to the museum at night, to see the masterpieces *in a stranger or more intimate context. Kings have had this privilege but only with a large escort. Security guards have the same experience, more intimately, every day. Others enjoy it, boldly and without restriction, through their imagination.*

At night, as we all know, the characters descend from their paintings. The painter Louis Béroud, in the last years of the 19th century and at the beginning of the 20th, was very successful at the Salon with his paintings combining the most famous figures of the Louvre, liberated from their frames. It was a spectacle of this kind that Roland Dorgelès (1885–1973) stumbled upon before being unmasked by Molière: the scenery of the "Wedding Feast at Cana" deserted by the banqueters, the Salon Carré full of guests, shipwrecked sailors from the "Medusa", gazing bright-eyed at a still life by Snyders . . .

❝Molière unmasked me; suddenly he realized. 'It's a man from the present, he shouted out . . . an attendant! watch out, everyone!'

Panic broke out. The alarm spread from the classical antiquities to the Salle Camondo, fear caught on like fire, everyone running, shouting, jostling, like some shady midnight party invaded by the police.

In a spin I saw saints go by, kings, naked women, prelates, moors, lute players. I was thrown against the wall, knocked over . . . . A Troyon herd passed over my body, all Delacroix's crusaders, Dutchmen in clogs, Corot's nymphs uttering sharp cries and that immense fellow Saint Michael who nearly poked my eye out with his lance . . . Under the huge frame of the *Wedding Feast at Cana*, crazed characters jostled, clambered, gave each other a leg up – Don't push, there are children here! Hey you, the man with the glove, you're in the wrong painting! And where is the Mona Lisa? gone off again . . . And suddenly, in the twinkling of an eye, nothing is moving, everything is back in place . . . . They have all found a place, somehow, haphazardly. However some of them have got into the wrong pictures. Saint Bruno, looking irritated, turning his nose up at the seraglio of Algerian women. Degas' laundress has left her attic and thrown herself, puffing and blowing, at the foot of Queen Elizabeth's bed (the latter regarding her with some distaste); with a single leap Velasquez's dwarf has leapt onto the Raft of the Medusa where he seems somewhat out of place, while Decamps' three bell-ringers, drunk as lords, are standing respectfully behind Napoleon who, still rather shaky from running, is crowning the Empress in front of a motley assembly in which I spotted the two thieves, Colbert, the gentlemen from the *Burial of Ornans* and a young martyr looking so terribly respectable despite her soaking wet dress.**"**

ROLAND DORGELÈS, "THE PALACE AWAKENED", *VIE PARISIENNE*, MAY 25, 1918

Sigmund Freud (1856–1939), visiting the Louvre during his stay in Paris in 1885, did not need a fiction like this to discover, as he wrote to his fiancée, "a dream world" (literally and in Freudian terms "a world as in a dream").

"I just had time enough left to look briefly at the Assyrian and Egyptian rooms, which I shall have to return to several times. There were Assyrian kings as tall as trees, holding lions in their arms as if they were toy dogs, winged bulls with human faces and magnificent curly hair, cuneiform inscriptions as clear as if they had been carved yesterday, Egyptian bas-reliefs painted in bright colors, colossal kings, real sphinxes, a world as in a dream (*eine Welt wie im Traum*).**"**

SIGMUND FREUD, LETTER TO MARTHA BERNAYS (OCTOBER 19, 1885),
IN *CORRESPONDENCE*, PUB. GALLIMARD, PARIS, 1979

A visit to the Louvre can inspire dreams of ownership. Napoleon asked his architect Fontaine if there was any way of moving his apartments in the Tuileries next to the museum, so he could have the Grande Galerie in his home . . . Michel Tournier (born in 1924) for his part, sees things less simply.

"The magic of the archaic Apollo of the Island of Paros! . . .I imagine what my life would be like if this god was in my home, owned by me night and day. And to tell the truth, no, I cannot imagine how I would bear the incandescent presence of this meteor landing by me, after twenty centuries of falling.**"**

MICHEL TOURNIER, *KING OF ALDERS*,
PUB. GALLIMARD, PARIS, 1970

PROFUSION AND CHAOS

*T*oo *many objects, of too many different types: the Louvre risks distracting the visitor's eye with the "indiscernible chaos" of its many juxtaposed works. Although the buildings and collections have been rearranged and reorganized at regular intervals, visitors still come up against a profusion of masterpieces, as well as the complexity of the museum itself. Regular visitors grow fond of this very abundance, even of the juxtapositions which are like those of a dream world.*

This is not the case with Paul Valéry (1871–1945) who has here just entered a sculpture room and attacks the very idea of a museum with such extreme criticism that it is impossible to imagine any progress which could alleviate his displeasure at this "combination of separate beauties".

❝I am in a commotion of deep-frozen creatures, each one of them demanding, but not obtaining, the inexistence of all the others. And I am not referring here to the chaos of all these sizes without a common measure, to the inexplicable mixture of dwarves and giants, of the perfect and the incomplete, the mutilated and the restored, of monsters and men ...

With a soul ready for suffering I move toward the paintings. Before me in the silence a strange organized disorder unfolds ... This combination of separate but conflicting beauties is a paradox; even when they seem most alike they are in fact the greatest of enemies.

Only a civilization without a sense of pleasure or reason could have set up this

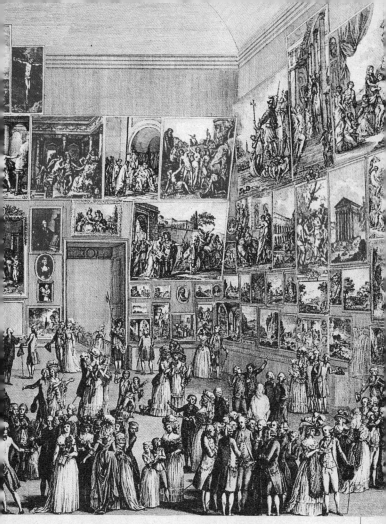

house of incoherence. The product of this proximity of dead visions is something senseless and indefinable. They quarrel jealously for the eyes that give them life. My undivided attention is called for in all directions, throwing into turmoil that internal magnet which draws the whole machine of the body towards what attracts it . . . No ear could bear to hear two orchestras at once. The mind cannot follow or conduct a number of different operations at the same time and there are no simultaneous thought processes. But the eye in the aperture of its optical angle and at the moment of perception, is obliged to take in a portrait and a seascape, a still life and a triumph and characters of the most diverse states and sizes; furthermore it is supposed to absorb completely incompatible consonances and styles of painting.

Just as the sense of sight is assaulted by that abuse of space which is called a collection, so the intelligence is no less insulted by the proximity of important works. The more beautiful they are, the more they are exceptional products of human ambition, the more separate they should be. These are rare objects, whose authors would want them to be unique. This painting it is sometimes said, just KILLS all the others around it . . .

I believe that neither Egypt, China nor Greece, all of them wise and refined cultures, had this system of juxtaposing works which consume each other. They did not arrange incompatible units of pleasure according to reference numbers and abstract principles. 99

PAUL VALÉRY, *THE PROBLEM OF MUSEUMS* (1923)
IN *OEUVRES II*,
PUB. GALLIMARD, PARIS, 1960

Élie Faure (1873–1937) called it an "irreducible chaos"; Julian Gracq (born 1910) described it even more cruelly as a stage-scenery merchant. How could this be remedied? More weeding out? Ingres had already called for this, in the name of his ideal of beauty. Baudelaire, more open-minded and generous, considered the profusion good and necessary, as without it there would be only general beauty, while the minor artists, with their particular beauties, "have good, sound and delightful qualities".

❝ A deep stupefaction, an immense confusion where shapes and colors fought it out in a comical, irreducible chaos, stayed with me after all my visits and often nearly discouraged me. I nearly dropped the Louvre, I nearly dropped painting . . . **❞**

ÉLIE FAURE: *EQUIVALENCES: CONFESSIONS OF A SELF-TAUGHT PAINTER*
(1ST EDITION, PUBLISHED POSTHUMOUSLY IN 1951),
IN *OEUVRES COMPLÈTES*, PUB. J.J. PAUVERT, PARIS, 1964

❝ The Louvre museum is still crammed full of grand old paintings like a stage-scenery merchant despite the reductions which have been made; often it seems like just an enormous, flabber-gasting provincial museum jammed full of state consignments. **❞**

JULIEN GRACQ,
LETTRINES, VOLUME 2,
JOSÉ CORTI, PARIS, 1967

The juxtapositions, the abundance and the chaos themselves become attractions for regular visitors to the Louvre. This is the view of Václav Vilém Štech, a Czech art historian, a professor of the Prague Academy of Arts from 1930 to 1945 and a student at the Sorbonne from 1912 to 1914. Among others of this opinion is Kenneth Clark, former director of the National Gallery and Surveyor of the King's Pictures in Great Britain.

❝ The Louvre has always been a chaotic museum. It grew for a long time without a plan for its development and without unity. But it is probably this anarchic abundance – so different from the synthetic character of the collections in Berlin, for example – that accounts for the living, unsettling attraction exercised by this testimony to humanity and humans. Here you can wander, compare, discover new visions and new worlds. **❞**

VÁCLAV VILÉM ŠTECH, *ZA PLOTEM DOMOVA (BEYOND OUR FENCES)*,
TRANSLATED BY A. NOVOTNA GALARD,
PUB. ČESKOSLOVENSKÝ SPOSOVATEL, PRAGUE, 1970

❝ Not only is the Louvre the largest collection of works of art in the world, but even its imperfections are endearing. The ordinary gaping tourists who are out of their depth in any art gallery must feel completely lost at the Louvre. However, once you have become used to its extraordinary juxtapositions (a spiral staircase takes us from the early Egyptians to French 19th-century painting), these excite your affection. To adopt a French custom, you could say that the Louvre is a very feminine institution – complex, unpredictable, sometimes exasperating, and always enchanting. **❞**

KENNETH CLARK, *THE OTHER HALF: A SELF-PORTRAIT*,
PUB. JOHN MURRAY, LONDON, 1977

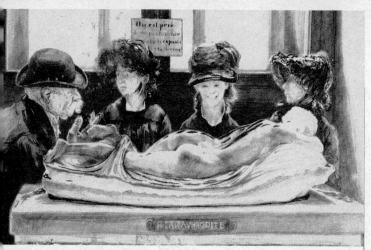

EROS

S *ome visitors are uneasy seeing figures and scenes which appear to be indecent.* *Their modesty is offended by the nudity on display. "The Louvre Museum: to be avoided by young girls" notes Gustave Flaubert in his "Dictionary of Received Ideas".*

Perhaps it should also be avoided by children suggests Julien Green (born 1900), thinking of the visits his mother took him on around 1910.

❝From time to time my mother took us to the Louvre, sometimes dragging us to the sculpture displays. She did not know what she was doing. She could not suspect that I came out of there in a sort of sexual intoxication which tortured me all the more because I did not know its precise cause. Nudity, criminal nudity, why was it permitted to see it like that, exalted, dominant, perched on pedestals and seeming to trample us underfoot? 'These are works of art' explained my mother, 'statues of false gods. Come on, let's go, don't stay there. We'll get the Passy-Hôtel de Ville bus to go home. If there aren't any spaces we'll go up to the Imperial.' Why do we take children to museums?❞

JULIEN GREEN, *LEAVING BEFORE DAYBREAK*, PUB. GRASSET, PARIS, 1963

Sergei Eisenstein (1898–1948) stayed in Paris in 1930 as part of a visit to France while shooting the film "Sentimental Romance". In his "Memoirs", he shudders at the memory of the Louvre and the dreams suggested by its "pernicious atmosphere".

❝I cannot remember the Louvre without shaking. It was reorganized during the pre-war years. But I still remember it, with all the suffocating splendor of its brightly colored rooms, and the turbulence of the indifferent multitude, somehow halfway between an opera foyer and a post office.

The walls were so closely packed with masterpieces it was as if they had been papered with postage stamps.

The women in the pictures seemed to be warming themselves on the animal heat of the sweaty herds of visitors.

The construction of the canvases seemed to highlight their bodies, whether these were plump, or ascetic in the early masters. And it seemed that in this pernicious atmosphere these Venuses, Dianas or Europas were ready to slide down from their frames, just as the cruelly spineless women of Degas' caustic pastels climb from their bathtubs, to grab the visitor with the big nose by the sleeve and draw him to them behind the flimsy olive-, puce- or cherry-colored curtains of the "foreground" where their drapery is abandoned. Ah, if these ladies of the past were not protected

● THE LOUVRE
THROUGH VISITORS' EYES

from visitors' eager hands by a lock and a grille ...
Such was the fate of the *Mona Lisa* after the infamous adventures of this illustrious mystery woman in the hands of international fraudsters. The grille and the lock suggest a chastity belt put on her for the next series of escapades. **99**

SERGEI EISENSTEIN, *MEMOIRS* (1964),
PUB. JUILLARD,
PARIS, 1989

And Salvador Dali (1904–89), being one of those who associate museums with eroticism (as does Michel Leiris in his book "The Age of Man") explains in his own style how "in an atmosphere like this" you can almost be driven, inescapably, to attack the "Mona Lisa".

66To explain the 'naive aggression' directed against the *Mona Lisa* with reference to the Freudian discovery of Leonardo's libido and his subconscious erotic visions relating to his mother, we would require the genius of Michelangelo Antonioni (unique in the history of the cinema) who would film the following sequence: a son, simple and innocent, unconsciously in love with his mother and ravaged by the Oedipus complex, visits a museum. For this more or less Bolivian innocent the museum is the equivalent of a public house, in other words a brothel; the resemblance is reinforced by the multitude of erotic objects he finds here: nudes, scandalous statues, Rubens. Amidst such sensual and libidinous promiscuity, the oedipal son is dumbfounded to find a portrait of his own mother resplendent in the epitome of idealized femininity. His own mother, here! And what is worse his mother is smiling at him in an ambiguous way which can only appear suggestive and shameful in this context. Aggression is the only possible response to a smile like that; unless he were to steal the painting to rescue it from the scandal and shame of being exhibited in a public house.
If anyone can offer any other explanations with reference to the attacks suffered by the *Mona Lisa*, let them cast the first stone at me. I shall pick it up and continue my work as builder of the Truth. **99**

SALVADOR DALI, "WHY THE MONA LISA WAS ATTACKED", *OUI 2*,
PUB. DENOËL, PARIS, 1971

In 1933 a Japanese pair, unsettled and oppressed by the cruelty in the pictures, experience nausea at the sight of the Rubens. Sanki Ichikawa is Professor of English Literature at the University of Tokyo.

66Going to the Louvre was quite a shock for me. It seems to me that I lack the ability to appreciate painting, almost as if I had an illness of some sort: therefore I shall say no more on this subject ... But, for example, taking that Saint Sebastian whose body and neck are pierced with arrows: if people do not see the ecstasy in his face, turned towards the sky, they are considered as abnormal. For my part I can only see a stupefied expression ... It is not that I am putting on airs and affecting a distaste for cruelty (I do sometimes get excited about bullfights), but this is a lost cause: not only do I not like this type of painting, it horrifies me to the point of giving me a migraine. The women painted by Rubens whose bodies would be nothing but sticky fat if you put them in a press, make me feel nauseous. I thought I would at least like a little the young girl painted by Greuze, but her eyes are like overripe fruit, beginning to go mouldy. **99**

SANKI ICHIKAWA, "PARIS, CITY OF FLOWERS", *OBEI NO SUMIZUMI*
(*IN THE FOUR CORNERS OF THE WESTERN WORLD*),
JUNE 1933

ITINERARIES
WITHIN THE LOUVRE

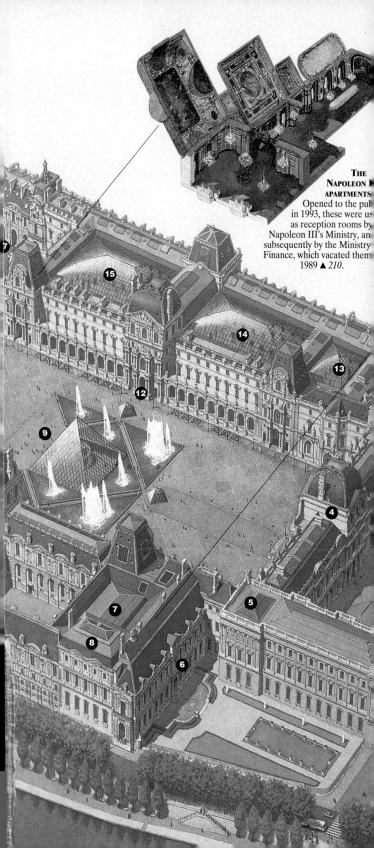

THE NAPOLEON III APARTMENTS

Opened to the public in 1993, these were used as reception rooms by Napoleon III's Ministry, and subsequently by the Ministry of Finance, which vacated them in 1989 ▲ *210*.

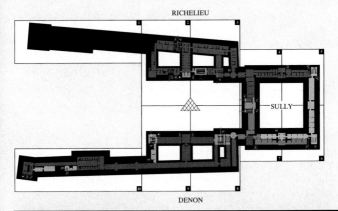

RICHELIEU

DENON

FIRST FLOOR

The first floor is divided into three separate zones. These are the Richelieu building, the north and west wings of the Sully building and the Galerie d'Apollon located in the Denon building, all reserved for *objets d'art* ■, the astonishing variety and wealth of which are among the revelations of the new Louvre. On the Sully side the rooms at the end of the Greek ■ and Egyptian ■ antiquities sections are currently being completed and will shortly be opened. On the Denon side, the principal feature is the Grande Galerie which houses the Louvre's collection of Italian art ■. The section containing larger-scale French paintings runs parallel on the north side; this and the Spanish painting section to the west are both indicated by the color ■. Also on this level are the Pavillon Mollien and the Pavillon Richelieu cafés in the former offices of the Ministry of Finance. The Graphic Arts rooms are indicated by the color ■.

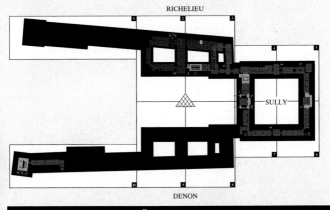

RICHELIEU

DENON

SECOND FLOOR

The second floor is principally devoted to French painting; this section is indicated by the color ■. It is laid out in chronological sequence starting in the Richelieu building and continuing all the way around the Sully building. From here you can return to the large-scale paintings on the first floor. The Dutch and Flemish schools are displayed in the Richelieu building, color ■. The rooms bearing the color ■ form part of the Graphic Arts section as on the first floor, while those of the Pavillon de Flore are reserved for the same department's temporary exhibitions. Fortunately abundant staircases, elevators and escalators make it possible for everyone, including handicapped visitors, to move easily between all four levels. The main escalator in the Richelieu building opened in 1993, offers the best access to the second-floor sales counters, and information rooms, clearly indicated by signs, are present on all four levels of the museum.

BIRD'S-EYE VIEW
OF THE LOUVRE

1. Colonnade
2. Cour Carrée
3. Pavillon des Arts
4. Pavillon de
l'Horloge
5. Pavillon du Roi
6. Petite Galerie
7. Cour du Sphinx
8. Salon Carré
9. Pyramide
10. Salle des États
11. Inverted Pyramide
12. Passage Richelieu
13. Cour Khorsabad
14. Cour Puget
15. Cour Marly
16. Pont du Carrousel
archways (*guichets*)
17. Rue de Rivoli
archways (*guichets*)
18. Arc du Carrousel
19. Carrousel
Gardens
20. Pont-Royal
21. Pavillon de Flore
22. Pavillon de
Marsan (Museum of
Decorative Arts)
23. Tuileries Terrace
24. Tuileries Gardens

THE GRANDE GA
The Louvre mus
with the Grande
originally extende
de Flore (21) ▲ *1*
for the most beau
Louvre – notably
Mona Lisa ▲ 262.

...ERIE
...m began
...Galerie which
...d as far as the Pavillon
...8, and is now a showcase
...iful Italian paintings in the
...eonardo da Vinci's

▲ FINDING YOUR WAY AROUND THE LOUVRE

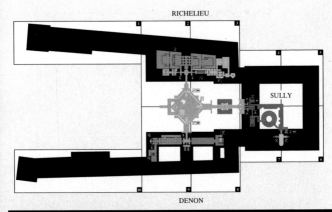

ENTRESOL

Visitors enter the Louvre at the entresol level beneath the Pyramide. From here you can proceed through the museum in any one of three directions, all of which are clearly marked: these are the Richelieu, Sully and Denon buildings. On this same floor level, on the Sully side of the building, are rooms devoted to the history of the Louvre and the Louvre in the Middle Ages, shown by the color ■. Passing through these rooms re-emerge in the Egyptian antiquities section, color ■, and the Greek, Etruscan and Roman antiquities sections, color ■, via the Sphinx crypt. On the Richelieu or north side, the Girardon crypt leads through to the lower levels of the French sculpture section, in addition to the Cour Marly and the Cour Puget, the color ■, and the Islamic section indicated by color ■. In the Denon building are foreign sculpture, denoted by this color ■, and the Greek, Etruscan and Roman antiquities ■.

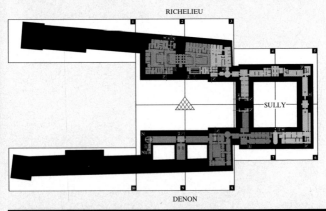

GROUND FLOOR

The ground floor is not directly accessible because the Hall Napoléon is in the way; you must take an escalator to reach this first level. Most of the museum's collections of antiquities are housed here on the Denon side and in the Salle des Cariatides on the Sully side. The Egyptian antiquities, color ■, in the Sully building is closed for restoration at the time of writing. Once reopened it will occupy part of the south wing and the whole of the Colonnade wing vacated by Oriental antiquities, denoted by color ■. The latter is now housed in the east side of the Richelieu building around the Khorsabad courtyard and in the west and north wings of the Sully building. Sculpture, see color ■; French sculpture is housed in the Richelieu building and foreign sculpture in Denon; both are accessible at this level. The former is displayed around the Cours Marly and Puget, and the latter around the former palace stableyards (opened in 1994).

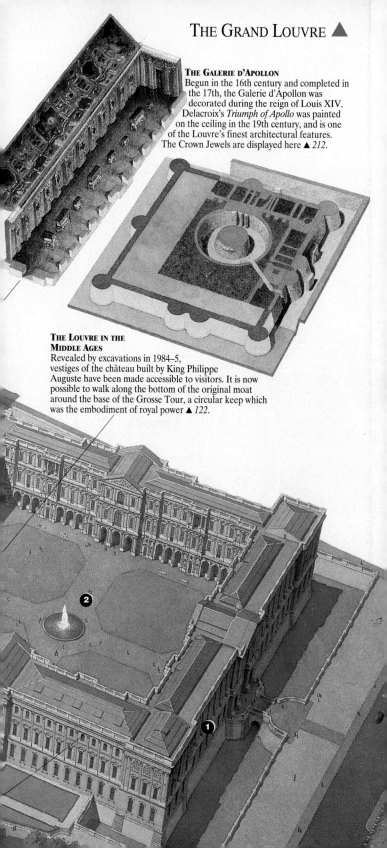

THE GALERIE D'APOLLON
Begun in the 16th century and completed in the 17th, the Galerie d'Apollon was decorated during the reign of Louis XIV. Delacroix's *Triumph of Apollo* was painted on the ceiling in the 19th century, and is one of the Louvre's finest architectural features. The Crown Jewels are displayed here ▲ *212*.

THE LOUVRE IN THE MIDDLE AGES
Revealed by excavations in 1984–5, vestiges of the château built by King Philippe Auguste have been made accessible to visitors. It is now possible to walk along the bottom of the original moat around the base of the Grosse Tour, a circular keep which was the embodiment of royal power ▲ *122*.

THE LOUVRE AND ITS HISTORY

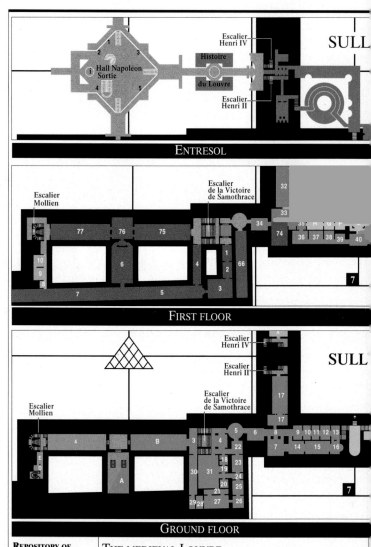

SULL

ENTRESOL

Escalier
Henri IV

Histoire
du Louvre

Escalier
Henri II

Hall Napoléon
Sortie

FIRST FLOOR

Escalier
Mollien

Escalier
de la Victoire
de Samothrace

GROUND FLOOR

Escalier
Henri IV

Escalier
Henri II

SULL

Escalier
Mollien

Escalier
de la Victoire
de Samothrace

**REPOSITORY OF
MASTERPIECES**
This itinerary gives an idea of the history of the museum and of its great decorative wealth and diversity – from the moats of the medieval Louvre to the modern Pyramide. It also offers an initial overview of how the collections are displayed which is developed more fully in the other itineraries.

THE MEDIEVAL LOUVRE

THE MOAT OF CHARLES V adjoins the Carrousel shopping area entrance to the Louvre. Originally fed by the waters of the Seine, it formed Paris' eastern defense line. The 14th-century earthworks were begun here by Étienne Marcel and completed by Charles V; the vestiges of the walls date from the early 16th century when the medieval fortifications were adapted to accommodate long-range artillery. The west wall was rounded by a low tower with an artillery platform on top. Note the long, well-preserved wooden beams on which the masonry rests and the traces of the water which once lapped at the stone foundations. To the west, the wall of the counterscarp served to retain the earth of the new gardens which were laid out for Henri IV in front of the Tuileries

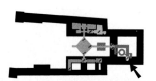

Palace. In the reign of Louis XIII the surrounding walls were pulled down and the moat was filled in.

The Hall Napoléon under the Pyramid, leads into the museum. The Sully aisle leads to the areas concerned with the Louvre's history. At the entrance are four powerful figures in

relief which originally decorated the attic story of the Renaissance Louvre ● *74*. They illustrate Charles IX's motto "piety and justice" and were sculpted at the workshop of Goujon. In the subsequent rooms, paintings by Hubert Robert form a coherent series of studies and meditations on the Louvre museum he loved so much ● *88–91*. His illustrations of the Grande Galerie and the changes it underwent, and the antiquities rooms where the copyists worked, offer fascinating insights into the huge effort made to create a museum here at the time of the Revolution. There is also a group of preparatory sketches for the museum's giant ceiling paintings.

The Bossage wall which you pass as you make your way toward the medieval Louvre, formed the facing for the moat; this was spanned by a bridge leading across to the Pavillon de l'Horloge. Built by Louis le Vau, this wall was discovered during the 1984–5 excavations. Not far away, in the Sully crypt a block of masonry and an outline on the ground indicate the position of the library tower where Charles V's library was located ● *35*.

Moats of Philippe Auguste's château. The sloping wall base in finely cut stone originally ran down to the water of the moats, through which visitors can now pass dryshod. The round towers dating from the time of Philippe Auguste ● *72* continue at regular intervals; there is also a massive square one built by Charles V. Only the north and east sides of the quadrilateral were exposed during the 1984–5 excavations, the other wings being covered over by later construction.

The keep (*donjon*), accessible via a recently opened passage through the wall, is perfectly circular. It can be skirted by way of the moat here, which was always dry. At the end of it is a molding of the ground covered in potsherds, a

The Flayed Judge
To illustrate the theme of justice on the Louvre's façade, the workshop of Jean Goujon ▲ *186* used the story of Cambyses who had a prevaricating judge skinned alive and obliged the son to dispense justice over his father's corpse (detail, left). The other themes are Roman charity (a daughter feeding her captive father from her breast), and Zaleucus, who condemned his own son to be blinded and put out one of the boy's eyes himself. These episodes were supposed to illustrate Charles IX's motto of "piety and justice", an ironic motto for the perpetrator of the St Bartholomew's Day Massacre.

The Medieval Moats
The stonework of the moats in the Carrousel area, like that of the keep and the main quadrilateral of the château (above and left), is remarkably well-bonded and trimmed; it still bears the marks left by the masons who built these features in the Middle Ages ■ *18*. Located during excavations carried out in 1866, the foundations were laid bare during the archeological research preceding the construction of the new Louvre facilities.

reconstruction of what the archeologists discovered. To the right is an overhang indicating the base of the great spiral staircase built in the reign of Charles V. A new passage continues from here beneath the Renaissance wing.

THE SALLE SAINT-LOUIS. Having passed through a vestibule in which ceramics discovered during the excavations are displayed, you enter the low room known as the Salle Saint-Louis. The perimeter walls here date from the time of Philippe Auguste. In the mid-13th century, these were altered: bases with grotesque masks sculpted into the masonry support the arches which rest on stout columns in the center of the room. In 1546 Pierre Lescot retained these substructures, but divided them up with walls and arcades (visible at the rear) to support his own construction, especially the stairway he had planned. This area is now used to display the pieces discovered in a well during the excavations, including plates with the arms of the dauphin and a gilded helmet. Described in a 1411 inventory, this helmet was probably stolen and scraped for its gold before being broken in pieces. By dint of careful work, its original shape and encircling crown of fleurs-de-lys have been restored. Note the

THE SALLE SAINT-LOUIS
This low room was found completely by chance under the Renaissance wing in 1882 in the course of work to install a heating system. It was subsequently opened to the public and for many years was the only visible part of the medieval Louvre. For a while it was called the Salle Philippe Auguste but was eventually renamed after Saint Louis because its capitals date from that king's time. Under Charles V there was already a Salle Saint-Louis in token of the dynasty's reverence for Louis IX. But his room must have been a large reception room, not a little-used basement area such as this one.

winged stags, heraldic emblems of Charles VI and Charles VII and their motto *"En bien"*.

THE RENAISSANCE

ESCALIER HENRI II.
Leaving the Salle Saint-Louis by way of the mezzanine of the Sully crypt, climb the staircase designed by Pierre Lescot to the end of the new Renaissance wing ● 74. The sober proportions of the banisters to the right are enlivened by a stone ceiling with strictly delineated compartments containing satyrs, dogs and a rendering of Diana the Huntress, the whole forming an elaborate allegory of Nature and the Chase.

THE SALLE DES CARIATIDES, the next room, is a huge reception area constructed under Henri II for official and religious ceremonies and entertainments ● *74*. At one end marked off by columns is the *tribunal*, a kind of throne room framed by two hemicycles. At its entrance is a musicians' gallery held up by four gigantic caryatids sculpted in white stone by Jean Goujon in 1550▲ *186*. The body of Henri IV lay in state here after his assassination by Ravaillac and the room remained in use until the reign of Louis XIV who came to see Molière act here. But from 1692 until the Revolution it became the Salle des Antiques, a repository for the royal collection of sculptures including antique originals, contemporary pieces commissioned by the government and casts. The original room which had a ceiling of plain wooden beams was arched over in the 17th century. After serving as the earliest venue for the Institut de France (1796–1806), it was entirely redecorated by Percier and Fontaine before being turned over

PIERRE LESCOT'S DESIGN
In the vaulting over the Henri II staircase (above), as in the celebrated musicians' gallery which is supported by caryatids, Pierre Lescot ● *74* gave sculpture a pre-eminent role in his architectural design (in this he was probably abetted by Jean Goujon). Lescot knew how to offset the highly wrought plasterwork which covers the ceiling surface with monumental figures inspired by texts of Vitruvius, which Goujon illustrated. The caryatids may have been modeled on Roman originals; the work is exclusively sculptural without a trace of color to relieve the whiteness of the stone.

to the museum as a gallery for its ancient sculptures. The great marble fireplace was also built at this time by Belloni, who re-used two figures by Goujon (1551) for the purpose. Turn right after the exit.

THE 17TH CENTURY

THE ROTONDE DE MARS begins the series of apartments used by Anne of Austria which were decorated in 1654–8 on the ground floor of the Petite Galerie and converted into a museum of antiquities following the arrival of works of art looted by the French armies in Italy in 1799 ● *40*. After the return to Rome of the celebrated Vatican

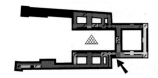

marbles *Laocoön* and the *Apollo Belvedere*, the room was turned over to Roman antiquities. The rotunda itself is a mixture of décors from several different periods: grandiose 17th-century stucco, early 19th-century medallions in relief (by Chaudet, Lange and Lorta) and a fresco by Blondel.

THE SALLE DES FLEUVES which comes next is even more eclectic with 1799 stucco medallions featuring the rivers of antiquity side by side with thoroughly kitsch paintings by Biennoury, typical of the Second Empire.

QUEEN MOTHER'S APARTMENTS. The main rooms have frescos by the Roman painter Romanelli, combined with lively stucco work by Michel Anguier. The Salle des Saisons precedes the vestibule whose walls were replaced in 1799 by columns removed from the rotunda of Charlemagne at Aix-la-Chapelle. Note the stucco figures of the four great rivers of France. Next comes the antechamber, which is decorated with scenes from Roman history, recounted in assorted frescos (*Mucius Scaevola*) and medallions (*Romulus and Remus*).

SALLE DES SAISONS
The ceiling frescos of the painter G.F. Romanelli (c. 1610–62) are framed by large atlas figures in stucco by Michel Anguier. The former was Roman by birth; the latter learned his art in Rome. The result is typical of Roman Baroque in the sober, rhythmical classical style which characterized the beginnings of the grand style under Louis XIV. The King's function as a protector of the arts is extolled on the pediment of the Cour du Sphinx by an image of the sun illuminating the emblems of the arts and sciences.

Last is the queen's bedchamber which was enlarged in 1799 to include the vestibule leading on from it toward the Seine. The period décor (paintings by Hennequin, stuccos by Dejoux) is combined with compositions by

Romanelli which show outstanding women in history framed by allegorical figures symbolizing the virtues of royalty. The Salle d'Auguste, which under Henri IV was the first Salle des Antiques, is a successful pastiche of the apartments of Anne of Austria. Its architect Lefuel employed the painter Matout (*Assembly of the Gods*) and the sculptor Duchoiselle (*Imperial Victories*) to produce decoration in the spirit of the 17th century.

COUR DU SPHINX. This covered courtyard may be entered by way of the Salle des Etrusques (Etruscan Room). On its east side is Louis Le Vau's façade for the Petite Galerie built in 1662. Take the broad staircase (unfinished by Lefuel during the Second Empire and only completed in 1934), and turn to the left past the *Winged Victory of Samothrace* ▲ *165* toward the Rotonde d'Apollon.

THE ROTONDE D'APOLLON, OR SALON DU DÔME. Built by Le Vau, this room was decorated with frescos in 1818–21. It opened onto the Galerie d'Apollon.

THE GALERIE D'APOLLON is closed off by an iron grille which originally came from the Château de Maisons. A long room lit from the

east, it was designed under Louis XIV by Le Vau and Lebrun in exaltation of Apollo. This sumptuous room, which is one of the earliest manifestations of Louis XIV style, owes its preservation and renewal to its occupation by the Académie Royale during the 18th century. The Académie commissioned several of the paintings here before the museum allocated the Salle d'Apollon for its collection of treasures and gemstones ▲ 212. The vaulting stuccos are original. Girardon and the Marsy and Regnaudin brothers executed the muses, the regions of the earth, the seasons and the signs of the zodiac. There is also a heavily restored *Triumph of Neptune* by Lebrun on the tympanum nearest the Seine. The other paintings date from 1766–80 (by Taraval, Callet, Durameau and Legrenée) and 1850–51 (by Müller and Guichard) when the architect Dubau installed the Delacroix's *Triumph of Apollo* (1849). Under the Second Empire, Gobelins tapestries were hung on the walls featuring the artists and kings who contributed to the Louvre.

THE TRIUMPH OF APOLLO
The Galerie d'Apollon was restored under the Second Republic which commissioned Delacroix, the most celebrated Romantic painter of the era, to execute its central panel (top). Delacroix made the connection with the ceiling perspective and lyricism of Lebrun by using a light-filled central panel with the chariot of the Sun bursting forth from a darker garland of bodies. Thirty years earlier, Blondel had used another solar theme for his *Fall of Icarus* (above) in the Rotonde d'Apollon.

127

THE SALLE DES BIJOUX (Jewel Room) is to the right of the gallery exit. This former vestibule to the apartment of Louis XIV was completely redecorated during the Restoration.
THE SALLE DES SEPT CHEMINÉES (Room of the Seven Fireplaces) originally included the Pavillon du Roi where the royal bedrooms were. An enormous salon was installed here which was converted by the architect Duban in 1851 and subsequently became the center of French painting. The stucco is by Duret.

THE MUSEUM IN THE 19TH CENTURY

SALLE DES BIJOUX
During the Restoration, quantities of precious objects were displayed here in ill-lit, rather tall cases. The other rooms of the Musée Charles X stretch away into the distance.

PERCIER AND FONTAINE STAIRCASE
This retrospective painting (below) shows the former entry staircase to the museum, with Napoleon reviewing his architects' plan. The main stairwell no longer exists, but one can still see the vaults of the landing which overlooks the Cour Carrée.

THE MUSÉE CHARLES X inaugurated in 1827 occupies the south wing of the Cour Carrée. The former apartment of the queen, it was reorganized by Fontaine to exhibit the antique vases and the Egyptian collection assembled by Champollion. The walls covered in stucco, the fireplaces by the mosaic craftsman Belloni and the tall windows by Jacob Desmalter go together to create a neoclassical ensemble of very high quality. Various painters were commissioned to execute scenes on the ceilings connected with the collections below. Ingres' *Apotheosis of Homer* ▲ 232 used to hang in the first room. Note the ceiling paintings on Egyptian themes by Picot and Pujol.
THE COLONNADE STAIRCASE at the far end of the Musée Charles X was designed by Percier and Fontaine as the access to the imperial apartments ● 81. On the left are the rooms which formed the Musée des Souverains under the Second Empire, which was devoted to relics of the French monarchy and empire. The first of these is a reconstruction of the council chamber at the Pavillon de la Reine at Vincennes; the rest contain woodcarvings from the Pavillon du Roi, relocated here in 1827. In the ceremonial bedchamber of Henri II, the ceiling by Scibecq de Carpi (1558) is characteristic of the

School of Fontainebleau, while Gilles Guérin introduced classical themes on the ceiling of Louis XIV's bedchamber (1654). From the window the façades of the Cour Carrée offer a fine demonstration of stylistic continuity: opposite is the Henri II wing built by Pierre Lescot; to its right is the Pavillon de l'Horloge and the wing designed by Le Mercier (1639–43); and to the rear are the wings by Le Vau, with their Empire pediments and circular Restoration *oeil-de-boeuf* windows.
THE GALERIE CAMPANA running parallel to the Musée Charles X bears the name of the collection acquired by Napoleon III in 1863, for which the huge showcases were specially made. The ceiling paintings are by Alaux, the younger Fragonard, Steuben, Heim and

Schnetz; they date from the reign of Louis-Philippe and their theme is the state's patronage of the arts.

THE HENRI II VESTIBULE. At the end of the Galerie Campana retrace your steps to the Salle des Sept Cheminées and turn right into the hall where Braque's *The Birds* (1953) is painted on the wooden ceiling. This was the first contemporary work to be incorporated into the Louvre. The other compartments are by Scibecq de Carpi (1557).

THE FORMER SALLE DES GARDES, adjoining, was used for royal audiences under the Restoration. Part of the column arrangement installed here by Fontaine still exists. From here, turn back to the staircase of the *Winged Victory of Samothrace* and after a quick look at the Cour Napoléon through the window, continue through the series of rooms awaiting you to the right of the *Winged Victory*.

THE SALLE PERCIER AND THE SALLE FONTAINE occupy the landing of a staircase built by these two architects then demolished during the Second Empire when most of the work

THE SALON CARRÉ
This room has no windows. A strong light from above illuminates the white and gold stucco of the ceiling, evoking palatial magnificence. Hanging on sober colored dados above black wooden paneling, the paintings are densely packed. At the center of the room is an immense circular seat which one critic compared to a

on the present stairs was carried out. On the ceiling of the third room, known as the Salle Duchâtel, the Restoration painter Meynier executed his *Triomphe de la Peinture Française,* which surrounds the bend of an arch: France's principal painters are represented here in a series of medallions. This glorification of national achievement acted as a counterbalance to the Salon Carré into which these rooms lead.

catafalque. All in all, this holy of holies of painting has a religious, quasi-mystical atmosphere which is quite unique.

THE ORIGINS OF THE MUSEUM

THE SALON CARRÉ (which is actually rectangular not square) has been devoted since 1914 to masterpieces of all schools of painting irrespective of nationality or period. This room has always been one of the kernels of the Louvre. Under the Ancien Régime, it gave its name (Salon) to the exhibition of

THE GRANDE GALERIE
Before 1861 the Grande Galerie was much larger than it is today, extending as far as the Pavillon de Flore. In sections demarcated by massive columns paintings were arranged according to school, with larger canvases above and smaller ones below. Views such as the exquisite watercolor by Nash, the English landscape painter (above), or else the meticulous record by Benjamin Zix (1810) of the wedding cortège of Napoleon and Marie-Louise of Austria (below), give an idea of this now vanished décor.

works by painters belonging to the Académie; later, it became a kind of judgement hall for painting, like the Uffizi in Florence. Duban decorated it lavishly in 1850–1; its white and gold stucco ceiling, sculpted by Simart, perpetuated the tradition of Anguier as seen through the prism of 19th-century eclecticism.

THE GRANDE GALERIE now looms ahead of you. There is no trace of Nicolas Poussin's *Labours of Hercules* painted on the vaulted ceiling for Louis XIII. Under the Ancien Régime the Grande Galerie became little more than a repository for relief maps of France's principal strongholds, used when teaching military tactics. Later, under Louis XVI, the room was earmarked as a museum, finally opening to the public on August 10, 1793. The paintings of Hubert Robert give an idea of the sheer austerity of the revolutionary museum: it was an immensely long vaulted corridor crammed with virtually every European masterpiece ● *29*. The classical exuberance of Percier and Fontaine (the architects of the Empire who added columns, arcades and a coffered ceiling) can also only be visualized by looking at old illustrations. In 1862 the gallery was again modified by Lefuel, who added skylights and reduced it to half its former size. To the section he rebuilt over the broad *guichets* (archways) fronting the Pont du Carrousel, he added two ornate rotundas. Here Rodin's master, Carrier-Belleuse, fashioned a bacchanal of white stucco against a background of gold. It was not until 1950 that the gallery acquired its present sober aspect inspired by the compositions of Hubert Robert. From the windows of the Grande Galerie there is a remarkable view across the Place Napoléon and the Place du Carrousel, at the center of which stands the Triumphal Arch of the Grand Army, erected in 1806. To the same era belongs the colossal wing opposite, which contrasts strongly with the highly decorative, ornate façades built by Lefuel under Napoleon III. Also visible is the

Jardin du Carrousel designed by Jacques Wirz, with box hedges radiating outward from its center. Halfway along the Grande Galerie, turn right into the suite of small rooms built under Napoleon III to house the minor French masters such as Lesueur and Vernet. From the window one can also see the inner courtyard, called the Cour Lefuel. Opposite, the wing constructed by the same architect contained the imperial riding school; of this there remains nothing but a splendid horseshoe staircase and an entrance whose tympanum displays an equestrian group by Rouillard. The right-hand façade is that of the Grande Galerie: the lower floor still retains the elevation and the type of décor that characterized the era of Henri IV but the upper levels are Lefuel at his most lavish.

L'ESCALIER MOLLIEN, the bulk of which was completed in 1857, makes a pair with the staircase of the *Winged Victory of Samothrace.* It originally served as an entrance to the picture galleries and was used by the imperial cortèges making their way to the Salle des États, the focus of the alterations made to the Louvre under Napoleon III. It was endowed with a richly decorated ceiling in 1868–70 under Lefuel's supervision; the side walls and the banister were completed by Gaston Redon in 1910. At the center, Müller was commissioned to paint an allegory of *Glory*, framed by stucco compartments representing painting, sculpture, architecture and engraving by Sanson, Janson, Duchoiselle and Hiolle. The atlas figures and caryatids of the tympana by Cavelier and Duchoiselle bear a resemblance to Anguier's stuccos.

THE SALLES MOLLIEN ▲ *234,* the next rooms you enter turning eastward, are broadly decorated in red, with interlacing gilt on the ceilings (painted by Denuelle). They were designed especially for Napoleon III's museum (1863).

THE SALON DENON occupies the entire area of the pavilion fronting the Cour Napoléon. It was originally designed as a vestibule for the Salle des États, in which Napoleon III received his administration (the room still bears this name, but its original décor has entirely vanished). The vault was painted by Müller in 1864. After a look through the window at the Cour Napoléon, take the elevator to the ground floor.

THE COUR DES ÉCURIES
This stableyard was surrounded by stables and lodgings for the grooms and the Master of the Horse. It led through to the riding school which the horses entered by way of a gently inclined staircase copied from the Cour des Adieux at Fontainebleau (above).

THE SALLE DES ÉTATS
This room was used for meetings of the joint assemblies (above). Its lavish décor by the painter Müller was destroyed in 1883. Under the Restoration the sessions took place in the present Salle des Bronzes ▲ 172. Napoleon III, having built this new room, planned another at the reconstructed end of the Grande Galerie.

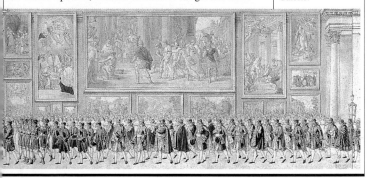

LARGE PAINTINGS
The Salle Daru (above right, in 1906) is one of the three rooms in which large-scale French paintings are displayed ▲ *234*.

THE STABLES
Now used to display the collection of

Italian paintings ▲ *194*, this area was originally designed to house the emperor's horses (above). The vaults are of brick, a reference to the style of Henri IV.

THE SALLE DU MANÈGE
The huge riding ring (right) was used by the Prince Imperial; Empress Eugénie often came to watch him here. The tall columns which support the brick ceiling have stone capitals sculpted with the heads of various animals: horses, donkeys, wolves, dogs, bears and birds. These were the work of the best animal sculptors of the time (Fremiet, Rouillard, Jacquemard); again their subject is the hunt, which is a theme found everywhere in the décor of the Louvre.

THE SALLE DU MANÈGE was built by Lefuel for the Prince Imperial's riding lessons. Today it displays the Louvre's antique sculptures restored or copied in the 17th century, and in particular those colored marbles which were the most prized features of the royal collections during the 17th and 18th centuries.

THE DENON VESTIBULE, a few steps higher, served for many years as the principal entrance to the museum. The view of the two galleries which lead away from it to the respective staircases is characteristic of the vast scale on which Napoleon III's new palace-museum was conceived. From here take the elevator to the Pyramide mezzanine.

THE HALL NAPOLÉON, Ioegh Ming Pei's magnificent brainchild, was opened in 1989. This area of the museum is all too often overlooked by visitors who tend to concentrate more on the spectacular glass pyramid which illuminates it. The same blend of technology and absolute simplicity, at once innovative and traditional, may be seen in the new Richelieu wing inaugurated in 1993. The light bathing the covered courtyards filters through a metal structure which is specially designed to soften its effect; the escalator leading to the upper levels is also a fine stroke of contemporary architecture with its great circular oculi. The Louvre is above all a museum of staircases and this applies especially to the Richelieu wing: here the Lefuel staircase is the most ambitious with its multiple flights and stone décor. An alternative route is by way of what is known as the Ministers' staircase, richly decorated with paintings by Daubigny, marbles and ornate banisters. From here you can proceed to the Napoleon III apartments (formerly used by the Ministry of State) ▲ *210*, whose lavish rooms illustrate the decorative richness of this stately palace, and conclude the tour of the Louvre's collection of paintings and *objets d'art*.

ORIENTAL ANTIQUITIES

RICHELIEU

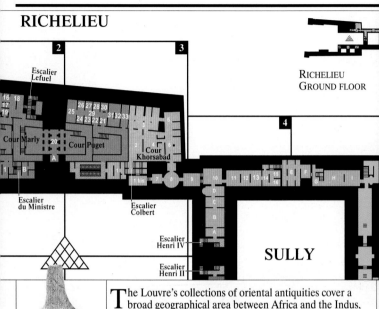

RICHELIEU
GROUND FLOOR

Escalier Lefuel

Cour Marly   Cour Puget

Cour Khorsabad

Escalier du Ministre

Escalier Colbert

Escalier Henri IV

SULLY

Escalier Henri II

The Louvre's collections of oriental antiquities cover a broad geographical area between Africa and the Indus, and they go back as far as 7000 BC. Their origins are threefold: Mesopotamia, around the Tigris and the Euphrates (in the Richelieu wing) and Iran and the Levant (the exhibition of the latter is currently being prepared in the Sully wing). These are completed by a section devoted to the art of Islam. Created in 1874, the Musée Assyrien has been considerably enriched by excavations carried out by French archeologists.

ANCIENT MESOPOTAMIA

Figurine of a woman (above) in painted terracotta (Halaf, c. 4500 BC).

THE BIRTH OF THE MESOPOTAMIAN CIVILIZATIONS (ROOM 1A). The neolithic revolution of the 7th millennium BC (in today's Iraq and Kurdistan) entailed the organization of the inhabitants into sedentary stable communities, and the invention of the ceramic process. One of these civilizations, the Hassuna, was known for the quality of its ceramic and its stoneware. With the civilizations of Samarra and Halaf in the 6th millennium, ceramics developed more sophisticated forms and decoration. Between 6000 and 4000 BC the Obeid civilization produced very fine terracotta figurines.

Sumerian tablet (above) covered with cuneiform inscriptions.
Sumerian priest-king (right), limestone, c. 3300 BC.

THE PRE-URBAN ERA (3500–2900 BC) was characterized by the birth of city-states, especially Uruk, which secured the growing

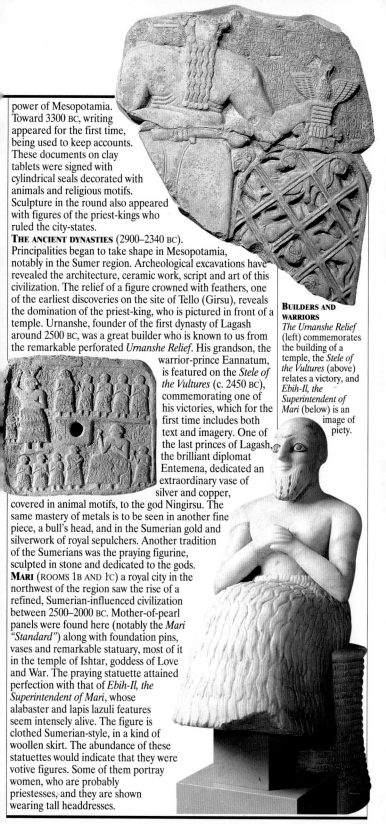

power of Mesopotamia. Toward 3300 BC, writing appeared for the first time, being used to keep accounts. These documents on clay tablets were signed with cylindrical seals decorated with animals and religious motifs. Sculpture in the round also appeared with figures of the priest-kings who ruled the city-states.

THE ANCIENT DYNASTIES (2900–2340 BC). Principalities began to take shape in Mesopotamia, notably in the Sumer region. Archeological excavations have revealed the architecture, ceramic work, script and art of this civilization. The relief of a figure crowned with feathers, one of the earliest discoveries on the site of Tello (Girsu), reveals the domination of the priest-king, who is pictured in front of a temple. Urnanshe, founder of the first dynasty of Lagash around 2500 BC, was a great builder who is known to us from the remarkable perforated *Urnanshe Relief*. His grandson, the warrior-prince Eannatum, is featured on the *Stele of the Vultures* (c. 2450 BC), commemorating one of his victories, which for the first time includes both text and imagery. One of the last princes of Lagash, the brilliant diplomat Entemena, dedicated an extraordinary vase of silver and copper, covered in animal motifs, to the god Ningirsu. The same mastery of metals is to be seen in another fine piece, a bull's head, and in the Sumerian gold and silverwork of royal sepulchers. Another tradition of the Sumerians was the praying figurine, sculpted in stone and dedicated to the gods.

MARI (ROOMS 1B AND 1C) a royal city in the northwest of the region saw the rise of a refined, Sumerian-influenced civilization between 2500–2000 BC. Mother-of-pearl panels were found here (notably the *Mari "Standard"*) along with foundation pins, vases and remarkable statuary, most of it in the temple of Ishtar, goddess of Love and War. The praying statuette attained perfection with that of *Ebih-Il, the Superintendent of Mari*, whose alabaster and lapis lazuli features seem intensely alive. The figure is clothed Sumerian-style, in a kind of woollen skirt. The abundance of these statuettes would indicate that they were votive figures. Some of them portray women, who are probably priestesses, and they are shown wearing tall headdresses.

BUILDERS AND WARRIORS
The Urnanshe Relief (left) commemorates the building of a temple, the *Stele of the Vultures* (above) relates a victory, and *Ebih-Il, the Superintendent of Mari* (below) is an image of piety.

A ROYAL SEAL
The manufacture of cylinders for use in signing the first written texts (these were plaques of clay) goes back to archaic times. The chlorite seal-cylinder of Sharkalisharri, King of Agade (c. 2200 BC, above left; molding at right) shows a scene from mythology featuring a naked hero.

THE MASTERPIECE OF AGADE ART
The *Victory Stele of Naram-Sin* (right) is a masterpiece of Agade art but is also an important historical document; an inscription in Akkadian relates the episode pictured in the relief. Another, written in Elamite in the 12th century BC by an Elamite king, informs us the stele was removed to Elam at roughly that time.

THE AKKADIAN EMPIRE 2340–2200 BC (ROOM 2). Sargon was the first monarch to forge an empire by uniting Sumer, Akkad and northern Mesopotamia. His sons Rimush and Manishtusu and his grandson Naram-Sin managed to hold this empire together, creating favorable conditions for a politicized form of art whose chief concern was the image of the all-powerful monarch whose palace was at Agade. The actual site of this town has yet to be discovered, but royal workshops were established here to produce monumental statuary – mostly in diorite, a hard black stone. The oldest steles dating from the reign of Sargon illustrate victories and battles, in a still-traditional archaic style which nonetheless shows early signs of the realism which was to characterize the sculpture of succeeding reigns. A fragment of a stele shows King Rimush in single combat with an enemy. Later with the reign of Manishtusu, more realistic lifesize royal figures were sculpted and installed in various towns of the empire. These statues, seated or standing, show the king wearing a long skirt with a shawl over his shoulders. The high point of the art of Agade was attained during the reign of Naram-Sin. His victory stele in pink sandstone offers a striking glimpse of the king,

followed by his army, climbing a mountain which is crowned by divine symbols. The delicacy of the relief, the expressions on the faces and the presence of a text commenting on Naram-Sin's victory over a tribe of mountain people from the Zagros region, make this stele one of the great masterpieces of the museum. After the fall of the dynasty, a century of instability followed. The display cases of ROOM 2 illustrate the importance of written text in the Akkadian civilization; eventually Akkadian became the principal language of the area, eclipsing Sumerian and annexing its ideograms. Numerous texts bear witness to contracts, treaties and historical events, but there are very few literary texts. The art of seal-making complemented the iconography of major sculpture by featuring the Akkadian pantheon in its entirety: the god of the Sea, the Sun god surrounded by flames, the god and goddess of Vegetation, the two gods of the Storm – and lastly Ishtar herself, the goddess of Love and War.

THE SECOND DYNASTY OF LAGASH (2150–2100 BC) managed to stem the tide of "barbarians" from the mountains and preserve in its southern capital a civilization which we know as neo-Sumerian. This civilization was famous for its literature, and has bequeathed us the longest poems written in Sumerian. The princes of Lagash are also familiar to us: diorite votive statues of Ur-Ba'u, Gudea and his son Ur-Ningirsu have come down to us. By now the realism of Agade sculpture had given way to a limited academic approach. Warrior kings were replaced by builders, and the inscriptions tell of labors of construction instead of military victories. In all there are about twenty statues of Gudea, seated or standing, with hands crossed, wearing a headpiece. One of these shows him carrying a fountain of water, clearly godlike. There are also a number of very beautiful female statuettes, among them the *Lady from Tello*, a libation vase of Gudea, and figurines of bulls with human heads. Most of this superb sculpture was found at today's Tello, the ancient site of Girsu. A certain number of objects evoke the architecture and construction of temples, the principal activities of the princes of Lagash.

There are also the *Cylinders of Gudea*, with text describing the construction of the temple of Ningirsu, foundation pins bearing figurines, and brick landfill used for seating four-cornered columns.

THE THIRD DYNASTY OF UR founded by Ur-Nammu, was distinguished for its political organization, as described in several texts.

GUDEA, KING OF LAGASH

Among the vestiges of the reign of Gudea, two statues bearing the name of the king show him seated (left) and bearing a vase that spouts water (below). The very similar *Lady from Tello* may have been his wife (below, left). A foundation figurine (above) evokes Gudea's achievement as a builder, while the libation vase decorated with serpents (facing page, lower left) also bears the name of the king.

▲ MESOPOTAMIA SECOND AND FIRST MILLENNIA

SECOND AND FIRST MILLENNIA

THE AMORITE KINGDOMS, 2000–1595 BC (ROOM 3). This was a period of instability which saw the fall of the kingdom of Ur (Sumer); it was also a time of intense creativity, especially in Babylon. Popular art forms, particularly terracotta work, described religious themes and scenes from everyday life. The princes of Eshnunna perpetuated the Sumerian idea of royal statuary in diorite, but with a realism that was entirely new. At Larsa literary texts were produced in the best Sumerian tradition. At Mari, an important crossroads for trade, Zimrilim took power in about 1800 BC and enlarged the royal palace (frescos from the state reception chamber). The palace was subsequently destroyed by Hammurabi, the powerful king of Babylon who had previously been Zimrilim's ally.

HAMMURABI
The *Law-Codex of Hammurabi* (detail, below) is a collection of exemplary royal pronouncements; it was found at Susa (Iran) where it had been taken as spoils of war c. 1200 BC. A fragment of a wall painting (above, center) from the palace of Zimrilim at Mari, destroyed by Hammurabi; (above) the *Worshipper of Larsa*.

THE FIRST BABYLONIAN DYNASTY (1792–1750 BC). Hammurabi, founder of this Babylonian dynasty, brought about the unification of Mesopotamia by his conquests. The stele entitled the *Law-Codex of Hammurabi* is a collection of court decisions written in magnificent language and represents an important piece of Babylonian literature. The king is depicted at the top of the stele, fixed in a hieratic attitude before Marduk, or Shamash, the solar god of Justice. A testimony to religious devotion, the *Adoration of Larsa* is a small bronze and gold statue on an elegant cup-shaped base in the form of three ibex.

THE KASSITES IN BABYLON (1500–1100 BC). The Kassite invaders who subsequently took control of Babylon soon assimilated Mesopotamian civilization. They gave many gifts of land to state officials which were recorded on engraved steles or *kudurrus* and placed under the authority of the gods. In the meantime Assyria to the north grew into a powerful empire which extended down to Babylon in the 13th century BC.

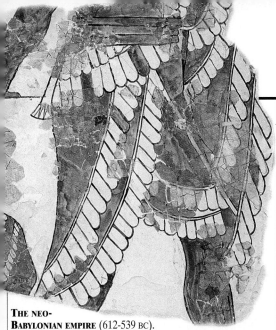

THE NEO-BABYLONIAN EMPIRE (612-539 BC).

The reign of Nebuchadnezzar II (604-562 BC) marked the apogee of this empire. While it lasted Babylon created its own sumptuous decoration; the Louvre now possesses fragments of this in the form of reliefs on terracotta bricks. Later the capital fell into the hands of the Persians followed by Alexander the Great. Hellenism blended with local traditions to produce a refined form of art including alabaster statuettes of women, one of which has retained its garnet-stone eyes and elegant golden jewelry.

ANATOLIAN CIVILIZATIONS (ROOM 5). Anatolia was another early seat of civilization, especially the neolithic site of Catal Huyuk. Here ceramics, bronzes and sculptures were extraordinarily refined. At the beginning of the second millennium colonies of Assyrian merchants established themselves in Cappadocia where they introduced cuneiform script; their ceramics show this in highly elaborate forms. Subsequently Anatolia passed into Hittite domination (1650 BC) before becoming the center of the empire of the Great Kings, who were patrons of an imperial form of art characterized by statuettes made of bronze and gold.

THE ASSYRIAN EMPIRE (ROOMS 4 AND 6) reached its high point in the first millennium under the great monarchs Ashurnasirpal, Sargon, Sennacherib and Ashurbanipal: these kings even subdued Egypt for a while, before their defeat by the Medes and Babylonians in 612 BC. The Louvre also possesses reliefs from the palaces of Khorsabad ▲ 140, Nimrod, Nineveh and other regional capitals.

ANATOLIA
This *Rython in the Shape of a Lion* (c. 1900 BC, below), is representative of art at the time of the Assyrian colonies of Cappadocia. A small *Pendant in the Shape of a God* (above) dates from the Hittite period which followed.

ASSYRIA
The royal capitals of Nimrod and Nineveh, like the regional capitals, have left numerous reliefs dominated by the features of the king and peopled by protective spirits. The high point of this art came with the building of the palace of Ashurbanipal II at Nineveh, a hymn to the glory of the conqueror of Elam. Among the most beautiful portraits is one of the king standing in his chariot, directing strategy (left).

The Louvre possesses a remarkable collection of decorative architectural fragments from the palace of Sargon II, King of Assyria, at Khorsabad. Discovered in 1843 by the French consul at Mosul, Paul-Emile Botta, this site revealed a forgotten civilization to the world. On May 1, 1847 King Louis-Philippe opened the Musée Assyrien at the Louvre. The bulls with human heads and the many murals were moved in 1993 to a new courtyard covered over with glass, with a view to displaying this Assyrian architecture in something like its original scale.

BOTTA AND PLACE
Paul-Emile Botta quickly understood the importance of his discovery but his identification of it was incorrect. He had found the remains of Dur-Sharrukin, one of the capitals of the Assyrian Empire, not Nineveh. His successor Victor Place (above) continued excavating after 1850, but the collection he assembled was lost in a shipwreck in 1855.

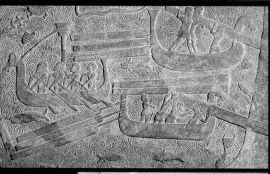

Among the reliefs on both the inside and the outside walls, those of the north walls (above, displayed in the Cour Khorsabad) form a fairly complete ensemble. Note the figures of Sargon and one of his dignitaries (left) and servants (right). *Transportation of Timber from the Lebanon* (top) is on the north wall of the courtyard.

Moving the remains from Mosul to Paris was by no means simple. In 1993 they were moved again, this time from the Cour Carrée to the Richelieu wing.

Photographs by Gabriel Tranchard show the various stages of the discovery.

RECONSTRUCTION
This attempt at a reconstruction of Sargon II's palace entrance was drawn by the architect Félix Thomas.

Model of an Elamite cultic site portraying *Sit Shamshi*, ceremony of the rising sun, found at Susa.

Original cultures came into being in Iran, enriched by exchanges with neighboring Mesopotamia and the Orient. Susa, a natural extension of the "land of the two rivers" in which an urban civilization had emerged as early as 4000 BC, has yielded important archeological remains. Mountain cultures like that of Luristan which was famous for its metals, and the civilizations of the plateau, evolved in parallel. The collections currently occupy rooms 7 to 10. Rooms 11 to 16 (Achemenid Persia and the Palace of Susa) are still in the process of reorganization.

Alabaster praying statuette from the Uruk period.

APÀDANA OF SUSA
The Louvre possesses one of these monumental capitals (right), from the Achemenid Persian period; they formerly crowned the columns of the Apadana (audience chamber) of the Palace of Darius at Susa (c. 520-500 BC) which was discovered by the French archeologist Marcel Dieulafoy in 1886. The Medes and the Persians, unified in the mid-6th century by Cyrus the Great, extended their empire throughout the Near East under Darius.

Ibex goblet of painted terracotta from Susa's foundation in about 4000 BC.

Female statuette in chlorite and white limestone (Bactria, c. 1800 BC).

PERSIAN VASE HANDLE
This handle in the shape of a winged ibex in gold and silver (Achemenid Persian era, c. 500 BC) shows the persistence of the zoomorphic tradition in the art of metalwork in Iran. At the base of it is a mask of Silenus, evidence of Greek influence.

THE IMMORTALS
The frieze of the *Archers of Darius*, called "the immortals", once decorated Darius' palace at Susa. The colors of the glazed brick remain as fresh as ever.

CHITECTURAL ORNAMENTATION
his ensemble of molded brick alled the *Panels of the Temple of Inshushinak*, shows the influence of Mesopotamian chitectural ornamentation on the brickwork of Iran, particularly in Susa.

LURISTAN BRONZE
This circular standard with four figures radiating from its center (early 2nd century BC) is highly representative of the bronzemakers' art, developed in the mountains far from urban civilization.

Nude holding a child, terracotta, Cyprus (c. 1400 BC).

The Mediterranean shore of the Near East, the Levant, was a cradle of civilization from the paleolithic era onward. Neolithic villages and cities of the third millennium have left behind a wealth of archeological material. The smaller kingdoms of the Levant were the link between Mesopotamia and Egypt and later with Mediterranean civilizations such as Greece. Rooms A to D display collections from Cyprus, from the Syrian–Lebanese shoreline, from Phoenicia, the Syrian interior and Palestine. Rooms E to I, now being completed in the Sully building, will house the rest of the Syrian collections (from Sidon and Palmyra in particular) as well as those of pre-Islamic Arabia.

FALCON PECTORAL (c. 1750 BC) Gold ornament discovered at Byblos modeled on an Egyptian original.

EARLIEST PALESTINE This hippopotamus ivory statuette of a naked male figure comes from Safadi in the Negev and shows the skill of Palestinian craftsmen in the fourth millennium BC.

PHOENICIAN PANTHEON This Mycenean-influenced *Fertility Goddess* was carved for the lid of a Phoenician ivory cosmetics box (above, late 13th century BC). Like the stele of the storm god Baal (right, 1350–1250 BC) it was found at Ugarit on the Syrian coast.

GODS OF PALMYRA
Palmyra was a crossroads between east and west, and its art was profoundly influenced by Greece and Rome. Above, the *Trio of Gods* (the Sky, the Moon and the Sun) are dressed as Roman officers (2nd century AD).

Model of a sanctuary decorated with nude goddesses, Syrian terracotta (13th century BC).

SEA-PEOPLE
The Egyptians called the Philistines of the Bible (who gave their name to Palestine), the "sea-people". This 9th-century BC model of a temple (left) from the region may be a likeness of the Temple of Jerusalem, built by Solomon a century earlier.

PUNIC STELE
This 2nd-century AD stele (right) bears witness to the continuing vitality of the religion of Carthage during the Roman occupation. The dedicatee, in the center, is placed under the sign of the goddess Tanit.

RICHELIEU
ENTRESOL

RICHELIEU

IVORY IN SPAIN
A masterpiece of 10th-century Cordoba sculpture on ivory, the *Pyx of Al-Mughira*, son of Caliph Abd-el-Rahman III, was cut from a single elephant's tusk (right).

CERAMIC PANEL IN THE FORM OF A MIHRAB (sacred wall of a mosque) is actually a funerary stele (Iran, Kashan, 13th century, below right).

THE BAPTISMAL FONT OF SAINT LOUIS
The large bowl (late 13th–early 14th century) below is one of the masterpieces of the Louvre's collection of Mameluke art. It is made of a single sheet of hammered brass with gold and silver inlay.

The rooms devoted to the Louvre's collection of Islamic art cover a broad panorama from the 7th to the 19th century, and from Spain to India. Ceramics, metal and glass, wood carving, ivories and books bear witness to a series of creative and refined civilizations.

THE BEGINNINGS OF ISLAMIC ART (ROOM 1). The Umayyads, founders of the first Islamic dynasty (AD 661-750), chose Damascus as their capital. Their art is filled with Christian, Hellenic and Iranian influences which are visible in architecture, ewers and lamps.

THE ABBASSIDS (ROOM 2). The art of this period (8th–10th centuries) blossomed thanks to the patronage of the caliphate of Baghdad (the new capital): it included palace decoration, art objects and ceramics with white opaque glazes and metal luster decoration.

THE FATIMIDS AND THE MUSLIM OCCIDENT (ROOM 3). The Fatimids (909–1171) set up their capital in Cairo in 969. They excelled in the crafting of rock crystal and wood. Their ceramics tended to be covered in luster decoration featuring animal motifs. After the conquest of

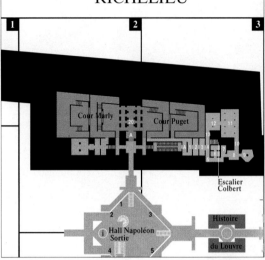

Ceramic lusterware was one of the finest products of the Fatimid period.

Spain in 711, the Umayyad emirs of Cordoba reigned over the region until the 11th century, at which time sculpture in ivory, as well as bronze and ceramic work, reached their highest levels.

THE IRANIAN WORLD in the 10th–12th centuries (ROOM 4) produced a style of ceramic with a creamy white background and marbled engraved decoration.

IRAN DURING THE SELJUK PERIOD 10th–13th centuries (ROOMS 5 AND 6) saw a number of innovations, represented here by scientific objects. The ceramic work and calligraphy produced at this time were remarkable. The art of metalworking, especially in Khurassan, produced inkstands, metal ewers, candlesticks and perfume-censers.

EGYPT, THE NEAR EAST AND ANATOLIA in the 12th and 13th centuries (ROOM 8) produced extraordinary treasures: decorated ceramics, enameled and gilded glass objects, metal bowls and ewers and miniatures.

THE MAMELUKES (ROOM 9) covered the years 1250–1517. They perpetuated the lavish traditions of the Fatimid caliphs, evolved a very elegant style of calligraphy and initiated the use of blasons on lamps of gilded and enameled glass.

MONGOL IRAN 13th–14 century (ROOM 10). This period is illustrated by ceramic wall coverings with geometrical and cruciform patterns, metal objects and fine ceramics. The Mongol school of miniatures is justly famous.

THE TIMURIDS, SAFAVID IRAN, QADJAR IRAN AND MOGUL INDIA (ROOM 11). Iranian carpet weavers reached high levels of perfection during the 16th century. One of the showcases here is devoted to the arms and armor of the Islamic world (10th–17th century). The works of Mogul artists – metal, glass and carpets – are outstanding in their refinement and their careful attention to detail.

THE OTTOMAN WORLD (ROOM 12). The Ottoman Empire, founded in the 13th century, reached its zenith under Suleyman the Magnificent in the 16th century. The ceramic pottery of Iznik is especially remarkable, with its cups, dishes and wall-panels. Also displayed are carpets and metal work from this period.

ROOM 13 is devoted to books and miniatures which are among the finest pieces in the Louvre.

Rose-patterned cup, ceramic, luster decorations against a blue glaze (Syria, early 12th century).

MANTES CARPET A detail of this asymmetrical weave, woolen carpet (below) from the collegiate church of Mantes-la-Jolie (Iran, late 16th century).

Hanap with floral décor (Iznik pottery, Turkey, 16th century, right); *Lamp from a mosque with the name of Sultan Hassan,* in enameled and gilded glass (Egypt or Syria, 14th-century, center); *Horse-head dagger* of jade, inlaid with gold, rubies and emeralds; steel blade (India, 17th century, left).

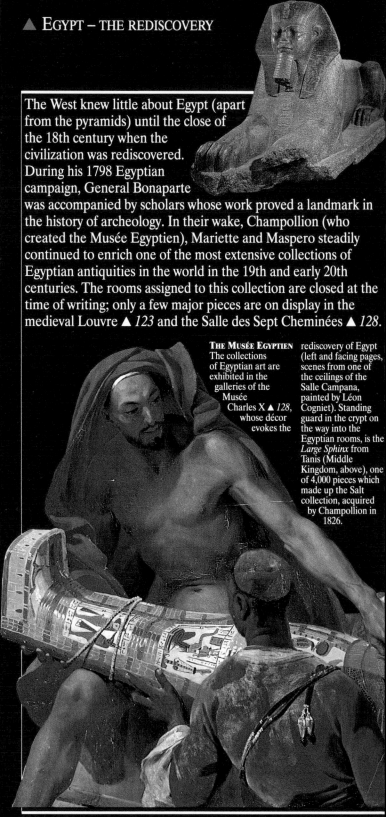

▲ EGYPT – THE REDISCOVERY

The West knew little about Egypt (apart
from the pyramids) until the close of
the 18th century when the
civilization was rediscovered.
During his 1798 Egyptian
campaign, General Bonaparte
was accompanied by scholars whose work proved a landmark in
the history of archeology. In their wake, Champollion (who
created the Musée Egyptien), Mariette and Maspero steadily
continued to enrich one of the most extensive collections of
Egyptian antiquities in the world in the 19th and early 20th
centuries. The rooms assigned to this collection are closed at the
time of writing; only a few major pieces are on display in the
medieval Louvre ▲ *123* and the Salle des Sept Cheminées ▲ *128*.

THE MUSÉE EGYPTIEN
The collections
of Egyptian art are
exhibited in the
galleries of the
Musée
Charles X ▲ *128*,
whose décor
evokes the
rediscovery of Egypt
(left and facing pages,
scenes from one of
the ceilings of the
Salle Campana,
painted by Léon
Cogniet). Standing
guard in the crypt on
the way into the
Egyptian rooms, is the
Large Sphinx from
Tanis (Middle
Kingdom, above), one
of 4,000 pieces which
made up the Salt
collection, acquired
by Champollion in
1826.

FRENCH EGYPT

During its struggle with Britain for control of the Mediterranean and the sea route to India, France occupied Egypt for nearly three years. Shown above is a painting of the 165 scholars and artists of the Commission des Arts et des Sciences, in Cairo.

THE TOMBS

The paintings of Léon Cogniet (below) illustrate some of the characteristic features of Egyptology: most of the discoveries involved tombs and the objects and funerary art that they contained. Death was an overriding preoccupation for the Egyptians, who made every possible effort to protect and preserve their mortal remains in the expectation of rebirth to eternal life. As it turns out, their memory has survived over the centuries and in that sense they have achieved a certain immortality.

THE EGYPTIAN EXPEDITION

Dominique Vivant Denon, the first director of the Louvre, was among the scholars commissioned by Bonaparte to measure and draw all the monuments of Egypt. Their work was eventually assembled in a monumental work of twenty volumes, *La Description de l'Egypte* (above, one of the original plates). When this work was published in Europe, the effect was electrifying; a vogue for Egypt was launched which led to a fresh wave of scientific expeditions and much uncontrolled looting.

THE NILE CIVILIZATION

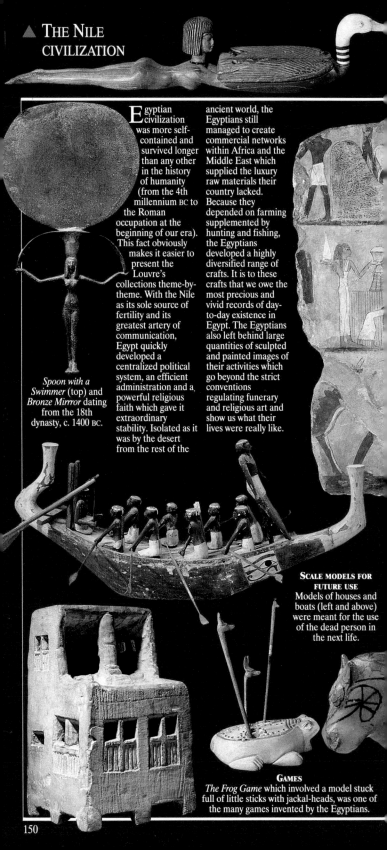

Egyptian civilization was more self-contained and survived longer than any other in the history of humanity (from the 4th millennium BC to the Roman occupation at the beginning of our era). This fact obviously makes it easier to present the Louvre's collections theme-by-theme. With the Nile as its sole source of fertility and its greatest artery of communication, Egypt quickly developed a centralized political system, an efficient administration and a powerful religious faith which gave it extraordinary stability. Isolated as it was by the desert from the rest of the ancient world, the Egyptians still managed to create commercial networks within Africa and the Middle East which supplied the luxury raw materials their country lacked. Because they depended on farming supplemented by hunting and fishing, the Egyptians developed a highly diversified range of crafts. It is to these crafts that we owe the most precious and vivid records of day-to-day existence in Egypt. The Egyptians also left behind large quantities of sculpted and painted images of their activities which go beyond the strict conventions regulating funerary and religious art and show us what their lives were really like.

Spoon with a Swimmer (top) and *Bronze Mirror* dating from the 18th dynasty, c. 1400 BC.

SCALE MODELS FOR FUTURE USE
Models of houses and boats (left and above) were meant for the use of the dead person in the next life.

GAMES
The Frog Game which involved a model stuck full of little sticks with jackal-heads, was one of the many games invented by the Egyptians.

The Egyptians were masters at making everyday objects in the form of animals (left) and at carving and modeling creatures for tombs (right, cattle).

WORK
Agricultural scenes are shown in tomb paintings (here, from the tomb of Ounsou, a grain accountant and scribe, New Kingdom).

MUSIC. One of the reliefs on the mastaba of Akhethep from the Saqqara burial ground shows harpists, flute players and singers.

Ceremonial chair of wood encrusted with ivory, and *Hippopotamus* of blue porcelain, evidence of great refinement.

▲ CHAMPOLLION AND THE HIEROGLYPHS

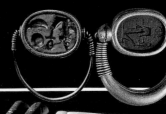

THE IMMORTAL NAME
The priority of Egyptian script was to preserve names, especially the name of the king. Two rings bear the cartouche of Amenhotep III (above) and a porcelain tablet with the same pharaoh's name (at left). An alabaster box and silver seal-cylinders from the reign of Mentuhotep I (above and right).

Papyri, but also monuments, statues and works of art, carry inscriptions that are of prime importance in the understanding of the political organization, religion and day-to-day life of Egypt. The script which began as hieroglyphs and later became hieratic and demotic, was the instrument of the scribes who belonged to one of the higher castes of Egyptian society. Thanks to Champollion who found the key to the hieroglyphs in 1822, we can now penetrate a form of literature which was hitherto a mystery.

THE SCRIBE
This statue has conferred eternal life on its model, or rather an illusion of life, with its anatomical realism and its eyes of rock crystal inset in copper. The *Seated Scribe* (c. 2620–2350 BC, below) is represented in the traditional position holding a stylus and a roll of papyrus in his lap.

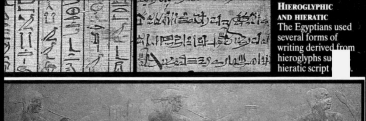

HIEROGLYPHIC AND HIERATIC

The Egyptians used several forms of writing derived from hieroglyphs su... hieratic script ...

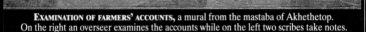

EXAMINATION OF FARMERS' ACCOUNTS, a mural from the mastaba of Akhethetop. On the right an overseer examines the accounts while on the left two scribes take notes.

THE ROSETTA STONE (original in the British Museum). Discovered in 1790, the year of Champollion's birth, the Rosetta Stone is engraved with the same text in hieroglyphic and demotic script with a translation in Greek. It became the key to the comprehension of Egyptian writing.

JEAN-FRANÇOIS CHAMPOLLION Born in Figeac and the son of a librarian, Champollion studied both living and dead languages from a very young age. In 1826 Charles X p... in charge of a ... section of th... museum devoted to Egyptian and oriental monuments.

THE SCRIBE'S EQUIPMENT A wooden tablet, a double inkwell in porcelain, a papyrus-cutter and a sheet of papyrus (above), a wooden palette with rush-stems and two cups for color blocks (left) make up a scribe's tools.

A PRECIS OF EGYPTIAN GRAMMAR Published after his death, the third work by Champollion entitled *An Egyptian Grammar, or General Principles of the Egyptian Language* completed his discovery. The page (left) shows equivalent words in hieroglyphic, hieratic and demotic Egyptian along with their translations into Greek and French.

153

COLOSSI
The origins of this statue (left), which is inscribed with the name of Ramesses II, are unknown. The 14-foot colossus of Sety I was found at Karnak (right).

Long forgotten, buried in the sands or transformed into dwellings, Egypt's temples have been the object of intense archeological interest since the 19th century. Most have now been unearthed, notably at Thebes (Luxor and Karnak). Whether they were funerary temples or religious sites dedicated to the gods, they were always richly furnished with narrative bas-reliefs and monumental statues of gods, pharaohs and private individuals. Capitals and columns, the principal features of Egyptian stone architecture, have survived thousands of years into our own time. Although the Louvre can offer no complete ensemble, its collection of monumental sculpture and architecture in the Galerie Henri IV affords a good introduction to the subject.

BULL-GOD
This statue of the god Apis comes from the Serapeum of Memphis, the burial ground of the sacred bulls. During their lives these bulls were revered as incarnations of the god Ptah.

FALSE DOOR
False door steles were symbolic passage-points between the worlds of the living and the dead. This one of limestone was dedicated by Queen Hatshepsut to her father, Thutmose I; it evokes the huge masonry columns which marked temple entrances.

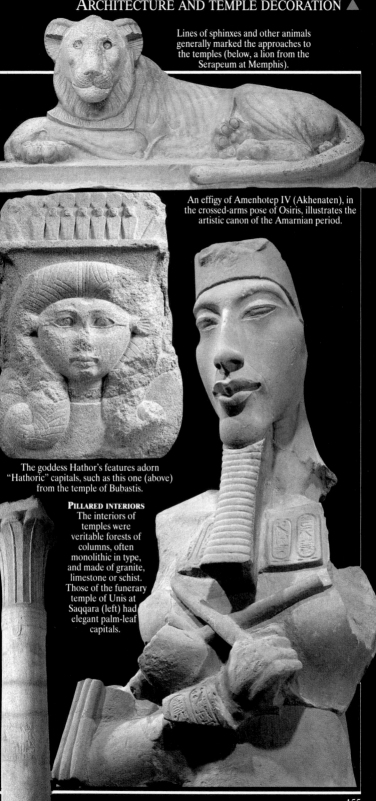

Lines of sphinxes and other animals generally marked the approaches to the temples (below, a lion from the Serapeum at Memphis).

An effigy of Amenhotep IV (Akhenaten), in the crossed-arms pose of Osiris, illustrates the artistic canon of the Amarnian period.

The goddess Hathor's features adorn "Hathoric" capitals, such as this one (above) from the temple of Bubastis.

PILLARED INTERIORS
The interiors of temples were veritable forests of columns, often monolithic in type, and made of granite, limestone or schist. Those of the funerary temple of Unis at Saqqara (left) had elegant palm-leaf capitals.

This amulet in the form of an "oudjat" eye was placed in the mummy's wrappings to ensure the integrity of the body in the next world.

For the Egyptians death offered not an end to life, but the promise of resurrection. This was one of the basic tenets of a religion whose pantheon of gods was remarkably diverse. Around the principal gods Re (or Amun) the Sun god, revolved Thoth, Anubis, Osiris, Isis and Horus. Creatures such as ibis, cats, rams, bulls, snakes, scarabs, falcons and crocodiles were sacred.

THE "BOOK OF THE DEAD"
The sacred text of the Egyptian religion is a collection of hymns to the gods, magic formulae to ensure the survival of the deceased. It was generally inscribed on papyrus (above).

RUSSIAN DOLLS
The multiple sarcophagi of the richer tombs are spectacularly decorative. That of the Lady Madja (below) and those of Tamutnefret, a singer of Amun (right) are in painted, stuccoed wood. The sarcophagi of pharaohs might even be in gold.

THE SACRED IBIS
This bird which still haunts the banks of the Nile, was revered as one of the incarnations of Thoth, the god of scribes.

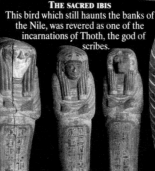

THE EGYPTIAN PANTHEON
This group of divinities is represented in the *Book of the Dead* of Khonsu (left). From right to left, Re-Hsrakhti, the principal god in the hierarchy crowned with the solar disc which is his symbol; Osiris, wearing the tall white crown of Lower Egypt is the resurrected god who protects the dead; Osiris' wife Isis who brought him back to life; and Nephthys. On the opposite page, from left to right, Bastet, the cat-goddess venerated at Bubastis; the god Bes; the lioness-goddess Sekhmet and Anubis, the jackal-god.

FUNERAL RITES

The dead were embalmed then carefully wrapped in linen bandages incorporating protective amulets. The mummy was then "dressed" in cardboard packaging and placed in one or more sarcophagi and put in a stone tank deep within the tomb. Above is the mummy of Pachery with its cardboard packaging; on the left is a funeral cortège from a *Book of the Dead*.

It was only later that animals were sacrificed and mummified like humans. Above right, a mummified cat.

PRE-DYNASTIC EGYPT: THE NAGADA PERIOD
The civilization which appeared on the banks of the Nile in the 4th millennium had not yet mastered the art of writing, but is known to us through the first fruits of its art: figurines of men (left), stone vases (right) and schist tablets with animal motifs (below left). The Louvre possesses a masterpiece from this period, the *Guebel el-Arak Dagger* covered with wonderful carved relief (right).

Egypt entered recorded history around 3000 BC, when writing appeared and the pharaonic civilization was founded. The first two dynasties, established at This, gave their name to the Thinite period. The *Stele of the Serpent King* (right) is remarkable from every point of view: it not only shows the image of a vanished palace, but also carries one of the first indications of a form of script, the serpent hieroglyph representing the pharaoh's name which is placed by convention above the palace. The falcon Horus, god of royalty, protects the pharaoh.

Plaque, of carved schist, used for grinding kohl, (c. 3200 BC).

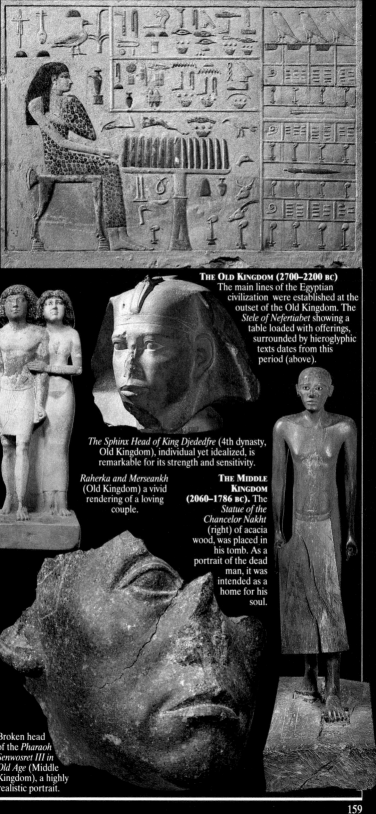

THE OLD KINGDOM (2700–2200 BC)

The main lines of the Egyptian civilization were established at the outset of the Old Kingdom. The *Stele of Nefertiabet* showing a table loaded with offerings, surrounded by hieroglyphic texts dates from this period (above).

The Sphinx Head of King Djededfre (4th dynasty, Old Kingdom), individual yet idealized, is remarkable for its strength and sensitivity.

Raherka and Merseankh (Old Kingdom) a vivid rendering of a loving couple.

THE MIDDLE KINGDOM

(2060–1786 BC). The *Statue of the Chancelor Nakht* (right) of acacia wood, was placed in his tomb. As a portrait of the dead man, it was intended as a home for his soul.

Broken head of the *Pharaoh Senwosret III in Old Age* (Middle Kingdom), a highly realistic portrait.

TUTANKHAMUN?
This little head in *pâte de verre* could be that of Tutankhamun, the last pharaoh of the 18th dynasty, whose tomb was discovered inviolate. Its treasures are now at the Cairo Museum.

QUEEN TIYI
This royal statuette of enameled schist (New Kingdom) is one of many Egyptian fig___ typifying a feminine ideal.

THE NEW KINGDOM (1555–1080 BC)

The period of the New Kingdom was a time of unprecedented artistic activity. Thebes was the capital of a powerful Egyptian empire and the 18th and 19th dynasties marked a high point of Egyptian civilization. A series of pharaohs called Amenhotep, Thutmose, Sety and Ramesses were among the greatest monarchs at this time. A painted limestone relief of Sety I and the goddess Hathor (above

RAMESSES II
Ramesses II reigned
for 67 years and was
one of the greatest
pharaohs of the 19th
dynasty. He is shown
(below) on a relief
being embraced by
the god Amun (Re).
A sumptuous pectoral
of electrum, colored
glass and turquoise
(left) bears his name
written in a
cartouche.

During the Roman era, the funerary
traditions of Egypt continued. Mummy
portraits became realistic, like this one of a
man (2nd century AD, below).

THE LOWER EPOCH
(1000 BC to the
Roman occupation).
Egyptian civilization
and religion resisted
Greek and later
Roman occupation
for many centuries.
Above, the *Osorkon
Group* (reign of
Osorkon II, 889–866
BC) in gold and lapis
lazuli, shows Osiris,
Isis and Horus.

Funerary Mask of a Woman in
painted plaster: Roman era,
from Antinoe.

161

Detail of the *Sabine's Shawl*: Cupid figures ride on the backs of crocodiles.

The roots of Coptic Egypt go back to the end of the Ancient World. The Copts (a distortion of the Greek word *aegyptos* meaning Egyptian) submitted to the Greeks of Byzantium and the subsequent triumph of Christianity renewed the iconography of their art. After the Arab conquest in AD 641, those Copts who did not convert to Islam turned to Byzantine and Islamic forms. Religious architecture is particularly well represented in the Louvre's collection, which will be exhibited in a new wing of the museum's Denon sector. Mosaics, fabrics, decorative sculpture and painting attest to an inventive civilization which found itself completely isolated within the Islamic world.

COPTIC WEAVING

Most Coptic fabrics were of linen and wool, decorated with brightly colored motifs. Their designers worked out an original formal language of their own, with strange proportions that owed nothing to perspective, but relied on graphic schematization and flat colors.

Among the many tapestries which illustrate the originality of Coptic art in the 5th century is this fragment showing the head of a dancing girl (left) and another highly graphic piece with geometrical, vegetable and figurative motifs (below, left).

THE SABINE'S SHAWL

Having abandoned the practice of mummification, the Christians buried their dead in rich fabrics decorated in the oriental style. The *Sabine's Shawl* (5th century, details left, right and top of page) was discovered in a tomb at Antinoe; it combines scenes from Greco-Roman mythology with Nilotic ones.

The *Birth of Aphrodite* in limestone relief, 5th–6th century AD.

The Copts built churches with highly original decoration: this capital from Baouit (left) blends vegetable motifs with the Christian cross.

CHRIST AND THE ABBOT MENA
The head of one of Egypt's many monasteries is shown in this painting on wood (6th–7th century AD).

VIRGIN OF THE ANNUNCIATION
This Virgin carved of fig-wood (late 5th century) may have been part of a piece of furniture illustrating scenes from the life of the Virgin, whose iconography was spreading through the Christian world at that time.

MOUNTED HORUS
Christian art assimilated some Egyptian motifs. This Saint George has Horus's falcon features and the dragon is a crocodile.

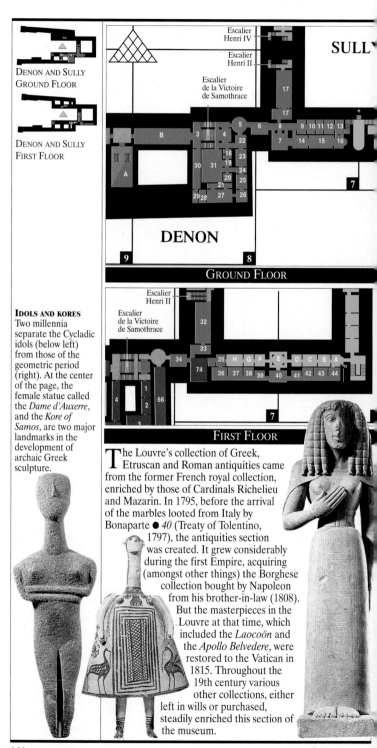

DENON AND SULLY
GROUND FLOOR

DENON AND SULLY
FIRST FLOOR

IDOLS AND KORES
Two millennia
separate the Cycladic
idols (below left)
from those of the
geometric period
(right). At the center
of the page, the
female statue called
the *Dame d'Auxerre*,
and the *Kore of
Samos*, are two major
landmarks in the
development of
archaic Greek
sculpture.

GROUND FLOOR

FIRST FLOOR

The Louvre's collection of Greek,
Etruscan and Roman antiquities came
from the former French royal collection,
enriched by those of Cardinals Richelieu
and Mazarin. In 1795, before the arrival
of the marbles looted from Italy by
Bonaparte ● *40* (Treaty of Tolentino,
1797), the antiquities section
was created. It grew considerably
during the first Empire, acquiring
(amongst other things) the Borghese
collection bought by Napoleon
from his brother-in-law (1808).
But the masterpieces in the
Louvre at that time, which
included the *Laocoön* and
the *Apollo Belvedere*, were
restored to the Vatican in
1815. Throughout the
19th century various
other collections, either
left in wills or purchased,
steadily enriched this section of
the museum.

THE PREHELLENIC AGE

The rooms devoted to the origins of art in the Aegean world, from the 4th millennium BC and the Cycladic period, are being arranged beneath the Galerie Daru (ROOMS 1, 2 AND 3). Especially noteworthy will be the marble Cycladic idols of the 3rd millennium, as well as items from the rich Minoan (Crete) and Mycenean civilizations. The geometric style was dominant from the 10th to the 8th century BC; this was softened in the 7th century by oriental influences which created what we know as the archaic style.

ARCHAIC GREECE

SCULPTURE (ROOM 4). Archaic Greek sculpture is characterized by two themes: that of the Kouros, the nude male of athletic build, and that of the Kore, a young girl, clothed. The conventions which govern these two types and which persisted throughout the archaic period, are the frontal, walking position of the body, with the left leg slightly in advance of the right. The female statue known as the *Dame d'Auxerre* is a prelude to the great Greek statuary in the exactness of its proportions and the sense of volume it displays. This piece probably came from Crete, c. 630 BC. The figure stands in an attitude of worship with one hand raised to her breast. A few traces of color remain on her dress, but none on that of the *Kore of Samos* (Samos, c. 570 BC) found in the shrine of Hera. This is one of the very earliest kores. She wears a ceremonial costume with a long, refined skirt or *chitra*; her right shoulder is draped with a shawl or *himation*. A kouros from the same period seems to be a portrait of Apollo, since it was discovered in his sanctuary at Action. This piece shows the extraordinary care Greek sculptors took in the rendering of anatomical detail. The *Rampin Horseman* (Athens, c. 550 BC) consists of an original head and a body which is a cast of the original in the Museum of the Acropolis in Athens. The hair and beard have beautifully sculpted tight curls. The smile is also an archaic convention. Equally archaic in form, the bronze *Piombino Apollo* ▲ 172 has certain characteristics of the 1st century BC, at which time sculptors developed a taste for representing sacred images in the archaic manner. The *Miletus Torso* (Miletus, c. 480 BC) marks the shift toward the Classical style; the figure is still frontal and rigid, but the hips are looser and more natural. Also displayed in this room are archaic ceramic vases (amphorae) painted with funerary scenes ▲ 174.

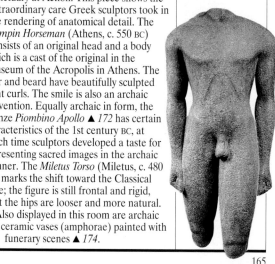

WINGED VICTORY OF SAMOTHRACE
Discovered during excavations on Samothrace in 1863, this statue originally stood on a terrace, probably commemorating a Rhodian naval victory in c. 190 BC.

IMMORTALS
"We never knew his magnificent head, with its ripening eyes. But his body still shines for us, like a candelabra: from it his inward eye still stares and glitters." This remark by Rilke, a propos of the Miletus torso, also applies to the *Kouros of Actium* (below). Top, the head of the *Rampin Horseman*.

THE ERGASTINES
This was the name given to the young girls who were chosen from the best Athenian families to embroider the tunic offered to the goddess Athena after the Panathenaic procession (right, the Ergastines and two leaders of the ceremony on the Parthenon frieze).

IDEALS OF BEAUTY
The canons developed by the Greek sculptors of the Classical era are models of perfection which artists have striven to equal ever since. They were mainly invented by Polykleitos (below right, *Male Torso of an Athlete at Rest*) and Praxiteles (below, the *Cnidian Aphrodite*). These two sculptures are Roman copies of Greek originals.

THE FIRST FRUITS OF CLASSICAL ART from the early 5th century are exhibited in the Rotonde de Mars (ROOM 5) ▲ *125*. The new severe style heralds the beginning of Classicism in which stiffness and hieratic poses give way to movement. The *Exaltation of the Flower* stele lies midway between Archaism and Classicism. The Salle de Diane is adjacent (ROOM 6).

CLASSICISM AND THE APOGEE OF ATHENS

THE PARTHENON (ROOM 7) was the most significant archeological achievement of the age of Pericles (5th century BC). At that time Athens was the dominant city of the Greek world, then emerging with redoubled confidence from the Medic Wars against the Persians (480 BC). Phidias and Polykleitos created sculptures that blended observation of the real with artifice in which ideal beauty was achieved by the approximation of forms to ideas. The *Frieze of the Panathenaic Procession*, whose subject is the great feast held by the Athenians in honor of their tutelary goddess, adorned the walls of the Parthenon's peristyle gallery. Most of this work is in the British Museum in London; designed by Phidias it marks a high point in the progress of Classical sculpture. The Louvre possesses a fragment which shows how the hang of the draperies subtly matches the slow, rhythmic march of the procession. Also visible are the little holes used for attaching accessories in bronze. After visiting this room, (which also contains the *Laborde Head*, a fragment of the decoration of a Parthenon pediment), return the way you came to ROOM 8. **GREEK FUNERARY ART** is displayed in the Pan corridor and in the two rooms following it (ROOMS 8, 9 AND 10). The most

ancient steles here (ROOM 7) were executed by artisans who worked on the Parthenon.

ORIGINALS AND COPIES. The old texts describe cities embellished with thousands of statues in bronze, but the only ones which have come down to us are marbles, most of them late copies of vanished pieces. Bronze ▲ 172–3, which was much used by artists who found in it a more pliable material than marble for the representation of movement, was melted down during the barbarian epochs. The marbles were frequently smashed and mutilated as well, but fortunately they were reproduced during the Roman era and resculpted from plaster casts of their originals. It should be noted that the Roman sculptors, who were much concerned with solidity, often contrived to modify the positions of the arms of sculptures, and added supports such as the one that links the thigh and wrist of the *Borghese Ares* (ROOM 17, ▲ 168) to maintain the equilibrium of bodies which were originally of much lighter bronze. In any case these Roman copies have contributed greatly to our understanding of Greek art.

THE CANONS OF CLASSICAL GREEK SCULPTURE. ROOMS 14, 15 and 16 (the Salles des Apollons, Athenas and Praxitèles) offer an overview of the developing canons of Classical Greek sculpture, from the austere style of Polykleitos to the more delicate, feminine manner mastered by Praxiteles at the end of the 5th century, which we mostly know from copies. The *Diadumenos*, after Polykleitos, the *Apollo* and *Athena* after Phidias and the *Aphrodite (Venus Genitrix)* after Callimachos, a late 5th century Athenian sculptor who made the link between Phidias and Praxiteles, represent the canons of the Classical style, both masculine and feminine (ROOM 14). The *Cnidian Aphrodite* (Roman copy, ROOM 16), all sweetness and modesty, is the prototype of the feminine figure evolved by Praxiteles in the 4th century. The *Arles Aphrodite* (ROOM 16) which was similarly copied from Praxiteles' lost original, has caught forever the suppleness of Phryne, a courtesan who was the sculptor's mistress

APOLLO
The graceful masculine type developed by Praxiteles (above, *Apollo Sauroctone*) may be compared with that of Polykleitos a century earlier (facing page).

OFFICIAL AND PRIVATE ART
Athena, the tutelary goddess of Athens (below) is a Roman replica of an original attributed to Alcamenes (late 5th century). Below left, funerary stele in the 4th-century Attic style showing a reunited family.

167

THE HELLENISTIC PERIOD

and favorite model. The *Apollo Sauroctone* by the same sculptor (ROOM 16) contrasts with the powerful athletes of Polykleitos: the subject here is a soft adolescent. The Classical art of the 4th century seems dominated by a gentler sensibility, perhaps more individualistically inclined, than that of the 5th century, hence the proliferation of portrait paintings. There is greater realism, and the athletes and divinities are engaged in precise actions which the sculptors' handling of anatomy seeks to reflect.

THE HELLENISTIC PERIOD

The sculptor Lysippos, the creator of the *Borghese Gladiator* (ROOM 13), was working at the end of the Classical and the beginning of the Hellenistic periods. He was clearly mindful of the lessons of earlier masters; his *Gladiator* (c. 100 BC) is in fact a Hellenistic work, much influenced by Classicism. It depicts a gladiator in combat; the shield strapped to the left arm and the sword in the right hand are left to the imagination. The Hellenistic period began at about the time of Alexander's death in 323 BC. It is characterized by a much greater emphasis on movement and by interpretations of elements such as childhood, old age, ugliness, suffering and fear. The Hellenistic sculptors also favored picturesque scenes, such as a child playing with a goose or a child perched on a centaur.

THE VENUS DE MILO (ROOM 12 ▲ *170–1*) is surrounded with works attesting to a period of Classical renewal (*Head of Aphrodite*, called the *Kaufman Head*); in addition, some Hellenistic works here echo a more severe earlier style. The sinuous rhythm and rendering of the body, the elaborate folds of the garment and the realism of the bust make it clear that the *Venus de Milo* is an original sculpture from the 2nd century BC; while the pose and facial expression remind us of Praxiteles and Lysippos.

THE SALLE DES PORTRAITS LAGIDES (ROOM 11) evokes the Ptolemaic dynasty to which Cleopatra belonged.

THE SALLE DES CARIATIDES (ROOM 17) houses sculpture of the Hellenistic period. A bust of Alexander stands at its entrance. Note the Roman replicas of lost works by Lysippos (4th century BC), one

THE CARYATIDS OF THE LOUVRE
The caryatids which support the gallery are a direct reference to Greek and Roman antiquity as reinterpreted by the Renaissance. This room (above right) is ideal as a showcase for the Louvre's collection of Hellenistic sculptures. *Artemis*, also called the *Diana of Versailles* (above), and the *Bust of Alexander* (below). To the right is the *Borghese Gladiator* (in ROOM 13) and on the facing page *Sleeping Hermaphrodite*, a replica of a (probably Alexandrian) original.

of the sculptors who represents the rejection of Classicism.
Of the 1,500-odd masterpieces he sculpted which were cast in
bronze, only copies by an unknown sculptor remain: on the
left as you enter the room, *Marsyas* hangs from a
tree waiting to be flayed alive on the command of a
wrathful Apollo. In the same vein as the famous
Cnidian Aphrodite is the *Aphrodite of the Capitol*,
the modest gesture of whose right hand echoes
the hand of the lost Eros resting on the
shoulder of the *Seated Aphrodite*. *Diana the
Huntress* which was copied many times
over, is itself a Roman replica of a 2nd
century BC adaptation of an original by
Leochares (4th century BC). At the
far end of the gallery lies the
exquisitely formed *Sleeping
Hermaphrodite*, discovered at the
beginning of the 17th century in
Rome. The marble mattress
was supplied by Bernini.
  The door behind the caryatids
leads to the Henri II staircase
(▲ *125*); from here, continue to
the rooms containing bronzes
and ceramics (▲ *172–5*).

(▲ *125*)
(▲ *172–5*)

EXPRESSION
Hellenistic sculpture
is distinguished by its

ability to express
passion. Above, the
tortured face of
Marsyas (Roman copy
from a Pergamon
original).

▲ APHRODITE OR THE VENUS DE MILO

Found in 1820 on the island of Melos, or Milo, in the Cyclades, this statue was taken to Paris in the following year. The lost arms have provoked speculation that she had one arm raised, was part of a group, or was with Mars, her lover. The style which is similar to that of the *Aphrodite of Capua* in the Naples Museum, suggests that the *Venus de Milo* was done by a sculptor from the Hellenistic period who worked in the Classical style.

THE WORLD'S MOST FAMOUS WORK OF ART
The *Venus de Milo* (right, in ROOM 12) shares the title of world's most celebrated work of art with Leonardo da Vinci's *Mona Lisa*.

THE ARMS OF VENUS
The right arm must have been held in front of the breasts and the left was probably raised.

Venus de Milo is featured on the ceiling painted by Mauzaisse in 1822 in the Salle Boscoreale (above); *Time Indicating the Ruination he causes, and the Masterpieces he allows to Re-emerge.*

170

Dumont d'Urville, then a ship's ensign, was one of the first to see the statue; he reported its discovery to the Marquis de Rivière, the French ambassador in Constantinople.

LA *VENUS DE MILO* EST TRANSBORDÉE DU NAVIRE *LE GALAXIDI* À BORD DE LA GOÉLETTE *L'ESTAFETTE*.

After negotiating with the Greek authorities of the island of Melos, the Marquis de Rivière (left) purchased the famous Venus along with all the other pieces found with it. He brought it back to France and presented it to Louis XVIII who immediately passed it on to the Louvre in May 1821.

MALE AND FEMALE
The statue of *Mithridates VI Eupator*, which belongs to the same period as the *Venus de Milo*, may also be by the same sculptor. It is displayed in the same room in the Louvre and has the same air of a deliberate return to Classicism inspired by Phidias and Praxiteles (Hellenistic period, 2nd–1st century BC).

VISITORS FROM ALL OVER THE WORLD
The *Venus de Milo* is a star feature of tours of the Louvre, both today and in the past. Above, a press engraving entitled *Nasser-Ed-Din at the Museum of Antiquities* in 1873.

Great statues were cast in bronze, but also in gold-plated wood and ivory (chryselephantine statues); few of these have survived. This is why we know Greek sculpture mainly from copies, most in marble but some in bronze and on a smaller scale. In Greece, as in Etruria and Rome, a rich tradition of metalwork evolved, of which one of the richest sources known to us is the treasure found at Boscoreale near Pompeii.

THE PIOMBINO APOLLO
The date of this bronze Apollo (left) has long been disputed; it is characteristic of the 5th century return to Classicism that marked the close of the Hellenistic period.

BRONZE
Bronze was also used to make everyday objects: (above) a 5th-century BC mirror-holder; (left) a gladiator's greave found at Herculaneum (1st century AD) and (below) a sconce from the 6th century BC.

GOLD
Gold was used to make coins, statues and jewelry as well as ritual vases like this sauceboat dating from the 3rd millennium (above). The treasure of Boscoreale (1st century BC), most of which was of silver, also included a gold bracelet in the form of a serpent (right).

BOSCOREALE
The destruction of the Campanian towns by the eruption of Vesuvius in AD 79 preserved quantities of evidence of a refined way of life. The magnificent treasure of silver discovered in a buried villa close to Pompeii includes (among other things) 109 pieces of tableware, mostly of gold and silver. The treasure was purchased by Baron de Rothschild who presented it to the Louvre.

One of the most beautiful pieces from Boscoreale was a partly gilded silver goblet decorated with skeletons (above).

VICTORIOUS ATHLETE
This bronze head of an athlete in the Classical style and manner of Polykleitos, dates from the 1st century BC.

The statue of Apollo found at Lillebonne, Normandy, is of gilded bronze.

GREEK CERAMICS

Perfumed oil flask in the form of a double head (6th century BC).

The collection of Greek ceramics in the Louvre, which is the most extensive of its kind in the world, is exhibited in the Galerie Campana on the first floor. Here the visitor can trace the development of forms, techniques and images. Painted ceramic work reflects something of what Greek painting must have been like, though no examples remain today. From the great funerary urns of the 8th century BC which were geometric in style, to the masterpieces of Classical art and magnificent kraters signed by the finest painters, the Louvre has an extraordinary variety of pieces on display.

CHALICE-SHAPED KRATER AND BELL-SHAPED KRATER
Left, *Hercules and the Argonauts* by the "painter of the Niobides" (Attica, c. 460 BC); right, *Massacre of the Suitors by Ulysses and Telemachus (*Campania, c. 310 BC); both are red-figured kraters.

AMPHORA (RITUAL VASE)
Attributed to the "painter of Anatolos", c. 700–680 BC. Transition period between the geometric and oriental styles in Athens.

THE LEVY OENOCHOE (WINE JUG)
Rhodes, c. 850 BC. Oriental style of decoration with dark figures against a clear background, animal and vegetable friezes.

HYDRIA (WATER JUG)
By a painter of the Archippe group, c. 550 BC. Black figures against an ocher background.

30–470 BC:
*tic ceramics,
d figures on
ack, austere in
yle, created by
e potter
ndokides.

470–400 BC:
Attic ceramics,
red figures,
Classical style.

400–320 BC:
Attic ceramics,
red figures.
**320 BC–1ST
CENTURY AD:**
Hellenistic
ceramics.

THE PAINTER EUPHRONIOS
Among the painters whose names we know,
Euphronios is one of the masters of the late
6th century BC, and one of the first to use
the red figure technique. The other side of the
krater featuring *Hercules and Antaeus*
(below) represents a music contest.

**THE APOGEE
OF CERAMICS**
This krater in the
shape of a chalice is by
the great painter
Euphronios, and is one of
the masterpieces of the
Louvre's collection. Made
in about 510 BC, it
dates from the
period immediately
after the
abandonment of
black figure painting. The red figures stand
out against the
black backdrop. The
anatomical details, the
force of the gestures, and
the terrified expressions of the
young women watching the
struggle between the
hero and the giant
show the virtuosity of
the painter, who
used the shape of the
vase to suit his purpose.

**HYDRIA
c. 520–510 BC**
*Achilles and Ajax
Playing Dice,*
black figures on red
ground.

LECYTHE (FUNERARY VASE)
By a painter of the "R" group,
last quarter of the 5th century.
Offering with Stele and *Charon
the Boatman,* red figure on
white background.

**RHYTON
(DRINKING HORN)**
shaped like a donkey's
head, c. 440–430 BC.
Red figure,
Classical style.

ETRUSCAN ORIGINALITY
On the way out of ROOM 20, note the small classical and Hellenistic bronzes, among them a classically-inspired vase in the shape of a young man's head (Gabies, c. 425–420 BC, below) and the filiform Aphrodite (Nemi, c. 350 BC, right), with a beautifully proportioned face and elongated body.

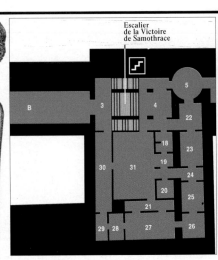

Escalier
de la Victoire
de Samothrace

UNITED FOR ALL TIME
The *Sarcophagus of a Married Couple* (far right), a masterpiece of Etruscan statuary, was discovered at Ceveteri (Caire in antiquity) in 1845. This piece came to the Louvre in 1863 with the Campana collection, to which the Louvre owes not only the greater part of its Etruscan objects, but most of its Greek vases as well. Above, facing page right, a cinerary urn with the same motif of a figure reclining for a banquet.

ETRUSCAN ART

The Etruscan civilization, the most brilliant of pre-Roman Italy, blossomed in the region between the valleys of the Arno and Tiber, and the Tyrrhenian Sea. At its zenith in the 6th century BC it extended as far as the plain of the Po and into Campania. Strongly influenced by Greek art whose development it broadly followed, Etruscan art was faithful nonetheless to its Italic roots. It evolved an original language of its own, excelling in terracotta, laminated bronze and goldwork.

ROOM 18 (9th–6th centuries BC). Villanovian culture supplied the prologue to Etruscan civilization. Characterized by the ritual of incineration, bronzework and geometrical decoration, it was distinctive for its *impasto* (rough clay) cinerary urns, vases and weapons. The history of ceramics between the 7th and the mid-6th century BC is illustrated in the Louvre collection by impasto ceramics and painted ceramics of Greek inspiration, and from the 7th century onward, by the appearance of *bucchero* ceramics (made with black clay, a typical feature of local production). The *Sarcophagus of a Married Couple* shows a man and a woman making the gestures of a perfume offering. This beautiful piece has the smiling grace of Ionian statuary whose influence was very strong in the late 6th century. The motif of the

reclining banquet is itself borrowed from Greek art. Etruscan terracotta is represented by a series of painted panels and by a series of architectural elements which were once colored. Two display cases contain small archaic bronzes made in Etruria.

ROOM 19 (6th–4th centuries BC). Another pair of cases in this room show some of the loveliest creations of Etruscan silversmiths and goldsmiths. Note the pendant in the form of a head of Achelous (the River god), with hair and beard skillfully detailed in filigree and granulation. The larger display cases follow the evolution of Etruscan ceramics between the mid-6th and 4th centuries (decorated with first black, then red figures). In the course of the 6th century, the forms of *bucchero* vases grew more ponderous. In one display case are some cinerary urns called *canopes* by association with the canopic jars in which the Egyptians placed the viscera of their dead. A lid in the shape of a head and handles that sometimes had moving arms, give these pieces an anthropomorphic character of their own. They are typical of the Chiusi region, as are the bas-reliefs, decorated with scenes of banqueting, dancing and exposure of the dead which adorned Etruscan *cippes*, the small monuments that marked their tombs.

ROOM 20 (4th–1st centuries BC). This room contains several sarcophagi, some in terracotta and others in stone, along with terracotta and alabaster urns. The art of portraiture, another field in which the Etruscans excelled, is represented by the head of a young man in bronze, from Fiesole (c. 200 BC).

METALWORK
The Etruscans who excelled in metalwork (*Achelous*, above), also applied their peculiar manual dexterity to the imitation of it. The 7th-century *bucchero sottile* (below), with its delicate outline, has the glint of metal.

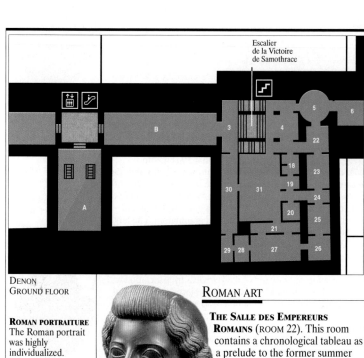

Escalier
de la Victoire
de Samothrace

DENON
GROUND FLOOR

ROMAN PORTRAITURE
The Roman portrait
was highly
individualized.

ROMAN ART

**THE SALLE DES EMPEREURS
ROMAINS** (ROOM 22). This room
contains a chronological tableau as
a prelude to the former summer
apartments of Queen Anne of
Austria, in which the Musée des
Antiquités was installed at its
creation and where the collections of
Roman sculpture are still housed ▲ *126*.
PORTRAITS AND HISTORICAL RELIEFS
(ROOMS 23, 24, 25 AND 26). Official
Roman art appeared at the end of the
first century BC, its ground having been
prepared in advance by a long Italic
tradition inherited in part
from the Etruscans and
influenced by the
Greeks. As a
manifestation of
political power its
goal was to serve
the gods, the state
and the emperor.
Its two principal
concerns were
portraiture and
historical relief. On
one of the most beautiful
reliefs of Republican Rome, the *Altar of Domitius
Ahenobarbus* (c. 100 BC), shows census-taking and
a sacrifice to the god Mars. *Marcellus*, a great
nude statue in the Classical tradition
(commissioned by Augustus in honor of his
nephew and son-in-law who died in 23 BC), carries
the signature of Cleomenes the Athenian.
The figure is both Greek and ideal, and a

A basalt
head of *Livia*, wife
of Augustus (right);
the Emperor *Caligula*
and *Agrippina*,
mother of Nero, in
marble (above). Far .
right, a statue of
Augustus whose head
and body were
sculpted at different
times.

> **"SOME HAVE CURLY HAIR, OTHERS HAVE IT STRAIGHT, TUFTED OR OILED; ALL HAVE MADE CAREFUL USE OF THE COMB, AND THERE ARE NO BALD PATES."** ROLAND BARTHES

thoroughgoing Roman portrait. The many busts offer an unexpected opportunity to study Roman coiffure: sophisticated bandeaux for the women and fine tresses and fringes for the men. This abundance of portraiture is linked to the cult of household gods, near whom the effigies of the principal members of a family would be placed. It was also linked to the deification of the emperors whose faces could be seen everywhere in public places. The new style introduced by each successive emperor had its effect on private sculpture: neoclassicism under Octavius (1st century BC), exaggerated expressionism under Nero (1st century AD), and realism in the second century, from Hadrian to Marcus Aurelius. A time of great diversity, it produced official and private portraits.

ROOM 27, the columns of the *Incantada,* fragments of a portico from the Agora of Thessalonika, are still a mystery. In the same room are portraits and reliefs from the beginnings of Christian art.

CHRISTIAN GAUL, ITALY AND SYRIA (ROOMS 28 AND 29). With the conversion of the Roman Empire to Christianity, a more provincial style emerges, especially funerary.

THE GALERIE DES MOSAIQUES (ROOM 30) illustrates the growth of private art: a few examples of very rare, fragile painting (*Winged Spirit* from Boscoreale near Pompeii, and vine branch decoration) as well as the most beautiful mosaics of antiquity, the celebrated *Triumph of Neptune and Amphitrite.* The superb *Phoenix* shining out from its bed of roses, a late mosaic (5th century) discovered in Antioch, capital of Roman Syria, is composed like a carpet. This piece is very different from the ordinary run of 2nd-century mosaics which were conceived like paintings (for example, the *Judgement of Paris,* a dining room decoration that is similar to Pompeiian paintings).

THE MOSAIC OF THE CONSTANTINE VILLA (COUR DU SPHINX, ROOM 31). The floor of this immense room which was originally a courtyard, is covered with a mosaic from a Roman villa dating from the last years of antiquity (4th century). The villa was situated at Daphne close to

AFTER CHRIST
Roman art had a prolonged period of creativity in the first centuries of our era, during which it kept up its tradition of portraiture – witness the busts of *Juba I* (left) the Numidian king who allied himself with Pompey against Caesar in the 1st century BC, and of *Hadrian* in the 2nd century (above). Above left, *Portrait of a Young Prince,* a 2nd-century marble sculpture found at Annaba in Algeria.

SACRIFICIAL ANIMALS
The relief below shows a sacrifice to Mars.

PAINTING IN MOSAIC
The great Roman mosaics are frequently paintings transposed into this form. Above, a fresco from Pompeii (1st century AD); below, a mosaic from Antioch of the *Judgement of Paris* (2nd century AD). At the top of the page, detail from the border of the *Phoenix* mosaic (5th century AD).

Achilles and King Lycomedes, sarcophagus relief, (3rd century AD, right).

Antioch, a city famed for its attractive gardens and springs. The decoration features the four seasons (in the corners) and hunting scenes (in the larger trapezoidal panels). On the walls, the *Frieze of the Temple of Artemis Leucophryena* from Magnesia dates from the early 2nd century. Likewise, spectacular fragments from the Temple of Didymian

Apollo give a clear indication of the proportions of the columns. From here, turn left.

SARCOPHAGI (ROOM B, GALERIE DARU). These works from Roman workshops (at the beginning of the 2nd century, burial supplanted cremation in Rome) carry fine mythological friezes. At first there was no specific choice of subject (*Apollo and Marsyas, The Nine Muses*); later themes touched on the bereavement (*Phaedra and Hippolyte, Achilles and Penthesilea*). There are also illustrations of mortals saved by the gods, as in *Ariana and Dionysos, Selene and Endymion*.

In the **SALLE DU MANÈGE** (ROOM A) are pieces from the Borghese and Albani collections: a wild boar, a lion, alabaster basins, statues in which the bust alone is antique, and an *Old Fisherman* (also called *Dying Seneca*), a Hellenistic copy. From the Daru vestibule, containing Piranesi's *Candelabra*, you can return to the Pyramide by the escalators, or continue through the rooms devoted to Italian sculpture ▲ *194*.

SCULPTURE

RICHELIEU/GROUND FLOOR AND ENTRESOL (GIRARDON CRYPT, COUR MARLY, COUR PUGET).

1 **2** **3**

RICHELIEU

Escalier Lefuel

Cour Marly

Cour Puget

Cour Khorsabad

Escalier du Ministre

Escalier Colbert

WOOD AND STONE The portal of Ste-Cécile d'Estagel (below) adorned with birds, foliated columns, palmettes and intertwining patterns.

The *Christ* (right) and the *Altarpiece of Carrières* (below) still show traces of their original colors.

The collection of French sculpture came to the Louvre at the time of the Restoration when works assembled during the Revolution at the Musée des Monuments Français and the Musée Spécial de l'École Française were merged. Added to very regularly since 1850, today's collection in the Richelieu building now offers a comprehensive overview of French sculpture from the Middle Ages to the mid-19th century.

ROMANESQUE SCULPTURE

FROM THE HIGH MIDDLE AGES TO THE 12TH CENTURY (ROOM 1). The portal of Ste-Cécile d'Estagel provides a visual introduction to the circuit that begins at the Cour Marly. The three vaults of the room are punctuated by foliated columns from the church of La Daurade in Toulouse and by capitals, one featuring *Daniel Among the Lions.* To the left is the plaque of a *Leper's Tomb.*

SALLE CLUNY, 12TH-CENTURY ROMANESQUE SCULPTURE (ROOM 2). The vestiges of color on the Christ figure in the *Descent from the Cross* remind us that these pieces were mostly polychrome to begin with, as is the elongated *Virgin and Child* from the Auvergne, behind glass nearby. *Saint Michael Killing the Dragon* was originally part of the tympanum of a chapel. The capitals – *Abraham's Sacrifice*, the *Combat of David and Goliath*, and scenes of grape harvesting – are placed higher up.

THE SALLE ST-DENIS, EARLY GOTHIC IN THE ÎLE-DE-FRANCE, SECOND HALF OF THE 12TH CENTURY (ROOM 3). The *Altarpiece of Carrières* is one of the oldest in France; the figures are almost completely detached from their background. The two statue-columns here, which come from Notre-Dame-de-Corbeil, apparently show *Solomon* and the *Queen of Sheba*.

GOTHIC SCULPTURE

CHARTRES, THE TRIUMPH OF GOTHIC (ROOM 4). The two principal sculptures here are *Saint Geneviève* from the church of the same name in Paris (c. 1230), and *King Childebert* from the old abbey of St-Germain-des-Prés (1240), which is more alive and natural in its gestures and in the way the clothing is handled. There is a similar elegance in the relief from the rood-screen of Chartres representing the *Angel Dictating to Saint Matthew the Evangelist*. Smiling like the angels at Rheims are some wooden angels behind glass which used to perch on the colonettes around medieval altars. If you look up you will see a set of gargoyles used to channel away the rainwater from the roofs of Gothic churches and cathedrals.

SALLE MAUBUISSON, 14TH-CENTURY ALTARPIECES (ROOM 5). The altarpiece of the Ste-Chapelle illustrates four scenes from Christ's passion; the one from the Abbey of Maubuisson (commissioned by the king in about 1340) is devoted to the Eucharist. The relief of *Canon Pierre de Fayel* from the tower of the choir of Notre-Dame-de-Paris, marks a trend toward individualizing images of people and a clear break with the frozen manner of religious art.

SALLE BLANCHELANDE, THE MADONNAS (ROOM 6). The wide variety of attitudes and styles displayed in this room shows the importance of the cult of the Virgin in the Middle Ages. The largest piece, from the Sens region, is a figure from a portal; here the Virgin is seen trampling underfoot an asp with a human head and a basilisk, another mythical reptile. *The Virgin of Blanchelande* with a hint of a sway in her hips, her delighted smile responding to the child's hand caressing her cheek, was the first medieval work purchased by the Louvre (in 1850). The *Virgin of la Celle* still shows traces of its original colors and inlaid *pâte de verre*. Also exhibited in this room are several marble Madonnas, a still more precious *Virgin of the Annunciation* made of alabaster, and an effigy of a child. This lovely piece is from the tomb of a daughter of Charles IV in the Abbey of Pont-aux-Dames.

GOTHIC MASTERWORKS
Major sculptures (like *King Childebert*, above) developed alongside the more mannered *Maubuisson Altarpiece (*below) and grotesque gargoyles (above left).

The white and polychrome Madonnas in the Salle Blanchelande.

FRENCH SCULPTURE
FROM THE GOTHIC PERIOD TO THE RENAISSANCE

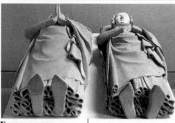

ETERNAL REST
The *Effigies of the De Dormans Brothers* and of *Charles IV and Jeanne d'Évreux* have open eyes anticipating resurrection.

THE PORTRAITIST'S ART
The face of *Jeanne de Bourbon* (above), Queen of France and wife of Charles V, is a delicate masterpiece.

FUNERAL CORTÈGE
The eight mourners of the *Tomb of Philippe Pot* (right and above) are a life-size transposition of the statuettes which were a feature of earlier tombs.

EFFIGIES. In the half-light of this tiny ROOM 7 lies a group of effigies. The effigies of the *De Dormans Brothers* have faces of marble and bodies of ordinary stone. On the left is the *Tombstone of Jean Casse, Canon of Noyon.* Clothed in his rich priestly vestments the cleric holds a chalice in his right hand; above his head is a rendering of the Last Judgement including his patrons the two Saint Johns. On the sides are other saints and two lay figures who may have been relatives.

THE TYMPANUM WITH A HEAD OF LEAVES (ROOM 8). Here the transition from the human face to vegetation is achieved imperceptibly.

SALLE JEAN DE LIÈGE (ROOM 9). The *Tomb of the Entrails of King Charles IV and Jeanne d'Évreux* (1372) is one of several separate tombs containing body, heart and intestines, which were customary at the time for important people. The statue of Charles V and his wife Jeanne de Bourbon (c. 1365–80) probably framed the east gate of the Louvre ● *34*; Charles V was one of the first kings to have himself portrayed by his own sculptor. The diminutive *Angel with Cruet, Saint Michael Killing the Dragon* and, above all the *Virgin and Child* are representative of the International Gothic style of the early 15th century.

ROOM 10 is arranged around the spectacular *Tomb of Philippe Pot* (made in 1480 during the subject's lifetime). Philippe Pot was the grand

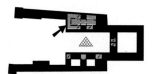

marshall of the Duke of Burgundy until his death in 1493. His monument is extraordinarily daring in conception. The room displays other notable pieces of Burgundian art such as the *Altarpiece of Nolay* and the *Virgins of Plombières and Dijon* and great funerary art like the *Effigy of Anne of Burgundy* by Guillaume Veluton. The coiffure and ornaments give an idea of mid 15th-century costume.

Saint George Fighting the Dragon by Michel Colombe.

THE EARLY RENAISSANCE IN FRANCE

SALLE MICHEL COLOMBE (ROOM 11). In the Loire Valley where Fouquet's art blossomed ▲ *215*, forms grew softer while remaining sculptural; witness the statue of *Saint John on Calvary*, in the rapt attitude of a figure at the foot of the cross. The group in the *Education of the Children* shows the Italian influence spreading into France. Between the candid simplicity of the *Virgin of Olivet*, and that of Ecouen which is more elegant, the contrast is clear. Michel Colombe, the great sculptor of the turn of the 15th century executed a marble altarpiece of *Saint George Fighting the Dragon* between 1504 and 1509 for the first great Renaissance building in France, the Château de Gaillon. Also in this room are several tombs, among them that of Renée d'Orléans Longueville, who is attended by the Virgin, saints and heraldic unicorns.

THE CHAPEL OF PHILIPPE DE COMMYNES, councillor and diplomatic agent of Louis XII, was built for the Couvent des Grands-Augustins in Paris. Dismantled during the Revolution it is evoked in diminutive ROOM 12; on the left, painted stone images of the dead man and his wife adorn a sarcophagus; underneath is stretched the *Effigy of Jeanne de Penthièvre*, their daughter. The decoration of the chapel is a blend of religious themes (Samson, the Tree of Jesse, the symbols of the Evangelists) and profane ones, such as Orpheus with mythological monsters.

IMAGES OF DEATH
Jeanne de Bourbon, Comtesse d'Auvergne (above); the *Dead Saint Innocent* (below), which until 1786 stood in the Cimetière des Innocents in Paris.

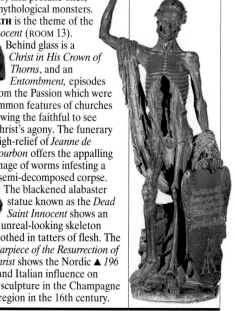

OBSESSION WITH DEATH is the theme of the *Dead Saint Innocent* (ROOM 13). Behind glass is a *Christ in His Crown of Thorns*, and an *Entombment,* episodes from the Passion which were common features of churches allowing the faithful to see Christ's agony. The funerary high-relief of *Jeanne de Bourbon* offers the appalling image of worms infesting a semi-decomposed corpse. The blackened alabaster statue known as the *Dead Saint Innocent* shows an unreal-looking skeleton clothed in tatters of flesh. The *Altarpiece of the Resurrection of Christ* shows the Nordic ▲ *196* and Italian influence on sculpture in the Champagne region in the 16th century.

THE FRENCH RENAISSANCE

JEAN GOUJON INTRODUCES MANNERIST ART (ROOM 14). His style was one of great fluidity, as we can see not only from the reliefs he executed for the Fontaine des Innocents (1549), but also in the draperies of his five reliefs for the rood-screen of St-Germain-l'Auxerrois ▲ *310*. Pierre Bontemps, an artist trained by Primaticcio at Fontainebleau specialized in funerary art; his *Charles de Maigny*, the captain of the Guard at the Porte du Roi protects his sovereign from beyond the tomb. Sculptors of the period liked to represent their dead subjects in everyday poses a bronze attributed to Rosso of *Albert Pius of Savoy, Comte de Carpi* shows him leaning on one elbow leafing through a book. On his effigy executed by Bontemps, the king's Chamberlain Jean d'Humières is also seen leaning on one elbow sleeping. The same insistence on sleep appears in the effigy of *André Blondel de Rocquencourt* who holds a poppy bouquet (attributed to Ponce Jacquiot).
GERMAIN PILON (ROOM 15A) begins with careful observation of reality and reinterprets it graphically and bitterly. On his *Tomb of Valentine Balviani*, he contrasts two effigies of his subject; in one she is alive, elegantly dressed and sculpted in the round, and in the other she is dead, emaciated and rendered in bas-relief. Pilon's *Resurrection of Christ* was sculpted for the Rotonde des Valois, a chapel built by Catherine de' Medici at St-Denis for Henri II and his descendants. Here the utterly bereft *Virgin of the Sorrows* expresses in her face all the anguish of the Passion.
BARTHÉLEMY PRIEUR (ROOM 15B). The simplicity of line is classically elegant in the *Monument for the Heart of Anne de Montmorency* and in the effigies of Montmorency and his wife. Prieur's contemporaries were not all as austere: the female nude was becoming a major theme. *Diane the Huntress of Anet* (1558–9 anon.) which is the oldest garden sculpture remaining in France, is a triumphant and unashamedly voluptuous figure. Near the window is the *Thorn-puller* by Ponce Jacquiot, a rare example of small sculpture from the French Renaissance.

THE COMING OF THE BOURBON DYNASTY

SALLE FRANCQUEVILLE (ROOM 16). The monument which Marie de' Medici sought to raise on the Pont-Neuf ▲ *308* to her husband Henri IV smacks of propaganda for the monarchy. Of the original ensemble, only the *Captives* which adorned the corners of the plinth of the king's equestrian statue have survived: these were sculpted by Francqueville and cast by his son-in-law Bordoni. Also in this room are two marbles by the same artist, *Orpheus* and *David*. ROOM 17, not yet completed, will display the works of the greatest sculptor of the Renaissance in Lorraine, Ligier Richier.

THE ANGUIER AND SARAZIN BROTHERS (ROOM 18). *Fame* by Pierre Biard is still powerfully Mannerist in tone. In contrast François Anguier brought back from Rome a more classical approach which is manifest in the four figures of the Virtues in his *Monument for the Hearts of the Dukes de Longueville.* This obelisk contained the hearts of Henri I who died in 1595 and Henri II who died in 1663. The *Monument for Jacques de Souvre* dissociates the dying body, naked in its shroud, from its useless breastplate. Other funerary monuments even more imposing in style occupy this room. That of the Duke and Duchess de la Vieuville expresses both the pride of the aristocracy (the figures have the ribbon of the Order of the Saint-Esprit around their necks) and Christian humility (expressed in their faces and attitudes). The same expression of radiant faith shines out of the Baroque statue of *Cardinal de Bérulle* by Jacques Sarazin.

THE MONUMENT OF PONT-AU-CHANGE (ROOM 19). This masterpiece by Simon Guillain was completed in 1647. The three statues represent Louis XIII, his wife Anne of Austria and their son Louis XIV. Formerly a statue of *Fame* crowned the Dauphin and the plinth was embellished with dolphins. Opposite stands a bust of Louis XIII by Francois Bordoni which is more realistic than respectful. Emerging in the Cour Marly you are met by *Children with a Goat* by Sarazin (1640). This group purchased in 1667 by Louis XIV and placed in the park at Marly on a Rococo pedestal, prepares the visitor for the majestic courtyard which celebrates the royal residence at Marly and the sculptures which once adorned its gardens ▲ *189*.

BRONZES
Two *Captives* by Francqueville (above and top left) and a fine head of Henri IV by Mathieu Jacquet (center). One of the builders of the Louvre, Henri IV commissioned the Grande Galerie among other things ● *76*.

THE "NOBLESSE DE ROBE" is very much present in the gigantic *Funerary Monument of Jacques Auguste de Thou*, president of the Parliament of Paris (below).

The glass roof which spans this former ministry courtyard avoids the inherent contradiction of displaying indoors those works that were made for the park of the Château de Marly. The Cour Marly is in the heart of the renewed Richelieu wing, the former ministry of Finance redesigned by the architect I.M. Pei. The most spectacular pieces here are the *Horses of Marly*: the two groups sculpted by Antoine Coysevox and Guillaume Coustou for the drinking-pond of Louis XIV's favorite château, surrounded by ble figures.

ESCAPED HORSES
Guillaume Coustou received an order in 1739 for two groups of sculpture for the empty plinths at Marly. Out of gigantic blocks of marble he sculpted his *Horses Restrained by Grooms*.

Mercury Riding Pegasus (above) and its twin *Fame*, sculpted by Coysevox in around 1700, were transported in 1719 to the entrance of the Tuileries ▲ 281. The sculptures were replaced by casts.

THE ART OF MOVEMENT
Hippomenes (above) and *Apollo* (below) were once placed in the middle of large ornamental ponds, as the sumptuous *Album de Marly* commissioned by Louis XIV shows.

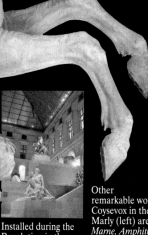

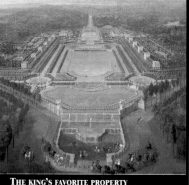

Installed during the Revolution in the Place de la Concorde, Coustou's *Horses* remained there until 1984 ▲ 281.

Other remarkable works by Coysevox in the Cour Marly (left) are *The Marne, Amphitrite* and *Neptune*, eroded by the salt-winds at Brest where they stood for many years; beside them *The Seine* which has been under cover since 1872 seems to be fresh from the sculptor's chisel. Much admired in the 17th century, the *Arria and Poetus* group is by Pierre Lepautre and the *Aeneas and Anchises* was even more famous. On the upper terrace Jacques Prou's *Amphitrite* combines the majesty of a classical face with Rococo curves.

THE KING'S FAVORITE PROPERTY
The various sculpted groups now in the Cour Marly once stood in the park at Marly (above) where they were centered on the king's pavilion. In the foreground, the drinking-pond and the *Horses* by Coysevox.

ROYAL SQUARES
The group of
sculptures in the Place
de Victoires in the
17th century. Today
they have been
supplanted by an
equestrian statue of
Louis XIV by Bosio
(19th century ▲ *300*).
These colossal bronze

compositions involved
the use of highly
sophisticated
techniques.

MILO AT VERSAILLES
Milo of Croton by
Puget (right) was
intended for the park
at Versailles, the
official residence of
Louis XIV.

THE GLORY OF THE SUN KING

THE GIRARDON CRYPT (ROOM 20) exhibits the
equestrian statue of Louis XIV, a smaller version of the
monumental statue executed by Girardon for Place
Louis-le-Grand (the present Place Vendôme
● 78). The king is dressed in Roman garb
but wears a fashionable contemporary wig.
The bust of the Prince de Condé by
Coysevox is a work of great expressive
force. Here also Puget's relief, the
*Meeting of Alexander and
Diogenes*, is enlivened by powerful
Baroque undertones; despite
the reference to the ancient
world, the expressiveness of
the attitudes and the
diagonal composition
somehow carry this scene.
THE COUR PUGET. On the
lower terrace are bronzes
by the Dutch sculptor
Martin van den
Bogaert (who
Frenchified
his name to
Martin
Desjardins);
these came
from the Place
des Victoires
▲ 300 where they
complemented the
pedestrian statue of
Louis XIV (destroyed during
the Revolution) and the
Chained Captives
representing the defeated
nations at the Treaty of
Nijmegen. On the wall at
right are bronze reliefs
entitled the *Precedence of
France Recognized by
Spain, The Crossing
of the Rhine, The
Conquest of Franche-
Comté* and the *Peace
of Nijmegen.* In
contrast to this
ensemble is

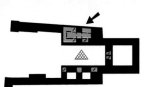

Hercules by Pierre Puget. The most famous work on the middle terrace is probably Puget's *Milo of Croton*. Its companion piece *Perseus and Andromeda* was brought to Versailles in 1685 and is the most Baroque piece in all the repertoire of French sculpture.

LOUIS THE WELL-BELOVED

Moving to the next terrace, in the Cour Puget, we pass from the reign of Louis XIV to that of Louis XV, whose favorite Madame de Pompadour had herself portrayed by Pigalle as *Friendship Offering Her Heart.* Her brother, the Marquis de Marigny, acquired *Two Children Playing with Flowers.* At the back of the courtyard above are reliefs by Clodion for the town mansion of the Princesse de Condé, *Scenes of a Childrens' Bacchanal.* At the top of the staircase is *Mercury Attaching His Heel Wings* by Bouchardon, a copy of an ancient statue.

Prince de Condé, bronze by Coysevox.

THE MARBLES OF THE ACADÉMIE
Among the reception pieces is Guillaume Coustou II's *Vulcan,* for his entry to the Academy in 1742.

THE GOLDEN AGE OF FRENCH SCULPTURE

TOMBS OF THE GREAT (ROOM 12). The funerary sculpture of the 18th century is represented by models for the tombs of illustrious men such as the Cardinal de Fleury, the *Mausoleum of the Comte d'Ennery* by Houdon, and the *Mausoleum of the Maréchal de Saxe* by Pigalle.
ÉTIENNE MAURICE FALCONET (ROOM 22). *Love's Threat* belonged to Madame de Pompadour ▲ *228* and the *Bather* to Madame du Barry. In the *Allegory of Music* is the score of *Aegle* by Pierre Lagarde, sung by the Marquise de Pompadour at the Théâtre des Petits-Appartements at Versailles in 1748.

BOUCHARDON (ROOM 23). This sculptor spent time in Rome and the influence of antiquity is clear. His *Love Carving a Bow from the Club of Hercules* (1750) inspired by an antique original, was judged vulgar because of its naturalism.
PIGALLE (ROOM 24). In this room is the statue of the unclothed Voltaire (1770) with its striking contrast between the inspired face and the scrawny body. Very much like this Voltaire is the bust of *Diderot as an Old Man* (1777) ▲ *229*.

CLASSICAL NUDE
Pigalle's *Voltaire,* portrayed naked at the request of Diderot.

RECEPTION PIECES

ROOM 25. The Académie Royale de Peinture et de Sculpture was founded in 1648. Members had first to be accepted and then were asked to execute a reception piece on a predetermined subject. In the 18th century these pieces, mostly taken from mythology, tended to be less than half-lifesize and were usually isolated nude figures. Most are displayed here according to the manner adopted by the Académie, whose headquarters was at the

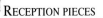

▲ FRENCH SCULPTURE:
NEOCLASSICISM AND ROMANTICISM

TWO AMERICANS
Benjamin Franklin (right) and *George Washington* (sculpted from life in the United States, seen here in profile); both portraits by Houdon.

THE REPUBLIC
Among the rare works surviving from the Revolution is this allegory of the *Republic* by Chinard, holding the tablets of the Law. The piece illustrates one of many attempts by artists to embody the French people in one individual. They have included Hercules, the Republic and finally France herself in the person of Marianne in her Phrygian bonnet. *La Marseillaise* by Rude (right), a study for the Arc de Triomphe.

Louvre until the Revolution ● *28*. The chronological succession emphasizes their stylistic evolution: the turbulence of Rococo at its apogee (*Neptune Calming the Waves* by Adam, or Slodtz's *Icarus*); the acme of feminine grace (*Leda and the Swan* by Jean Thierry); then the transition to neoclassicism in mid-century. Falconet's *Milo of Croton,* still in the Baroque mode, was coolly received in 1754 in contrast to the same piece by Dumont who was accepted in 1768. The panorama ends with pure classicism (Julien's *Dying Gladiator*). Behind glass are some studies in terracotta.

IN HONOR OF GREAT MEN AND THE PEOPLE

CAFFIERI (ROOM 26). Many of Caffieri's busts (done between 1770 and 1790) are displayed here, among them the jovial *Canon Alexandre-Gui Pingré.*

PAJOU (ROOM 27). To the left is a fine bust of *Madame du Barry,* Louis XV's mistress. Here also is his *Psyche Abandoned,* whose plaster cast caused a scandal at the 1785 Salon on account of its total nudity and dramatic facial expression. Behind glass is a small terracotta piece entitled *Ariana Abandoned*, a later variant on the theme.

HOUDON (ROOM 28). A consummate portraitist Houdon earned a substantial income from his busts of the famous. He did likenesses of nearly every eminent man of his time including Diderot, George Washington, Benjamin Franklin, Buffon, Rousseau and Voltaire. In a display case are intimate works such as the children of the architect Brongniart, and the artist's own daughters. Houdon was also a fine monumental sculptor: see his *Mausoleum of the Comte d'Ennery* (ROOM 21) and *Diana the Huntress* (ROOM 29).

GALERIE DES GRANDS HOMMES (ROOM 29). In the center of the room are ten of the twenty-eight statues of great men commissioned in 1776 by the Comte d'Angiviller for the Grande Galerie which later became a museum ● *29*.

CLODION'S work is exhibited in ROOM 20, notably the major reliefs in fine stone which once adorned the bathroom of the Baron de Besenval and some terracotta pieces, among them the *Comtesse d'Orsay,* who with her dying breath shows her husband the son she has borne him. *Egyptian woman at the Naos*

recalls the late 18th-century vogue for ancient Egypt.

REVOLUTION AND EMPIRE (ROOM 31). Sculptures from the Revolutionary period ● *38* are rare, mostly ephemeral products of a troubled time. The official art of the Empire, *Napoleon in his Coronation Robes* by Claude Ramey, or Peace by Antoine-Denis Chaudet, is classical and severe. It coexisted with another trend which was marked by the gracefulness of Canova ▲ *195*, and exemplified by Chaudet's *Love* or Marin's the *Bather* Meanwhile the art of portraiture persisted (*Madame de Verninac as Diane* by Chinard).

TOWARD ROMANTICISM

ROOMS 32 AND 33. There is less Romanticism than late Neoclassicism in the work of Cortot or Foyatier while Pradier's *Three Graces* is more sturdily naturalistic. The really Romantic pieces here are by such artists as François Rude (his pieces for the Arc de Triomphe are well known, but *Mercury Attaching His Heel Wings* and *Young Neapolitan Fisherboy Playing with a Tortoise* are not). Other major Romantics are David d'Angers (*Child with a Bunch of Grapes, 1845*), and Antoine-Louis Barye, whose *Jaguar Devouring a Hare* exists in three versions: the original plaster study; the master version used for casting; and the first version cast and engraved by the artist himself. The same goes for the neo-Mannerist *Angelica and Roger Mounted on the Hippogriff*. There is also a bust of *Alphonse de Lamartine* by David d'Angers who specialized in medallions of celebrities.

THE UPPER TERRACE OF THE COUR PUGET houses the monumental sculptures. The *Dying Soldier at Marathon* (Cortot, 1834), like Bosio's bronze group of *Hercules Fighting with Achelous in the Form of a Serpent*, is classical, but *Orlando Furioso* by Duseigneur, exhibited at the 1831 Salon, is a manifesto for Romanticism. The final piece is Barye's *Lion Fighting a Serpent*: the lion's fearsomely realistic fangs are said to have terrified Alfred de Musset.

NEOCLASSICAL GRACE, ROMANTIC EXPRESSION
At the beginning of the 19th century airy neoclassicism persisted in the work of Ruxtiel (*Zephyr and Psyche*, left) while the expressionism of the Romantics (for example, Jehan Duseigneur's agonized *Orlando*, below) was emerging. This latter brand of sculpture has close affinities with the paintings of Géricault ▲ *232*.

**IN SEARCH OF
ANTIQUITY**
The marble *Head of
an Empress*
(Ariana?), the first
piece of Italian
sculpture on this
circuit comes from
Rome and dates from
the early 6th century.

TUSCANY
Jacopo della Quercia
(Siena, 1374–1438), a
seated *Virgin and
Child* (below right)
and Donatello
(Florence 1386–1466)
Virgin and Child
(below) were the
most celebrated
Tuscan sculptors of
the Quattrocento.

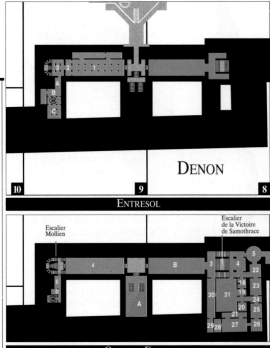

DENON

ENTRESOL

Escalier
Mollien

Escalier
de la Victoire
de Samothrace

GROUND FLOOR

The Louvre's collections of sculpture from other countries
are displayed in the Denon building: in the Galerie
Mollien, in the former vaulted stables of Napoleon III, and
(in the case of the Northern schools) in the rooms adjoining.
Though the collections are less complete than those of French
sculpture, they nevertheless offer a wide variety of pieces
ranging from the high Middle Ages to neoclassicism.
THE GALERIE DONATELLO (ROOM 1) contains Italian sculpture
from the Byzantine era to the 15th century. The first bay is
reserved for the Byzantine period, with among other things, a
very fine *Head of an Empress*. The next three bays are filled
with Roman and Gothic works, notably a 13th-century
Umbrian *Descent from the Cross* and a *Virgin of the
Annunciation* by Nino Pisano. The beginnings
of the Renaissance are represented by Lucca
della Robbia and the Sienese sculptor
Jacopo della Quercia (look for his large
polychrome wooden statue of a seated
Virgin and Child). At the center of the
gallery are works by Donatello and his
school, in particular a *Virgin and
Child* in gilded and painted
terracotta: the background
drapery which emphasizes the
long graceful neck of the Virgin
combines with the curves of the
seat in the foreground to give
this piece a remarkable illusion
of depth. Certain other late
Renaissance Italian artists are
represented here including Mino
da Fiesole (several Madonnas, a
bust of the humanist *Dietisalvi
Neroni* in antique dress, and a
fragment of the tomb of Paul II);

Desiderio da Settignano (a *tondo* featuring *Christ and John the Baptist as Children*, and *Julius Caesar*); and Agostino di Duccio (the *Rothschild Madonna* and the *d'Auvillier Madonna* executed for Piero de' Medici). Other sculptors are represented by a few isolated masterpieces such as Benedetto da Maiano's *Bust of Filippo Strozzi* and Francesco Laurana's *Unknown Princess*.

BOTTEGA DELLA ROBBIA (ROOM 2) contains examples of the enameled terracotta sculptures which made the fortune of the Della Robbia family.

SPANISH SCULPTURE (ROOM 3) occupies the vacated areas under the Denon staircase; here the most remarkable pieces are a *Door with an Annunciation* from Valencia and a statuette of the *Body of Saint Francis in His Tomb*.

GALERIE MICHEL-ANGE (ROOM 4). On the floor above where Benvenuto Cellini's *Nymph of Fontainebleau* echos the distant *Winged Victory of Samothrace*, is the monumental *Door* of the Palazzo Stanga. In the center of the gallery are Michelangelo's *Slaves,* which were destined for the monumental tomb of Pope Julius II in Rome but were never completed. There is disagreement among the experts about the symbolic meaning of these *Slaves*; some think they evoke the human soul trapped in the body. Also in this gallery are a *Young River God* by Pierino da Vinci, full of grace and hedonist poetry which manages to combine psychological depth and Mannerist virtuosity, as well as a fine group of works by Gian Francesco Rustici. *Mercury in Flight* by Giambologna, *Bacchus* by Susini and *Mercury Abducting Psyche* by Adriaan de Vries (a Dutchman trained by Giambologna) are characteristically Mannerist.

Baroque sculpture is represented by the most important Italian sculptor of the 17th century, Gian Lorenzo Bernini ● *79*, including *Angel Bearing the Crown of Thorns*, a study for *Truth* and busts of *Richelieu* and *Pope Urban VIII*. The neoclassical period in Italy is illustrated by Canova's exquisitely polished marble of *Psyche Revived by the Kiss of Eros*. No wrinkle mars the perfect bodies of these adolescent lovers. Bartolini's *Nymph and Scorpion* which featured in the 1837 Salon can also be seen here.

Michelangelo's two *Slaves*: the *Dying Slave* (left) and the *Rebellious Slave* (below).

BAROQUE TO NEOCLASSICISM
Bernini's view of the world (left, *Angel Bearing the Crown of Thorns*) was very different to Canova's (below, *Psyche Revived by the Kiss of Eros*). But both sculptors sought to give movement to the dead matter of marble and terracotta.

195

▲ NORTHERN EUROPEAN SCULPTURE

The *Altarpiece of the Passion* from the church at Coligny (right). In its center is the *Crucifixion* with the *Bearing of the Cross* on the left and

the *Descent from the Cross* on the right. In the lower register are the *Nativity* and the *Adoration of the Magi*. An alabaster bust of Otteimrich, Count and Elector Palatine

(1502–59) attributed to Dietrich Schro (above) is here also.

REPENTANCE
Gregor Erhart's *Saint Mary Magdalen* (right) is portrayed nude with long fair hair. At far right is *Venus Holding an Apple* by Thorvaldsen.

The Louvre's collection of northern European sculpture has a number of gaps, but nevertheless the museum possesses many masterpieces in the field. Northern European sculpture occupies a suite of five rooms in the Denon building on two different levels.

ENGLAND (ROOM A) is represented by 15th-century alabaster reliefs.

THE SALLE DES BELLES MADONES (ROOM B) is devoted to the International Gothic style which dominated all of Europe around 1400. It contains a number of graceful, supple Madonnas and in particular a *Virgin of Piety* in alabaster by the pupils of the master altarpiece maker of Rimini.

LATE GOTHIC (ROOM C) contains sculptures of the late 15th and early 16th centuries from the Netherlands and the Holy Roman Empire. The *Virgin and Child* of Issenheim is a major example of the new style in German sculpture, with its tumultous drapery carved from limewood (a material which can be worked to a high standard of finesse). Tilman Riemenschneider's *Virgin of the Annunciation* illustrates the delicate lyrical art of this great master from Würzburg. But the unquestioned masterpiece of the German section is *Saint Mary Magdalen* by Gregor Erhart. Sculpture from the Low Countries is represented by the Antwerp altarpiece from Coligny, statuettes and reliefs from Malines, Brussels and Utrecht, and the monumental Nivelles *Calvary*.

ROOM D which is accessible by way of the former Grand Écuyer staircase contains sculptures belonging to the northern European Baroque and Rococo schools of the 17th and 18th centuries.

THE GALERIE THORVALDSEN (ROOM B) completes this tour with works by the Swedish sculptor Johan Tobias Sergel and the Dane Bertel Thorvaldsen, characteristically neoclassical in inspiration.

196

DECORATIVE ARTS

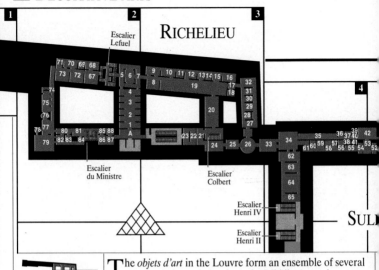

RICHELIEU

SUL

FIRST FLOOR /
RICHELIEU AND SULLY

Pendant *"Bulle"* of
Empress Maria.

Alpais Ciborium
(Limoges, c.1200), gilt
brass, chiseled and
engraved, precious
stones (right).
Serpentine Paten
(below). Gold,
precious stones and
9th-century cloisonné
motifs; 1st-century
saucer.

The *objets d'art* in the Louvre form an ensemble of several thousand pieces dating from the Middle Ages, the Renaissance (Richelieu building) and the 17th and 19th centuries (Sully and Richelieu buildings). They come from many different sources and include the treasury of the Abbey of St-Denis, bronzes from Louis XIV, the royal collection of furniture, collections bequeathed by amateurs or purchased by the French state and (more recently) from bequests in lieu of death duty.

TREASURES OF THE MIDDLE AGES

SALLE CHARLEMAGNE, THE HIGH MIDDLE AGES.
ROOM 1 between the Cour Marly and the Cour Puget, introduces the high Middle Ages – from the last years of the Roman Empire (porphyry columns surmounted by the bust of an emperor) and the beginnings of Christian art (the *"Bulle"* of the Empress Maria, made in about AD 400, found in Rome in 1544). The *Chest Decorated with Rosettes*, made in Constantinople in the 10th century, shows the legacy of antiquity. The same richness is visible in several psalter-bindings and in the *Jewels of Queen Aregonde*, wife of Clothair. Ivory was much prized in Constantinople: examples are the *Barberini Ivory* (6th century) in honor of Justinian, and the *Harbaville Triptych* (10th century). The Carolingian emperors of the 8th and 9th centuries were also partial to ivory; in their time bindings were made of this material for the *Dagulf Psaltery* and the plaque known as the *Earthly Paradise*, in which imaginary animals are pictured with more familiar ones. The bronze *Equestrian Statuette of Charlemagne* was made in the reign of his son Charles the Bald, whose features it may have borrowed (the horse is a reused piece made in antiquity). This room also exhibits Western pieces

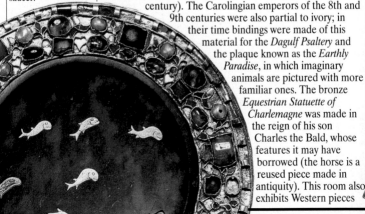

Detail from the *Barberini Ivory* (left) of Christ blessing Justinian.

(the *Serpentine Paten*), Byzantine objects like the *Reliquary of the Stone of the Holy Sepulchre*, mosaic-decorated pieces (*Icon of the Transfiguration*) and painted icons.

SALLE SUGER, 10TH–12TH CENTURY. ROOM 2 bears the name of the abbot who founded St-Denis, a building which heralded the birth of Gothic architecture. It contains fine ivories such as *Christ with a Child* and the *Feeding of the Five Thousand* (c. 968), along with ivory hunting horns, gaming counters, and other pieces of Limoges enamelwork. Gold items include a binding-case representing the *Crucifixion* with precious stones and gilded silver as in the *Arm-Reliquary of Charlemagne*. Gilded silver is shown combined with rock crystal, as in the *Vase of Eleanore*, or otherwise in the forms of a chalice and ewer which are typical of Fatimid art in the 10th and 11th centuries. There is also a masterpiece in porphyry, the famous *Suger's Eagle*, one of the abbot's many treasures. The hilt of the *Sword of Charlemagne* known as *La Joyeuse* is gold. Copper is combined with champlevé enamel on the "*Vermiculated Background*" *Reliquary*, and on the reliquary celebrating the *Assassination and Burial of Thomas à Becket*, the archbishop who was killed in 1170. However the high point of Limoges enamelwork in the Gothic style is the *Alpais Ciborium*. Alpais is one of the few artists of that period whose name has come down to us. The Salle Suger contains not only French pieces such as the *Apostle* carved from a walrus tusk, but also Italian (a superb plaque of *Cain and Abel*), Spanish (two magnificent ivory *Crosses*) and above all German pieces (*Reliquary of Saint Henry*, a memorial to the Emperor Henry II who was canonized in 1146). The final decades of the 12th century saw the blossoming of a new style, seen in the *Double Cross* made for Abbot Hugo, and a Limoges *Saint Matthew*.

SALLE JEANNE D'ÉVREUX, THE STYLE OF 1200 (ROOM 3). In this room are a number of important Limoges pieces, notably the *Reliquary of Saint Francis of Assisi* and the *Casket of Saint Louis.* In the reign of Louis IX the quality of ivory work improved considerably: the *Virgin and Child of Ste-Chapelle* is skillfully crafted around the naturally curving elephant's tusk. The groups depicting the *Descent from the Cross* and the *Coronation of the Virgin*, left, whose polychrome features lend emphasis to its perfect craftsmanship, represent the summit of the art of Parisian ivory carvers. This Parisian style spread throughout northern France (for example, the *Polyptych of Floreffe* probably came from the Ile-de-France). The metal *Arm Reliquary of Saint Luke* is made in the shape of the evangelist's arm and that of the *Finger of Saint Lawrence* depicts the saint on the gridiron of his martyrdom.

RICHNESS AND VARIETY OF MATERIALS Rock crystal and gilded silver for the *Arm reliquary of Saint Luke* (below left), porphyry and silver gilt for *Suger's Eagle* (above), ivory heightened with gold for the 13th-century Parisian *Descent from the Cross* (below).

199

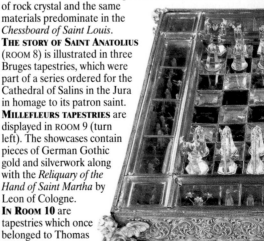

Salt-cellar which belonged to Louis XIV (right) and two *Angel Reliquaries*, which belonged to Anne of Brittany (center).

GOTHIC ART, THE SCEPTER-ROOM OF CHARLES V (ROOM 4). The king enthroned at the point of the scepter is Charlemagne; his inscription is engraved in the golden orb studded with precious stones. Bone is the material used for the *Great Altarpiece* and ivory for the diptych illustrating *Scenes from the Life of the Virgin*, and of the *Childhood and Passion of Christ*. The *Ring of John the Fearless* is of gold and enamel, its raised outline cut from white chalcedony. The marquetry caskets depict subjects such as the *Loves of Paris* and the *Legend of Griselidis* while a lovely painted box relates the *Triumph of Venus* (a Sienese example of International Gothic). Midway between sacred and profane is the *Tapestry of the Heart's Offering* which illustrates the courtly love of the *Romance of the Rose*. The *Bear Tapestry* which is somewhat later, celebrates the Orsini family.

NEW TECHNIQUES, NEW DECORATION

Scepter of Charles V.

THE SALLE ANNE DE BRETAGNE (ROOM 6) between Valencia corridor (ROOM 5, left, Spanish ceramics) and the Faenza corridor (ROOM 7, right, Italian ceramics and metalwork) displays 14th and 15th century treasures against a backdrop of Flemish tapestries. These include a pair of *Angel Reliquaries*; a gold and agate *Salt-cellar*; and the *Self-portrait of Jean Fouquet* the first great name in French painting. In this piece, the earliest known self-portrait by a Frenchman, the copper support was first covered with black enamel, then with grey-brown enamel before being hatched with gold. The *Reliquary of the Flagellation* with its plinth in blue enamel covered with gilded embossed silver, has a vase of rock crystal and the same materials predominate in the *Chessboard of Saint Louis*.

Self-portrait by Jean Fouquet (above) and *Reliquary of the Flagellation* (below).

THE STORY OF SAINT ANATOLIUS (ROOM 8) is illustrated in three Bruges tapestries, which were part of a series ordered for the Cathedral of Salins in the Jura in homage to its patron saint.

MILLEFLEURS TAPESTRIES are displayed in ROOM 9 (turn left). The showcases contain pieces of German Gothic gold and silverwork along with the *Reliquary of the Hand of Saint Martha* by Leon of Cologne.

IN ROOM 10 are tapestries which once belonged to Thomas Bohier, Chamberlain

of Charles VIII who began building the Château de
Chenonceaux in 1515.

SALLE LOUIS XII, PAINTED ENAMEL ON COPPER (ROOM 11).
This technique was current at Limoges in the last years of the
15th century. The *Coronation of the Virgin* by the
same master who did the triptych of
Louis XII, is a fine example.

THE ITALIAN RENAISSANCE

THE ART OF BRONZEWORK (ROOMS 12
TO 14). Donatello, though not himself a
bronze-worker created a number of works for
casting in that material, notably a *Crucifixion*
exhibited in ROOM 12 beside pieces by his pupil
Bartolomeo Bellano (*Saint Jerome and the Lion*).
From the Padua studio of Andrea Briosco known as
Riccio, came a number of small bronzes inspired by
mythology and fables of antiquity, among them
Arion (by the master himself), who is depicted
enchanting the dolphins with the music of his lyre.
One of Riccio's major works displayed in ROOM 13
is the tomb of Marcantonio della Torre (about 1511)
who was a professor of medicine at
the University of Padua: this explains
the themes of some of the bas-
reliefs. The medallions in ROOM 14
served as memorials to Italy's great
families – d'Este, Gonzaga, Malatesta. Pisanello
(c. 1380–1455) was the first to distinguish himself
in this branch of decorative art.

THE SALLE DU MAÎTRE DE L'"ÉNEIDE" (ROOM 15)
presents an array of magnificent French enamels
from the first half of the 16th century. The eleven
Aeneid Plaques were made in about 1530.

ROOM 16, THE REIGN OF FRANÇOIS I (see on the
door to the left, the king's salamander emblem).
The *Tapestry of Saint Mammès* is a Parisian piece
dating from 1544, after Jean
Cousin. The furniture,
dressers and caskets blend
Gothic tradition and
ornament with the
Italian taste for
arabesques and
vegetable motifs.

GLASSWORK. After
this cross the Passage
des Nielles (ROOM
17) to visit the
diminutive
ROOM 18.
Charles
Sauvageot
bequeathed to
the Louvre his
collection of
Venetian and
German glass.

**THE ART OF THE
EVERYDAY**
A detail from a 16th-
century French
tapestry (above) *Fruit
Pickers*. A *Feeding
bottle* (left) made at
Rheims c. 1500 is very
much an everyday
object. *Saint Jerome
and the Lion* by
Bellano shows how
small sculptures can
still have monumental
overtones.

CRYSTAL
The *Chessboard of
Saint Louis* (center,
below) is in rock
crystal, a material
which was surpassed
from the 15th century
onward by Venetian
glass (below, *Venetian
Gourd* from the 16th
century).

The *Curse of Rome*, a majolica dish by Xanto Avelli (Urbino, 1532).

Baroque pearl mounted as a dragon's breast (Spain, 16th century).

APOGEE OF PAINTED ENAMEL
Objects in painted enamel became very fashionable in the 16th century. *Moses and Jethro*, a dish painted by Pierre Reymond in grisaille (above).

Anne de Montmorency, Constable of France by Leonard Limosin (1556).

Spherical Watch by Jacques de la Garde (1551, right). *Vermeil Basin with Reptiles, Frogs and Crayfish* (c. 1550), below.

THE CENTURY OF CHARLES V

THE GALERIE DES CHASSES DE MAXIMILIEN (ROOM 19) is devoted to tapestries illustrating the twelve months of the year with twelve hunting scenes from the forest of Soignes near Brussels, the capital of Flanders and of the art of tapestry. At the center of the room is a display of majolica – faience from Italy or in the Italian taste – dating from the 16th century.

Istoriato, majolica illustrating themes from history, originated in Faenza and Urbino; it is represented here by a dish from the *Service of Isabella d'Este* (1525) signed by Nicola d'Urbino. More ornamental is the style of Castel Durante, the rival of Urbino where grotesques, flowers, fruits and landscapes are all mixed into the equation. To this school was attached that of the portrait of the *Belle Donne* (Deruta), which produced plates of a yellowish, coppery sheen, as distinct from the dark blood-red of Gubbio.

THE EIGHT TAPESTRIES OF THE GALERIE DE SCIPION (ROOM 20) were woven in the late 17th century by the Gobelins factory, commissioned by Louis XIV to reproduce a series of 16th-century tapestries which were destroyed during the Revolution. They were inspired by Livy's history of the Second Punic War and the exploits of Scipio Africanus. Also in this room are some pieces of Limoges enameled porcelain painted in grisaille by Pierre Reymond (1513–84), a service by Pierre Courteys (who died c. 1581) and work by the Penicaud family (also shown in ROOM 15).

ENAMELS AND CERAMICS (ROOM 21). The enamel portraits executed by Leonard Limosin of Limoges who invented this genre, are amazingly vivid (to achieve the maximum finesse, Limosin applied his enamel with a thin brush). At center are 13 pieces of rare St-Porchaire pottery, the largest collection of its kind in the world. Everything about these first Parisian experiments in French porcelain is original: the white, sonorous clay, the technique used for the decoration and even the shapes.

THE SALLE HENRI II (ROOM 22) contains various enamels (panels of altar-screens with portraits of François I and Henri II), tapestries and stained glass.

SALLE PAUL GARNIER, CLOCKS (ROOM 23). The watch was invented in the second half of the 15th century and very soon jewelers and clockmakers became obsessed with it. Miniaturized to an extreme degree the earliest watches were meticulously ornamented combinations of precious metals, enamel and rock crystal and were worn like jewelry around the neck or waist. The *Spherical Watch* by

March (top) is the first hanging in the series entitled *Maximilian's Hunt* (at the time March was officially the first month of the year in Flanders). The city in the background is Brussels with the ducal palace on the left and the towers of the church of Ste-Gudule on the right. The rider in red is Charles V. *December* (center and bottom, with detail and preparatory sketch by Bernard van Orley) shows a boar-hunting scene and the confrontation between the rider and the beast. A medallion at the top of each tapestry gives the signs of the zodiac.

A necklace decorated with scenes from the *Passion* (left) and a pendant of the *Annunciation* (below), are two treasures from the Rothschild collection.

Jacques de la Garde (1551) is the oldest in the Louvre. Several are displayed open, showing mechanisms of astonishing complexity. Some of the German and French table clocks are as delicate as the watches, while the Renaissance jewelry exhibited in the same room gives an idea of the sheer luxury of contemporary courts: crosses and enameled gold pendants with inlaid baroque pearls and precious stones. In one case there is a collection of *Busts of the Twelve Caesars* cut from gemstones.

SALLE CHARLES QUINT (ROOM 24). The tapestries here celebrate Hercules, an omnipresent character in the 16th and 17th centuries. A number of treasures demonstrate the wealth of the Renaissance Habsburg Empire (Flanders, Spain and Germany), most of which derived from the wealth of the Americas: the *Sword and Dagger of the Grand Master of the Order of Malta*, with golden knotwork; *Vermeil Basin with Reptiles, Frogs and Crayfish* by Wenzel Jamnitzer; *Ewer and Basin of Charles V* in enameled vermeil; and finally Hercules again, with the *Centaur Abducting Deianira* in vermeil and silver.

TOWARD CLASSICISM

ADOLPHE DE ROTHSCHILD bequeathed his collection of religious gold and silverwork to the Louvre (ROOM 25) in 1900 along with funds to display it. These funds made it possible to acquire and install a 16th-century coffered Venetian ceiling. Particularly admirable here is a pendant representing the *Annunciation* and a necklace made up of cartouches of the *Passion of Christ*; there is also an archbishop's crozier illustrating the *Annunciation to the Shepherds*. Behind glass are bronzes combining religious motifs (*St Francis of Assisi*) and pagan figures such as *Atlanta* or *Hercules*. The porcelains come from Florence. For centuries porcelain was imported from China but in 1575 Duke Francesco de' Medici established a factory in Florence. All the pieces were decorated in blue, to rival oriental porcelain.

THE BRONZES OF THE ROTONDE JEAN BOULOGNE (ROOM 26) were cast in Florence for the Medici family. The most famous is probably *Nessus and Deianira*. *Morgante* the celebrated dwarf-jester of the Florentine court is represented here as Bacchus astride a barrel.

(for Karolus) alternates with oval medallions in cloisonné enamel. In the center is the *Victory of Marius over Jugurtha, King of Numidia*.

A *Mantle of a Knight of the Order of the St-Esprit* (right) a 17th-century mantle from this order with embroidery around the border and the collar.

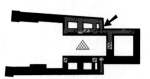

Monkey from the collection of small bronzes by Giambologna (Jean Boulogne).

SALLE HENRI III (ROOM 27; turn left past the corridor) displays the lavishness of the order of the St-Esprit (founded in 1578 by Henri III), the most important of France's royal Orders. A ciborium, some cruets, a holy water pail and various candlesticks are among the exhibits; all are made with rock crystal, gilded metal and precious stones. In the same room are the helmet and shield of Charles IX, the latter with the monogram K (Karolus) around the rim alternating with medallions in cloisonné enamel.

THE ORDER OF THE ST-ESPRIT (ROOM 28). In an evocation of the Order's chapel, this room exhibits a collection of its *mantles* made of black velvet embroidered with gold flames. In the corridor to the right is a tapestry of the *Battle of Jarnac* which celebrates a victory of Henri III over the Protestant forces.

ROOM 29 displays typical furniture from the second half of the 16th century including a pair of armchairs and an English tapestry from Mortlake (c. 1630).

BERNARD PALISSY, MASTER OF FRENCH FAIENCE (ROOM 20). Here are displayed Palissy's dishes decorated with reptiles, shells and plants cast from life – fabulous schemes which refer to one of the great literary successes of the 16th century, Francesco Colonna's *Hypnerotomachia* (Venice, 1499). Palissy was inspired by this novel to build a grotto in the gardens of Catherine de' Medici's Tuileries, which he peopled with green creatures ● 75. Alongside these striking works are others celebrating the *Nymph of Fontainebleau,* the *Judgement of Paris* and the *Triumph of Galatea*. Among the figurines from the workshops of Avon is an *Equestrian Statue of Louis XIII*.

THE SALLE HENRI IV (ROOM 31), contains in addition to some beautiful choir-stalls, a wardrobe illustrating the *Seasons* and a casket with the arms of Marie de' Medici. There are also some bronzes, among them *Girl Drawing out a Thorn* and the *Milkmaid*, attributed to Bathélemy Prieur who also did a likeness of *Henri IV as Jupiter.*

THE SALLE D'EFFIAT (ROOM 32). Louis XIII commissioned the tapestry of *Moses in the Bullrushes* from Simon Vouet. The ebony cabinet displayed with it has bas-reliefs with religious, mythological and historical themes. The bed and the armchairs of the Château d'Effiat (in the Puy-de-Dôme) are typical of the mid-17th century.

THE SALLE MAZARIN (ROOM 33) on the far side of the rotunda, contains the *Deborah Tapestry*, painted on silk with gold and silver embroidery, which once belonged to Cardinal Mazarin. In the middle is a *Casket*, a masterpiece of the French goldsmith's craft. From here continue through the Sully building, back into the Richelieu wing for a tour of the furniture and decorative arts of the 18th and 19th centuries (ROOMS 35 to 73 ▲ *206*); this ends with the Napoleon III apartments (ROOMS 74 to 88 ▲ *210*).

GLAZED EARTHENWARE
French potters of the 16th century made a specialty of glazed earthenware, while the Italians concentrated on ceramics. The inspiration for the former came from Fontainebleau, as is shown by the dish called the *Nymph of Fontainebleau* (left) after a work by Rosso Fiorentino. The same movement affected French painting ▲ *218*.

THE BIRTH OF FRENCH CABINETMAKING
The ebony-veneered cabinet with an ivory interior is representative of German cabinets of the 17th century which inspired the first Parisian "ebenistes". A new rich era in the history of French furniture was about to begin.

Silver *salt-cellars* (1734–6) by
François-Thomas Germain.

The Louvre's collection of French furniture was assembled very
late, at the fall of the Second Empire when the furniture from
the Tuileries and St-Cloud palaces was moved to the museum
and thereby saved from destruction by fire. After 1900 this basic
collection was reinforced by pieces from the Mobilier National
followed by sundry gifts, bequests and purchases. Today the
collection offers a complete panorama from the 17th century to
the 1830's, from Boulle to Jacob by way of all the greatest
cabinetmakers of the 18th century.

The introduction into
France in the early 17th
century of the German
"ebenisterie" technique
(veneer) brought about a
revolution. Paris
cabinetmakers devised lavish
polychrome decorative
schemes, using wooden
marquetry and even
blending wood, tortoiseshell
and metal, as in the work of
André-Charles Boulle
(1642–1732) who gave his
name to this technique.

Eight-footed Table-console (c. 1715). The use in furniture-making of
gilded wood (here it is oak) was widespread in the reign of Louis
XIV, in the second half of the 17th century. This table acquired by
Napoleon III was frequently copied at the end of the 19th century.

Monkey Commode by
Charles Cressent
(c. 1745). The reign of
Louis XV saw the triumph of the curve:
Cressent, who was a trained sculptor, took
special care over his bronze decoration (at
center, children with a monkey on a swing).

Commode by Matthieu Criaerd
(c. 1742) using the Martin
veneer technique to imitate
oriental lacquer. Created for the blue
bedroom at the Château de Choisy, it was
used in an apartment at Versailles under
Louis XVI.

Mechanical Table by
Jean-François Oeben (c. 1755)
the royal cabinetmaker. A
mechanism makes the top draw
back, pushing forward a large
drawer which in turn reveals other
drawers and pigeonholes. Some
parts are of mahogany, a type of
wood then only just coming into use.

Cylinder Desk
by Jean-François Leleu
(c. 1768–70), with plaques of
Sèvres porcelain. The cylinder
desk was a new design that had
been perfected ten years earlier
by Oeben.

Surtout (1758) cast in silver and worked by François-Thomas Germain for Joseph I of Portugal. Appearing at the end of Louis XIV's reign, *surtouts* generally incorporated salt-cellars, oil-jugs etc. This one is purely decorative.

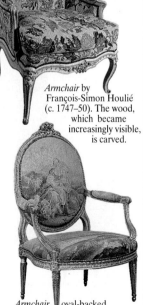

As the king's gold and silversmith, Germain was given lodgings at the Louvre but he did work for all the courts of Europe.

Wardrobe by André-Charles Boulle (c. 1700) allying polychrome flower-marquetry on a tortoiseshell background with Boulle marquetry in brass, tin and stained horn.

Armchair (1690–1700). From the 1650's onward, the Spanish-Flemish style of chair gradually assumed the name of "arm-chair" as its comfort increased.

Commode by Jacques-Philippe Carel (c. 1750) embellished with Chinese lacquer champlevé panels, called "Coromandel" panels. This piece has two doors, a rarity for the time.

Armchair by François-Simon Houlié (c. 1747–50). The wood, which became increasingly visible, is carved.

Commode by Leleu (1772), made for the Prince de Condé. In the 1760's the Greek style with straight lines and Greco-Roman bronze decoration became popular.

Armchair oval-backed, c. 1770–5 by Philippe Poirié.

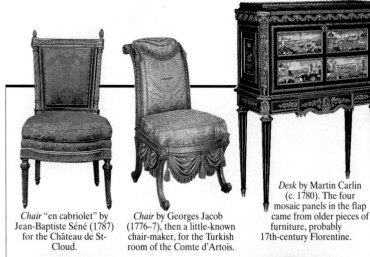

Chair "en cabriolet" by Jean-Baptiste Séné (1787) for the Château de St-Cloud.

Chair by Georges Jacob (1776–7), then a little-known chair-maker, for the Turkish room of the Comte d'Artois.

Desk by Martin Carlin (c. 1780). The four mosaic panels in the flap came from older pieces of furniture, probably 17th-century Florentine.

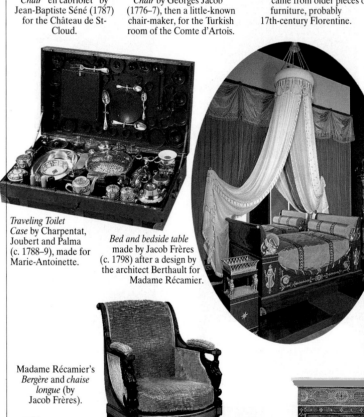

Traveling Toilet Case by Charpentat, Joubert and Palma (c. 1788–9), made for Marie-Antoinette.

Bed and bedside table made by Jacob Frères (c. 1798) after a design by the architect Berthault for Madame Récamier.

Madame Récamier's *Bergère* and *chaise longue* (by Jacob Frères).

The bergère is the one on which Madame Récamier sat for her portrait by Jacques-Louis David in 1800 ▲ *230*. The painter brought back drawings of antique furniture from Rome and the cabinetmaker used these as his model.

Lower section of a bookcase by Georges-Alphonse Jacob-Desmalter

Writing table by Adam Weisweiler (1784) for the inner cabinet of Marie-Antoinette at the Château de St-Cloud. The sides are of steel, the feet are of bronze adorned with caryatids, and the slender lines are characteristic of Weisweiler.

Cylinder desk by Jean-Henri Riesner (1784) furniture maker to the king from 1774 to 1784. At the center of the cylinder a trophy celebrates the attributes of poetry.

Above, *Athénienne* made by Martin-Guillaume Biennais (1800–4) for Napoleon I, a washbasin of yew wood and gilt-bronze which the Emperor took with him to St Helena. At right, the *jewel cabinet* (1809) of Empress Josephine designed by the architect Charles Percier and made by F.H.G. Jacob-Desmalter.

(1832). The shape is still in the Empire style, but a marquetry of hollywood and rosewood has replaced mahogany and gilt bronze.

Dressing table and chair from the shop "À l'Escalier de Crystal" which specialized in objects of crystal mounted in gilded bronze (c. 1819).

The Louvre, as completed by Napoleon III, was used for sumptuous state receptions which were formerly given in the Tuileries Palace (now vanished) and in the apartments of the Ministry of State, which had been installed in the new north wing along the Rue de Rivoli, today's Richelieu building. Occupied by the Ministry of Finance from 1871 to 1989, this wing was opened to the public in 1993, displaying the restored apartments in all their glory. The paintings, the stucco, the gilded furniture with its silk coverings, and the marble and bronze of the fireplaces constitute one of the greatest achievements of the Napoleon III style, on a par with the Paris Opéra by Garnier.

MASKED BALL AT THE LOUVRE
A masked ball was given for the inauguration of the Ministry of State apartments in 1861. This engraving emphasizes the colossal proportions of the Grand Salon which was designed to contain guests in very large numbers at official receptions.

> "THE BROCADE-STYLE ORNAMENTATION OF THE VAULTING, THE VAULT ITSELF AND THE WALLS OF THE ORCHESTRA DECORATED WITH TRELLIS-WORK ACCENTED WITH GOLD, COVERED WITH FLOWERS AND FOLIAGE AGAINST A SKY THAT GIVES THE EFFECT OF NIGHT . . ."
>
> LAURENT-JAN, ARTIST, 1861

DIFFERENT ROOMS, DIFFERENT FUNCTIONS
Each room in the apartments corresponds to a precise function, a fact which distinguishes them from the undefined rooms of the 18th century. Below, the Galerie

d'Introduction, and left the Grand Salon with furniture in the style of Louis XV. Below, left to right, the "niche" of the Petite Salle à Manger, the Salon-Théâtre and a detail of the décor of the Grand Salon, a homage to the builders of the Louvre, in this case François I, with a model of the façade designed by Pierre Lescot for the Cour Carrée.

Diadem of
Empress
Eugenie
(1853).

From the outset, the Galerie d'Apollon (on
the floor above the Petite Galerie built
by Henri IV) was intended as a
backdrop for the French Crown
Jewels, as part of the Decorative
Arts department. The décor here
was arranged by Le Vau and
Lebrun for Louis XIV; it was
steadily enriched right up to the
time Delacroix's *Triumph of Ap*
was installed on
its ceiling in 1851. The
grille that closes it off
originally came from the
Château de Maisons.

**THE CROWN OF
LOUIS XV**
This remarkable piece
contains no fewer
than 282 diamonds
and 64 other precious
stones.

Throughout history
French monarchs
accumulated
treasures by direct
purchase, as gifts
from foreign princes
or as spoils of war.
They also hoarded
the various ritual
objects used for their
coronations, along
with the emblems of
monarchy. The oldest
pieces are now in the
Decorative Arts
section of the Lo
▲ 198 and the m
recent ones are in
the Galerie
d'Apollon
(left).

THE REGENT
This 140-carat diamond, bought in
1717 is considered to be the world's
most beautiful diamond. It was part of
Louis XV's personal crown (above) as
well as that of his son Louis XVI; later it
adorned Napoleon I's sword and the crown
used for the coronation of Charles X.

THE SANCY
A 56-carat
diamond (below) one
of the many crown
jewels.

*Vessel with a
Statuette of
Neptune*
in rock crystal
and lapis lazuli
with enameled
mounting.

EUROPEAN PAINTING

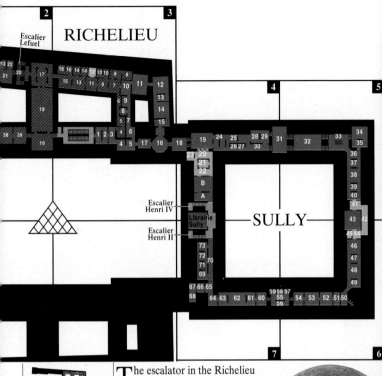

RICHELIEU

2   3   4   5

Escalier Lefuel

SULLY

Escalier Henri IV

Librairie Sully

Escalier Henri II

7   6

SECOND FLOOR / RICHELIEU AND SULLY, AND FIRST FLOOR / DENON (LARGER PAINTINGS).

T he escalator in the Richelieu building leads to the second floor and the rooms assigned to French painting. Assembled from the time of Louis XIV, the royal collections form the kernel of this section; to these were added the works confiscated during the Revolution. In the 19th and 20th centuries acquisitions, bequests and donations helped complete this unique ensemble of pictures.

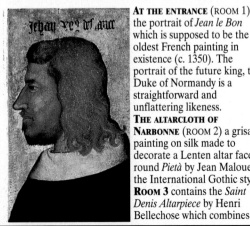

MEDIEVAL TRADITION TO THE RENAISSANCE

INTERNATIONAL GOTHIC
Malouel's large circular *Pietà* (right) illustrates the style called International Gothic of which Burgundy was one of the most active centers.

jehan roy dy frãt

PORTRAIT OF JEAN LE BON
This picture is said to be the oldest French portrait in existence.

AT THE ENTRANCE (ROOM 1) is the portrait of *Jean le Bon* which is supposed to be the oldest French painting in existence (c. 1350). The portrait of the future king, then Duke of Normandy is a straightforward and unflattering likeness.
THE ALTARCLOTH OF NARBONNE (ROOM 2) a grisaille painting on silk made to decorate a Lenten altar faces a round *Pietà* by Jean Malouel in the International Gothic style.
ROOM 3 contains the *Saint Denis Altarpiece* by Henri Bellechose which combines

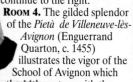

realism with the Gothic style. In the *Calling of the Virgin* the clumsily-handled perspective and the disproportion between the Virgin and the architecture are typically medieval. From here, continue to the right.

ROOM 4. The gilded splendor of the *Pietà de Villeneuve-lès-Avignon* (Enguerrand Quarton, c. 1455) illustrates the vigor of the School of Avignon which emerged in the 14th century with the installation of the Papacy in that city. The *Pietà* is also the most celebrated French painting of the 15th century. A diptych by Nicolas Froment evokes Provence and its "good king" *René of Anjou*, a lamentable politician but an intelligent patron of the arts.

ROOM 5 contains the richly expressive and dramatic *Three Prophets* assigned to the same Provençal school and is near the great *Boulbon Altarpiece* (c. 1450).

JEAN FOUQUET (ROOM 6). A native of Tours, Fouquet traveled to Italy in about 1445, where he discovered the painting of the Italian Renaissance and the techniques of perspective. His *Charles VII* with its diamond pattern of construction is a monumental royal portrait which reveals the man as much as it exalts the power of the prince. The Flemish Jean Hey (the "Master of Moulins") was a portraitist of great talent (see *Suzanne de Bourbon* and his picture of the Dauphin, *Charles-Orlant*). The *Altarpiece of the Parliament of Paris* depicts the capital in the 15th century, with the Cité at right and the Louvre on the left, before the Pont-Neuf was built ▲ *308*.

PORTRAIT OF FRANÇOIS I BY JEAN CLOUET (ROOM 7) was one of the rare French paintings owned by that king. During his Italian campaigns, François employed Italian artists, among them Leonardo da Vinci ▲ *262* convincing them to come to France to stimulate the artistic renewal then underway at Fontainebleau. Jean Clouet overshadowed other French portraitists of his time, who espoused the fashionable realism of the 16th century. Their work ▲ *216* is displayed in ROOM 8.

The *Three Prophets* (c. 1480, below, and detail above).

Guillaume Jouvenel des Ursins by Jean Fouquet, a painter of the French Renaissance.

THE SCHOOL OF AVIGNON
Avignon produced paintings of great austerity and emotion like the *Pietà de Villeneuve-lès-Avignon* by Enguerrand Quarton (c. 1455, left), but also with singular expressive force (as in the *Three Prophets* above). In the *Villeneuve Pietà* the canon who commissioned the picture is shown in prayer behind Saint John. At the time, the few portraits being done were of people who commissioned religious paintings and had themselves included in them.

Two trends emerged in the art of French portraiture in the 16th century. The first played on allegory or mythology to flatter its models (ROOM 9 ▲ 218). In ROOM 8 where the atmosphere is intimate and precious, are works belonging to the second movement: realist portraits painted by Jean Clouet and his son François, both of them painters to the king, and by Corneille de Lyon. These are very different from Mannerist Italian pictures and form a definite French type of small portrait. Shown here are portraits of the royal family: the last of the Valois dynasty up to Henri III by François Quesnel, and a picture of Catherine de' Medici (anonymous), all of whose children came to the throne but failed to produce direct descendents. Opposite them, the court is represented, notably the Guise and Lorraine families, familiar through such Dumas novels as *La Reine Margot* and *Les Quarante-cinq*. There are also some intriguing unknowns whose faces alone are familiar to us.

FATHER AND SON
From the studio of François Clouet, portraits of *Henri II* (left) and *Charles IX* (right), the husband and the son of Catherine de' Medici.

A ROYAL PATRON OF THE ARTS
François I, King of France by Jean Clouet (perhaps in collaboration with his son François?) painted c. 1530. The king is richly dressed in the Italian style and the composition is not unlike that of Fouquet's *Charles VII*.

CORNEILLE DE LYON
Among the rare portraits definitely attributed to Corneille de Lyon are those of the poet *Clément Marot* and *Jean de Bourbon-Vendôme* (above). *Jean d'Albon, Seigneur de St-André* (left) is the work of several different hands.

Pierre Quthe, Apothecary by François Clouet, indicates a change of style.

A LITTLE-KNOWN QUEEN
The portrait of Elizabeth of Austria by François Clouet reveals a largely forgotten French queen, the daughter of Maximilian II and wife of Charles IX.

Corneille de Lyon was a Dutch painter who settled in Lyon in 1547. He did a number of small portraits on panel, in which the subjects are represented half-length against a blue or green background. While his technique had much in common with that of the Clouets – realistic features, narrow framing of the bust, three-quarters or full face, single-toned background – Corneille's meticulous brushwork reveals his northern origin. A number of portraits which are probably by pupils are displayed alongside his work: among these is *Pierre Aymeric* painted in 1534 (above).

LAVISH FRAMES
The works of Corneille de Lyon were placed in frames originally made for mirrors, probably during the 19th century. His studio produced *Anne Stuart* (above) and he himself painted the *Portrait of a Young Man* and *Mellin de St-Gelais* (right).

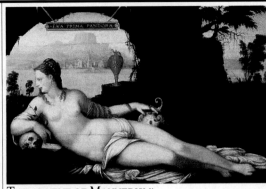

EVA PRIMA PANDORA

THE ADVENT OF MANNERISM

THE SCHOOL OF FONTAINEBLEAU (ROOMS 9 and 10) shows the influence on French painters of the period by artists from the other side of the Alps who were attracted by François I to Fontainebleau. Theirs is a delicate courtly art, full of references to Italian Mannerism. The theme of Diana is very much present, perhaps in homage to Henri III's mistress Diane de Poitiers: indeed Diana became a regular feature in paintings of courtly love. *Diana the Huntress* owes much to the idealized elegance which the French perceived in Italian art. The reference to mythology and history suggests a personality type more

218

than an individual likeness. *Eva Prima Pandora* was painted in about 1550 by Jean Cousin, one of the few Parisian painters whose name is well known to us even though he was relatively independent of the Court. Using a pose reminiscent of Cellini's sculpted *Nymph of Fontainebleau* ▲ *195*, the picture associates the biblical theme of original sin with the myth of Pandora. Her left hand rests on the vase she should never have opened. Fontainebleau remained

the center of French art throughout the second half of the century, which was scarred by the Wars of Religion ● *36*. The surreal, icy violence of Antoine Caron's work of great Mannerist refinement, the *Massacres of the Triumvirate*, evokes the killings perpetrated during the Second Triumvirate of Octavius, Antony and Lepidus (43 BC). But the real theme was the contemporary massacre of French Protestants. Very similar is the spatial arrangement of Caron's *Sybil of Tibur* in which the prophetess shows the Emperor Augustus the Virgin and Child and enjoins him to worship them. For Augustus read Charles IX, and for the Sybil, Catherine de' Medici. Nobody knows who painted the enigmatic double portrait of *Gabrielle d'Estrées and One of Her Sisters*. One of the women's delicately pinching the nipple of the other would seem to imply the illegitimate daughter Henri IV had with his beautiful mistress, while the theme of the bath legitimizes the

sensuality of the two figures framed by the red folds of a curtain. Already the period was becoming embittered. In the anonymous *Funeral of Love* a funeral cortège featuring all the greatest poets mourning the death of Eros, mark the drowning of gallantry

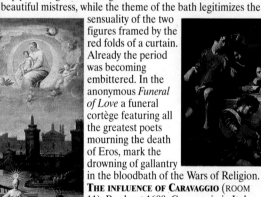

in the bloodbath of the Wars of Religion.
THE INFLUENCE OF CARAVAGGIO (ROOM 11). By about 1600, Caravaggio in Italy ▲ *268* was producing spectacular effects of chiaroscuro, with realistic dramatization of scenes that had nothing to do with the idealization then so prevalent in religious art. The painters who followed his lead, known in France as the "Caravagesques" included Claude Vignon, Valentin de Boulogne and even Simon Vouet at the outset of his career. The light which falls on the body of Nicolas Tournier's *Christ on the Cross* and on the faces of the women beneath him, blazes out dramatically from the shadowy background in which the colors of the draperies are barely visible.

CHIAROSCURO
Valentin de Boulogne who spent most of his life in Rome was one of the most faithful followers of Caravaggio – an artist who made a point of having no pupils. Above, *Concert* (c. 1622–5), a work of refined chiaroscuro in which the ordinariness of the figures and the perfection of the expressions pay homage to the great Italian.

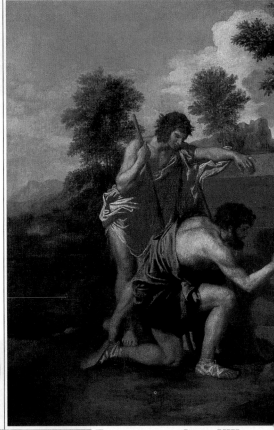

"I HAVE NEGLECTED NOTHING." (POUSSIN)
On the tomb in his *Arcadian Shepherds* (left) are the words "Et in Arcadia ego", a reminder of the presence of death even in Arcadia. Poussin (below, detail from his *Self-portrait*) avoided official honors to devote himself entirely to his art. He preferred Rome to Paris and spent most of his life there, yet eventually he was attracted back to France by Louis XIII and Richelieu who wanted him to paint the Grande Galerie at the Louvre. This project never came to fruition.

SUMMER
At the end of his life Poussin turned his attention to landscapes. In his *Four Seasons* the light seems to emanate from the countryside itself. *Summer* (above) is one of the four canvases displayed in the rotunda which bears Poussin's name.

THE PAINTERS OF LOUIS XIII

SIMON VOUET (ROOM 12), inspired by Caravaggio while visiting Italy, came back to France on the orders of Louis XIII. There he became the king's favorite painter and was loaded with commissions including the *Presentation at the Temple* and channeled French painting toward a clear, frank palette and broad, lyrical treatments; his canvases *Charity, Virtue* and *Wealth* seem to make yellow and blue fabrics glint with Baroque iridescence. In his time the Louvre was the palace of Louis XIII ● *76,* whose portrait was painted by Philippe de Champaigne for the Galerie des Hommes Illustres du Palais Cardinal (now the Palais-Royal ● *77*), the residence of Richelieu whose portrait upstages that of the king with its glorious purple.
NICOLAS POUSSIN (ROOMS 13 and 14), who was in Rome at this time, was building a reputation with paintings like the *Inspiration of the Poet* (1630). Poussin found in his mythological sources (*Triumph of Flora, Echo and Narcissus, Bacchanals*) a pretext for the depiction of beautiful bodies as well as everything else to do with the pleasures of life: wine,

In the works of Poussin and Vouet there are similar harmonies of yellow and blue.

dance and music in particular. With his *Self-portrait* (ROOM 14) Poussin appears as a man with a character of his own, poised between the seductions of mythology (*Arcadian Shepherds*) and the austerity of the Bible (*Plague of Ashdod*).

WITH CLAUDE LORRAIN came the loveliest sunsets in all painting and the idea of landscape as a separate genre (ROOM 15). Claude's pictures are hymns to light, set in realistic Roman landscapes or imaginary ports of the ancient world. Titles include *Ulysses Restoring Chryseis to Her Father* (1644) and *The Disembarkation of Cleopatra at Tarsus* (1642).

THE ROTONDE POUSSIN (ROOM 16) shows Poussin's *Four Seasons* painted for the Duc de Richelieu between 1660 and 1664. *Winter* featuring the Flood is dramatic; *Spring* shows an earthly Paradise; *Summer* and harvest time is illustrated by the story of Ruth and Booz; while *Autumn*, replete with bunches of grapes evokes the Promised Land. On the right is an information and documentation room (ROOM 17); continue your circuit by way of the Salle Poussin (ROOM 18) and the *Love of Apollo and Daphne,* Poussin's final unfinished canvas.

ROYAL DECORATION
Victory and *Wealth* by Simon Vouet (above).

SUNSET in the *Disembarkation of Cleopatra at Tarsus* by Claude Lorrain.

CHURCH DECORATION
The similar formats of Eustache Le Sueur's 22 paintings of the *Life of Saint Bruno*, founder of the Charterhouse Order, create an odd cartoon-like impression clearly intended for a public which seldom knew how to read. Above,

left to right, *Dream of Saint Bruno*, *Saint Bruno Taking the Monk's Habit*, *Saint Bruno Teaching Theology at Rheims*, and *Death of Saint Bruno*.

FROM ALLEGORY TO REALISM

The great altarpieces of the 17th century (ROOM 19) were the prerogative of the painters of the Académie Royale de Peinture et de Sculpture founded in 1648. Alongside the large canvases of Eustache Le Sueur (the *Sermon of Saint Paul at Ephesus*) are such works as *Virgin and Child* by Laurent de la Hyre and Poussin's *Saint François Xavier* which depicts the Jesuits in Japan. Most of ROOMS 20 to 23 exhibit the cartoons of Lebrun, preparatory drawings for ceremonial décors such as the Ambassadors' staircase and the Grande Galerie at Versailles; all exalt Louis XIV.

ROOM 24 holds the twenty-two paintings done by Eustache le Sueur to illustrate the *Life of Saint Bruno*. In his *Plan of the Charterhouse of Paris* you can pick out the Louvre, the Pont Neuf ▲ *306* opposite, and in the background, the spire of Ste-Chapelle and the towers of Notre Dame.

ROOM 25 has some of the canvases commissioned for private mansions in Paris, such as the Galerie

PRIVATE TOWNHOUSES
The building of many new private townhouses in Paris under Louis XIII meant an abundance of commissions for painters. Most of the décor of the Hôtel Lambert (above, the Cabinet de l'Amour) on the Île St-Louis has now been transferred to the Louvre: in particular, canvases and panels by Le Sueur. (Right, the *Birth of Eros*).

des Muses and the Cabinet d'Amour at the Hôtel Lambert (Le Sueur).

CABINET PICTURES (ROOM 26). This type of painting was intended specifically for private collectors; it mostly consisted of genre scenes, still lifes and small landscapes. Examples here are by Claude, Patel and Jacques Stella.

STILL LIFES (ROOM 27) often involved food as in Lubin Baugin's *Still Life with Wafer Biscuits* but they were not devoid of sensuality, as in *Strawberries and Cherries* by François Garnier, *Grapes* by Pierre Dupuis and *Half-opened Pomegranates* by Jacques Linard. This tradition took hold during the 17th century under the influence of Flemish painters. The art of the still life sometimes allied itself with the theme of the *vanitas*, with such images as skulls accompanied by the symbols of vain hopes.

THE SALLE LA TOUR (ROOM 28). An artist from Lorraine who went unrecognized for many years, Georges de la Tour was much influenced by Caravaggio. His night scenes (*Saint Joseph*, the *Adoration of the Shepherds*, the *Mary Magdalen*, and *Saint Sebastian Tended by Irene*) are illuminated by candlelight; his daytime scenes are strikingly different, bathed by a colder sheen (*The Cheat*).

THE LE NAIN BROTHERS (Antoine, Louis and Mathieu) worked together often on the same

canvases and signed them with their family name only. Their scenes of peasant life brought them special fame. ROOM 29 contains their principal works notably the *Peasant's Repast* and *Peasant Family*. The dignity of their subjects, the simplicity of their composition and the austerity of their palette show a deliberate rejection of the picturesque. Take seven steps down to ROOM 31.

Above left, *Peasant Family* by the Le Nain brothers.

JANSENIST PIETY
The *Ex-Voto of 1662*
(below), the
masterpiece of
Philippe de
Champaigne.

THE GLORY OF THE SUN KING

PHILIPPE DE CHAMPAIGNE (ROOM 31). The seven steps from the previous room lead down to a harsher world peopled by great lords and ravaged by the religious warfare which shook

France in the 1650's. Philippe de Champaigne who had lived among the Jansenists at the Abbaye de Port-Royal, painted the portrait of *Mère Angélique Arnauld*, the mother superior at the convent, along with *Arnauld d'Andilly* and above all the remarkable *Ex-Voto of 1662.* His terrifyingly realistic *Christ on the Cross* and *Dead Christ* is a reminder of the austere faith of the Jansenists. In the portraits which made his reputation (*Portrait of a Man*, 1650) Champaigne showed his exceptional skill at making his models lifelike. The king and the church were the protectors of painters at that time: thus Lebrun, a pupil of Vouet, was successively employed by Séguier, Richelieu, Fouquet, Mazarin and Louis XIV. The accession of Louis in 1661 gave Lebrun primacy among his painter colleagues allowing him to impose a newer, less somber style of his own.

CHARLES LEBRUN (ROOM 32) ● *78*. This room houses the monumental canvases painted by Lebrun between 1665 and 1673 in celebration of Alexander the Great. The golden, sunlit sheen of the the young conqueror's armor makes it clear that the painter's real

TRIUMPHS
Chancellor Seguier
(above) and
*Alexander the Great
Entering Babylon*
(right) by Charles
Lebrun.

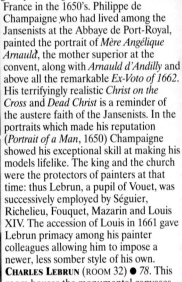

subject is the Sun-King himself, who enjoyed comparisons of himself with Alexander. In 1665, Racine dedicated his play of Alexander the Great to the young king. Lebrun painted these four pictures at the same time as his work on the Galerie d'Apollon at the Louvre (1665) ▲ *127* and on the Hall of Mirrors at Versailles (1673).

JEAN JOUVENET (ROOM 33). This artist, a Norman by birth, painted his *Raising of Lazarus* and the *Miracle of the Fishes* in 1706 for the Benedictine priory of St-Martin-des-Champs; for the latter painting he sketched Dieppe fishermen from life

THE PAINTER ...
Charles Lebrun
"premier peintre" to
the king, painted by
Nicolas de
Largillierre (left).
Lebrun exercised the
functions of a virtual
minister of fine arts
and played a decisive
role in the training of
the artists of his time.

**... AND THE
MONARCH**
The purple drapery
surrounding Louis
XIV in his portrait by
Rigaud lends
theatricality to his
pose.

PAINTERS OF LOUIS XIV (ROOMS 34 and
35). The paintings of Charles de la Fosse
reveal a charming, innovative style which
rejects the austerity of the later years of
Louis XIV and ushers in the 18th century
(*Moses in the Bullrushes*). In the *Arrival of
Louis XIV at the Siege of Maastricht*,
Adams van der Meulen portrayed the
king appearing on the battlefield where
the musketeer d'Artagnan was killed. In
his portrait by Hyacinthe Rigaud in 1701,
the King is still in excellent form, his
shapely leg clothed with silk: this is truly
the apogee of the formal state portrait.
Pierre Mignard became "premier
peintre" in 1690; his *Self-portrait* contrasts
with *Lebrun* by Nicolas de Largillierre.
The portrait of *Bossuet*, the "Eagle of
Meaux" also by Rigaud, seems to make a
pair with that of the king: the two great
powers of the century, temporal and
spiritual, are seen in identical
compositions. Nearby, the double
portrait of *Madame Rigaud* (right profile and three quarters
left) is ample proof that the official court painter was also a
vigorous portraitist. By contrast Antoine Coypel's *Democritus*
seems to mock at the instability of a world which he views as
no more than a shifting mass of matter. As to Jean-Baptiste
Santerre's *Susannah Bathing*, the flesh-tints of the central
figure are of such porcelain loveliness that one can well
understand the emotion of those old men in the Bible who
were so little discouraged by her legendary chastity.

The King is
surrounded by the
symbols of monarchy:
crown, scepter and
golden fleurs-de-lys
on the great mantle
lined with ermine. He
is also highly
idealized: at 63 he was
already ravaged by
disease.

225

THE REIGN OF LOUIS THE WELL-BELOVED

PILGRIMAGE TO CYTHERA
Watteau's famous painting (above) also called the *Embarkation to Cythera* is the masterpiece of the *peinture galante* of the 18th century; it is also the work which the artist produced on admission to the Academy in 1717.

CROSSING TO HADES
Charon Ferrying Souls Across the River Styx by Pierre Subleyras (below) contrasts in its melancholy subject-matter with the sensual surroundings of Boucher and Watteau.

WATTEAU (ROOMS 36 AND 37). Jean-Antoine Watteau entered the Louvre in 1869 with a major donation from Doctor La Caze. In 1715 Louis XIV died and was succeeded by a Regent: the time had come, after the religious excesses of the old king's last years, to make a new start (with Philippe d'Orléans), epitomized by Watteau's *Pilgrimage to Cythera* (1717) – the island of Venus. With this painting Watteau gained admission to the Academy ● 66 at the age of 33, using a new approach to the idea of the *fête galante*. This theme originated with the theater and consisted of a meeting of honest folk in pastoral surroundings. *Nymphs and Satyrs* like *Diana Bathing* unveil and celebrate the female body. If Watteau's masterpiece *Pierrot* (which used to be called *Gilles*) appears grave and enigmatic this is because his role in the Commedia dell'arte is exactly so. The *Two Cousins* or the *Indifferent Lover* celebrates the voluptuousness of life; Watteau excels at suggesting the graceful line of a girl's neck, or the undulating movement of her dress. In the same room, note Coypel's *Young Negro* and *Young Girl*.

THE PAINTERS OF LOUIS XV (ROOM 38) embarked on the themes of lightness and gallantry: this was dubbed Rococo. Small paintings were commissioned in ever greater numbers by individuals. François Lemoyne portrayed his *Hercules* subdued by the distracted grace of Omphale, his club metamorphosed into a distaff. Nicolas Lancret celebrates the *Delights of the Bath* while François Boucher's *Diana Rising From Her Bath* is yet another pretext for a study of the female nude. With the contrast between the blue velvet and the flesh tints of the women's bodies, and the second contrast between the hunting trophy and the obvious sensuality of the pose, everything is in place for a celebration of the freeing of both minds and bodies. The hunting scenes and *déjeuners champêtres* of Jean-François de Troy or Carle van Loo depict the amusements of the court which have nothing in common with Subleyras' *Charon Ferrying Souls Across the River Styx*

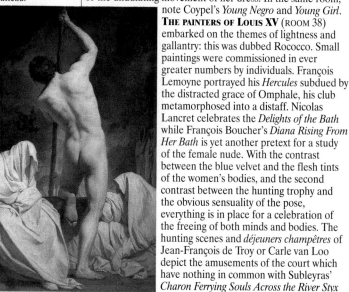

"Chardin, what you mix on your palette is neither white, nor red, nor black; no, what you place on the tip of your brush and put to the canvas is the very substance of things. It is azure. It is light."
Diderot

CHARDIN'S ART OF THE ORDINARY
In paintings like his *Young Man with a Top* Chardin draws attention to ordinary objects which he raises to the level of sentient beings. He does this for cauldrons, pipes, glasses, copper fountains, cooking pots and pieces of porcelain which he traces with a deep love of form and shape, and with tender half-tones (left, his still life of a *Basket of Peaches, with Nuts, Knife and Glass of Wine*). Even more famous are his genre scenes such as *Grace* (1740, below).

nor with Chardin's tragically realistic *Skate*, a forlorn triangular dead fish.

JEAN SIMÉON CHARDIN is exhibited in ROOMS 39 and 40 which contain his *Poor Meal* and *Rich Meal* framing an attentive *Young Draughtsman Sharpening His Pencil.* The painter's *Young Man with a Top* is equally absorbed with his toy while the *Dead Rabbit* confronts a similarly lugubrious *Dead Hare*. The still lifes are complemented by genre scenes, such as Boucher's the *Lunch*.

The new rooms for the French painting section were designed by the Italian architect Italo Rota.

PAINTINGS OF THE ENLIGHTENMENT

PASTELS AND MINIATURES. In ROOM 41 the Graphic Arts Department ● *62* exhibits its finest pastels by rotation for conservation reasons. In the Couloir des Poules (ROOM 42) – the name probably comes from the Rue des Poulies and has no connection with chickens – there is a permanent display of miniatures. These are tiny portraits which girls give to their lovers in the plays of Marivaux. There are also mid-sized pastel portraits, mostly of artists and their close relatives. Two oculi here offer a view of Perrault's Colonnade ● *78*.

PENTECOST by
Jean Restout (right).

*La Marquise de
Pompadour*, a friend
to many philosophers
and artists by
Delatour.

"What would you
have that artist put
on canvas? Whatever
he has in his
imagination. And
what can a man's
imagination contain
who spends his life
among the lowest
prostitutes?"

Diderot on the
subject of Boucher

HISTORY PAINTING (ROOM 43) – in this case
religious in tone – was not abandoned;
indeed it maintained its position as the
noblest genre as Jean Restout's *Pentecost*
(1732) shows. Restout was a master of great
religious themes and royal or church
commissions were abundant in the 18th
century. *The Hermit* by Joseph Marie Vien
seems still to believe in a world freed from
the constraints of the flesh.

A FEW FINE PASTELS are displayed in ROOMS
44 and 45 in rotation; among these are two
portraits, *La Marquise de Pompadour* and
D'Alembert by Maurice Quentin Delatour.

RETURNING TO BOUCHER (ROOM 46) and
history painting (here the subject matter is
drawn from mythology) we find the *Rape of Europa*; never
was any rape accomplished in such an atmosphere of good
humor if the face of the girl astride the bull is anything to go
by. The same is true of the *Forge of Vulcan*: the subject is epic,
the treatment idyllic. Two *Views of Naples* by Joseph Vernet,
one showing the smoking Vesuvius, illustrate the evolution of
landscape painting. And in a fine hunters' return scene by
Jean-Baptiste Oudry (*Bittern and Partridge Guarded by a White
Dog*) the painter has skillfully included a single shaft of light
coming from the background to strike the dog's white neck.

The *Forge of Vulcan*
(right and details
above).

228

DIDEROT AS ART CRITIC

ROOM 47 contains the favorite painters of Diderot, the first art critic, grouped around his portrait by Louis Michel van Loo. Diderot liked still lifes, sentimental genre paintings and bourgeois pathos (as in Greuze's the *Village Betrothal* of which he said: "one feels oneself touched by a gentle excess of emotion as one gazes at it". And he liked his paintings suggestive, as in *The Dead Bird* by Greuze which implies the loss of virginity. "The subject of this small poem is so refined that many people have not perceived it: they thought this girl was weeping for no greater loss than that of her canary," he wrote about another picture with a similar theme.

ROOM 48. Greuze achieved the same effect with *The Broken Jug*, a pair to his *Milkmaid*. Diderot also liked Fragonard, his portraits above all (see *Diderot, Inspiration* and the *Abbé de St-Non*, the latter painted with brio "in one hour"). Fragonard's skies also found favor with Diderot (the *Storm*, the *Tivoli Cascade* and *Women Bathing*. To paint his *Port of Marseilles* Vernet went out in a boat to work, while Hubert Robert specialized in ruins (the *Pont du Gard*, the *Maison Carrée* and the *Arenas of Nîmes* ● 90).

ROOM 49. Jean Honoré Fragonard was also a painter of the triumph of the flesh as in his *Love's Oath,* the *Stolen Chemise* and *The Bolt.* "That is beautiful, very beautiful, sublime", said Diderot of the *Paternal Curse* by Greuze (ROOM 51).

LOST INNOCENCE
The Bolt by Fragonard graphically conveys the moment of temptation, through its bold diagonals. *Diderot* (center) by Louis Michel van Loo shows the writer in the dressing gown given to him by Catherine II, on which he never dared wipe his pens. Below *The Broken Jug* by Greuze.

229

▲ FRENCH PAINTING
DAVID AND NEOCLASSICISM

NEOCLASSICAL AUSTERITY
The *Interior of David's Studio* (center) by Cochereau evokes a time when artists under the king's protection were lodged in the lower floors of the Louvre, below the Grande Galerie ▲ *130*. The rooms devoted to smaller-scale works by the painters of the transition period between the 18th and 19th century include some exquisite portraits: above right *Portrait of a Negress* by Marie Guillemine Benoist; below *Portrait of a Young Man in Hunting Clothes* by Anne-Louis Girodet-Trioson (purchased in 1994) and below *Bonaparte at the Bridge of Arcole* by

Antoine-Jean Gros: already in 1796 the outlines of the Napoleonic legend were being drawn.

NEOCLASSICISM

ROOM 52 contains the remarkably vivid portraits by Mme Vigée-Lebrun with works by other women painters such as Anne Vallayer-Coster and Adelaide Labille-Guiard. In *Night*, a canvas by Vernet the full moon seems to be a reflection in the sky of the fire lit by the men.

THE SO-CALLED GREEK STYLE (ROOM 53) was initiated by Joseph-Marie Vien in 1763 followed by François-André Vincent. The most beautiful example of this kind of neoclassicism is *Psyche and Eros* by François Gérard, a famous portraitist of the time. The inconstancy of love is symbolized by a buttterfly hovering above the girl's head.

DAVID AND HIS PUPILS. David was the principal painter of the years 1780–1820 and a master of neoclassicism and the quest for ideal beauty. His works are displayed in ROOM 54 (along with those of his pupils) and in the rooms for large-scale paintings (Daru, Denon and Mollien ▲ *234* to *237*). The extraordinary *Madame Trudaine* in ROOM 54 is noteworthy; as is the *Wounded Roman Soldier* by Drouais, David's favorite pupil who died in 1788 at the age of 25. Antoine-Jean Gros, a future baron of the Empire, is represented here by a study for the famous *Bonaparte at Arcole* as is Girodet by his portraits. Vincent, another founder of neoclassicism (*Zeuxis*, 1789, ROOM 53) who was also a painter of battle scenes has contributed a *Battle of the Pyramids* in grisaille.

LANDSCAPES, GENRE PAINTINGS AND PORTRAITS. ROOM 55 has a rotating exhibition of the 125 *Studies of Italian Landscapes* by Pierre-Henri de Valenciennes, a fascinating repertoire of

> # "UNDER HIS HANDS, WHICH RIVAL THOSE OF THE GODS,
> THE CANVAS BLAZES INTO ELOQUENT LIFE."
>
> ANDRÉ CHÉNIER, 1791

THE SALLE DAVID
The large-scale masterpieces of David are exhibited in rooms in the Denon building; nonetheless ROOM 54 is a preparation for these since it contains sketches for such pictures as *Belisarius*, and the *Oath of the Horatii*. There are also a number of portraits, notably *Madame Charles-Louis Trudaine* (left), painted about 1791 but unfinished, in which the patrician lady's silhouette is set against a strange red background.

skies and landscapes which is a reminder of how important it was for all these painters to travel to Italy. On the right, in ROOM 57, are genre paintings from around 1800, notably the *Convalescence of Bayard* by Pierre Révoil (exaltation of the troubadour style which haunted the first generation of romantics who had read Walter Scott). There is also a very rare piece by Daguerre, an *Interior of a Chapel* in which the consummate light effects remind us that this painter later became a photographer. The portraits and genre scenes of around 1800 are assembled in the Salle Boilly (ROOM 58) and include *Meeting of Artists in Isabey's Studio* (1798) by Louis-Léopold Boilly. Likewise, the *Rain Shower* gives us a glimpse of the streets of Paris, not yet paved in which pedestrians had to pay a toll to those who laid down planks for crossing the mud. ROOM 59 exhibits the landscapists of the same period, especially a fine *Interior of the Coliseum* by Marius Granet.
THE SALLE PRUD'HON (ROOM 56) is dominated by the theme of love (*Venus Bathing*); but Pierre-Paul Prud'hon was also a painter of portraits, who specialized in dignitaries of the imperial court such as *Empress Josephine*, the *King of Rome* and the Egyptologist *Baron Vivant Denon*, the first director of the Louvre under Napoleon ● *68*. The antithesis of David, Prud'hon found his inspiration in hellenistic Greece and Leonardo da Vinci ▲ *262*. He was one of the masters of early Romanticism.

THE ITALIAN REFERENCE
Villa Farnese: Two Poplar Trees, a composition by Pierre-Henri de Valenciennes.

ROMANTICISM VERSUS ACADEMICISM

JEAN AUGUSTE DOMINIQUE INGRES. In the first half of the 19th century there was a controversy between the colorists whose champion was Delacroix, and the draftsmen whose leader was Ingres, a pupil of David, who said "Drawing does not mean simply reproducing contours; drawing is not merely line. Drawing is expression, the inner line; it is planes and reliefs." The works assembled in ROOM 60 display the relief and the line perfected by Ingres: the *Small Bather* and the larger *Valpinçon Bather* demonstrate the art of a painter who saw himself above all as a follower of Raphael. Baudelaire wrote very unkindly that Ingres' figures "looked like very

correctly shaped dolls, swollen with some kind of soft, dead matter entirely foreign to the human organism". On the contrary, these (bathers) are marvelous studies of the female body, and the rounded composition of Ingres' *Turkish Bath* is one of perfect harmony. Ingres was also a major portraitist of the new bourgeoisie in France; see his *Louis-François Bertin*, director of the *Journal des Débats* or *Edme Bochet*.

THE IMPOSSIBLE
GALLOP
The *1821 Derby at
Epsom* (left) by
Theodore Géricault
shows the vogue for
horse-racing on the
English model, and
the contemporary
state of research into
the mechanics of
movement. The
unreal landscape and
the fantastic
atmosphere of this
painting are a far cry
from the realism of
contemporary
English painting.

THE PAINTER OF MADNESS. Géricault is best known for his *Raft
of the Medusa* ▲ 238, painted in 1819, a sketch of which is
shown in ROOM 61. But he was also a painter of horses which
were both his passion and his nemesis; he died at 33 as a
result of a fall from a horse. The gliding thoroughbreds of his
Epsom Derby are a striking example of this aspect of his art.
In his portraits of human beings (the *Compulsive Gambler*)
the people are handled like horse-portraits with the same
sense of volume and the same nervous, flaring nostrils. And
the smoke that rises above Géricault's *Plaster Furnace* is not
unlike the disquieting clouds of the *Raft of the Medusa*.
EUGÈNE DELACROIX was the greatest of the Romantic
painters; his major works are displayed with other large-scale
canvases elsewhere, but otherwise he appears for the first
time in ROOM 62 with a *Portrait of Frédéric Chopin*, *Self-portrait*
and *Jewish Wedding in Morocco*. The dramatic *Assassination of
the Bishop of Liège* reminds us that the younger generation in
1830 were captivated by the works of Sir Walter Scott, while
Hamlet and Horatio is inspired by Shakespeare. The above
painters are also present in ROOMS 71 and 72 (the Georges
Thomy-Thiery and Étienne Moreau-Nélaton Collections
▲ 242) and ROOMS 75 to 77 (Daru, Denon and Mollien ▲ 238).

Self-portrait (above)
and *Jewish Wedding in
Morocco* (below) by
Eugène Delacroix.

The large-scale canvases of French painters, from the neoclassicists to the Romantics, are displayed in the Salles Daru, Denon and Mollien in the Denon building. They range from David to Delacroix by way of Ingres and Géricault, and from the 1780's when the Revolution began, to the 1850's which saw the coming of the Second Empire. Indispensable as they are to an understanding of this period they are much more than a complement to the rooms where these schools are presented in detail; they are outstanding both in their quality and in their celebrity. The *Coronation of Napoleon I* by David, the *Raft of the Medusa* by Géricault and *Liberty Leading the People* by Delacroix are the prime examples. Most of the others are what the French call *grandes machines* in terms of their sheer scale, the hugeness of their themes and their theatrical approach; they come complete with male virility, female grief and dolor, glory personified by great men and abundant historical and dramatic narrative.

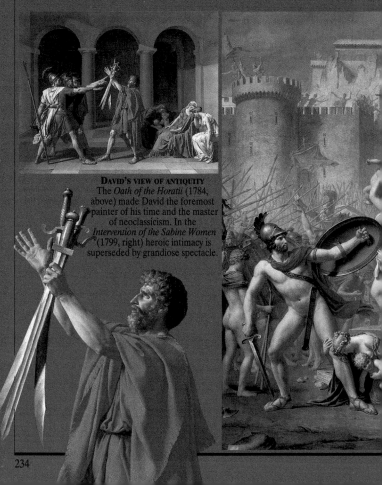

DAVID'S VIEW OF ANTIQUITY
The *Oath of the Horatii* (1784, above) made David the foremost painter of his time and the master of neoclassicism. In the *Intervention of the Sabine Women* (1799, right) heroic intimacy is superseded by grandiose spectacle.

INGRES.

A MANIFESTO FOR COLOR
The *Death of Sardanapalus* by Eugène Delacroix, painted in 1827 is one of the major works of French Romantic painting; it refers to the suicide of a king of Babylon who preferred this end to dishonorable surrender.

THE APOGEE OF LINE
Two works by Ingres, the strange *Roger Delivering Angelica* (right), commissioned to go above the door of the Throne Room at Versailles, and the *Great Odalisque* (right) painted in 1814 for Caroline Murat, Queen of Naples.

The same desolation is present in modern subjects like Gros' *Napoleon Visiting the Plague-stricken at Jaffa* (bottom and detail right), and classical ones like Guérin's *Marcus Sextus* (below).

> I WANT TO WORK IN THE PUREST GREEK STYLE. I FEAST MY EYES ON THE STATUES OF ANTIQUITY, AND I MEAN TO IMITATE SOME OF THEM."
>
> JACQUES-LOUIS DAVID, 1799

NEOCLASSICAL IDEAL

...classical painting set ...to illustrate the ...es of antiquity: ...grity and respect for ...es (*Marius ...isoned* by Germain ...n Drouais, above ...t), fidelity to death ...*ombment of Atala* by ...e-Louis-Girodet- ...son, center right, ...details) and justice ...*ice and Divine ...eance Punishing ...e* by Pierre-Paul ...l'hon, right). The ...tion of the *Return of ...cus Sextus* by Pierre- ...cisse Guérin (top) ...ys that neoclassicism ...far from cold and ...nsitive as some have ...d it.

Th. Géricault

Although Gros and Girodet were the first to free themselves from the influence of David, they could hardly have foreseen the revolution that the Romantics Géricault and Delacroix were to bring about. These two set themselves up in opposition to the partisans of classicism, led by Ingres (below right, his *Great Odalisque*, in strong contrast to Delacroix's *Death of Sardanapalus*, center). The Romantics stressed emotion, not virtue, and glorified the individual as opposed to the state. Once freed of the "antique" repertoire, they found new sources of inspiration such as contemporary history and the literature of the Middle Ages and the Renaissance. Nature found a place in their work which the neoclassicists had denied to her, preferring their theatrical decorative schemes. Stormy seas, misty horizons and jagged rocks were part of the new backdrop for Romantic drama. Two of the best-known paintings of the French Romantics were inspired by two pivotal events in the history of France: the *Raft of the Medusa*, (Géricault 1819, below) was prompted by the wreck of a frigate in 1816 and the subsequent abandonment of 149 sailors, who drifted off the coast of Africa for twelve days on a raft. This caused an international scandal and discredited the restored monarchy. *Liberty Leading the People* (Delacroix 1830, right), which evoked the *Trois Glorieuses*, the three days of Revolution in late July 1830 which precipitated the fall of Charles X.

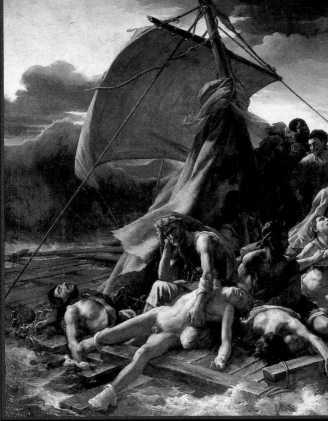

DANTE REREAD BY THE ROMANTICS
The *Souls of Francesca da Rimini and Paolo Malatesta Appearing to Dante and Virgil* (1855, right) by Ary Scheffer is taken from an episode in Dante's *Divine Comedy* (early 14th century).

THE MEDIEVAL VEIN
The Middle Ages and the Renaissance along with their tragedies were rich sources for the Romantics. The *Princes in the Tower* (1830) was inspired by history and a play by Shakespeare. Paul Delaroche (right) portrays the youthful Edward V of England and his brother Richard who were assassinated in 1483 by their uncle Richard III, himself the subject of a Shakespeare play.

241

The *Weir at Optevoz* by Charles-François Daubigny (1859, above).

Andromeda Chained to a Rock by the Nereids by Chassériau (1840, below) and *Young Man Sitting by the Sea* by Flandrin (1836, bottom).

TOWARD ECLECTICISM AND IMPRESSIONISM

LINE AND COLOR (ROOM 63), the two conflicting tendencies in French art, remained at odds as the 19th century wore on but sometimes they came together. A demonstration of pure form came with Hippolyte Flandrin's *Young Man Sitting by the Sea* which shows the legacy of Ingres. The supremacy of color was celebrated by orientalism with its realistic or idealized images of the East that was opening up to Western travelers: examples are Alexandre-Gabriel Deschamps' *Caravan* and Adrien Dauzat's *Convent of Saint Catherine on Mount Sinai.*

Théodore Chassériau's lines were bold enough but he was tempted by color contrast in his earlier paintings with their growing sense of movement: *Esther at Her Toilette*; *Andromeda*; and *Apollo and Daphne* in which the young girl is caught at the moment when her metamorphosis begins.

LANDSCAPE ART became a major genre in 19th-century France. The painters of the Barbizon School (ROOM 64) who took their name from a village near Fontainebleau, celebrated nature; Théodore Rousseau was the leading light among this new group of young artists. The *Chestnut Avenue* framed to accentuate its somber vaulting effect was refused by the 1841 Salon, but applauded by the Romantics. Rousseau's subsequent *Way Out of the Forest at Fontainebleau*, a state commission, was enthusiastically received in 1850; his skies were thought especially remarkable. By contrast Narcisse Diaz de la Peña, a Barbizon painter and the future master of Renoir, enlivened his landscapes to emphasize their sensual side (*Folles Filles*, ROOM 65). Another major figure of the same school was Charles-François Daubigny (*Weir at Optevoz*, 1859, ROOM 66).

COROT AND THE ART OF LANDSCAPE PAINTING
View of St-Lô (above), like the bathroom décor of his friend François-Parfait Robert at Mantes (left, above), shows Corot's passion for nature. He was in the habit of painting from life and then completing his canvases in his studio. The bathroom décor with its Italian scenes, reminds us that Italy was still an essential stage in a French painter's training. The *Woman in Blue* (left) shows another side to Corot. Below, a photograph of the painter at his easel in the open air, c. 1871–2.

JEAN-BAPTISTE COROT AND HIS COLLECTORS (ROOMS 65 to 73). The Louvre owes its Corot collection to two donors: Étienne Moreau-Nélaton (1859–1927) and Georges Thomy-Thiéry (1823–1902). Moreau-Nélaton bequeathed twenty-nine Corots to the museum, covering the painter's entire career from his first visit to Italy (*Castel Sant'Angelo and the Tiber*) to the landscapes of the Île-de-France (*Bridge at Mantes*, the *Tower at Montlhery* and the *Church at Marissel*, ROOM 69). There were also paintings by Delacroix: the *Taking of Constantinople, Knights in Combat* and the *Orphan-girl at the Cemetery*, a study for the *Massacre at Chios*. Georges Thomy-Thiéry donated the works of 1830's painters, including Ernest Meissonier and Delacroix and some antique tragedies, among them the *Wrath of Medea* which is simply a mouth, a silent shriek and wild eyes staring through the darkness. Thiéry's collection also included paintings by Decamps, Millet and Daubigny in addition to Corot's *Woman with a Pearl*, a study of the *Mona Lisa*, a pensive *Woman in Blue* and *Souvenir de Mortefontaine* bought by Napoleon III. This last comes very close to Impressionism.

243

SECOND FLOOR /
RICHELIEU

RICHELIEU

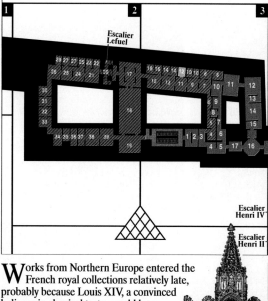

Escalier
Lefuel

Escalier
Henri IV

Escalier
Henri II

Works from Northern Europe entered the French royal collections relatively late, probably because Louis XIV, a convinced believer in classical taste, would have found them little short of grotesque. It was not until the late 18th century that d'Augiviller ● 29, the Royal Director of Buildings, amassed for Louis XVI a collection worthy of the name which was later enriched by purchases and bequests. Today this is exhibited in the Richelieu building.

Portrait of an Old Woman by Hans Memling, right-hand side of a panel which also featured a *Portrait of an Old Man.*

BURGUNDIAN FLANDERS
Jan van Eyck was one of the first painters to get away from the International Gothic style (exemplified here by the *Chapelle Cardon*, early 15th century, far right) and to imagine an art much closer to reality, made possible by the technique of oil painting. His *Madonna of Chancelor Rolin* (right) was commissioned by the Duke of Burgundy's chancellor for his family chapel at the church of Notre Dame at Autun. Burgundy and Flanders formed a single political entity at that time.

INTERNATIONAL GOTHIC (ROOM 3). Cross the two first rooms of French painting to ROOM 3 where the *Chapelle Cardon* is displayed. The glass case to the left contains a Bohemian Virgin and Child (15th century).

VAN EYCK AND VAN DER WEYDEN (ROOM 4). Jan van Eyck (c. 1400–41) so influenced his contemporaries that he was thought by them to have invented painting in oils. In the *Madonna of Chancelor Rolin*, one of his greatest works, van Eyck included a portrait of the donor himself; above the chancellor's head the capitals illustrate human weaknesses (*Adam and Eve Driven from Eden, Cain and Abel,* the *Drunkenness of Noah*). Between Rolin and the Madonna is an empty space in which the prayer of the man and the blessing of the Christ-Child are exchanged against a background of a landscape and an idealized city divided in two by a river. In the left-hand glass case is a superb anonymous diptych, a *Saint John the Baptist* and a *Madonna and Child* in grisaille done according to a technique which brings painting and sculpture close to one another. Quite as remarkable is Rogier van der Weyden's *Annunciation*; here everything has symbolic meaning with the three corollas of the blossoming lilies suggesting both virginity and the Trinity, the ewer and basin implying purity and the phial on the chimney piece transfixed by light evokes virginity and the approaching birth of Christ. The *Triptych of the Braque Family* by the same painter was a portable altarpiece used for the family's devotions when it was traveling. This is the first example in Flemish painting of half-length figures. If you view the triptych from behind, you see the *vanitas* on the reverse: on the back of the left panel is a skull – *Memento Mori* – and on the back of the right, the Cross.

HANS MEMLING (ROOM 6). The Louvre possesses an extraordinary *Portrait of an Old Woman* and the *Madonna of Jacques Floreins* painted by Hans Memling for a Bruges spice merchant in about 1490.

On the wall to the left are several beautiful triptychs, along with the *Ship of Fools* by Hieronymus Bosch, a composition on the vices of gluttony and drunkenness heavily laced with anticlericalism.

THE STUDIOLO OF URBINO. ROOM 6 juxtaposes 14 of the 28 portraits of famous men painted in about 1475 for the *Studiolo* of Duke Federigo da Montefeltro at the Palace of Urbino (acquired for the Louvre by Napoleon III in 1863). These portraits are the work of the Flemish Justus of Ghent and the Spaniard Pedro Berruguete.

Triptych of the Braque Family (c. 1480). Center panel: Christ the Redeemer, the Virgin and Saint John the Evangelist; left panel, Saint John the Baptist; right panel, Saint Mary Magdalene.

A PANTHEON OF FAMOUS MEN
As though talent made great men part of a single family, all the great originators of the Renaissance in Italy feature in the *Studiolo* of Urbino, from Plato to Dante by way of Aristotle and Saint Augustine (above, Ptolemy and Plato).

SATIRE
The *Ship of Fools*, the only work by Hieronymus Bosch in the Louvre, was inspired by the book of the same name published in Basel in 1494 by the Alsatian Sébastian Brant. It shows the fools embarking for the land of folly, Narragonia.

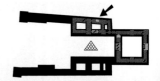

THE PORTRAIT, A GENRE IN ITS OWN RIGHT
Above, left to right: *Erasmus Writing*, by Holbein, is caught in profile engaged in his intellectual calling (Erasmus' *Commentaries on the New Testament* epitomize the return to the old texts then championed by humanism); Albrecht Dürer *Self-portrait* (the thistle in his hand was a token of fidelity from his fiancée); Lucas Cranach's *Portrait of Magdalena Luther*.

GERMANY IN THE 15TH AND 16TH CENTURIES

In **ROOM 7** the Seine and the Louvre appear in the *Pietà* painted (c. 1500) by the master of St-Germain-des-Prés ● *26*. Bartolomaus Zeitblom was the painter of an altarpiece with four panels centered on an *Annunciation* and Ulrich Apt the Elder of another, centered on an *Adoration* scene which is a fine example of late Gothic portraiture. The German schools, without forsaking the Gothic tradition represented by the great Flemish altarpieces and portraits of donors, were heavily influenced by the Italian Renaissance. Iconographic themes developed, spurred on by the Reformation, and the isolated portrait became a genre in its own right.

THE TWO CABINETS IN ROOM 8 contain some breathtaking marvels: Holbein's portraits of *Erasmus* and *Anne of Cleves*, the fourth wife of Henry VIII of England; Lucas Cranach's *Portrait of a Lord of Kockeritz, Portrait of Magdalena Luther* (the daughter of the reformer Martin Luther), and the celebrated *Venus in a Landscape* (1529) with her transparent veil. A winged serpent concealed in the décor holds a ring, the signature of Lucas Cranach. Lastly there is the extraordinary self-portrait of Albrecht Dürer. In the second cabinet is *Christ Blessing the Children* attributed to the Master of the *Griffon's Head*).

THE LOW COUNTRIES IN THE 16TH CENTURY

ROOM 9 contains the *Banker and His Wife* by Quentin Metsys. The figures have nervous faces and hands that seem full of life. Metsys was the first of a long line of Antwerp painters; this picture is dated 1514 on the manuscript on the shelf behind the couple. A Virgin by the same artist known as the *Rattier Madonna*, has

a face reminiscent of Leonardo. There is also a *Madonna and Child* by Joos van Cleve which is noteworthy for its medieval background and for the Dominican monk, a witness of the purest faith who accompanies the Virgin. Saint Dominic in his 12th-century sermons had imposed the idea of austere virtue through his monastic Order (the Dominicans controlled the Inquisition at that time). The theme of religion had become a pretext for painting landscapes, a genre which acquired ever-greater importance; it also sanctioned portraits of women (the Madonna, Saint Barbara and Saint Catherine of Alexandria painted by Ambrosius Benson, an Italian who worked in Flanders. Heavily influenced by the Italian Renaissance is the *Carondelet Diptych* (1517) by Jan Gossaert known as Mabuse. The donor of this masterpiece who was doyen of the church at Besançon and a councelor of Charles V is shown praying beside the Virgin; on the back of the diptych is a magnificent trompe l'oeil of a skull, with a precept of Saint Jerome.

IN THE TWO SMALL CABINETS OF ROOM 10 are landscapes by Simon Bening rendered with an attention to detail that

ITALIAN INFLUENCES
The *Carondelet Diptych* (1517, top) by Mabuse, like the *Banker and His Wife* (above) by Quentin Metsys, show the influence of Italian art on the Northern schools. The *Banker* illustrates the tremendous economic development underway in Flanders, but it is also a kind of still life whose realism is illusory.

A PROTEST
Bruegel the Elder's *Beggars* (1568) with their fox brushes and carnival disguises represent a muted protest against the Spanish occupation of Flanders. On the back is written "Legless cripples, take heart, may your affairs prosper".

Left page, bottom, a *Vanitas* on the back of a mid 15th-century Flemish triptych.

247

NORTHERN MANNERISM
David and Bathsheba by Jan Massys from Antwerp (above) and *Perseus Rescuing Andromeda* by Joachim Wtewael of Utrecht (below) are perfect illustrations of

betrays the miniaturist; *Saint Mary Magdalene Reading* by the master of half-figures; Pieter Huys' monster-filled *Temptation of Saint Anthony* (1547); and the elder Bruegel's *Beggars* (1568). *Lot and His Daughters* (School of Leyden) is a superb composition showing the wrath of God smiting Sodom.

IN ROOM 11 the splendors of the flesh dominate *David and Bathsheba* by Jan Massys. The subject is drawn from the Bible: Bathsheba in Hebrew means the "opulent one" who is noticed in her bath by the ageing David who will shortly become a sinner and a criminal (Samuel II, 11 and 12). The same room contains the *Dwarf of Cardinal Granvelle* who foreshadows Velasquez' degenerate buffoons and reminds us of Spain's long occupation of Flanders. The artist, Mor van Dashorst, went by the name of Antonio Moro when he worked for the Spanish court.

ROOM 12 consigned to the museum's Department of Graphic Arts, exhibits by rotation the designs for the tapestries of *Maximilian's Hunt* from the studio of Bernard van Orley, one of the first Flemish artists to embrace the Italian style. The tapestries are in ROOM 19 on the first floor of the Richelieu building ▲ *203*.

16TH-CENTURY MANNERISM

Mannerism which came from Italy and spread throughout Europe. These paintings exemplify the curving lines, Baroque rhythms and refined materials of the genre to which Northern painters added sumptuous landscapes.

(ROOM 13). The second Italian Renaissance influenced by Mannerism ▲ *265* found echoes all over Europe. Line, stylization, affectation and rhythm were its principal characteristics. The foreground of Joachim Wtewael's *Perseus Rescuing Andromeda* contains a mass of shells whose tones echo the pearly flesh of the princess. In Paul Bril's *Diana and Her Nymphs* the surroundings also contribute to the narrative, as they do in Valckenborch's *Temptation of Saint Anthony*, where an overwhelming forest over which an imaginary monster soars, seems to crush the saint.

17TH-CENTURY FLANDERS

IN ROOM 14 cabinet 1 are more pictures by Paul Bril and some beautiful landscapes (on the right at the entrance), notably a wonderful *View of a Seaport* attributed to Anton Mozart and a *Winter Landscape* by Denys van Alsloot. In cabinet 2 is the *Battle of Arbelles* (in which Alexander the Great crushed Darius and the Achemenids) painted with considerable dash by Jan Bruegel (the Elder "Velvet" Bruegel) to whom we also owe a *View of Tivoli*. The Italian landscape had by now become an esential reference in European painting.

"VELVET" BRUEGEL also features in ROOM 15 with an *Earthly Paradise* awash with wild animals and nostalgia. In addition to a *Church Interior* by Van Steenwyck, a portrait of Queen Marie de' Medici (in whose portrait Frans Pourbus seems more interested in the clothes than in the face) foreshadows the Baroque extravagance of Rubens.

POURBUS reappears in ROOM 16, cabinet 1 with *Henri IV King of France in Black Costume. Diana Discovering the Pregnancy of Callisto* is more memorable for its landscape by Denys von Alsloot than for its figures by Hendrick de Clerck.

RUBENS (ROOMS 17 and 18) was the most influential Flemish painter of the 17th century, when his home city of Antwerp was one of the world's greatest ports. A consummately European artist, trained in Italy where he met with the first glimmerings of Baroque, Rubens worked for the courts of Paris, Madrid and London. A first great Rubens, among many others, dominates ROOM 17: this is *Tomyris, Queen of the Scythians, Plunging the Head of Cyrus into a Pitcher filled with Blood.* The series of paintings done by the artist illustrating the history of Marie de' Medici may be seen in the Galerie Médicis (to the left, ROOM 18, ▲ *250–1*).

JACOB JORDAENS (ROOM 19 at the end of the Galerie Médicis) was Ruben's best pupil. This room contains a number of his tumultuous, joyous canvases, notably *Jesus Evicting the Merchants from the Temple* (nobody in this picture seems too worried about what is happening), the *King Drinks* and the *Child Jupiter* in which the god is eclipsed by the goat Amalthea who nourished him on Mount Ida. Go back to ROOM 17 to continue the circuit.

FLEMISH GRACES
In the *Baptism of Christ* (above) by Cornelis van Haarlem the subject of the picture is relegated to the deep background behind a group of cunningly executed Italianate nudes. Left, an *Imaginary View* of a landscape packed with Italian architecture by Jan Bruegel the Elder.

Tomyris, Queen of the Scythians (below) by Rubens entered Louis XIV's collection in 1671.

The Coronation of Marie de' Medici at St-Denis (painting X, below) which inspired David's *Coronation of Napoleon I*, two hundred years later.

The group of twenty-four canvases painted by Rubens between 1622 and 1625 for the Galerie Médicis in the Luxembourg Palace constitute a phenomenal achievement; over 300 square yards of painting done by a single artist. The work is a series of allegories on the life of Marie de' Medici, wife of Henri IV, who was regent after his death until her son Louis XIII came of age. In this masterpiece of Baroque art, realism and fantasy are blended in a series of compositions which display wonderfully fluent dynamism and unearthly light.

Birth of Marie de' Médici in Florence April 26, 1573 (painting II).

Education of Marie de' Medici (painting III).

Marie de' Medici Landing at Marseilles November 3, 1600 (painting VI).

The Triumph of Juliers September 1, 1610 (painting XIII).

Happiness of the Regency (painting XV).

The Majority of Louis XIII October 20, 1614 (painting XVI).

*The King Meets Marie de'
Medici at Lyons* November
9, 1600 (painting VII).

*Birth of Louis XIII at
Fontainebleau* September 27,
1601 (painting VIII).

*Henri IV Goes to War in Germany
and Entrusts the Government of
His Kingdom to the Queen*
March 20, 1610 (painting IX).

*The Queen Flees from the
Château de Blois* on the
night of February 21–2,
1619, (painting XVII).

The Treaty of Angoulême
April 30, 1619 (painting XVIII).

Conclusion of the Peace at
Angers, August 10, 1620
(painting XIX).

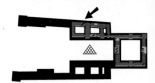

THE PAINTER'S FAMILY
The portrait of *Hélène Fourment and Her Children* (right) by Rubens (husband and father) was bought in 1784 for the collection of Louis XVI.

FROM THE HUMBLEST TO THE GREATEST
Joos van Craesbeeck's *Smoker* may be a lively self-portrait. *Charles I of England* by Antony van Dyck (below) acquired by Louis XVI in 1175, shows the English monarch at the hunt in a simple composition painted with enormous sensitivity. Charles epitomizes the elegant, enlightened prince. The cane is his symbol of royalty along with his rich costume which contrasts vividly with the landscape.

RETURN TO ROOM 17 and take time to look at the landscapes of Bril, a *Cat Discovering Game* from an unexpected angle by Jan Fyt and the *Holy Family During the Flight from Egypt*, a lovely night landscape lit by the moon. The Lefuel staircase (ROOM 20) leads on through to ROOM 21, which contains more works by Rubens.

RUBENS APPEARS AGAIN in ROOMS 21 and 22. In ROOM 21 are two portraits of *Hélène Fourment*, the artist's wife. In one, she wears black with a striking tonal contrast to the red doublet of the child on her left. In the other, she is in white. The cluster of fat-bottomed *putti* surrounding the *Madonna and Child* are echoed by the whirling figures of the *Village Wedding*; all Baroque art is here with its perpetual motion and tumult of colors.

ROOM 22 contains a collection of Rubens sketches, among them one for the *Raising of the Cross* (this altarpiece is at Angers). There is also a fine *Cavalry* by David Teniers the Elder with some powerful light effects.

TENIERS. There are more painting by this artist in ROOM 23, notably caricatures, along with Joos van Craesbeeck's *Smoker*. The man depicted was the baker

at the prison in which Adriaen Brouwer was imprisoned for debt. Brouwer was Ruben's favorite painter; the prisoner so thoroughly won over the baker that he made him his disciple in both his paintings and his debauches. Tavern scenes were a frequent and well-worn theme of Flemish painters.

MONUMENTAL PORTRAITS BY VAN DYCK occupy ROOM 24. Here the atmosphere changes, with formal portraits of aristocrats such as a *Gentleman with a Sword* or the beautiful *Marquesa Geromina Spinola-Doria* from Genoa. The Flemish painter lived in England from 1632 until his death in 1641, shortly before the destruction of the world he had painted. Van Dyck's portraits of *Charles I* and *James Stuart* are full of life as well as being profound psychological studies.

IN ROOM 25 are two tiny church interiors by Pieter Neefs the Younger. Dutch painters were masters of the art of illustrating architecture because of their mastery and close application of the laws of perspective.

VAN DYCK IN ROOM 26. He reemerges with a double portrait of the *Dukes of Bavaria and Cumberland*. In *Rinaldo and the Enchantress Armida* the tangled bodies show how much Van Dyck owes to Rubens and Jordaens, his masters. *The Dessert* by Jan Davidsz. de Heem, illustrates the care taken by Dutch painters in rendering such things as fruits, dishes and silver.

FOR THE DELECTATION OF AMATEURS
The extraordinary *Dessert* by Jan Davidsz. de Heem (1640, left and detail above) is one of the greatest masterpieces of 17th-century still life. A genre in its own right, still life is above all decorative; as such, it was often commissioned by aristocrats. Later it became symbolic, not unlike the "vanities" of an earlier era. With de Heem it acquired a Baroque dimension on account of his luxuriant composition, details and spectacular mastery of trompe l'oeil.

NORTHERN CARAVAGGISM
The *Clown and His Lute* (below) by Frans Hals painted between 1620 and 1625, shows a strong influence of Caravaggio: the piece is a miracle of cheek, pictorial verve and expressive realism.

THE 17TH CENTURY IN HOLLAND

ROOM 27. To the right in cabinet 1 are those favorite characters of Baroque writers, *Pyramus and Thisbe,* painted by Leonaert Bramer: their story formed the basis for the play of Romeo and Juliet. Beside them, the dress of the *Lady at Her Toilette* by Pieter Codde, is altogether admirable. In the second cabinet are the magnificent ruins of *Campo Vaccino*, among other Italian landscapes by Cornelis van Poelenburgh. There is also a superb *Ham* spiked all over with cloves (spices were then a supreme luxury in cooking) by Floris van Schooten.

ROOM 28 contains a series of remarkably detailed portraits – *Portrait*

Although his masters knew Italy, Rembrandt never visited that country; nevertheless he developed an art in Amsterdam which blended the magnificence of Baroque painting with an inward-looking somberness. This gave his work a tragic dimension. Everything in Rembrandt is absolutely unique, including his mastery of light, his dark glazes, his dull-golds and his brushwork, which began with great precision and later grew troubled. Always a reflective artist, he painted many self-portraits – the Louvre alone has three – illustrating the sense of deep introspection that he was to cultivate until his death in 1669 at the age of 63. Although he remained aloof and independent of official commissions, he won immediate fame: his influence on art was enormous, even in his own lifetime.

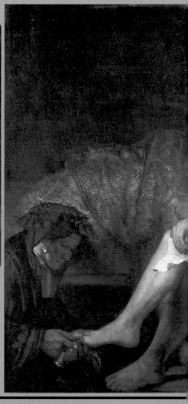

The Flayed Ox Carcass was bought very cheaply by the Louvre in 1857 because its subject matter offended bourgeois taste. "The sordid butcher's cellar is illuminated with the gold and ruby sheen of the bloody carcass," writes Charles Sterling in his *The Still Life, from Antiquity to the 20th Century* (1985). Delacroix, Daumier and (in 1925) Soutine were all inspired by this provocative painting, which has parallels with Chardin's painting, *The Skate* ▲ 227.

The three *Portraits of the Artist* at the Louvre. Rembrandt painted the ones on the left and right when he was 27 and the one in the middle when he was 54.

REMBRANDT VAN RIJN ▲

LIGHT ABOVE ALL THINGS
Confronted by *Bathsheba* (1654, left) the spectator sees with the eyes of King David who is not in the picture; the beauty of the young woman is breathtaking. The *Philosopher* (top) with its pronounced chiaroscuro approaches the monochromatic. The *Archangel Gabriel Quitting Tobias and His Family* (above) seems to be sucked upward by the light, an impression that is strengthened by the dark void in the lower right hand corner.

SCENES OF DAILY LIFE
Despite their different ways of treating their themes, we find the same interest in ordinary existence and the same meticulous detail in the work of Adriaen van Ostade (*Portrait of a Family*, top of facing page, details above), Gerard Dou (*Self-portrait with Palette*, right) and Vermeer, two of whose most celebrated works the Louvre possesses. These are the *Lacemaker* (below) and the *Astronomer* (facing page, center right).

of a Man by Frans Hals, *Portrait of a Woman* by Pieter Soutman. The *Lady Musicians* by Gerrit van Honthorst, the *Gypsy Girl* and the *Clown with His Lute* by Frans Hals are characteristic of the influence of Caravaggio on Dutch painting in the first half of the 17th century: these are not so much portraits as subjects; the handling is broader and the brushwork similar to Caravaggio's.

FRANS POST (ROOMS 29 and 30) went to Brazil with Prince Maurice of Nassau's expedition between 1637 and 1648. He was the first European artist to paint these landscapes of the New World. A rodent in the estuary of the *Rio San Francisco*, cactuses, negros – Post was depicting something completely different, so much so that his works were eventually used as patterns for West Indies wall-hangings. Also in ROOM 29 is a *Church Interior* by Saenredam, a coldly geometrical piece; the same high finish may be seen in the portraits of Nicolaes Elias (called Pickenoy) with lace that is a pretext for an exercise in painterly virtuosity.

In ROOM 30 there is a *Portrait of a Child of Twelve* by Wybrand de Geest, and a fine *Still life with a Silver Goblet* by Willem Clausz. Heda which clearly indicates that this genre – the allegory of passing time contrasted with human vanity – was a major feature of 17th-century Holland. Landscapes are also represented by the works of Nicolaes Berchem.

ROOM 31 is entirely given over to Rembrandt ▲ 254. The most famous of the master's paintings to be seen in the Louvre is *Bathsheba*.

ROOM 32 contains *Bathsheba Receiving King David's Letter* by Willem Drost, a pupil of Rembrandt; more nudes in Nicolaes Maes' *Bathers* and dramatic light effects in Frans de Halst's *Castle*.

IN ROOM 33 a young *Dutch Prince Drawn in a Coach by Miniature Goats* is the subject of a canvas by Ferdinand Bol, one of Rembrandt's favorite disciples. Adriaen van Ostade who was a follower of Frans Hals, was the author of the fine *Portrait of a Family* displayed here: note also the beautiful portraits by Nicolaes van Helst (*Unveiled Woman Lifting a Drape*). Finally the simple *Bush* painted by Jacob van Ruisdael somehow has the motion of a flame. Note also a *Young Man and a Procuress* by Michael Sweerts.

THE OUDEKERK AT DELFT (ROOM 34) is the subject of a superb architectural study by Hendrick van der Vliet. Nearby, the *War Fleet Close to Shore* is rendered in dramatic black and white tones (Van de Velde), a reminder that Holland was a maritime nation (under attack in this case by the France of Louis XIV) and that for the Dutch the painting of seascapes was a genre in its own right.

GERARD DOU (ROOM 35). Apart from his *Self-portrait*, Dou's the *Gold-weigher*, the *Trumpet Player*, the *Cook*, the *Dutch Housewife* and the *Grocer's Wife* offer intriguing insights into the occupations and callings of ordinary people. The *Dropsical Woman* is fascinatingly realistic with scintillating fabrics, fine light and exquisite detail.

ROOM 36. The *Meal of Herrings* and the *Herb Market* by Gabriel Metsu (1629–67) give another glimpse of life in Amsterdam. The latter is remarkable in that it is an open air scene, combining the themes of love and the still life.

IN ROOM 37 hangs Jacob van Loo's *Half-clothed Woman* and a *Still life with Fruits* by Abraham Mignon.

TWO GREAT VERMEERS, the *Lacemaker* and the *Astronomer* occupy ROOM 38. Both protagonists are involved in their tasks, haloed in diffuse light. Here also is Pieter de Hooch's *Young Woman Drinking* with her striking scarlet skirt, and various Dutch landscapes – in particular Jacob van Ruisdael's superb *Ray of Sunlight*, seascapes (*Storm at Sea* by Aelbert Cuyp, the "Dutch Claude Lorrain") and city scenes (the *Herengracht in Amsterdam* by Jan van der Heyden).

THE DUTCH COUNTRYSIDE (ROOM 39) with its astonishing skies is represented in the paintings of Wouwerman (*Wooden Bridge over a Torrent*), in Adam Pynacker's *Landscape at Sunset* with the horn of a goat catching the last rays of the sun, and in Meindert Hobbema's *Watermill* and the *Farm*.

A MARITIME POWER
The wealth of the Low Countries was founded on trade in which the Dutch merchant fleet played the principal role. Seascapes were a genre in which Ludolf Backhuyzen was the outstanding figure (*Dutch Vessels off the Port of Amsterdam*, below).

The Louvre's collection of Italian paintings originated in the royal collection, thanks to the acquisitions made by François I and Louis XIV. Its presentation is to be modified within the same chronological framework (12th to 18th century), principally in the Grande Galerie. It begins with the primitive painters – among them Cimabue and Giotto – who were rediscovered at the close of the 18th century, and whose works were brought to the Louvre by Vivant Denon. The purchase of the Campana collection by Napoleon III in 1863 gave the *Trecento* – the Italian 14th century – the place it deserved in art history. Then came the early Renaissance paintings of Fra Angelico, Filippo Lippi and Paolo Uccello.

Despite its intense focus on religious themes, Italian painting of the 13th century and the early 14th century offers clear insights into contemporary society. At that time Florence was a major artistic center, as evidenced by the *Virgin and Child in Majesty* by Cimabue (above right, c. 1270), borrowed from Byzantine iconography but handled with a more supple sense of line. Thirty years later, Giotto's *Saint Francis of Assisi* (left) exhibited a totally new approach to figurative expression. In the 1420's, Brunelleschi's perfecting of perspective created a revolution in the painter's art, as may be seen in the *Martyrdom of Saints Cosmos and Damian* by Fra Angelico (1438, right).

Saint Francis of Assisi Receiving the Stigmata, a detail of Giotto's altarpiece dedicated to the patron saint of birds and the meek.

The *Presentation at the Temple* by Gentile da Fabriano (1423, left).

The *Carrying of the Cross* by Simone Martini (c. 1335, left) exemplifies the Sienese school in the *Trecento*. In his *Portrait of Sigismondo Malatesta* (above, c. 1450) Piero della Francesca follows the formula of the head and chest in profile borrowed from traditional Gothic style.

APPLIED PERSPECTIVE
Two details from the
Battle of San Romano
(below) show the
progress made by
Paolo Uccello. Note
the alternating planes
of color which give
the illusion of depth
and the *mazzochio*, a
ring-shaped, check-
patterned head-dress,
which is an exercise in
virtuosity for
draftsmen.

The art of the 15th century (the *Quattrocento*) is characterized by new themes, both sacred and profane, and new representations. Right, from top to bottom, *Portrait of an Old Man and a Boy* by Domenico Ghirlandaio; *Madonna and Child with Two Angels* called the *Virgin with the Pomegranate* by Filippino Lippi, and *Christ by the Column* by Antonello da Messina. Linear rhythm and tender colors served the classical ideal of Botticelli in his 1483 frescos for the Villa Lemmi, near Florence (opposite page, center). In *Venus and the Graces Offering Gifts to a Maiden* the terrestrial world represented by the young girl contrasts in its simplicity with the fluid outlines of the immortals. At the close of the 1430's, Paolo Uccello painted a group of three panels (one of which is at the Louvre) entitled the *Battle of San Romano* (opposite page, bottom) in which he put into practise his researches on perspective; in addition to the sense of confusion demanded by the subject, the organization of the painting is entirely ruled by an obsession with depth (see details, below left). Mantegna's *Calvary* of 1459 (above left) is another masterpiece of perspective.

Calvary by Andrea Mantegna (above) formed the central scene of the lower part of an altarpiece for a church in Verona.

The *Mona Lisa* has had a checkered history: stolen in 1911, she was recovered two years later. Today she is as coveted and praised as ever and is closely protected.

The *Portrait of Lisa Gherardini*, also called *La Gioconda* or *Mona Lisa*, was the principal jewel of François I's collection and has long been the most celebrated painting in the Louvre.

Leonardo da Vinci was a painter, a scholar and a theoretician: his art marks the apogee of the Renaissance. He came to live in France in 1516, at the request of François I ▲ *215* and died there three years later. A mysterious poetry flows from his paintings, most of which contain

elaborate compositions, delicate reliefs, a serene misty light and enigmatic smiles. Above right, the *Virgin and Child with Saint Anne* (above, a sketch for *Saint Anne* in the Graphic Arts Department ● *62*), remarkable for its movement and the interaction between the figures. Right, *Saint John the Baptist*; facing page the *Mona Lisa*, also known as *La Gioconda*.

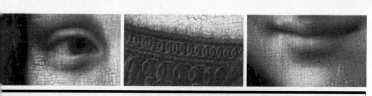

La Belle Jardinière and *Balthazar Castiglione* by Raphael.

Madonna and Child with Sai

I taly in the 16th century was a breeding ground for genius: Leonardo da Vinci; Michelangelo, the painter of the Sistine Chapel, (represented in the Louvre by his sculptures ▲ *195*) and Raphael, who laid the groundwork for what was to become the classical style. The Louvre possesses a fine array of Raphael's work initiated by François I. The *Virgin and Child with Saint John the Baptist*, known as *La Belle Jardinière* (above left), and the *Portrait of Balthazar Castiglione* (left) are among the most famous. Raphael represents the triumph of Italian painting, unrivaled in Europe.

and Four Saints by Pontormo.   *Portrait of a Sculptor* by Bronzino.

In the mid-16th century Italian painting evolved in the direction of Mannerism. The new sinuous lines, unreal light, strange proportions, meticulous refinement and extravagant colors have been viewed as signs of a growing insipidity: but artists like Pontormo (*Madonna and Child with Saint Anne and Four Saints* above left) and Bronzino (*Portrait of a Sculptor* above) achieved a balanced synthesis and produced paintings of rare intensity. Venice witnessed the growth of an expressive form of art: Lorenzo Lotto's *Saint Jerome* (left) is a poetical, nostalgic work in the manner of Giorgione.

Venice, the metropolis of northern Italy, a trading city and an international maritime power, was a focus of creativity in the 15th and 16th centuries. Venice favored coloration over the art of draftsmanship exemplified by the Florentines and Venetian painting came to define a type of classicism whose

VERONESE
The *Wedding Feast at Cana* (right) painted by Veronese in 1562–3 for the refectory of the monastery of San Giorgio Maggiore measures close to 21 feet by 30 feet. This huge canvas had to be restored in situ between 1989 and 1992 because its sheer size made it impossible to move. The restoration uncovered the original

influence was just as strong as its rival's. In the second half of the 15th century, Giovanni Bellini was the greatest exponent of this science of light. Bellini with his lucid, brilliant palette, later gave way to a second generation of painters heavily influenced by Leonardo da Vinci, who came to Venice in 1501. First Giorgione, then Titian worked to soften outlines and use light and broad masses of color to give dramatic intensity to their compositions, portraits, religious and mythological themes, and major pieces commissioned for Venice's churches and religious institutions. Among the most famous of these are Veronese's *Wedding Feast at Cana*, Tintoretto's *Paradise* and Vittore Carpaccio's *Sermon of Saint Stephen at Jerusalem* (1514, above).

colors under the various touchings-up and grime (far right, top to bottom, the same detail of the steward before restoration, X-rayed and after restoration).

TITIAN
Three masterpieces by Tiziano Vecellio (known as Titian), court painter to the Emperor Charles V: *Man with a Glove* (above), *Christ Crowned with Thorns* (right) and *Concert Champêtre* (center, opposite) were attributed to his master Giorgione for years. Titian's motto was "Art is stronger than Nature".

TINTORETTO. The Louvre possesses the sketc[h] made by Tintoretto for his *Paradise* (right) which once decorated the Council chamber [at] the Doge's Palace but was destroyed in a fir[e]

"THE DANCE OF REFLECTIONS AND ATOMS, WHICH IS INTEGRAL FROM CORNER TO CORNER OF THE PAINTING, THE RIGHTNESS OF THE VALUES, THE CONTINUITY OF THE VOLUMES . . ."

ÉLIE FAURE, ON VENETIAN PAINTING

267

The Renaissance was followed by several parallel movements, Baroque, classicism and Caravaggism, while Venice and Florence yielded their primacy to Rome and Naples. One dominant personality emerged at the turn of the 16th century; this was Caravaggio, a tormented violent painter who sought his inspiration and his models among ordinary people. Though he had no pupils and was always on the move, Caravaggio achieved enormous influence throughout Europe ▲ *219, 263* and *271*. But other painters who received the favor of princes and popes (the brothers Agostino and Annibale Carracci from Bologna, Guido Reni, Guercino and Domenichino) moved Mannerism toward a form of classicism that bordered on the academic.

There is no similarity between Caravaggio's *Death of the Virgin* (1605–6, above) and *Romulus and Remus Recovered by Faustulus* by Pietro da Cortona (c.1634, left). The first is about grief and death, a dramatic reality peopled with grave silhouettes; the second recounts a legend using conventional figures, decorative colors and well-worn classical references.

"FOR THE FIRST TIME IN THE HISTORY OF PAINTING THE PRINCIPAL OF REALITY IS IMMATERIAL: IT HAS SUBSTANCE, BUT IS NOT MADE FLESH."

R. LONGHI, ON CARAVAGGIO

Saint Cecilia with an Angel Holding a Musical Score (above) by Domenichino, and *Deianeira and the Centaur Nessus* (above right) by Guido Reni. The two female figures, graceful but unearthly, belong to a different world to that of the *Virgin* of Caravaggio, who used the body of a girl drowned in the Tiber as his model.

Venice in the 18th century was in steep decline though the prevailing atmosphere was one of perpetual carnival. The genre scenes of Gian

Domenico Tiepolo (the *Tooth Puller*, above) and Guardi's painting of the carnival (*La Salute*, middle right of the page) reflect this.

269

Still Life with Figs b...
Luis Eugeni...
Meléndez (1716–80...

The vogue for Spanish painting came late to France, impelled by th[] Romanticism of the 19th century. The works "collected" or rather looted by Napoleon I were restored to Spain after the fall of the Empire; another collection assembled by Louis-Philippe had a powerful impact on French art but was unfortunately sold under the Second Empire. The Louvre's acquisition policy and a number of major donations have made it possible to reconstitute an ensemble of paintings that is representative of Spanish art from the Gothic period onward, from Martorell to Goya (late 18th century), by way of Mannerism and El Greco. When the current reorganization is completed the Spanish School will be displayed in the Pavillon des États.

A GREEK IN SPAIN
Domenico Theotocopoulos called El Greco (1541–1614), a native of Crete, moved to Toledo at the end of the 16th century. Trained in Italy by the Mannerists he was the painter of agony and ecstasy, sinuous line and extreme austerity of color as exemplified by his *Christ on the Cross Adored by Donors* (left).

THE MARTYRDOM OF SAINT GEORGE
The *Flagellation of Saint George* (above) is one of four paintings by Bernardo Martorell (c. 1427–52) which formed the side panels of an altarpiece centered on a portrayal of *Saint George and the Dragon*.

THE RIGOR OF ZURBARÁN
Francesco de Zurbarán (1598–1664) painted a four-part series on the life of Saint Bonaventura, the moral reformer of the Franciscan order. Two of these pictures are in the Louvre, among them *Saint Bonaventura on His Deathbed* (right). Austerity and spirituality characterize this "Caravaggesque" painter.

THE 17TH CENTURY IN SPAIN
Jusepe de Ribera (1591–1652) and Bartolomé Esteban Murillo (1618–82) were among the greatest painters of their age. Influenced by Caravaggio and Flemish painters their works have an astonishing realism which shows a darker aspect of the Spanish Golden Age. See Ribera's *Club-footed Boy* (1642, left) and Murillo's *Young Beggar* (above).

THE CARLOS DE BEISTEGUI COLLECTION
This rich collection was bequeathed to the Louvre in 1942 and is displayed in the Sully Wing. It includes a number of masterpieces of European painting, among them the portrait of the *Contessa del Carpio*, Marquesa de la Solana (above), by Francisco de Goya y Lucientes (1746–1828), the elegant and serious portraitist of the king and Madrid aristocracy.

▲ ENGLAND AND GERMANY: 18TH AND 19TH CENTURIES

Lady Macbeth Sleepwalking (1784) by Henry Fuseli (1741–1825).

The galleries of German and English painting will be adjacent to the Northern schools of painting in the future westward extension of the Richelieu wing. These works illustrate English 18th-century portraiture, with fine examples by Thomas Gainsborough and Sir Thomas Lawrence, and the development of Romanticism in Germany and England in the canvases of Fuseli, Friedrich and Turner.

ROMANTICISM
The leader of the Romantic movement in German painting was Caspar David Friedrich. His *Tree of Crows* (left) shows a leafless oak which grows on the burial mound of a forgotten hero, a symbol of the vanity of human pretensions picked at by the crows. Even so, the light in the background lends an aura of hope.

ENGLISH PORTRAITS
Conversation in a Park (below) by Thomas Gainsborough, similar to the *fêtes galantes* of Watteau, shows the painter and his wife in a park in the year of their marriage (1742). The temple in the background would seem to be that of Hymen. The carefully depicted park shows the painter's love of landscape. Sir Thomas Lawrence gained fame for portraits such as *Mr and Mrs Julius Angerstein* (1792, below). Angerstein, art-lover and friend of Lawrence who did several portraits of him, was also one of the founders of Lloyds, the marine insurance company.

ITINERARIES AROUND THE LOUVRE QUARTER

▲ THE CARROUSEL

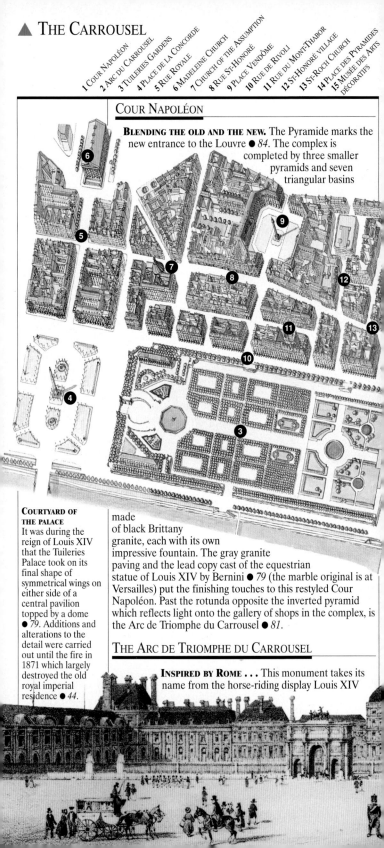

COUR NAPOLÉON

BLENDING THE OLD AND THE NEW. The Pyramide marks the new entrance to the Louvre ● *84*. The complex is completed by three smaller pyramids and seven triangular basins

COURTYARD OF THE PALACE
It was during the reign of Louis XIV that the Tuileries Palace took on its final shape of symmetrical wings on either side of a central pavilion topped by a dome ● *79*. Additions and alterations to the detail were carried out until the fire in 1871 which largely destroyed the old royal imperial residence ● *44*.

made of black Brittany granite, each with its own impressive fountain. The gray granite paving and the lead copy cast of the equestrian statue of Louis XIV by Bernini ● *79* (the marble original is at Versailles) put the finishing touches to this restyled Cour Napoléon. Past the rotunda opposite the inverted pyramid which reflects light onto the gallery of shops in the complex, is the Arc de Triomphe du Carrousel ● *81*.

THE ARC DE TRIOMPHE DU CARROUSEL

INSPIRED BY ROME . . . This monument takes its name from the horse-riding display Louis XIV

organized in 1662 ● *52* on the parade ground which had previously been the site of the Tuileries' old private garden. The architects Charles Percier and Pierre-François-Léonard Fontaine drew their inspiration for this monumental entrance to the Tuileries Palace courtyard from the Arch of Septimius Severus in Rome. This splendid example of Empire architecture built between 1806 and 1808 is flanked by eight Corinthian columns of red and white marble from the Languedoc. Six marble bas-reliefs depict victories by Napoleon. Over the cornices the arch is topped by eight soldiers dressed in the uniform of Napoleon's Grande Armée.

... WITH CONTRIBUTIONS FROM VENICE. A chariot driven by *Victory* and *Peace* bearing the *Emperor Napoleon I* was intended to crown the arch. The sculptor Frédéric Lemot carved the three figures, but the emperor vetoed the plan to erect the statue. The four antique gilded bronze horses on the Basilica of San Marco in Venice removed in 1797 as spoils of war, were then hitched to the chariot ● *40*. The horses were handed back in 1815 and it was not until 1827 that the chariot in place today was rebuilt from a design by Percier with a copy of the famous chariot and four

horses, along with a figure of the Restoration by Bosio. On both sides of the arch on tall pedestals are the stone statues of *History* (on the left) and *France Triumphant* (on the right), carved in 1814 by Antoine Gérard. From the arch looking north can be seen the façade of alternating pilasters and pediments which Percier and Fontaine began to build in 1806, and the wing rebuilt by Lefuel in 1875 to match the one on the south side put up some ten years earlier. The Tuileries Palace stood between the Pavillon de Marsan to the north and the Pavillon de Flore to the south.

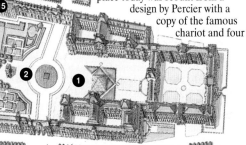

NAPOLEONIC POMP
To win over the masses who liked pomp and ceremonial, Napoleon reintroduced the splendors of the court of the Ancien Régime. The new dynasty set about refurbishing the decoration and furniture in the imperial residences. In this scene painted by Fontaine, Napoleon and the Empress Marie-Louise receive the homage of their courtiers on the day after their wedding in 1810 in the king's chamber where Louis XIV granted his audiences. This same chamber was used to lay out the body of France's last king, Louis XVIII, who had died in the Tuileries Palace. The painted decoration on the ceiling dates from the 17th century.

PARADES AND PROPAGANDA
Parisians were deeply impressed with uniforms and the emperor entertained them with numerous military parades, using uniforms as valuable propaganda.

THE TUILERIES PALACE

A COUNTRY RESIDENCE. Catherine de' Medici commissioned Philibert Delorme to build a country residence on land occupied by a sewage outlet and factories producing tiles and bricks from the clay on the banks of the Seine. Work on the palace began in 1564. Between 1659 and 1666 Louis Le Vau completed the palace, preserving the original proportions between the main pavilions and the wings. The interior has undergone constant alterations over the centuries. The theater known as the Salle des Machines was built in 1659 and housed the first performance of an opera in France; in 1793 it was rebuilt as a meeting chamber for the Convention ● *39.*

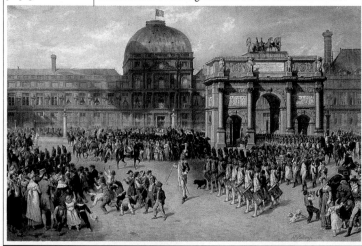

SYMBOL OF THE MONARCHY. The palace was burned down by the Commune in May 1781 and stayed in ruins until 1883. Several plans for its restoration were drawn up but in spite of the sound state of the shell of the building, the Republic decided to get rid of this reminder of the monarchy for political reasons, destroying the "grand design" perfected by Napoleon III. The stone remains are scattered as far away as Saint-Raphäel, Corsica and Bulgaria. Bits of stone were even cut up into paperweights and given away to subscribers to the *Figaro* newspaper.

VIEW TOWARD THE ÉTOILE. From the terrace spanning the Général-Lemonnier underpass the eye stretches to the Arc de Triomphe at the Place de l'Étoile and beyond that to the Défense. Two enormous urns mark the entrance to the Tuileries Gardens.

THE TUILERIES GARDENS

CATHERINE DE' MEDICI'S GARDEN. Covering some seventy acres, the Tuileries offer long walks within a formally planted garden setting right in the heart of the most historic part of Paris. The enclosed gardens of Catherine de' Medici, separated from the palace by a public pathway, consisted of elaborate Italian-style flower-beds with basins, statues and pavilions. Recent excavations in the Carrousel courtyard have uncovered remains of the kiln used by Bernard de Palissy as well as certain items of enameled terracotta from a rustic grotto used to decorate the garden ● 75 and ▲ 205. Nature was the theme of the decoration which featured various types of moss and water plants, frogs, serpents and tortoises.

Henri IV planted mulberry trees for his silkworms on the side of what is today the Rue de Rivoli and built silkworm breeding houses in the Orangerie. When the king was not there, the gardens were opened to the public.

A MASTERPIECE BY LE NÔTRE. In 1664 on the site of this first garden, André Le Nôtre designed an open garden running east to west ● 79. The main features of his classical layout can still to be seen today. Bordered to the north along the Rue de Rivoli by the Terrasse des Feuillants and to the south, facing the Seine by the riverbank terrace, the garden is laid out in three main sections. On the east side separated by a ditch are the private gardens of Louis-Philippe and Napoleon III, decorated with two symmetrical basins, then the Grand Carré where flower-beds surround the large round basin on which children hire and sail model boats in summer. The second section

THE GRAND STAIRCASE
Built by Fontaine in 1837, this staircase escaped the ravages of the great fire and, in spite of the narrow stairwell, looked imposing thanks to its three landings and connecting Corinthian columns.

CREATING A THROUGHWAY
André Le Nôtre (bust on left) was the amiable creative spirit behind the plan for a major east-west axis which thereafter decided the planning format for the extension toward the west of Paris. Currently there is a plan which aims to double this major route, extending it beyond the terrace of the Château of St-Germain-en-Laye.

includes the large shaded area (Grand Couvert) thickly
wooded with irregular rows of chestnut and lime trees around
the lawns. The third section is on the west side from the large
octagonal basin right up to the railings on the Concorde side
and includes two semicircular walkways leading up to the
Octagone where splendid views can be had from the terraces.
PLEASURE GARDEN. During the Ancien Régime the Tuileries
Gardens were the most colorful walk in Paris but also a mecca
for prostitutes and clandestine male encounters. Decorated
with a constantly changing array of designs fashioned out of
wood, plaster and painted canvas, and lit with lanterns and
firework displays, it was used as a venue for welcoming
dignitaries and for holding splendid receptions. During the
Revolution the flower-beds just missed being turned into
vegetable patches but the plan was never put into operation.
In 1794 Jean-Jacques Rousseau's ashes were kept on a small
island built in the middle of the large basin for a short time
before finally being taken to the Panthéon.
FLAVOR OF THE SECOND EMPIRE. A pavilion was built during
the Second Empire on both the esplanades which form the
western boundary to the gardens on the Place de la Concorde.
To the south, the Orangerie was built (1853) which today
houses the Walter Guillaume collection of Impressionist
paintings and the *Water Lilies* by Claude Monet; to the north
is the Jeu de Paume (1861), once the museum of Impressionist

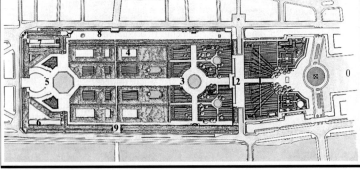

painting (1958–91); it was redesigned in 1991 by Antoine Stinco to house exhibitions of work from the last thirty years.

OPEN-AIR MUSEUM. A large number of sculptures can be seen in the Tuileries Gardens. From the Ancien Régime right up to the 1980's new works have been continuously added. The variety of the pieces covering four centuries of creative output has made this collection into a veritable open-air museum of sculpture.

A NEW LIFE. Because of the dilapidated state of the Tuileries and Carrousel Gardens, the Louvre was given the task in 1989 of carrying out a complete renovation program. After an international competition, the designs submitted by Jacques Wirtz for the Carrousel Gardens and Pascal Cribier, Louis Bénech and François Roubaud for the Tuileries were approved. Restoration work began in 1991 and is due for completion in 1995. The aim of this huge undertaking is to revive and give meaning to the gardens' history – the main avenues, the water basins and statues – while introducing contemporary ideas of landscaping. There is a plan to introduce a wider variety of plants as well as more recreation and refreshment facilities with tearooms and play areas.

MERCURY AND FAME. From the Place de la Concorde is a view of one of the finest pieces of urban design and planning in the world. Above the gate on either side stand the equestrian statues of *Mercury* and *Fame* by Coysevox who originally designed them for the Château de Marly. They were replaced in 1986 by copies ▲ 188.

ON THE TERRACE DE FEUILLANTS
The new beds (above) bring a contemporary note to these gardens whose layout had not been altered for a long time and which had become somewhat neglected. At the beginning of the last century, tubs of orange trees set off the Terrace des Feuillants (left) beautifully.

PLACE DE LOUIS XV

PLACE ROYALE. The city of Paris wanted to contruct a square bearing the name of Louis XV. The king, mindful of financial problems, made a gift of a piece of land outside the capital and his architect Jacques-Ange Gabriel conceived this square as a wide open four-sided shape like the square in front of a palace surrounded by ditches. To the north (on the Rue Royale side) he drew his inspiration for the two palaces with their Corinthian colonnades built between 1757 and 1770, from the Colonnade du Louvre ● 78. At the intersection of these two perpendicular axes of the square was placed the equestrian statue of Louis XV begun by Edme Bouchardon and finished by Jean-Baptiste Pigalle. In 1792 the statue was melted down (only the right hand survives and is on display in the Louvre) and the square, renamed the Place de la Révolution, was the setting for executions including those of Louis XVI and Robespierre.

PAVILLON DE L'ORANGERIE
Built during the Second Empire, it houses Impressionist paintings which complement the collections in the nearby Musée d'Orsay on the Left Bank.

EXORCIZING THE PAST. First given the name Concorde in 1795, under the July monarchy this name was fixed once and for all. As part of his policy of reconciliation Louis-Philippe decided to redesign the square in 1835 in order to remove the political implications and symbolic significance this square held for the opposing parties. The architect Jacques-Ignace Hittorff gave it the character of a central square with two huge fountains and eighteen raised gilt-painted decorative lampposts. He placed allegorical statues of the main towns in France as lookouts in the ditches. The Strasbourg statue carved by

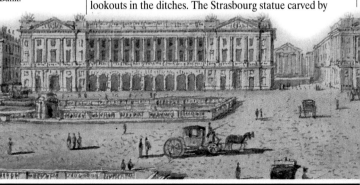

James Pradier has the features of Juliette Drouet, muse and mistress of Victor Hugo; from 1870 to 1914 the statue was revered as a place of patriotic pilgrimage and was draped in black.

A 3300-YEAR-OLD OBELISK AT THE CENTER. In 1836 no less than 200,000 spectators watched the obelisk from the Temple of Amun in Luxor being erected. These very complex operations are described on the base of this monolithic structure which is over 3300 years old and weighs 220 tons. The square is used for national celebrations and military parades and in 1934 also witnessed the bloody riots which almost brought down the Third Republic.

TO THE WEST, THE MARLY HORSES. The entrance to the Champs-Elysées has been guarded since 1795 by two *Horses Restrained by Grooms*. The original works created by Guillaume Coustou came from the drinking-pond at Marly near Versailles, and were replaced in 1984 by copies; the originals are in the Louvre ▲ *188*.

TO THE SOUTH, THE PONT DE LA CONCORDE. Built in 1791 partly from stones of the demolished Bastille, the width of the bridge was more than doubled in 1931. It leads to the Palais Bourbon on the Left Bank, whose façade in the style of an ancient temple, dates from the First Empire and echos the front of the Madeleine Church.

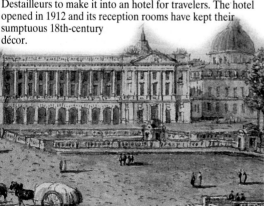

TO THE NORTH, TWO COLONNADED PALACES. These palaces were initially intended as residences for special ambassadors. The palace on the right was used as a depository for royal furniture and today is the headquarters of the French Naval Ministry. The one on the left was quickly let to members of the aristocracy, and part of it has now become one of the capital's luxury hotels. The company which acquired the *Hôtel de Crillon* in 1907 (it had previously been a private residence), asked the fashionable architect Walter Destailleurs to make it into an hotel for travelers. The hotel opened in 1912 and its reception rooms have kept their sumptuous 18th-century décor.

THE SENTRIES ON THE PLACE DE LA CONCORDE
The architect Hittorff borrowed from Gabriel the idea of erecting this series of statues of women symbolizing the major towns in France: Lyons and Marseilles, Bordeaux and Nantes, Rouen and Brest, Lille and Strasbourg (above).

Louis XV passing in front of his own equestrian statue (left).

MARLY HORSES
At the instigation of the painter Jacques-Louis David, the Marly *Horses* by Guillaume Coustou have stood over the entrance to the Champs-Élysées on the west side of the Place de la Concorde since 1795.

On either side of the palaces are two mansions
set well back: the one on the left, built in
the 1930's was modeled on the one on the
right which belonged to Prince Talleyrand.
Both buildings house the US diplomatic
and consular offices. Go north up the
Rue Royale.

AROUND THE RUE ROYALE

CHURCH OF THE ASSUMPTION
Crowned by a dome, the church is the last remnant of a convent of Augustinian nuns. On the site of the convent today stands the Audit Office. At the apex of the coffered dome is the *Assumption of the Virgin* by Charles de La Fosse (1676). It is the only piece of original decoration left since all the rest was either destroyed or scattered during the Revolution.

RUE ROYALE. From 1758 onward this prestigious
thoroughfare was lined with identically fronted mansions
following a design proposed by Jacques-Ange Gabriel to keep
the harmony of the Place de la Concorde. The ground was the
subject of speculation on the part of architects like Louis Le
Tellier and Étienne-Louis Boullée. Some of the buildings have
kept their neoclassical interiors from the late 18th century but
since companies use them as offices today, it is difficult to
visit them. Some of the world's leading names, however, still
carry on business in this street including Christofle the
silversmiths, the crystal houses of St-Louis and Lalique,
Lachaume the florists and that world-famous restaurant
Maxim's, whose windows and Art Nouveau interior date from
1899. The Ladurée tearooms at no. 16 which opened in 1862
has a 1890's décor and the reputation for fine macaroons.

**THE MADELEINE CHURCH – TO THE GLORY OF NAPOLEON'S
GRANDE ARMÉE.** Recently cleaned and restored, it is
impossible not to look in closer detail at
the imposing façade of the Madeleine
sitting at the end of the Rue Royale with
all the air of an ancient temple. Building
was begun in 1764 but the church
remained unfinished for some time. In
1806 the church was dedicated to the
glory of the Grande Armée and was
finally finished in 1842 by Vignon the
last architect to work on it. In the
triangular pediment, there is a *Last
Judgement* by Philippe-Henri Lemaire.

RUE ST-HONORÉ. To the right take the Rue St-Honoré, the
only road which cuts across the Rue Royale. Until the Rue de

Rivoli was opened at the beginning of the 19th century, it was the only main east-west thoroughfare in Paris. Right up to the Place Vendôme there are numerous shops selling antique jewelry. At the first crossroads on the right, the Rue St-Florentin contains fine buildings which as far as the Place de la Concorde, make up a very impressive collection of urban architecture. At no. 263 bis a square opens up with the Church of Our Lady of the Assumption.

NOTRE-DAME DE L'ASSOMPTION. The church and its convent were the headquarters of the order of the Sisters of the Assumption (Dames de l'Assomption) known as the Nouvelles Haudriettes. It was built between 1670 and 1676 by the painter and architect Charles Errard who was director of the brand new Académie de France in Rome. The rotunda with its porticoes takes its inspiration from the Pantheon in Rome; the lack of symmetry might be attributable to the clumsy interpretation of the plans by the builder while the architect was away. Inside the dome is an *Assumption* painted by Charles de La Fosse (1676). Since 1850 it has been the parish church of the Polish community in Paris.

RUE CAMBON. On both sides of the Rue St-Honoré, the Rue Cambon is lined with buildings from the 18th and 19th centuries; banks and large business concerns, the offices of the Ministry of Justice and an annexe to the Ritz hotel. Rue Cambon owes its world-wide renown to the boutique opened at nos. 29–31 in the 1930's by Coco Chanel which still houses the famous couture house. Continue along the Rue St-Honoré as far as nos. 362–4. It was the architect Ventre who in 1934 designed the buildings whose private courtyard is used as a public walkway during the day. The whole is characteristic of the neoclassical revival of the inter-war period with its bas-reliefs and stylized capitals. The passage leads to the Place Vendôme.

LUXURY SHOPS
Toward the west end of the Rue du Faubourg-St-Honoré are the great names of haute couture and their boutiques ● *54* (Lanvin); on the Rue St-Honoré are jewelers, fine leather workers and perfumiers (Guerlain); on the Rue Royale are crystal and porcelain (Christofle, Lalique, St-Louis). The house of Chanel on Rue Cambon has kept its mirrored staircase designed by an exiled Russian grand duke and the apartment with the Coromandel lacquered screens belonging to Coco Chanel, who preferred to live in the Ritz hotel. On the Rue Royale is Lachaume the florists, while Maxim's restaurant maintains the traditions and pleasures of the Belle Époque. This restaurant founded in 1891 is named after the person who created it and anglicized it to follow fashion. An identical copy of the original Paris décor can be found in an offshoot of the Paris restaurant – in Beijing.

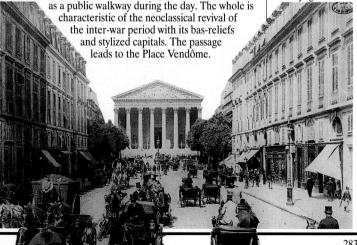

283

PLACE VENDÔME

AN ENCLOSED SALON. The old Louis-le-Grand square occupies the site of the mansion belonging to the Duke of Vendôme. Minister Louvois initially planned a huge center for institutions like the Académies or the Mint. In 1686 Jules Hardouin-Mansart designed a square with three sides, the fourth being left open on the south side. To increase the area to be built on, the square gradually became octagonal from 1699 ● 78, closed and completed with its two openings facing the convents of the Capucines and the Feuillants which have now been replaced respectively by the Rue de la Paix and the Rue de Castiglione. Designed as a sort of enclosed salon the square has arched windows with fantasy stone figure decoration at ground level, two upper stories joined by Corinthian pilasters and large attics with dormer windows. The sides are cut at angles and a forward section with a triangular pediment supported by columns is used to ornament the center of each of the main sides.

THE VENDÔME COLUMN. The equestrian statue of Louis XIV dressed as a Roman emperor was designed by Girardon who began work on it in 1699 and it was sent for casting in 1792. Napoleon gave orders for it to be replaced by a monument to the glory of the victors of the Battle of Austerlitz. The architects Gondoin and Lepère, who based the design on Trajan's column in Rome put up the column between 1806 and 1810. It is made of stone, reaches a height of 145 feet and is covered with 425 bronze plaques weighing 251 tons altogether. These were made from the 1,250 pieces of artillery taken from the Austrians and Russians. The 850-feet bas-reliefs which rise in a spiral tell the story of 1805. Originally the statue of *Napoléon Imperator* made by Chaudet in 1810 sat at the top of the column, whereas the one currently there is a copy put up by Napoleon III in 1803. In 1871 under the Commune the pins were taken out of the column and it was knocked down at the instigation of the painter Gustave

HISTORIC IRONY
The seventy-six bronze bas-reliefs (above) curl round the central stone body which hides a staircase leading to a spectators' platform. Carved by thirty-two sculptors, they represent the victories of Napoleon over the Austrians. The monument was unveiled very discreetly in 1810 because the emperor had just married an Austrian ● 41. The parts damaged during the Commune were eventually recast. Ordered to pay the rebuilding costs from his own pocket, the painter Gustave Courbet was often caricatured as above: "Courbet sets about work on the Vendôme column himself so that he can employ one workman less. At least that's a little bit less to pay!"

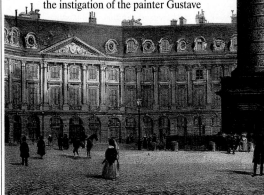

Courbet who called it *le mirliton* (carnival whistle). He was later made to rebuild it at his own expense ● *44*.

MECCA FOR JEWELRY. The public cannot see many of the

interiors of the magnificent houses all round the Place Vendôme which include the Chancery or Ministry of Justice at no. 13, the famous Ritz hotel at no. 15, the Evreux mansion at no. 19, where the Crédit Foncier has offices and which moreover owns much of the property on the Place. World-famous makers of luxury goods, particularly jewelry, are still based at Place Vendôme and to the north along the Rue de la Paix as far as the Place de l'Opéra. Since 1992, the square (700 feet long and 405 feet wide) has been paved with gray granite flagstones in the shape of a checkerboard. Stone or steel posts show the demarcation areas for automobiles and pedestrians.

DETOUR THROUGH NEOCLASSICISM. The sightseer can go straight down the Rue de Castiglione as far as the Rue de Rivoli or on the left, go along the Rue du Mont-Thabor with its rows of buildings whose strict neoclassical style is a feature of the Restoration period. At no. 6 a plaque recalls that the poet and writer Alfred de Musset died in this building in 1857. Turning right after that into the Rue d'Alger leads back to the Rue de Rivoli with, in the distance, the Hôtel de Ville to the left and the Place de la Concorde to the right.

RUE DE CASTIGLIONE. The street which opened in 1802, was formed from the old walkway linking the Rue St-Honoré to the Tuileries Gardens and separated the convents of the Feuillants and the Capucines. It took in a part of the room known as the Salle du Manège where the First Republic was proclaimed in 1792 ● *39*. Here are the same buildings with their arcaded open sidewalks as in the Rue de Rivoli. At no. 3, the Continental was one of Paris's first luxury hotels to offer all modern comforts. It was built in 1878 by the architect Henri Blondel for the Paris Universal Exhibition on the site of the Ministry of Finance which was burnt down under the Commune ● *44*. The reception rooms retain their rich Napoleon III décor; the Salles des Fêtes is a listed building.

RUE DE RIVOLI

A MODEL OF RESIDENTIAL PROPERTY. The Rue de Rivoli opened bit by bit between 1802 and 1835 from the Place de la Concorde to the Place du

ON THE PLACE VENDÔME
The top Parisian jewelers left the Palais-Royal after the July monarchy and set themselves up on the Place Vendôme and Rue de la Paix at the turn of the century. Behind the wonderful showcases and the luxurious shops themselves are workshops which carry on centuries-old traditions.

NOSTALGIC EMPRESS
The gilt bronze torchères of the Hôtel Continental were installed when the hotel was originally built. Even when she reached an advanced age, the Empress Eugénie came as an ordinary guest to the hotel to look down from the balcony of her bedroom onto the empty space left by the destruction of the Tuileries Palace.

MOSAIC ARCADES
Many of the walkways in the arcades of the Rue de Rivoli are decorated with mosaic medallions and arabesques, seen here at the corner of the Rue de Castiglione.

Palais-Royal and was intended to be used as a main east–west thoroughfare to complement the old Rue St-Honoré. The apartments, built only on the north side of the street facing the Tuileries and the Louvre, sit on top of colonnades designed by Percier and Fontaine ● *81*. The attics, rounded off in shape and made of zinc, were to become an architectural feature of residential apartments in Paris. Some of them have been heightened since then, breaking the line of the frontage. Between 1848 and 1850 the street was extended eastward to the Hôtel de Ville and then on into the Marais as far as the Rue St-Antoine, but with different façades.

ESSENTIAL STOPS ALONG THE WAY. Amidst the souvenir shops and travel agencies, is the Galignani bookstore at no. 224, the first English bookshop established on the Continent, in 1802. At no. 226 there is the Angelina tearoom (the old firm of Rumpelmeyer, founded in 1903) with its neo-Louis XVI white and gold décor. It is an institution among gourmands and is famous for its hot chocolate and its *Mont-Blanc* (whipped cream and chestnut purée).

HÔTEL MEURICE. At no. 228 the Hôtel Meurice, opened in 1907, has kept a magnificent series of 18th century-style reception rooms on the ground floor designed by Henri-Paul Nénot, architect of the new Sorbonne. At the time a sign of grand luxury was that each suite had its own private bathroom. The hotel was equipped with central heating and elevators designed to look like Marie-Antoinette's sedan chairs. The biggest novelty which brought it enormous success was its open-air roof garden restaurant with its incomparable view of the Tuileries Gardens and the Left Bank. The Meurice was a favorite with kings and princes between the two world wars and on June 14, 1940 was requisitioned to provide headquarters for the *Gross Paris*, the German chiefs of staff who commanded Paris.

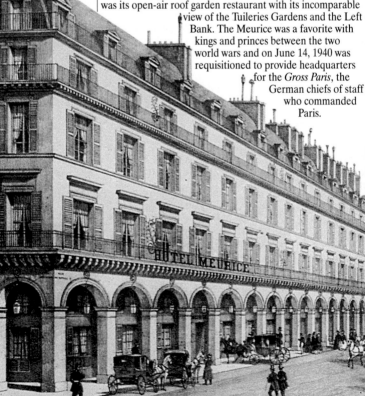

VILLAGE ST-HONORÉ. Turning left into the Rue du 29-Juillet, (so named after the last of the three days in July 1830 known as *Les Trois Glorieuses*) and then into the Rue du Marché-St-Honoré, the visitor goes into a "village" which has managed to maintain its typical character with its little shops and traditional grocery stores. On the Place du Marché-St-Honoré, a multi-level garage and fire station which in the 1950's replaced the old covered market, are due to be replaced by a glass shopping arcade and office complex designed by Ricardo Bofill, the Catalan architect who champions an up-dated version of neoclassicism. All round the square with its modest façades – witnesses to domestic architecture in the 18th

468. - PARIS. - Le Marché St-Honoré. - G. I.

century – have sprouted various restaurants (especially Japanese) and some fashion houses like Jean-Charles de Castelbajac and Philippe Model. On the corner of the Rue St-Hyacinthe, the Rubis is an attractive wine bar. Return to the Rue St-Honoré by way of Rue de La Sourdière which has kept something of the flavor of Paris during the Ancien Régime.

CHURCH OF ST-ROCH

PARISH CHURCH OF THE TUILERIES. A church was first built here at the end of the 16th century. In this area which owes its rise to the proximity of the Tuileries Palace, the church's reconstruction as one huge building was intended to mark its elevation to the status of parish church. Jacques Le Mercier, architect of the Sorbonne, drew up the plans but because of the lie of the land, was forced to change the positioning of the church; the chancel faces north rather than east as tradition normally dictates. Louis XIV laid the first stone in 1653. In 1690 the chancel, transept and nave were finished and in 1705 Jules Hardouin-Mansart was commissioned to complete the church. To the apse he added the Lady Chapel whose

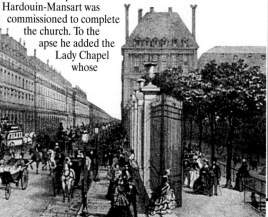

▲ St-Roch to the Place des Pyramides

1ᵉʳ ARR.

RUE
Sᵗ ROCH

**A CHURCH WORTHY
OF THE LOUVRE**
The carved classical
façade of the church
of St-Roch, destroyed
at the time of the
Revolution, was
partly restored
between 1873 and
1943. The interior of
the church is a
veritable museum of
17th- and 18th-
century religious and
funerary sculpture
from churches that no
longer exist. The
huge chancel has four
barrel-vaulted bays
with lunettes richly
decorated in gilt.
These have recently
been cleaned. At the
rear the Lady Chapel
has a dome in which
there is an
Assumption painted
in 1756, while a *God*

in Majesty, inspired by
St Peter's in Rome
decorates the vault
behind the huge altar
and completes the
dramatic visual effect.

elliptical nave is surrounded by an ambulatory; a series of
rather daring arches and a large amount of light give a
definitely theatrical feel to the whole structure. In 1722 the
financier John Law, inventor of the banking and financial
system which proved a resounding failure, gave 100,000 livres
to finish the nave.

BAROQUE AND CLASSICAL FAÇADE. Robert de Cotte drew up
designs for the main façade onto the Rue St-Honoré which
was built between 1738 and 1739 ● *80*.
This façade has two levels with a set of
Doric columns on the lower and
Corinthian pillars with wide entablatures
on the upper; it combines the principles
of the Baroque with the heavier features
of French classical architecture.

**JEAN-BAPTISTE MARDUEL, CURATE OF
ST-ROCH.** During the second half of the
18th century, Fr. Jean-Baptiste Marduel
undertook a large-scale program to
enrich the church. In 1754 Étienne-Louis
Boullée built a Chapel of the Crucifixion
onto the north side which extends and
connects to the interior of the church.
In 1756 Jean-Baptiste Pierre painted an
Assumption on the dome of the Lady
Chapel. The sculptor Étienne-Maurice
Falconet decorated the gallery behind the
altar in the Lady Chapel with a *God in
Majesty* inspired by Bernini's depiction of
the same subject in St Peter's in Rome. The priest also had a
pulpit built in 1758 and the transept was decorated with a
series of paintings and sculptures from the best artists of the
day which were completed in 1767. During this period Boullée
redesigned the altars and reredos at either end of the transept.

MUSEUM OF RELIGIOUS ART. St-Roch houses treasures which
make it a veritable museum of sacred art between the 17th
and 19th centuries; some of these come from buildings
previously destroyed and were brought here. A number of
artists who were parishioners are buried here; in the chapels
can be seen busts of *Mignard* by Lemoyne and of *Le Nôtre* by
Antoine Coysevox. The church itself and St-Sulpice on the
Left Bank are the finest extant examples of a major parish
church built in the classical style.

UNDER ATTACK FROM NAPOLEON. The church is also famous for having undergone very heavy cannon and gunfire attack by order of Bonaparte on September 5, 1795. He was leading forces of the Convention whose aim was to dislodge the royalist rioters who had made it their stronghold. Continue along the Rue St-Honoré as far as the Rue des Pyramides which leads onto the square of the same name to the right.

PLACE DES PYRAMIDES

FROM SIEGE TO BATTLE. The square, opened in 1802 on the site of the royal mansion of the Grandes-Écuries, was called the Place de Rivoli until 1932. It echoes the theme of arcaded houses and identical frontages of the Rue de Rivoli. In the middle stands the gilt bronze statue of Joan of Arc by Emmanuel Frémiet. The place where the statue stands is the spot on which Joan is alleged to have been wounded during the fruitless siege of Paris. The Hôtel Régina, at no. 2, has kept the décor of the reception rooms as designed by the architect Armand Sibien; in the entrance lobby there are clock faces showing the time in the world's major capital cities. From the back of the square runs the Rue des Pyramides which opened in 1802 as far as the Rue St-Honoré and extended in 1877 as far as the Avenue de l'Opéra. Its name recalls the victory Napoleon won in Egypt in 1798 ▲ *148*. The Administration of France's museums (DMF) has its headquarters in the old annexe of the Hôtel Régina. Cross the Rue de Rivoli after that to reach the Musée des Arts Décoratifs ▲ *290*, the second of the two major museums housed in the Louvre, in the Marsan pavilion and wing.

JOAN OF ARC
The statue of Joan of Arc by the sculptor Emmanuel Frémiet was erected in 1874. Since then leagues, groups and parties involved in nationalist activities have used it for march pasts. The saint represented resistance to the enemy and symbolized the spirit of revenge after the loss of Alsace-Lorraine (1870). The original gilding has been restored and its base still has hooks for hanging commemorative wreaths.

HÔTEL RÉGINA
This hotel which opened in 1903 was one of the few decorated in Art Nouveau style; the smart set usually preferred "Louis-style" decoration.

PAVILLON DE MARSAN
This pavilion was rebuilt from 1874 onward by the architect Lefuel who used a modern metal frame for the roof. Its monumental pediments are decorated with allegorical subjects.

▲ MUSÉE DES ARTS DÉCORATIFS

Founded after the Universal Exhibitions in the 19th century, the Musée des Arts Décoratifs has brought together various collections, series of objects and masterpieces in a wing of the Louvre. The museum is devoted to the industries involved in art, crafts and design. It is a reminder of decorative arts from the Middle Ages to our own day but there is also a place for contemporary works. The collections of furniture, *objets d'art*, paintings and drawings complement those in the Louvre since they are set up in a completely different sort of museum environment based on a chronological presentation of the pieces on display.

AN IMMENSE NAVE . . .
The museum's exhibition areas mainly open out from the large central hall of the Louvre's Marsan wing. Built by Gaston Redon it has housed the museum since 1905.

. . . UNDER A GLASS ROOF
The administration, the Departement of Drawings and the Musée de la Publicité are on the upper floors which were reorganized in 1985. The Library is on the ground floor.

THEMATIC DISPLAYS
The collections are displayed thematically: above, the room devoted to the Middle Ages. Bequests have played an important part; among the most significant benefactors were Émile Peyre, Mlle Grandjean and the Marquise Arconati-Visconti.

18TH-CENTURY POMP
The Salon Barriol contains, along with the Louvre and the Musée Nissim-de-Camondo (part of the Musée des Arts Décoratifs), one of the finest collections of Louis XVI furnishings including wood paneling, furniture, *objets d'art*, silks, bronzes and chandeliers.

ON PAPER TOO . . .
The museum conserves works of reference on the beginning of the 19th century, the souvenirs of daily life and the plans of designers of everyday objects such as cups (above). An Empire-style traveling case made by Napoleon I's silversmith Biennais can be seen here (left) ▲ 209.

JEANNE LANVIN AT THE MUSEUM

At the time of the demolition of the grand couturier's townhouse ● 54 in the Marais, Prince Louis de Polignac donated to the museum the furniture and decorative schemes used in the private apartments, which had been commissioned from Armand Rateau around 1920. The boudoir (above) and the bathroom (below left) are Art Deco masterpieces and rank among the finest exhibits in the Musée des Arts Décoratifs.

THE 1900 EXHIBITION

The pavilion designed by Georges Hoenstchel using wood as its theme has been reconstructed. Its display cases contain fine glass, porcelain and metalware from the 1900's.

ART DECO TREASURES

Jeanne Lanvin's reconstructed bathroom shares center stage with works by Lalique, Gallé, Pierre Chareau, Charlotte Perriand, not to mention Percier and Fontaine, Delacroix, Guimard and a marvelous collection of old toys.

CONTEMPORARY WORKS

The museum is a real treasure-house of contemporary furniture unique in France. The collection is constantly enriched. Above can be seen examples of chairs from 1980 to 1985, a theme which has been taken up by numerous other museums.

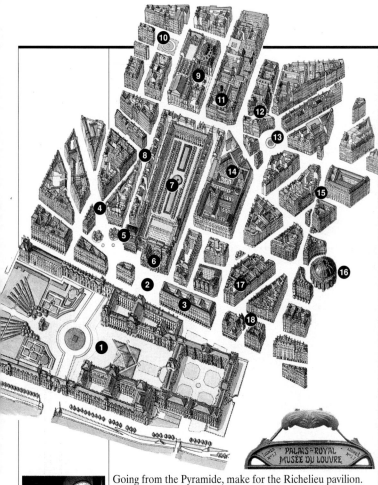

**FROM PALACE
TO TOWN**
Cour Marly and the
Pyramide seen from
the Richelieu passage.

Going from the Pyramide, make for the Richelieu pavilion.
At the entrance to the passage, on the left is the Café Marly,
whose Second Empire décor sits well with contemporary
furniture and evokes literary café society of the past. From
the second room there is a view down onto the Cour Marly.
PASSAGE RICHELIEU. The eye is drawn by both the richness of
the decorative carvings in the vaults and the side bays opening
up onto the Cours Marly and Puget ▲ *188*. When the Ministry
of Finance took over this part of the Louvre, the Richelieu
passage was reserved for the exclusive use of the minister and
the two open-air courtyards were jam-packed with official
cars. Cross the Rue de Rivoli to get back to the Place du
Palais-Royal. The Metro station entrance with its cast-iron
Art Nouveau decoration is one of eighty-six public restrooms
still surviving from the 141 designed by Hector Guimard at
the beginning of the century. Today they are officially listed.

PLACE DU PALAIS-ROYAL

Originally built in 1648 the square was enlarged several times
during the 18th century and on the south side even featured a
decorative water tower which ironically burnt down during
the 1848 Revolution. It was not until the Second Empire,
however, that it acquired the appearance it has today. It owes

its name to the Palais-Royal whose entrance is marked by the Cour de l'Horloge. The façade of the Palais-Royal built in 1763 by Moreau-Desproux was rebuilt to its original design after the devastation caused by the Commune ● *44*. To the right on the corner of the Rue de Valois and the Rue St-Honoré a plaque commemorates the site of the Petit-Cardinal theater where Molière and

THE SQUARE IN 1910
The Hôtel du Louvre and the Théâtre-Français from left to right and the Cour de l'Horloge on the right which leads to the Palais-Royal, seat of the Conseil d'État.

his troupe of actors performed from 1661 onward. It was here on February 17, 1673 that Molière died while he was giving a performance of *Le Malade Imaginaire*. The Académie Royale de Musique then occupied the premises until 1780. On the east side of the square stands the Louvre des Antiquaires and on the west the Hôtel du Louvre. On the south the façade of the Louvre has a magnificent decorative sculpture with two pairs of caryatids supporting the front and several decorative symbols of imperial power.

THE LOUVRE DES ANTIQUAIRES. This collection of buildings bounded by the Rue de Rivoli, the Rue Marengo, the Rue du Faubourg-St-Honoré and the Place du Palais-Royal belongs to a wealthy British post office pension fund and contains, apart from offices, three floors of antique shops which make up a commercial center unique in Europe. It is constructed along the same lines as the Rue de Rivoli with its arcaded freestone buildings as designed by Percier and Fontaine during the Empire. The brainchild of financier Émile Pereire, it initially housed the Grand Hôtel du Louvre which opened in 1855 for the first Universal Exhibition in Paris and subsequently, from 1878 onward, the large stores known as the Grands Magasins du Louvre. As early as the first decade of this century, they were the first shops to put up electric Christmas and New Year decorations. One of the founders of this temple to trading, Alfred Chauchard, donated his collection of paintings including Millet's *Angelus* to the Louvre .

The Metro station entrance designed by Hector Guimard.

HÔTEL DU LOUVRE. On the left of the square turn west and go along the side of the Hôtel du Louvre. On the ground floor, looking onto the Place Colette, are the Delamain bookstore and the Civette tobacco shop. At the crossroads, looking right to the far end of the Avenue de l'Opéra designed by Haussmann, can be seen the Palais Garnier, a perfect example of the Napoleon III style of architecture. It was built between 1862 and 1875 by Charles Garnier and until recently was the main home of the Paris Opéra ● *83*.

ORATOIRE DU PRINCE NAPOLÉON. Cross over the Rue St-Honoré and

TEMPLE OF BUSINESS
The Louvre des Antiquaires (above) occupies buildings which were once the Grands Magasins du Louvre (below).

THE THÉÂTRE-FRANÇAIS
A large chandelier with fifty oil lamps lit the sumptuous interior of the theater designed by Victor Louis. The current decoration formed part of the reconstruction carried out by Julien Guadet after the fire in 1900.

THE BUREN COLUMNS
The black and white columns in the ceremonial courtyard of the Palais-Royal. Shown at night (below) lit from below by illuminated underground water and colored lamps; (below that) the columns by day.

pass beneath the arcades of the Comédie-Française to join the Nemours passage. The two first-floor windows on the left are decorated with stained glass; this is the neo-Gothic oratory of the emperor's cousin, Prince Napoleon (1822–91) and his wife Princess Marie-Clotilde de Savoie who took up residence in the Palais-Royal after their marriage in 1859.

THE PALAIS-ROYAL

THE DISSONANCE OF ANCIENT AND MODERN. The visitor comes out onto the ceremonial courtyard where there is series of black and white striped columns surrounded by a pattern of grilles through which can be seen an underground fountain. The whole is lit after dark by red and green lights. This contemporary work by Daniel Buren erected in 1986 gave rise to the same debate as the Pyramide by Pei ● 84.

The Galerie d'Orléans covered with its glass roof as it was last century.

THE PALAIS CARDINAL TO THE PALAIS-ROYAL. The façades of the buildings overlooking the ceremonial square reflect the complex history of the palace which was originally built in 1634 for Cardinal Richelieu by Jacques Le Mercier, the architect responsible for the Pavillon de l'Horloge at the Louvre ● 76. All that remains today is the Galerie des Proues on the east side where the maritime artefacts on display – rostrums, anchors, ropes and rigging – remind us that Richelieu was in charge of supervising navigation in 1626. It took the name of Palais-Royal in 1643 when Anne of Austria stayed there and in 1692 was given over to the exclusive use of the Orléans family who kept the whole property until 1848.

A CONTINUAL PROCESS OF EMBELLISHMENT. Louis XIV's brother, the Duke of Orléans and then his son the regent, commissioned the greatest artists of the day (architects Hardouin–Mansart, Antoine Lepautre and Gilles-Marie Oppenord and painters Noël and Antoine Coypel) to extend and make the palace more ornate. It was in his apartments that the Regent entertained his roué friends to grandiose supper parties which were the talk of the town. His son who succeeded him in 1723 retained the services of the cabinetmaker Cressent, the goldsmith Thomas Germain and the sculptor Slodtz. In the 1750's, Pierre Contant d'Ivry redesigned the apartments of the Duchess of Orléans. The elegant front pavilion with its wrought-iron balcony and façade looking out over the Rue de Valois dates from the period of these works.

REBUILDING. The fire at the Opéra on April 6, 1763 utterly destroyed the east wing of the palace and a part of the main building. The building was then completely rebuilt adjoining the Valois wing in 1770 by Pierre-Louis Moreau-Desproux, superintendent of buildings for the city of Paris. He also designed the new façade of the front courtyard on the Place du Palais-Royal. Contant d'Ivry rebuilt the frontage onto the ceremonial courtyard and decorated the new apartments. On the terraces stand four statues carved by Pajou (1766): *Military Talents*, *Prudence*, *Liberality* and the *Arts*.

THE COMÉDIE-FRANÇAISE AND THE GARDEN APARTMENTS. In 1780 the Duke of Orléans made a gift of the Palais-Royal to his son the Duke of Chartres, who for all his huge fortune was suffering from truly chronic debts. The area was short of places of entertainment after the fire at the Opéra de Moreau and the prince decided to build a theater west of his palace, which the Comédie-Française today uses as its base. The grounds surrounding the gardens were to provide the necessary space to extend the palace. Overseeing the work was put in the hands of the architect Victor Louis who had just finished the Grand Théâtre in Bordeaux. To give the gardens an attractive setting, he built sixty apartments for renting

THE ARCADES OF THE PALAIS-ROYAL
The arcades (bottom, in a model) were designed by Victor Louis with the intention of taking maximum advantage of the piece of land. From the Duke of Orléans to Louis-Philippe, they contained gaming rooms and brothels, cafés and cabaret halls to which tourists from all over Europe flocked in pursuit of pleasure, helped by numerous and very explicit guides. Shops selling fashionable clothes and novelty items lived side by side in the gallery (below, in a model), whose use of a multicolored decoration was inspired by antiquity.

between 1781 and 1784, occupying the space of three arcades. The uniform façades featuring large Corinthian pilasters, balustrades and decorative urns make up a total of 180 arched arcades on the ground floor, with a mezzanine level of galleries and boutiques, a floor of commemorative windows, another mezzanine and a top-floor attic ● *80*. Streets called after members of the Orléans family, Valois, Montpensier and Beaujolais, were later opened up around the outside perimeter to the great displeasure of the occupants in the apartments who had formerly enjoyed an uninterrupted view over the gardens. Between these and the ceremonial courtyard was built the Camp des Tartares, huge temporary wooden and glass galleries given over to boutiques. Gaming clubs and brothels proliferated in the atmosphere of the Palais-Royal which acquired an international reputation for debauchery. This promenade, the most popular in Paris, was also a meeting place for revolutionary activists up to 1794. **RESTORATION.** When he returned in 1815 Louis-Philippe Duke of Orléans, commissioned Fontaine to restore the palace. The architect added on the Galerie d'Orléans (1829–31) with a double portico separating it from the palace. During the inter-war years the gallery acquired its current layout and its two square basins were decorated in the early 1980's by steel spherical mobiles designed by Pol Bury.

THE MIDDAY CANNON SALUTE
The Palais-Royal's small cannon has recently been restored and tells Parisians the exact time.

The classic order of the galleries, and a chair designed by Wilmotte.

THE GARDENS IN THE PALAIS-ROYAL

The gardens of the Palais Cardinal were in their day the biggest private gardens in Paris. Le Nôtre began altering them in 1674 to please the distinguished people who often visited them. His nephew Desgots, the king's architect undertook the task again in 1730: trellises with architectural themes surrounded the gardens which were decorated with statues. A large circular pond was dug in the center and, for the first time ever, hoses were used to water the huge flower-beds which had been laid out.

A HAVEN IN THE CITY. Having only just escaped road-building plans at the beginning of the present century, the gardens whose rectangular shape covers a around 2½ square acres, offers a haven of peace in the center of town. Always

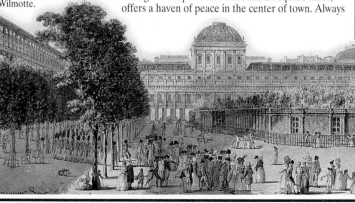

at the ready, facing the Galerie d'Orléans , the famous cannon gun has gone off at noon every day since 1786. Four double rows of lime trees trimmed into a sort of tent offer visitors shade during the summer. The metal seats available for the public to sit on were designed by Jean-Michel Wilmotte ● *64*. The two wide lawns on either side of the fountain have been newly planted with more colorful and attractive flower displays designed by landscape gardener Mark Rudkin. At night the galleries are closed to the public; only residents and owners have the key to the gates of this state-owned property.

THE GRAND VÉFOUR AND THE THÉÂTRE DU PALAIS-ROYAL. At the northern end of the garden in the Beaujolais gallery is one of the loveliest restaurants in Paris, the Grand Véfour. First called the Café de Chartres, it was opened in 1784 although the rich style of its decoration dates from the Restoration. Turn left in to the Rue de Montpensier and the Théâtre du Palais-Royal. Originally a puppet theater then a venue for fairground entertainment, it has been famous since it was rebuilt in 1830 for the light comedies that are put on there. Climb the steps of the Passage de Beaujolais to reach the Rue de Richelieu.

RUE DE RICHELIEU, A MEMORIAL TO MOLIÈRE. This road was opened by Cardinal Richelieu in 1634 in a straight north-south axis which was something new in Paris at the time. Keep to the left side of the street. At no. 37 the Molière fountain commemorates the great comic actor who died at what is today no. 40. The fountain was built in 1844 by public subscription and keeps alive the Parisian tradition of corner fountains set into houses. It was designed by Louis Visconti and decorated with an engraving of *Molière Seated* by Charles-Émile Seurre and of figures from *Serious Comedy* and *Light Comedy* by James Pradier. Go back along the Passage de Beaujolais and turn left toward the Rue Vivienne, crossing the Rue des Petits-Champs on the way. Go along the side of the garden railings to enter the Bibliothèque Nationale.

LE GRAND VÉFOUR
The old Café de Chartres which became the Véfour restaurant (above) at the beginning of the 19th century is famous for its beautiful painted panels fixed under glass. Café du Caveau at the time of the Revolution (left).

The metal fire escapes of the Théâtre du Palais-

Royal themselves form part of the decoration on the Rue de Montpensier.

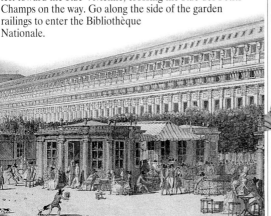

Colette and Jean Cocteau made the Palais-Royal a haunt for intellectuals right up to the 1950's.

The gourmet Grimod de La Reynière represented on a sign.

THE BIBLIOTHÈQUE NATIONALE

IN THE GARDENS. Set back and parallel with the street is the brick and stone building which formerly housed Cardinal Mazarin's treasures, displayed in two galleries sitting one on top of the other. Part of the original décor can still be seen in these galleries that are now used for temporary exhibitions. The statue of a man leaning forward at the bottom left is philosopher Jean-Paul Sartre. Go through the door on the right to the Mansart wing and reach the famous Salle de Lectures des Imprimés on the left.

ONE OF THE RICHEST LIBRARIES IN THE WORLD. First the Royal and then the Imperial Library, the Bibliothèque Nationale covers an area of approximately 20,000 sq. yards. It is one of the world's richest libraries and its treasures are spread over twelve departments including prints, manuscripts, engravings, maps and plans, music, medals, coins and antiques. Most of the collection is due to be transferred to what is to become the Bibliothèque de France being built by Dominique Perrault; the Bibliothèque Nationale will then become the Institut National des Arts.

THE SALLE DE LECTURES DES IMPRIMÉS. Set up in the Rue Richelieu in 1725, the library owes its basic structure to the architect Henri Labrouste. Its real gem is the reading room called the Salle de Lecture des Imprimés which can be seen through the glass door at the entrance. It opened in 1869 and can accommodate 360 people. Its rationalist architecture is shown in its nine metal domes, each crowned with a circular window and decorated with colored ceramic plaques set on eleven 30 feet-high slender cast-iron pillars. The walls covered in books on three-tiered shelving are decorated at their highest level with paintings and Sèvres medallions. The two caryatids at the back of the room stand guard at the entrance to the main repository. By crossing the main courtyard, access can be gained to the Square Louvois off the Rue de Richelieu, which occupies the site of the Opéra where the Duc de Berry was assassinated on February 13, 1820. He was second in line to the throne of France. Retrace the same walk to return to no. 2, rue Vivienne.

GALERIE COLBERT. This magnificent covered market, whose name reminds us that a private hotel on this spot was owned by Colbert, was designed in 1826 by the architect J. Billaud. The property company who commissioned it wanted to set it up as a rival to the adjacent Vivienne gallery and take advantage of the hustle and bustle of the nearby Palais-Royal. Today the complex houses annexes belonging to the Bibliothèque Nationale. Come out at no. 6, rue des Petits-Champs. On the opposite sidewalk the small passageway set at an angle to the Deux-Pavillons was arranged by the owner of the Galerie Vivienne in such a way as to waylay to his own advantage people coming from the Palais-Royal, in whose path lay the entrance to the Galerie Colbert. Turn left at no. 4, rue des Petits-Champs to turn into the Galerie Vivienne.

THE BIBLIOTHÈQUE NATIONALE Labrouste's rationalist architecture inside an historical exterior; the corner rotunda on the Rue des Petits-Champs (top) and the famous reading room (above). The Molière fountain (below) brightens up a congested part of town.

The Galerie Colbert with its columns of imitation marble and its neo-Pompeiian rotunda contains the statue of *Eurydice Being Bitten by a Serpent* (1822) by Charles Lebœuf-Nanteuil.

The Grand Café Colbert with its typical Paris brasserie décor is enobled by neoclassical friezes. The old bookstore in the passage links the Colbert and Vivienne galleries.

There is a restrained and yet bright quality to the various features of the Galerie Vivienne, making it an elegant setting for its luxury shops.

Marble, paintings, mahogany and bronze blend in the Galerie Véro-Dodat.

Notre-Dame-des-Victoires.

Statues of Louis XIV by Bosio (1822) and Desjardins (1686) demolished in 1792.

GALERIE VIVIENNE. This glass-roofed shopping arcade designed in 1823 for a Paris lawyer, was laid out by the architect François-Jean Delannoy in the neoclassical style. Wands of Hermes, anchors and cornucopias, the mottos of trade, are found around the windows set in a half-moon on the mezzanine level with goddesses and nymphs in the rotunda. The gallery's success was short-lived and it was nearly demolished in the middle of the 20th century. Today the Institut de France, which owns the gallery, has restored it to its original elegance. The bookstore specializing in antique books remains as it was at the beginning of the century. A perpendicular passageway leads to the Galerie Colbert. Returning to the Rue des Petits-Champs, take the small passage which comes out onto the Rue de La Banque. Go into the passage of the Petits-Pères.

NOTRE-DAME-DES-VICTOIRES

THE PETITS-PÈRES. The Place des Petits-Pères keeps alive the memory of the barefoot Augustinian monks or *petits pères*, whose Order was established in 1628 and whose monastery stood on this site until the Revolution. The buildings were destroyed in 1859 with the exception of the chapel which is now the parish church. Its dedication records Louis XIII's gratitude for his battle successes, particularly at La Rochelle. **A CENTURY OF WORK.** The architect Le Muet built the chancel between 1629 and 1632, Jacques Bruant the transept and the last bay of the nave between 1642 and 1666 and finally Sylvain Cartault crowned the whole building with vaulting and put in the main door between 1737 and 1740. Three doors on the lower level with Ionic pillars, an arched bay at the upper level with Corinthian columns and two inverted consoles cushioned by two obelisks and a pediment decorated with the arms of France make up a façade

whose classical style is echoed in the church's interior design and décor. From 1796 to 1809 the church was the headquarters of the Bourse (stock exchange).

PLACE OF PILGRIMAGE. On the right of the transept is the chapel of the Très-Saint-et-Immaculé-Cœur-de-Marie with its statue of the Virgin. Twenty thousand plaques and silvered metal hearts cover the walls of this place of pilgrimage instituted in 1836. The chancel's long shape is a reminder that the church was first used by a religious community. It contains seven pictures painted by Carle van Loo between 1748 and 1755 telling the story of Saint Augustine. This set of pictures is one of the few to remain in the place for which it was created ▲ 226. In the second chapel on the left stands the memorial to Jean-Baptiste Lully, superintendent of music to Louis XIV and composer of *Au Clair de la Lune*. His bust by Jean Collignon is surrounded by the figures of *Poetry* and *Music* by Pierre Cotton.

SHOPS FROM A BYGONE ERA. At no. 8, rue des Petits-Pères stands the last remaining shop (called Au Coeur Immaculé de Mairie) to sell religious objects. Alongside at no. 6 bis the Maison Bleue shop window has been preserved as a reminder of the type of business which once flourished in the area. At no. 10 an old baker's shop has kept its late 19th-century decoration with its colored ceramic tiles.

PLACE DES VICTOIRES

A NEW MODEL FOR ROYAL SQUARES. The Place des Victoires was the first to be dedicated to Louis XIV and was to become the model for royal squares throughout France. Maréchal Duc de La Feuillade asked the principal architect to the king, Hardouin-Mansart, to devise an Italian-style circular area in 1685 which had not existed before in Paris. This type of town architecture was intended to highlight the statue of the king on a plinth commissioned as early as 1679 after the victory at Nijmegen from the courtier and sculptor Martin Desjardins. The huge statue whose very height determined the axis of the

square's layout, was unveiled in 1686. Louis, dressed in a coronation cloak, was portrayed crushing a three-headed dog symbolizing the Triple Alliance. A gilt bronze figure of *Winged Victory* was presenting him with a crown of laurels and at the base four male figures seated and in chains, represented the captive nations Holland, Germany, Spain and Turkey. At the corners four lanterns set atop columns decorated with medallions burned day and night. None of the streets running into the square was ever extended into another street in order to give the illusion of an enclosed area and thus make the royal effigy stand out against the buildings. The identical façades feature pilasters, the "court dress" of architecture in the Grand Siècle. At ground level there were walled arcades, which prevented pedestrians from looking upward.

RUE DE LA BANQUE connects the Bank of France to the Bourse. At nos. 2 and 4 a 1905 apartment block was the headquarters of the Louis-Dreyfus Bank.

At no. 1 Legrand's (top of page), which keeps alive the tradition of gourmet groceries, was set up in a residential apartment block from the period of Louis XVI. Victor Ballard who built the metal market chambers in Les Halles also built the *Mairie* (town hall) of the 2nd arrondissement (1850) at no. 8, the Petits-Pères barracks at no. 12 and the Hôtel du Timbre (1844) at nos. 9–13.

ROYAL COMMEMORATION
A medallion featuring a copy of the royal equestrian statue decorates the corner of a shop which dates from the partial rebuilding of the Place des Victoires at the end of the 19th century.

FROM ONE STATUE TO ANOTHER. Louis XIV's statue was sent to be melted down under the Revolution. Today all that remains are the four slaves in chains which can be seen in the Cour Puget in the Louvre Museum ▲ *190*. The existing equestrian statue of Louis XIV by François-Joseph Bosio was erected in 1822. It replaced the statue of General Desaix, shown as a nude from antiquity which was melted down to make the equestrian statue of Henri IV at the Pont-Neuf!

SUCCESSFUL TOWN LANDSCAPING. Looking up the Rue Catinat, the visitor can see the front entrance of the Bank of France. In spite of excessive alterations and out-of-proportion reconstructions which have compromised the original harmony of the square, the Place des Victoires remains a successful piece of urban landscaping and the reputation of its high-class shops has been maintained since the end of the last century.

RUE DU MAIL FOR FURNISHING FABRIC. This street was opened in 1636 on the site of the croquet game set up along the old Charles V ramparts. Its main attraction lies in the large number of showrooms run by some of the best-known manufacturers of furnishing fabrics. Return toward the Place des Victoires.

RUE D'ABOUKIR, SOUVENIR OF EGYPT. The street partly occupies the site of the wall and ditches of the Charles V ramparts destroyed after 1634. It took its name in 1807, and like those of the other streets in the district (Cairo, Nile and Damiette) commemorates Napoleon's expedition to Egypt ▲ *148*. No. 4 is a fine example of neoclassical residential property from the 19th century ● *81*. Then go along the Rue Étienne-Marcel, opened in 1858 between the new Boulevard de Sébastopol as far as the Place des Victoires which opens up on the east side. The first main crossroad brings the visitor into the Rue du Louvre.

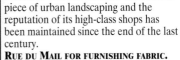

RUE DU LOUVRE

TRIUMPH IN METAL AND CONCRETE. The road was built in sections between 1854 and 1906 from the Quai du Louvre as far as the Rue Montmartre. It is in typical Haussmann style and cuts right through the traditional

THE NEW POST OFFICE
With its hydraulic lifts, its steam-powered machines to ensure the proper functioning of the pneumatic telegraph system and its generator room to supply electricity, the new Post Office building became *the* symbol of the modern

townscape of the Palais-Royal and Les Halles districts. Lined on both sides with office buildings, it offers a comprehensive view of the various styles of architecture possible with metal and concrete.

POST OFFICE, BEACON OF MODERNITY. This model of rationalist architecture (nos. 48–52) was built between 1880 and 1886 by Julien Guadet on a small piece of land created by the opening of the Rue Étienne-Marcel and the Rue du Louvre. The building is four-sided with its longest side measuring some 425 feet and a surface area of some 10 acres. Its six stories rise around a steel structure partly built by the firm of Eiffel. Behind the classically ordered façades the floors are laid out on very wide metal frames. Next door at no. 46 bis the old Paris telephone exchange built between 1890 and 1892 by the architect Jean-Marie Boussard, stands out thanks to its corner rotunda covered with pale-blue glazed bricks.

BEGINNING OF THE CENTURY. Take the second street on the right, the Rue Coquillière. At the corner of the Rue du Bouloi, the café A. Gutenberg has kept its décor of glass paintings dating from 1913. From here you can see one of the wings of the Bank of France which goes onto the Croix-des-Petits-Champs, with its pediment decorated with an allegorical sculpture by Pierre Carrier-Belleuse.

COUR DES FERMES. At no. 15, Rue du Louvre behind a door surrounded by figures of Atlas, there is a complex of offices, shops and apartments. This is the Cour des Fermes built in 1889 by the architect Henri Blondel. A second entrance on the Rue du Bouloi opens onto an impressive metal frame with exposed rivets. Continue toward the south. At the next crossroad on the left is the Bourse du Commerce.

age at the end of the 19th century. With its attractive bright layout and pleasant airy atmosphere for both workers and clients alike, it was to become the model for post offices throughout France. The sorting office (above left) and a cross-section of the old Paris telephone exchange around 1893 (below left).

▲ THE BOURSE

BOURSE DU COMMERCE. The Bourse (stock exchange) is circular in shape and occupies the site of the old Corn Exchange. It was built in 1767 and the wooden frame which covered the central courtyard was replaced in 1811 by an iron dome covered in brass leaf then glass panes. In 1887 Blondel reworked the building to make it into an exchange hall for commodities. The huge dome, painted in 1889, celebrates the virtues of trade. On the pediment at the front of the building the allegorical group by Onésime Croissy, *Town of Paris Protecting Commerce and Industry*, is characterized by its late 19th-century monumental sculpture. On the east side the fluted column, a relic of the mansion belonging to Catherine de' Medici, is reputed to have been used as an observatory by her astronomer Ruggieri. Cross the Rue du Louvre and take the diagonal Rue Jean-Jacques-Rousseau as far as no. 19 and the Passage Véro-Dodat.

PASSAGE VÉRO-DODAT. Built on the initiative of two butchers after whom it is named, this is one of the prettiest galleries in Paris. Inaugurated in 1826 the gallery caused a sensation thanks to the refinement of its decoration: checkered tiling, alternating glass and painted ceilings, copper window and door frames and panels of mirrors, wood painted to look like

THE ORATOIRE DU LOUVRE
The buttresses on the apse and sides of the Oratoire, together with its gables make a very attractive building. The main façade onto the Rue St-Honoré, a French interpretation of the Jesuit style, saw its rich decorative sculptures dating from 1745 disappear during the Revolution.

mahogany and small trompe l'oeil onyx columns. Its gas lamps were a great novelty. Today the gallery houses antique shops, boutiques and a restaurant. Take the Rue Jean-Jacques Rousseau again as far as the Rue St-Honoré and turn left.

ORATOIRE DU LOUVRE. The church was first built in 1621 as a chapel in the monastery of the Congregation of the Oratory of France, an Order of priests dedicated to preaching and teaching which was founded in 1611 during the Counter-Reformation. Designed by Clément Métezeau and Jacques Le Mercier ● 76, it was not finished until 1745 by Pierre Caqué. Louis XIII is reputed to have wanted to incorporate it within the Palais du Louvre which he was keen to extend. Bossuet, Massillon, Bourdaloue and Malebranche preached in this church. A munitions' store under the Revolution and then the Opéra's costume storeroom, it became a Protestant church in 1811.

ART NOUVEAU ARCHITECTURE. Continue along the Rue St-Honoré as far as the crossroads with the Rue du Louvre where at no. 32 the Paris headquarters of the firm of Saint-Frères, previously the owners of the jute mills in Picardy was situated. Still in the Rue du Louvre at no. 16 is an example of late Art Nouveau built in 1912 by Frantz Jourdain, architect of the Samaritaine ● 85. Its bow-windows which go up to the fourth floor, its stylized decoration, wrought iron balconies and plaques of multicolored enameled tiles are typical of this period.

APSE OF THE ORATOIRE. Turn right into the Rue de Rivoli just by the apse of the Oratoire, to see the monument to Admiral Gaspard de Coligny. Cross the Rue de Marengo and go back via the arcades of the Louvre des Antiquaires until you are back in the Place du Palais-Royal.

The monument to Gaspard de Coligny, head of the Protestant party, assassinated during the St Bartholomew's day massacre in 1572, is the work of the sculptor Gustave-Alphonse-Désiré Crauk (1889).

THE "GUICHETS" AND THE BRIDGE

Go in the direction of the arched gates of the Carrousel, pass beneath the pavilion called Lesdiguières which juts out on the left side then cross the Quai du Louvre toward the bridge. Below, a stroll along the river bank offers a splendid view across to the embankments on the Left Bank of the Seine.

THE PAVILLON DES GUICHETS
The pavilion was rebuilt in 1868 by Hector Lefuel. At the foot of the arcades are two groups of stone carvings, the *Merchant Navy* and the *Military Navy,* by François Jouffroy; on the pediment the *Spirit of the Arts*, a high-relief in beaten copper by Antonin Mercié (1877) has replaced an equestrian statue of Napoleon III by Antoine Louis Barye.

A NEW BRIDGE. At the end of the 1930's the Pont du Carrousel replaced the metal bridge designed in 1834 by the engineer Antoine-Rémy Polonceau. With its reinforced concrete structure, stone facing and three arches stretched very low, the bridge looks a bit like a hunchback. The groups of sculptures carved by Louis Petitot in 1846 have been replaced at the four corners: *Industry* and *Plenty* on the Right Bank and *The Town of Paris* and *The Seine* on the Left Bank. At both ends the lampposts, which used to have variable heights of 40 feet during the day and 70 feet at night, were made by Raymond Subes a famous craftsman of wrought-iron objects active during the interwar years. Continue eastward along the Quai du Louvre.

GALLERY AT THE WATER'S EDGE

THE GRANDE GALERIE was built for Henri IV between 1595 and 1610 by Louis Métezeau to link the "Old Louvre" to the Tuileries ● 76. On the first floor, the windows have been blocked to give prominence to overhead lighting. In 1848 Félix Duban restored the façades which have remained unchanged since then. Virtually all the decorative sculpture dates from that time. The mezzanine level was crammed with the studios of artists enjoying the king's protection but they were kicked out by Napoleon in 1806. The Lefuel door opens onto the courtyard with its double balustraded staircase in the riding school and the emperor's stables ▲ 132.

FOOTBRIDGE OF THE ARTS
Rebuilt in 1981 after the original design but in steel and with seven rather than nine arches, the bridge with its exotic wooden boards is used by strollers, artists and tourists who enjoy one of the best views along the Seine.

PAVILLON DU SALON CARRÉ. The first and second floors house the Italian-style Salon ● 28 where exhibitions were periodically put on.

PETITE GALERIE. Coming back from the square, the Petite Galerie was originally a passage linking the Louvre to the Grande Galerie in which Louis Le Vau redesigned the first floor in 1661 to accommodate the Galerie d'Apollon. In 1849 Félix Duban restored the façades and at the far south end added the loggia decorated with Anne of Austria's monogram. The single-color decoration relieved with some gold embellishments

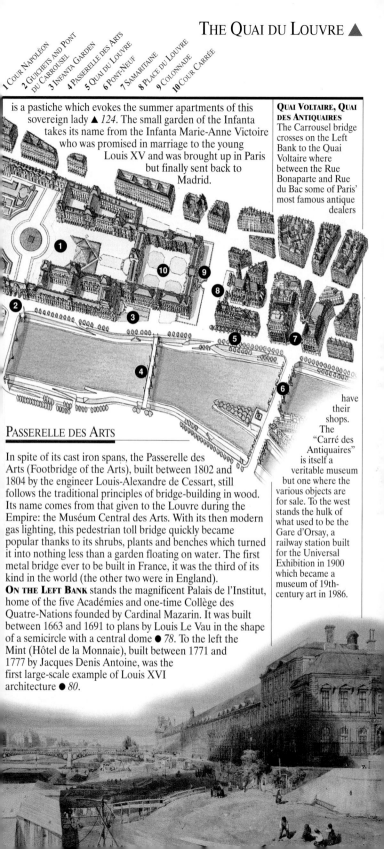

is a pastiche which evokes the summer apartments of this sovereign lady ▲ *124*. The small garden of the Infanta takes its name from the Infanta Marie-Anne Victoire who was promised in marriage to the young Louis XV and was brought up in Paris but finally sent back to Madrid.

QUAI VOLTAIRE, QUAI DES ANTIQUAIRES
The Carrousel bridge crosses on the Left Bank to the Quai Voltaire where between the Rue Bonaparte and Rue du Bac some of Paris' most famous antique dealers have their shops. The "Carré des Antiquaires" is itself a veritable museum but one where the various objects are for sale. To the west stands the hulk of what used to be the Gare d'Orsay, a railway station built for the Universal Exhibition in 1900 which became a museum of 19th-century art in 1986.

PASSERELLE DES ARTS

In spite of its cast iron spans, the Passerelle des Arts (Footbridge of the Arts), built between 1802 and 1804 by the engineer Louis-Alexandre de Cessart, still follows the traditional principles of bridge-building in wood. Its name comes from that given to the Louvre during the Empire: the Muséum Central des Arts. With its then modern gas lighting, this pedestrian toll bridge quickly became popular thanks to its shrubs, plants and benches which turned it into nothing less than a garden floating on water. The first metal bridge ever to be built in France, it was the third of its kind in the world (the other two were in England).
ON THE LEFT BANK stands the magnificent Palais de l'Institut, home of the five Académies and one-time Collège des Quatre-Nations founded by Cardinal Mazarin. It was built between 1663 and 1691 to plans by Louis Le Vau in the shape of a semicircle with a central dome ● *78*. To the left the Mint (Hôtel de la Monnaie), built between 1771 and 1777 by Jacques Denis Antoine, was the first large-scale example of Louis XVI architecture ● *80*.

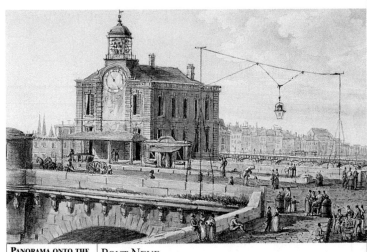

PANORAMA ONTO THE LOUVRE
Designed by five
architects including
Jacques Androuet du
Cerceau, the Pont-
Neuf has two sets of
arches, one with five
spans and the other
with seven joined in
the middle by an
artificial platform
built on two small
islands and today
called Square du
Vert-Galant. On the
esplanade Lémot's
equestrian statue of
Henri IV (1818) has
replaced that made
by Giambologna
which was destroyed
during the
Revolution.

Old-style grandeur at
the Samaritaine.
(facing page center
right and cross-
section above).

PONT-NEUF

THE OLDEST BRIDGE IN PARIS. The Pont-Neuf was built to
make it easier for the king to cross from the Louvre Palace to
the Abbey of Saint-Germain-des-Prés; Henri III laid the first
stone on May 31, 1578. Work was not completed till 1606 and
it was Henri IV who gave it the name of Pont-Neuf. Spanning
almost 900 feet it is still one of the longest bridges in Paris.
Under the Ancien Régime popular sideshows were constantly
held there. In the summer of 1985 the artist Christo wrapped
it in white sheeting tied with ropes. For a period of two weeks
hordes of people crowded onto the bridge to rekindle the
spirit of traditional popular entertainment.

LA SAMARITAINE

Opposite the Pont-Neuf on the right bank stands the
Samaritaine, the biggest department store in Paris whose
name evokes the pump installed on the bridge from 1603 to
1813. Its style is a catalog of industrial and commercial
architecture from 1900 to 1930.
EVEN THE RIVETS CAN BE SEEN. Between 1905 and 1910
the architect Frantz Jourdain built a revolutionary building.
between Rue de la Monnaie, Rue des Prêtres-St-Germain-
l'Auxerrois, Rue Baillet and Rue de l'Arbre-Sec (the
back part of today's store no. 2). The metal structure with
its exposed rivets supports large bay windows.

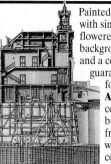

Painted bright blue, it was decorated with single-color strips: mosaic signs in flowered enameled tiles on an orange background. Inside it had glass tile floors and a central area covered in glass guaranteed maximum illumination for the interior.

AN ART DECO FAÇADE. The municipal council opposed the design for a building with a completely metal frontage and so Frantz Jourdain worked together with his young colleague Henri Sauvage to design the huge frontage onto the Quai du Louvre which they finished in 1928. The metal frame rising to eleven stories is hidden behind a stone facing decorated with bow windows and recesses. The Samaritaine thus joins the ranks of the "monuments" and is in fact the only large Art Deco façade in Paris.

PANORAMA. From the belvedere on the eleventh floor with its orientation map there is an exceptional view across Paris and onto the Louvre.

THE BELLE JARDINIÈRE. To the right of the Samaritaine, a number of old stores collectively known as the Belle Jardinière, were famous for their array of working clothes, particularly liveries for domestic servants.

THE QUAI DE LA MÉGISSERIE. Until the seventeenth century, tanners prepared skins along this quay which is well known today for its shops selling plants and domestic animals of all sorts. Booksellers ply their trade on the Seine side of the road. Return to the Samaritaine and turn into the Place de l'École on the right and then on the left, the Rue des Prêtres-St-Germain-l'Auxerrois to reach the church of the same name on the Place du Louvre.

This painting from 1666 shows how busy the Pont-Neuf was even then.

THE BELFRY was built between 1858 and 1862 by Théodore Ballu who delved deep into northern Gothic art for his inspiration. The three faces on a background of blue enamel and the gold lettering on the clock tell the time, day and date as well as the moon's phases. Originally the architect Jacques Ignace Hittorff planned to put a Gothic spire on top of the belfry (see drawing below).

SACRED OR PROFANE? Behind the central rose window of the 1st arrondissement Mairie (town hall) is the room where marriages are performed.

VICTOR HUGO. The author compared the outline of the church, belfry and town hall to a cruet set!

CHURCH OF ST-GERMAIN-L'AUXERROIS

Few monuments have undergone so many transformations in their history as this church, which became a royal parish church when the Valois settled in the Louvre in the 16th century. Founded at the end of the 7th century and rebuilt in the 12th, it was extended in the 13th century. It is from this period that the chancel, apse and main central door date. The nave and transept were built between 1420 and 1425, the porch between 1435 and 1439. During the night of August 24, 1572 it was the bells of St-Germain which announced the St Bartholomew's Day Massacre. In 1710, to make it easier for processions to pass, the central pillar with its statue of Saint Germain and the recessed pediment of the *Last Judgement* in the central door (13th century) were taken down. In 1728 the stained glass was replaced by clear panes of glass. In 1754, Claude Bacarit and the sculptor Louis-Claude Vassé adapted the central nave of the chancel to bring it in line with the taste for classicism; they knocked down the rood-screen of which five pieces can be seen in the Louvre ▲ *186*. The church was restored between 1838 and 1855 by Jean-Baptiste Lassus and Victor Baltard.

BURIAL PLACE OF ARTISTS. From the 17th century artists under the king's protection were buried here: the architects Le Vau, de Cotte, Gabriel; the sculptors Desjardins, Coysevox, Coustou, Vassé; the painters Coypel, Desportes, Restout, Boucher, Van Loo and Chardin. The link with the arts is kept alive today with the service of the Ashes offered for artists, the almshouse of the École des Beaux-Arts and the exhibition of current works of religious art.

MASTERPIECES. Notable are two early-Renaissance Flemish altarpieces, the royal family pew carved between 1682 and 1684 to designs by Charles Lebrun, *Christ* in the nave by Bouchardon and the Louis XVI organ case which came from Ste-Chapelle. The Lady Chapel is neo-Gothic; the architect and restorer Lassus designed the altar and reredos, Eugène Viollet-le-Duc designed *The Stem of Jesse* and the painter Eugène-Emmanuel Amaury-Duval decorated it with paintings inspired by the primitives.

PLACE DU LOUVRE

A HAUSSMANN CREATION. As early as 1660, some forty plans had been devised for a square between St-Germain-l'Auxerrois and the Louvre. Such a square was declared to be in the public interest in 1855 and it owes its creation to the program of decorative improvements headed by Baron Haussmann. In 1854 as a suitable frame for the new square on the clearing between the two monuments, Haussmann built two buildings on the Seine side of the Rue de Rivoli based on those Percier and Fontaine had designed for the Rue de Rivoli . Between 1857 and 1859 he added on the building which is Mairie of the 1st arrondissement. The architect Jacques Ignace Hittorff took his inspiration from the medieval outline of the neighboring church but drew on the architectural vocabulary of the Renaissance. To correct the misalignment of the church the architect thought of building a belfry on a street planned between the church and the Mairie. It was on this square in 1881 that the Town of Paris installed the first of around a hundred public restrooms, a worthy attempt at hygiene which continued with the famous public circular urinals (known somewhat more romantically in French as "vespasiennes") which have now been replaced by "superloos". At the corner of the square on the Seine side the Cadort teashop (founded in 1896) has retained its pretty gold and white decoration and Corinthian columns.

THE BELLS
The famous set of bells installed in 1878 and renovated in 1982, are in the belfry; thirty-eight bells cast in 1862 each give out a different sound; the heaviest weighs 2 tons and the lightest 35 lbs. At 11am the bells play pieces by Couperin and Rameau and a tune written by Marie-Antoinette.

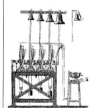

TRUE GOTHIC AND FALSE RENAISSANCE
The entry to the church is the only Gothic doorway in Paris, apart from that at Ste-Chapelle. It borrowed a certain flamboyance from Burgundian architecture, along with five unequal bays and a complex system of vaulting.

THE WING ON THE COLONNADE

The wing was restored between 1756 and 1757 by Jacques-Ange Gabriel who took inspiration from it to build the palaces on the Place Louis-XV (Concorde). The surrounding area was cleared but a plan for a monumental square had to wait until the Second Empire. In 1808, Lemot carved on the pediment a *Minerva* surrounded by the *Arts* and *Victory* crowning Napoleon's bust, which the Restoration replaced with a bust of Louis XIV. Ditches planned were not finally dug till between 1964 and 1967. They are 80 ft wide and 25 ft deep and relieve the huge foundation area, setting the colonnade in its proper proportions. The bridge leading to the palace's main entrance was designed from 17th-century drawings with the foundation stones from the first plan made by Le Vau.

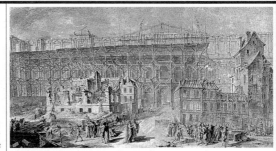

THE COLONNADE DU LOUVRE

A MONUMENTAL FAÇADE. Louis XIV wished the east side of the palace to have a grand entrance as part of an architectural east-west axis. A first design by Louis Le Vau, begun in 1661, was abandoned in 1664. A year later there was a design by Bernini which was considered too Baroque and then in 1667, a second design by Le Vau was put forward and accepted by the king. However the architect was so absorbed in building the château at Versailles that he was unable to see it through. Part of the work then passed to Claude Perrault. The most striking element in this 550 feet long façade is the range of Corinthian columns ● *78*.

THE COUR CARRÉE

THE HEART OF THE PALACE. The Cour Carrée is the result of extensions and decorative improvements carried out from the time of François I to Napoleon III. The west wing begun in 1546 by Pierre Lescot ● *74* is the oldest. His successors have respected the Renaissance architecture remarkably well. Recent restoration makes it easier to read the pediments. On the east side spirits support a cock surrounded by a serpent; on the north side the *Genius of France* with the features of Napoleon evokes the *Gods of Peace* and *Law*; on the south side, *Minerva* is accompanied by the *Sciences* and *Arts*. At night the courtyard is magnificently floodlit.

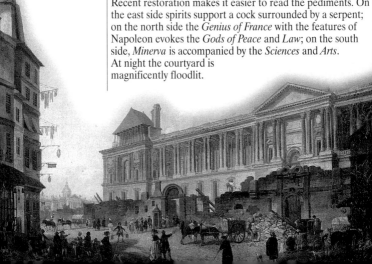

PRACTICAL INFORMATION

◆ GETTING TO THE LOUVRE

Modernized and extended with the opening of the Richelieu wing, the Louvre has become the world's largest museum. The number of visitors is constantly on the increase and later opening hours to some of the collections give the visitor the option of visiting the museum in the evening. A new ticket system reduces waiting time and makes it easier for visitors to circulate through the museum.

GETTING TO THE MUSEUM

BY BUS
Numerous bus routes go to the Louvre:
◆ 21
(Gare St-Lazare–Porte de Gentilly)
◆ 27
(Gare St-Lazare–Porte de Vitry)
◆ 39
(Gare de l'Est–Porte de Versailles)
◆ 48
(Gare du Nord–Porte de Vanves)
◆ 68
(Gambetta–Champs-de-Mars)
◆ 72
(Pont de St-Cloud–Hôtel de Ville)
◆ 95
(Porte de Montmartre–Gare Montparnasse).

BY METRO
The Louvre can be reached from the following stations (in order of proximity):
◆ Palais-Royal/Musée-du-Louvre (lines 1 and 7)
◆ Louvre-Rivoli and
◆ Tuileries, both on line 1 (runs Château de Vincennes–La Défense)
◆ Finally, east of the museum, the subway and suburban RER

station at Châtelet-les-Halles is an interchange between subway lines 1, 4, 7, 11 and RER lines A, B, D.

PARKING LOTS
There are a number of parking lots around the Louvre.
1 hour costs around 12F; 12–24 hours costs 85F (120F for the Carrousel-Louvre).
◆ Entry is sometimes limited to certain times of the day but drivers can collect their cars 24 hours a day.
◆ Carrousel–Louvre parking bay (7am–11pm); access by the underpass on ave. du Général-Lemonnier from the Quai des Tuileries or Pont Royal. Tel. 01 42 44 16 32
◆ St-Germain-l'Auxerrois parking bay (8am–8pm); entrance at 1, place du Louvre.
◆ Croix-des-Petits-Champs parking bay (open 24 hrs); entrance on Rue du Colonel-Driant between the Bourse du Commerce and

the Banque de France.
◆ Vendôme parking bay (open 24 hrs); access on Place Vendôme.
◆ Pyramides parking bay (open 24 hrs); access at no. 15, rue des Pyramides or 21, ave. de l'Opéra.
◆ Harlay/Pont-Neuf

parking bay; access on Rue Harlay/Quai des Orfèvres.
◆ St-Eustache parking bay (open 24 hrs); access on Place de la Bourse du Commerce.
◆ Les Halles garage parking bay (open 24 hrs); access at 10 bis, rue de Bailleul.

HOW TO GET INTO THE MUSEUM

◆ The Pyramide is the main entrance and nerve center to the museum and covers the Hall Napoléon. To get there from the Rue de Rivoli go through the Passage Richelieu.
◆ The museum is also accessible from the Galerie du Carrousel reached by taking the staircases in the garden on

either side of the arch. The gallery can also be reached through no. 99, rue de Rivoli along the Avenue des Pyramides (from the parking bay on Avenue du Général-Lemonnier) or from the Palais-Royal metro station.
◆ Entrance in the Passage Richelieu is for groups only.

PRACTICAL INFORMATION

◆ Mailing address: Musée du Louvre, 34–6, quai du Louvre, 75058 Paris Cedex 01.
◆ Answerphone: 01 40 20 51 51 or Minitel: 36 15 LOUVRE

or 36 15 CULTURE (to obtain the museum's program) Information desk: 01 40 20 53 17 Disabled persons: 01 40 20 59 90 Internet: http://www.louvre/fr

OPENING TIMES

The museum is open every day except Tuesday; it is closed on certain public holidays. PERMANENT COLLECTIONS Open 9am–6pm, late opening until 9.45pm Wednesday (entire museum) and

Monday (part of the museum). TEMPORARY EXHIBITIONS IN THE HALL NAPOLÉON Open 10am–9.45pm.
◆ Room closing time starts at 5.30 pm (9.30pm late opening) THE MEDIEVAL LOUVRE 9am–9.45pm on opening days.

In 1995, 4,700,539 visitors came to admire to the 26,000 works on show. Temporary exhibitions are held to show the 136,000 drawings, engravings and prints from the Graphic Arts Department.

Beneath the Pyramide is the Hall Napoléon.

Multilingual reception: copies of the museum Plan-guide are available free of charge.

Tickets are on sale inside the Pyramide (Hall Napoléon).and are valid for the whole day even if the visitor leaves the museum.

◆ Sale of tickets: till 5.15pm (9.15pm on Monday and Wednesday, late closing days)

◆ 1996 admission prices: 45F 9am–3pm; 26F after 3pm and on Sunday. Entrance tickets including entry to temporary exhibitions 60F before 3pm, 40F after 3pm.

FREE ADMISSION

◆ Those under 18; people with major disabilities; school, student or teachers' groups; certain professions such as journalists, artists, professional staff from other museums; art school students all enjoy free admission to the permanent exhibitions in the museum and the temporary exhibitions in the Hall Napoléon upon presentation of identification.

◆ Unemployed persons, or those on low income or receiving social security (who must produce evidence of this claim), military conscripts, conscientious objectors, deputies, senators and members of the European Parliament can visit the permanent

TICKETS

collections free of charge.

◆ Admission to the permanent collections is free for all visitors on the first Sunday of the month.

GROUPS

Groups are not admitted on the first Sunday of each month, after 1pm on other Sundays, and on public holidays. Independent groups with their own guide are asked to book in advance on:
Tel. 01 40 20 57 60
Fax 01 40 20 58 24;
to book a guide from the Museum:
Tel. 01 40 20 51 77,
Fax 01 40 20 54 46.
Group reservations: 150F.

THE CARTE LOUVRE JEUNES

This card is for those under the age of 26 and in the teaching professions. Cardholders are allowed free entrance to both permanent and temporary exhibitions and can buy reduced-price tickets for lectures.
Cost: 100F
Tel. 01 40 20 51 04

FRIENDS OF THE LOUVRE

This independent association works to increase the museum's funds through gifts from members and benefactors. Membership (300F a year, 450F for two people living at the same address) gives free admission to the

permanent collection and temporary exhibitions and priority entrance through the Passage Richelieu. Members receive a free copy of the museum's program and the Friends' Bulletin. They enjoy reduced price entry to the Musée d'Orsay, the Georges-Pompidou Center, other French museums and those run by the town of Paris and exhibitions put on by the RMN as well as in certain private and municipal museums. Yet another advantage is a 5 percent discount in the bookstores at the Louvre, at Paris' Modern Art Museum and at Galignani, Delamain and Arcturial and a 10 percent discount in the restaurant *Le Grand Louvre* (booking essential).
Tel. 01 40 20 57 55

MUSEUM AND MONUMENTS CARD

Valid for 1, 3 or 5 days (70F, 140F or 200F), it reduces the time spent standing in line and gives access to the permanent collections of 65 French museums and sites. Cards are on sale at ticket offices in the museum, the gallery shop of the Carrousel de Louvre, main metro stations, the Paris Tourist Office and main-line railway stations.

INVITATION TO THE MUSEUM

Every year during October a promotion is carried out to encourage the public to visit France's museums, particularly families and students. Special events allow the visitor to really discover the treasures in the museum.

CHOOSE YOUR TIME CAREFULLY

To get maximum advantage from your visit to the museum, go along at opening times or at the end of the afternoon on late closing days; avoid the midday rush and school holidays.

It is impossible to see everything in just a few hours.
The wealth of exhibits and the sheer size of the building can be
overwhelming and the visitor may prefer either to see exhibits
of particular personal interest or simply stroll around the museum.
With the added facilities now in place and the very clear sign
indicators, finding your way around is so much easier.

*By using earphone guides, the visitor can enjoy commentary on the most important
works in the museum and plan the visit according to personal preferences.*

PREPARATIONS

PLAN AND SIGNS
Pick up a free copy of
the booklet *Plan-
guide* at the
information desk,
which is printed in
six languages.
It contains a plan of
the museum and sign
indicators for finding
your way around the
various rooms.

**VISITORS WITH
MOBILITY DIFFICULTIES**
A special guidebook
(in English and
French) and
wheelchairs are
available at the
information desk.

EARPHONE GUIDES
These are available
in six languages and

may be obtained from
the desks on the
Entresol levels
(Richelieu, Sully and
Denon entrances) for
30F. Commentary on
more than 130 works
on view in the three
wings is available,
and their position in
the museum is shown
on the accompanying
leaflet. You will find
the commentary you
require by using a
numbered code so
that your visit can be
organized in the way
you would like it.

GUIDEBOOKS
Destination Louvre,
coll. "Chercheurs
d'art", for children
from the age of 11

written by the cultural
department of the
museum (84 pages,
90F), and the *Guide
du visiteur pressé* for
the adult visitor in a
hurry (20F, available
in 12 languages) can
be bought from the
museum's bookstore.
They allow a visit to
be planned and
suggest several
guided tours, shorter
or longer.

THE ROOMS
At the entrance to the
main rooms, leaflets
in several languages
explain some of the
works on display or
comment on the
techniques and major
schools in the history

of art. If structural
work is in progress,
video screens in the
entrance hall
announce which
collections can be
visited.

PLEASE NOTE
Smoking, drinking
and eating are
forbidden in the
museum.
Animals are not
allowed in and the
use of flashbulbs is
strongly
discouraged. There
is a free cloakroom
for personal
belongings except
items of value.

VISITS WITH LOCAL TOUR OPERATORS

Cityrama or Paris
Vision offer guided
tours to the museum
sometimes as part of
a guided walk around
the neighborhood.
◆ Cityrama organize
a guided tour of the
Louvre in French,
English, Japanese,
Italian and Spanish
every day except
Tuesday.

Meet: 9.30am at
Cityrama's office,
4, place des
Pyramides.
Duration: around
3½ hours.
Cityrama:
147, rue St-Honoré
75001 Paris.
Tel. 01 44 55 61 00.
◆ The tour *Paris
artistique* by Paris
Vision takes in a visit

to Notre-Dame and
the Louvre with a
qualified guide-
interpreter.
Monday, Thursday
and Saturday at
9.30am.
Duration: around
3½ hours.
Paris Vision also
organizes a walk
Louvre and Tuileries
every Wednesday

and Friday at
9.30am.
Duration: around
2½ hours.
Departure point for
both trips in front of
the offices of
France Tourisme
Paris Vision
214, rue de Rivoli
75001 Paris
Tel. 01 42 60 95 06
or 01 42 60 31 25.

Oriental antiquities
Islamic arts
Egyptian antiquities
Greek, Etruscan and
Roman antiquities

Decorative arts
Sculpture
Graphic arts
Paintings
Medieval Louvre

ORIENTATION

◆ The Louvre is divided into three main sections: Denon to the south running along the road bordering the Seine, Richelieu to the north along the Rue de Rivoli and Sully to the east around the Cour Carrée.

◆ The museum is made up of seven departments: Oriental antiquities and Islamic arts; Egyptian antiquities; Greek, Etruscan and Roman antiquities; Decorative arts; Sculpture; Painting; and Graphic Arts (this department puts on temporary exhibitions and allows access to the rooms containing permanent exhibitions).

◆ The rooms corresponding to each department are color coded.

◆ The exhibits are spread over four levels, each one of which is subdivided into ten areas. These areas contain several rooms numbered in the direction of the visit. Rooms are identified either by a letter of the alphabet or their own name.

◆ Arrowed pictograms show the most important works in the museum such as the *Venus de Milo* (Denon – ground floor), *Mona Lisa* (Denon – first floor) or the *Crouching Scribe* (Sully – ground floor).

◆ On each level, detailed plans show the layout of the collection. The small panels with a pyramid on them indicate the exit.

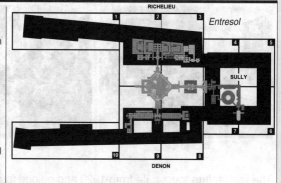

Entresol

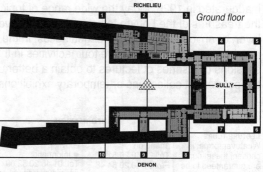

Ground floor

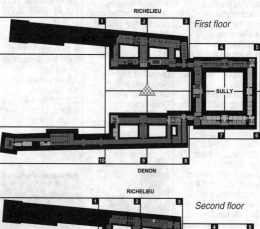

First floor

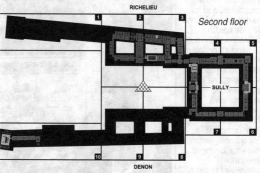

Second floor

◆ TOURS, LECTURES AND ACTIVITIES

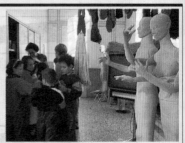

Lecture tour.   *Activities in the studio.*

The first lecture tours date from 1920 and guided tours were inaugurated in 1926; today the wide range of topics on offer allows the treasures of the Louvre to be explored as never before. The art lover, or anyone who is afraid of getting lost in the maze of rooms, may choose between a lecture tour, activities in the studio, one-off sessions or a series of lectures to obtain a better understanding of the permanent collections or temporary exhibitions.

INFORMATION

LECTURE TOURS
Whatever format is chosen, these tours are guaranteed to be carried out by a state museum lecturer.
◆ Duration: around 1½ hrs
◆ A fee on top of the standard museum admission charge is payable.
Sale of tickets and meeting point: group welcome area (Hall Napoléon).
◆ Individual visitors: 33F (full rate); 22F (reduced rate for under-18's, people with serious disabilities and their attendants, and for holders of the Louvre Jeunes card).
◆ Groups (maximum 30 people): on top of the reservation fee of 150F: 600F (full rate), 400F (reduced rate for over-60's, students, and teachers), 250F (disabled), 200F (schools).
For schools, lecture tours are arranged at times most convenient to them.

Groups must book ahead on:
Tel. 01 40 20 51 77, Fax 01 40 20 54 46.
◆ Some lectures are set aside for the deaf and hard-of-hearing. Information:
Tel. 01 40 20 59 90.
◆ Dates and times of guided tours are posted in the Hall Napoléon where brochures are also available.
To obtain a copy of the program, contact the museum in writing or check

Minitel (36 15 LOUVRE).
◆ Information: Tel. 01 40 20 52 09 (individual visitors) or Tel. 01 40 20 51 77 (groups).
ACTIVITIES IN THE STUDIOS
◆ Duration 2–2½ hrs depending on subject.
Price per session: 43F (full rate), 28F (under-18's, holders of the Louvre Jeunes card).
Groups: 750F (adults), 400F

(reduced rate for over-60's, teachers, students, and holders of the Louvre Jeunes card), 250F (disabled), 200F (schools).
◆ Subscription options
Adults:
Four sessions 145F (reduced price 95F)
Eight sessions 290F (reduced price 190F).
Children:
Four sessions 95F.
◆ Sale of tickets and meeting point: group welcome area.
◆ Visiting times for schools: Monday, Wednesday, Thursday, Friday, Saturday at 9.45am or 10.30am; Monday, Thursday, Friday at 2.15pm.
Registration essential Tel. 01 40 20 51 77.
◆ Information and registration for individual children (on the morning for that afternoon): Tel. 01 40 20 52 63.
◆ Studios are open to disabled groups
Information : Tel. 01 40 20 59 90.

Visitors and copyists in the Grande Galerie during the last century.

GENERAL VISITS

Two visits, one at 11.30am to the Sully and Denon wings and the other at 3.30pm to the Richelieu wing, except Tuesday and Sunday, are enough to give an overview of the museum's masterpieces.

ENGLISH-LANGUAGE TOURS

English-language tours are held with variable frequency: three per day

December to March, four per day October and November, six per day April to June and September. In July and August they are at half-hourly intervals each day (except Tuesday and Sunday) from 10am to 11.30am and from 2pm to 3.30pm (general tour), and at 11am (Richelieu wing only).
Information:
Tel 01 40 20 52 09.

IN-DEPTH SERIES

These consist of a detailed study of the collection seen from a chronological or thematic point of view; they are available several times a week or spread across a three-month period. Depending on subject there are five or ten sessions.
◆ Daily except Tuesday and Sunday.
◆ As they require a

degree of commitment on the part of the art lover, registration is by subscription only. To obtain a copy of the series program write the Service Culturel, Visites-conférences, 75058 Paris Cedex 01.
Fee: 140F (five sessions), 280F (ten sessions). Reductions available for holders of the Carte Jeune.

MONDAY EVENING THEMES

The Richelieu wing is open on Monday evening and the visitor can see exhibitions on particular themes: "Dutch Still Life", "Poussin and Antiquity", "Masterpieces of Byzantine Art", "Ivories from the Middle Ages" (7.30pm).

TOURS OF THE COLLECTIONS

These are held in French and are usually on one or two themes each day (the Italian Renaissance, 17th-century French painting, Medieval Louvre . . .).
◆ Daily except Tuesday, at 11.30am, supplementary sessions: Monday and Wednesday at 7.30pm and Saturday at 2.30pm.

VISITING TEMPORARY EXHIBITIONS
Times are posted up in the entry hall.

ARTISTS' MONOGRAPHS

A study of the life and work of one artist (such as Rembrandt, Titian, Veronese, Palissy, etc). Monday, Thursday and Friday at 2.30pm, Wednesday at 2.30pm and 7pm.

ONE HOUR, ONE WORK

A presentation and study of a single work from the museum's collection. Monday, Thursday and Friday at 12.30pm, Wednesday at 12.30pm and 7.30pm.

ACTIVITIES

These are held in all departments of the museum. About thirty different themes are offered to adults and children ◆ *331*; the activities develop certain aspects relating to the running of the museum, art history and techniques, and give visitors a chance to experiment with earlier techniques or make models. Some themes studied at the adult classes have included "The Architecture of the Louvre", "Building an Exhibition", "First Steps in Ancient Scripts", "Perspective and Space in a Picture" and "Filming a Work of Art".

◆ THE LOUVRE: AUDITORIUM

Details of events are posted at the doors to the auditorium.

"Perfumes, colors and sounds mingle," wrote Baudelaire, a connoisseur of the Louvre. He frequently arranged to meet people there as he felt it to be the best place in Paris for holding a conversation. It is this mingling that the Louvre auditorium wants to to revive the link between the different arts by offering concerts, movie shows, lectures and debates. The moviegoer observes the painter, the silent movie finds its musical score, and literature speaks on art.

A MULTIPURPOSE HALL

The auditorium in the Louvre is multipurpose and seats up to 420 people. It is reached from the Hall Napoéon under the Pyramide. Movies, concerts, lectures and debates all take place here. Between September and June there is often more than one event a day taking place.

◆ One-off tickets and subscriptions can be bought at the ticket booths from 9am to 7.30pm (9am to 5.30pm on Saturday) except Tuesday and Sunday.

◆ Auditorium information:
Tel. 01 40 20 51 86
Recorded program message:
Tel. 01 40 20 52 99.

LECTURES AND DEBATES

The numerous events which take place in the auditorium include series of lectures given by experts from France and abroad, and various debates. Topics include movements in the history of art, certain artists, and themes covering the permanent collections and temporary exhibitions in the museum.

◆ Tickets :
25F per session,
15F reduced price.

COME AND LISTEN

Debates are free of charge depending on the seats available.

CONCERTS

The auditorium also puts on a varied program of chamber music concerts. These concerts begin at 8pm. Information:
Tel. 01 40 20 51 86
◆ Tickets:
130F (full price), 85F (stand-by tickets for the under-26's: these can be purchased at least 30 minutes

before the concert, subject to availability).
◆ Tickets: available at the auditorium box office and at FNAC stores.
◆ Reservations (two weeks before the concert) on
Tel. 01 40 20 52 29 (from 2pm to 5.30pm on Monday, Wednesday, Thursday and Friday). The auditorium offers various attractive rates for regulars and subscribers.

In the 420-seat hall, silent movies are accompanied by music written by contemporary composers.

SCREENINGS

DOCUMENTARIES AND FICTION

In the auditorium documentaries on art and series of feature movies are screened: "The Silent Screen Set to Music". Classics of the silent era (Renoir, Griffith, Cecil B. DeMille, Pabst), played against a background of old music just rediscovered or new compositions.

♦ Ticket:
The price for documentaries and features is 25F per performance, 15F reduced price. Series features and concerts cost from 50F to 100F, depending on the movie.

A WORK OF ART IN CLOSE-UP

Every month from September through June there is an opportunity to study a major work from the museum in the auditorium.
A curator comments on the work, which is filmed in the most minute detail. The large-scale video projection makes it possible to examine the richness of the tiniest detail.

♦ Ticket price:
25F per one-hour presentation, 15F reduced price.

FREE SCREENINGS

Every day (except Tuesday from 9am to 6pm) the Louvre holds screenings of movies about art made by the museum itself. (*Palettes, La Ville Louvre, Contes et Légendes du Louvre*). They are held in the audio-visual room on the north side located under the Pyramide opposite the bookstore.

READINGS

From October to June, the Louvre chooses six different texts related to themes of works in the collection; these texts are played out by actors.
♦ Ticket prices: 35F to 50F.

DEBATES

AROUND THE MUSEUMS
As well as holding international debates on the history of art and archeology, the Louvre offers a day's debate on the theme of the international museum in today's world on one Wednesday every month. Curators, architects and specialists take part in these debates on museum architecture, the structuring of collections, restoring and presenting works of art and mounting different types of exhibitions.
♦ Ticket prices: 25F to 40F.

LUNCHTIME AT THE LOUVRE

This is an informative way to spend a lunch hour (55–60 minutes). There are eighty-eight meetings which take place between September and June at 12.30pm.
♦ There is a weekly program. Monday, a movie about art; Wednesday, a lecture in the "Around the Museums" series on the current state of international museums; Thursday, a concert; and Friday, a lecture on the history of art.
♦ Ticket price: 15F to 60F according to the type of event and variety of reduced price tickets. A yearly season ticket is available at a cost of 300F (reduced price 200F).

L'ÉCOLE DU LOUVRE

The Louvre School of Art, Archeology and Epigraphy is the most famous in France. Its students are the future researchers, curators and scientific staff in museums. It is possible to join the general history course and the specialized courses as an unregistered student. The School runs evening classes and has a variety of art courses from prehistoric times up to the present day as well as free courses open to the public on the artistic heritage of the French capital (organized in conjunction with the city of Paris).
♦ Reception is open Monday to Friday from 9.30am to noon and 1.30pm to 5pm.
♦ Information: 34, quai du Louvre 75001 Paris
Tel. 01 40 20 56 14.
Answerphone:
Tel. 01 42 60 25 50.

It would be a pity to go home empty-handed after a visit to the Grand Louvre, especially since a huge shopping gallery has opened in the Carrousel selling objets d'art, perfumes, scarves and ties, jewelry and luxury designer items. The museum itself offers reproductions of exhibits which can be bought as postcards, slides, books, prints, reproductions and even casts of items of sculpture. Buy a copy of the *Mona Lisa* to hang on your wall at home; take a copy of the *Victory of Samothrace* as a present for a friend; or get the video of the highlights of the Louvre to play back as a reminder of your trip.

THE LOUVRE BOOKSTORE

◆ A basic range of publications, slides and video cassettes on the museum can be purchased at the sales counters situated at the entrance to the collections on the Entresol level.

◆ The museum's bookstore under the Pyramide offers a huge selection of books covering all areas of art (over 20,000 works of which 4,000 are in foreign languages, ranging from English to Japanese, Italian, German and Spanish). There are books on the collections in the Louvre itself and on those held in other museums, both in France and abroad, as well as exhibition catalogs, teaching kits and a range of material for children.

◆ The bookstore also sells multimedia interactive programs combining text and visuals in the following forms: CD-ROM, photo-CD, Macintosh- and PC-compatible disks, and CDI. They cover various national museums, artists and schools of art. (*Le Louvre, Paintings and Palace*; *Delacroix, his*

THE LOUVRE AND MULTIMEDIA

journey to Morocco). Some are multilingual although some video discs work in the French Pal system, English, Spanish and Japanese.

◆ Slides are sold in series of ten, twenty or forty and are grouped according to department, artist, period or else contain a collection of the major works in the museum.

◆ Since 1990 an area on the Entresol level has been set aside for children. Various children's books, magazines, drawings, toys and video cassettes,

Mémoires du Louvre

including the children's series *Fairy Tales from the Louvre*, are on sale here.

INFORMATION: The Louvre Bookstore, Tel. 01 40 20 52 06. Open every day except Tuesday, from 9.30am to 9.45pm.

THE LOUVRE AS PUBLISHER

The publishing firm Réunion des Musées Nationaux (RMN) produces an up-to-date *Visitor's Guide* series. The series aims to provide the visitor with an insight into various departments while visiting the museum room by room.

◆ On the occasion of the Louvre's bicentenary, Réunion des Musées Nationaux joined forces with Montparnasse Publications to bring out a boxed set of three video

tapes (*In the Louvre with the Masters*; *The Louvre, A Museum and its Time*; *The Louvre, the Great Museum*). These works can be obtained from the bookstore.

INFORMATION

BY MAIL

Prints, engravings, jewelry, gifts and casts of sculptures can be obtained by mail order. For catalogs write to: Boutiques du Musée du Louvre 75058 Paris Cedex 01

BY PHONE

Information on the bookstore, boutiques and brass rubbing: Tel. 01 40 20 52 06.

The museum's international bookstore.

Engravings and brass rubbings.

SOUVENIRS OF THE LOUVRE

BOOKS AND REPRODUCTIONS

◆ On the first floor of the bookstore there are copies of nearly two hundred pieces of jewelry ranging from Egyptian, Etruscan and Greek, to Roman and Merovingian Gaul.

◆ The *Hidden Jewelry* (*Bijoux dérobés*) range is a refashioning of items used by painters in their pictures.

◆ It is also possible to buy reproductions of objets d'art and copies from national collections at a reasonable price.

REPRODUCTIONS ON PAPER

◆ Next door to the bookstore a number of specialist stores sell reproductions of paintings and sculpture.

◆ With no less than sixteen thousand plates in the museum, it is easy to study and purchase brass rubbings and engravings by artists such as Arp and Poliakoff, ranging from 17th-century work to the present day. An on-site video disc shows 6,000 engravings from the collection.

NATIONAL MUSEUMS

Souvenirs of the Louvre and other national museums can also be bought from the Réunion des Musées Nationaux (RMN) (49, rue Étienne-Marcel, 75001 Paris) and the store at the Musée Halles (Forum des Halles, Berger door, level 2, 75001 Paris).

SHOPPING IN THE CARROUSEL

Lit by the upside-down pyramid designed by leoh Ming Pei, the Carrousel du Louvre extends underground from the Quai des Tuileries and the Arc de Triomphe du Carrousel to the Rohan and Flore wings in the Louvre Palace. There are two areas combining the commercial with the cultural; an immense shopping mall lies alongside an area designed for specific events such as trade fairs, congresses and shows.

THE SHOPPING MALL

This shopping mall contains fifty stores selling goods ranging from gourmet foods to high-class boutiques for jewelry, perfume, beauty products, fashion and fine crystal, from fine table decorations to designer accessories. The selection is vast and the stores include names such as Natures & Découvertes, Body Shop, Aridza Bross, Courrèges, a fashion store run by Réunion des Musées Nationaux and a Virgin Megastore.

◆ Note: remember to keep your valid museum ticket as certain stores within the shopping mall will give you a discount on presentation of this ticket.

USEFUL TIPS

◆ There are several pedestrian entries to the Carrousel. These are located through the main entrance hall in the museum, by the staircases on either side of the Arc de Triomphe du Carrousel, by no. 99, rue de Rivoli or direct from the Palais-Royal/Musée du Louvre metro station (lines 1 and 7) and by the exit doors at the Carrousel parking lot.

◆ Access by car: two parking lots (capacity 620 cars) have been built under the Carrousel Garden, both of these are accessible from the underground walkway on Avenue Lemonnier.

◆ Opening times: the Carrousel is open every day from 8.30am to 11pm and the stores from 10am or 11am until 8pm every day except Tuesday.

◆ General information: Tel 01 46 92 47 47 and no. 11 on Minitel.

NOT TO BE MISSED

◆ NATURES & DÉCOUVERTES sells ecological and environmental products such as solar-powered calculators, astronomers' telescopes, wooden decoys and books. *Allée de Rivoli*

◆ Everyone knows VIRGIN MEGASTORE for its compact discs but you can also buy books and video tapes of feature and children's movies there. *Galerie Commerciale.*

The well-informed visitor to the Louvre can combine the pleasures of the art-lover with those of the gourmet without ever having to leave the museum. Visitors may go straight from the exhibit rooms to the restaurants and cafés. The entry ticket to the museum is valid all day and it is possible to make a phone call, change money or even to arrange automobile rental without ever leaving the building.

WHERE TO EAT

IN THE MUSEUM
It is possible to have some refreshment and something to eat inside the palace itself in either the Café Mollien (1st floor, Denon wing) or the Café Richelieu (1st floor, Richelieu wing) designed and decorated by Jean-Michel Wilmotte, Daniel Buren, Jean-Pierre Raynaud and Francis Giacobetti, the photographer. Both are open at the same time as the museum's permanent collection.

UNDER THE PYRAMIDE
There are several restaurants and cafés here: the Café du Louvre, the Café Napoléon on the Mezzanine level beside the Richelieu wing and a self-service cafeteria as well as *Le Grand Louvre* restaurant. The chef Yves Pinard offers dishes

typical of the southwest of France such as foie gras, duck soup, *andouillette de poisson*, duck à l'orange) as well as grilled meats, fish and seafood. The fixed menu costs 178F, lunchtime and evening. À la carte you may expect to pay around 250F. Open until 10pm, except Tuesday.
◆ Table reservations Tel. 01 40 20 53 63.

BY THE RICHELIEU WING
When the Grand Louvre was opened, the Café Marly on the Richelieu side attracted a sophisticated clientele who began their day by having breakfast here. Part of the attraction is the interior

Café Marly terrace underneath the arcades.

decoration by Olivier Gagnère, its Napoleon III design and the summer terrace under the arcades. There is a splendid view onto the Cour Marly and Pyramide at all times of the day but especially during the evening when the Pyramide is illuminated. Dishes include foie gras and haddock à l'anglaise. Expect to spend 160F per person. Access is through the Cour Napoléon. It is open from 8am to 2am.
◆ Reservations Tel. 01 49 26 06 60.

GALERIE DU CARROUSEL
The Carrousel has a brasserie, an international buffet

table and a tearoom – these are all open from 8.30am to 11pm. The Élisée Louvre brasserie seats 150 and looks out onto the Charles V moat. The average cost of a meal is 130F.
◆ Reservations Tel. 01 40 20 96 06. *Universal Resto* is

a large room with enought seating for 650 people, which serves a dozen French and foreign fast-food counters. This type of catering offers a wide range of dishes: vegetarian, crêpes, pizzas, Tex-Mex, Italian, Chinese, Lebanese, sandwiches and snacks, wine bar etc. for an average price of 50F. Ragueneau, the pastry chef, set up business at the end of 1994 near the entrance to *Universal Resto*, accessible from the Rue de Rivoli.

Take a break between exhibitions.

One of the rooms of the Café Richelieu.

Food from around the world in the Carrousel.

FACILITIES IN THE LOUVRE AND THE CARROUSEL

As well as numerous stores, cafésand restaurants, the Louvre and the Carrousel also offer a variety of extremely useful facilities. These include:

♦ A post office is open during museum hours (closed on Tuesday but open on Sunday).

♦ A bank, two cash dispensers and a bureau de change are open from 10am, along with an Independent Châteaux Hotels travel agency. Tel. 01 40 15 00 99.

♦ All types of vehicles can be rented at the Hertz desk. Tel. 01 47 03 49 12.

♦ The Virgin Megastore has a stand selling no less than 1,200 magazines and 150 daily newspapers from various countries around the world. The visitor can pick up a favorite magazine and reserve seats for any cultural event. Tel. 01 49 53 52 90.

♦ In the time that it takes you to go around the Carrousel, Foto-Quick develops the snaps you took in the museum (1-hour service). Tel. 01 47 03 40 52.

♦ The Carrousel has three payphones (one of which takes credit cards) at the bottom of the Allée de Rivoli escalator.

One of the four multipurpose rooms, set up for a fashion show.

RECEPTIONS AT THE LOUVRE

♦ The Carrousel offers four rooms for business seminars, product launches and displays. There is a total area of 9,000 square yards. The size of the rooms can be varied and they have retractable seating, a bar and a welcome desk for press and organizers – a total of 725 square yards of fully equipped offices.
Tel. and Fax 01 46 92 47 47

♦ For special events you can rent the Pyramid, the medieval Louvre and certain rooms such as the Richelieu mezzanine or even the auditorium which is ideal for a symposium or film show. The Hall Napoléon can accommodate between 400 and 1,000 for lunch and up to 3,000 for a cocktail party. Renting the Pyramid for an evening costs between 150,000F and 300,000F.
Tel. 01 40 20 51 87
Fax 01 40 20 54 52

FASHION SHOWS AT THE CARROUSEL

Fashion designers used to present their couture and ready-to-wear collections in marquees in the Cour Carrée of the Louvre. Nowadays these take place in the section of the Carrousel reserved for special events (see "Receptions at the Louvre", left).

AN IDEAL SPACE

The Grand Louvre is dedicated to Parisian culture and chic, and offers an ideal setting for prestigious events such as fashion shows. The venue is almost tailor-made for this type of presentation – its enormous area can be split up according to the client's needs. There are adjustable tiers of seats around an amphitheater, stage lighting and pits for photographers. Major fashion designers such as Chanel were immediately won over by the Carrousel's salons because they provide an excellent space to show off their creations and their models to superb effect. Shows take place in January and July for couture fashion and during March and October for ladies' ready-to-wear fashions (the autumn-winter and spring-summer collections). There are also shows for young designers and ready-to-wear for men. These shows are not open to the general public.

325

This tour has been designed for the person in a hurry who wants to see as many of the exhibits as possible without having much time to do so. The visitor is led quickly from one room to another, guided around the museum's wings and levels, directed toward particular works and thus permitted to see as many works of art as possible within a limited amount of time. The tour covers the majority of the museum's departments – including the medieval Louvre – by selecting the most important landmarks or best-known of the works on display.

A TO Z OF THE LOUVRE

The letters (from A to Z) shown alongside each work or group of works chosen refer to the plans and show where they are to be found in the museum. For greater details on the works, refer to the *Guide for the Visitor in a Hurry* published by the Louvre museum ◆ 316.

DENON WING

A set of two escalators leads to ground level and the Salle du Manège. Leave the room and turn left.

A THE SLAVES (1513–15) by Michelangelo are two statues carved for the first design of Pope Julius II's tomb. (*Denon 9, ground floor*)

Take the Mollien staircase up to the second floor to take you to room 77.

B THE RAFT OF THE MEDUSA (1819) painted by Théodore Géricault depicts the shipwreck of the frigate *Medusa* with only fifteen survivors on board a raft. (*Denon 9, 1st floor, room 77*)

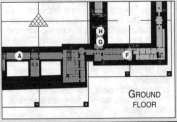

GROUND FLOOR

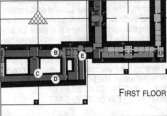

FIRST FLOOR

DENON WING

Go through room 76 and turn right into room 6.

C **WEDDING FEAST AT CANA** (1562–3), painted by Veronese, was commissioned for the refectory of the monastery of San Giorgio Maggiore in Venice. *(Denon 9, 1st floor, room 6)*

Leave room 6 and cross over left to the Grande Galerie.

D **MONA LISA** (1503–6) by Leonardo da Vinci, is the portrait of the wife of the eminent Florentine Francesco del Giocondo, which explains its other name of *La Gioconda*. *(Denon 9, 1st floor, room 6)*

At the end of the Grande Galerie, cross the Salon Carré and turn left.

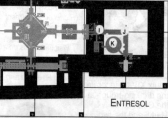

E **THE VICTORY OF SAMOTHRACE** (c. 190 BC) was discovered on the island of Samothrace in the Aegean Sea. *(Denon 8, 1st floor, Daru staircase landing)*

Go down to the ground floor. Turn right and go as far as room 13 and then straight ahead.

F **APHRODITE, KNOWN AS THE VENUS DE MILO** (end 2nd century BC) was unearthed in 1820 on the island of Milos. It is considered one of the masterpieces of art from antiquity. *(Sully 7, ground floor, room 13)*

Retrace your steps and turn right into room 17.

This is **G** the **SALLE DES CARIATIDES** with its collection of works from the Greek Hellenic period copied by the Romans.

HERMAPHRODITE is **H** the right. The Caryatids support the musicians' gallery used during balls given at the time of Henri II. *(Sully 6, ground floor, room 17)*

Walk in between the Caryatids and go down to the bottom of the staircase. Turn right to see the remains of the medieval Louvre. You will also see some pieces from Egyptian antiquity temporarily on display*.

SULLY WING

I **THE MEDIEVAL LOUVRE**

Continue into the moats.

J **THE MOATS**, ditches filled with water, separated the fortress built by Philippe Auguste (on the right) from the Paris city walls (on the left).

Go past several towers to arrive at the donjon or keep.

K **THE DONJON** of the Louvre was demolished in 1528 by order of François I.

Continue into the room containing exhibits found during the excavations. A passage between the display cases leads to the main staircase. Go down as far as the mezzanine level of the Hall Napoléon in the Richelieu wing. Turn right.

ENTRESOL

*NOTE

The major work going on to rearrange the Grand Louvre's collection has necessitated closing the department of Egyptian Antiquities until the end of 1997. A selection of items will, however, be exhibited temporarily in the moats of the Louvre (the large pieces of sculpture from the Old Empire to the Middle Empire), and in the Salle des Sept Cheminées (Sully 7, 1st floor, room 74) are those from the Middle Empire to the Late Period.

◆ The Louvre for the Visitor in a Hurry

Richelieu Wing

Go into the crypt which leads onto two large courtyards. Go into the left-hand courtyard, the Cour Marly.

L **The Marly Horses** is the collective name given to four groups of sculptures: the two groups by Coysevox (1706), *Fame* and

Mercury, commissioned by Louix XIV to decorate the drinking-trough at the Château de Marly, and the two groups by Coustou (1745) which replaced the first group originally used at the pond. (*Richelieu 2, ground floor, Cour Marly*)

Go back into the crypt and walk to the right-hand courtyard, the Cour Puget.

M **Milo of Croton** (1670) was sculptured by Pierre Puget for the park at Versailles. (*Richelieu 3, between the basement and*

Entresol levels on the right of room 20, Cour Puget)

Near Milo of Crotona a passage and corridor lead to the Islamic collection.

N **The Baptistery of Saint Louis** (late 13th–early 14th century) shows just how rich the illustration in Mameluke art was. (*Richelieu 3, Entresol level, room 8*)

Visit the rooms on this level devoted to Islamic art. Go back to ground level and turn right to reach room 3.

O **The Law-Codex of Hammurabi** (c. 1790–70 BC), engraved on a stele erected by the King of Babylon, is one of the first works ever devoted to the rights of man. (*Richelieu 3, ground floor, room 3*)

In the next room, on the right stands the Cour Khorsabad, room 4.

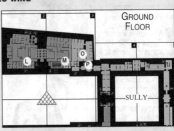

GROUND FLOOR

SULLY

P **Cour Khorsabad** houses reliefs of the palace of Sargon II. Included are five winged bulls with human heads, the good spirits protecting the palace. (*Richelieu 3, ground floor, room 4*)

Go between the two bulls on the right. Continue through rooms 2 and 1 to reach the escalator. Go to the second floor and walk past the staircase.

Q **The Lacemaker** by Vermeer. This small painting is a romantic depiction of domestic life. (*Richelieu 2, second floor, room 38*)

R **Portrait of the Artist at his Easel** (1660) by Rembrandt is a self-portrait of the artist while painting. (*Richelieu 2, second floor, room 31*)

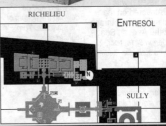

RICHELIEU   **ENTRESOL**

SULLY

RICHELIEU WING

Continue and after a high staircase, turn right.

In the **GALERIE MEDICI** **S** the cycle in the life of Marie de' Medici (1622–5) is shown. The work was commissioned by her from Rubens for her the Luxembourg Palace. (*Richelieu 2, second floor, room 18*)

Return to the escalator and walk past it. Go into room 1. Keep going straight ahead.

T **PORTRAIT OF KING JOHN THE GOOD** (c. 1350), anon., is the first known French portrait to have been painted on an easel. (*Richelieu 3, second floor, room 1*)

jehan Rey def auãt

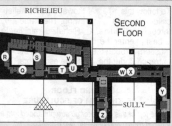

RICHELIEU

SECOND FLOOR

SULLY

After room 3, turn left.

U **THE NORTHERN SCHOOLS**

Go into room 4.

V **THE VIRGIN OF CHANCELLOR ROLIN** (c. 1435) is the work of Jan van Eyck, who painted at the court of the Duke of Burgundy. (*Richelieu 3, second floor, room 4, the Northern Schools*)

Keep going to reach room 7, turn right then cross rooms 12–16. Turn left. This is the Sully wing.

SULLY WING

W **THE CHEAT** (c. 1635) by Georges de La Tour is similar in style to the works of Caravaggio, who was extremely influential during this period. (*Sully 4, second floor, room 28*)

X **THE PEASANT FAMILY** (c. 1643) by the Le Nain brothers gives a certain nobility to peasant life. (*Sully 4, second floor, room 29*)

Y **THE SKATE** (1728) by Jean-Baptiste-Siméon Chardin is one of the two paintings by the artist for which he was elected to the Académie royale de peinture. (*Sully 5, second floor, room 38*)

Pass through the paintings of the French School. Stop at room 73.

Among Corot's pictures note especially **Z** **MEMORY OF MORTEFONTAINE** (1864) a masterpiece by this landscape artist. (*Sully 7, second floor, room 73*)

To leave the building go to the bottom of the staircase and follow signs showing a pyramid.

Within the maze of the Louvre there are plenty of treasures for young art lovers, but in the proliferation of works, periods, schools and styles how can a young visitor find them? The following itinerary has been put together to enable children to pick their way through this world treasury of culture. It takes shortcuts, jumps across the ages and does not observe strict chronology. Instead it wanders through the various rooms to pick out various milestones, and provide something of an overview of world art to the young visitor.

To follow this children's route through the Louvre, it is best to enter the museum through the entrance under the Pyramid and walk toward the Richelieu wing. The name Richelieu, minister to Louis XIII, is written above one of the three escalators.

GROUND FLOOR
THE KINGDOM OF SCULPTURE

At the top of this escalator go straight ahead into a vaulted room lying between two glass-covered courtyards.

Go into the left-hand courtyard, the Cour Marly.

A THE MARLY HORSES
There are four of these. The two furthest away were made by Coysevox by order of Louis XIV to decorate the drinking-trough at his Marly Palace; the two nearest groups were designed by Coustou for Louis XV and replaced the earlier ones at the pond. All these horses have long since left Marly and are now housed in the pollution-free safety of the Louvre.

Go back through the vaulted room to reach the right-hand courtyard, the Cour Puget.

B MILO OF CROTON has his hand deep in a tree trunk and is being attacked. Milo was an athlete who thought he was invincible and one day decided to split with his own hands a tree which was already partly split. The two sides of the trunk closed up again and kept one of his hands trapped on the inside. Milo was devoured by a wolf which the sculptor Puget here depicted as a lion. The animal's claws are dug deep into the man's flesh and his whole body cries out in pain.

C THE KHORSABAD BULLS are a little further on.

To reach them, take the left-hand staircase which leads to the upper level of the Cour Puget. Go into room 33 which adjoins the first room of oriental antiquities. Enter this room and then turn right into the following room.

These enormous bulls with human heads guarded the palace doors of Sargon II, King of Assyria.

Take the large escalator (pass between the two Khorsabad bulls on the right, turn right into room 2, then left into a room with information indicators and cross this room to the right).

FIRST FLOOR
VERY PRECIOUS OBJETS D'ART

On first floor, go straight ahead and then right.

D THE LITTLE STATUE KNOWN AS CHARLEMAGNE welcomes the visitor who then goes on into a series of rooms where a number of finely crafted pieces demonstrate the skill of craftsmen in the Middle Ages.

Retrace your steps and take the escalator up to the second floor.

SECOND FLOOR
STILL LIFE AND GENRE SCENES: REALIST PAINTERS

Go past the escalator and go through five rooms dedicated to the Northern School.

E GENRE SCENES by Gerrit Dou and Pieter de Hooch are in room 35. These 17th-century Dutch painters favored scenes taken from everyday life, as is evident from the names of the pictures: *Dutch Housewife, Woman Drinker, Village Grocer.*

Retrace your steps, cross over the landing and go straight ahead.

FRENCH PAINTING F begins here with *John the Good.*

Go through three rooms, cross over to the right and then go through eight rooms.

STILL LIFE is the name given to paintings depicting inanimate objects. The beautiful baskets of fruit are particularly noteworthy **G** room 27.

A little further on, turn left.

GEORGES DE LA TOUR H room 28 and the **LE NAIN BROTHERS I**, are called realist painters because they depicted intimate family scenes. *The Cheat* by Georges de La Tour portrays a scene where everything is said through the play of hands and eyes. Close by, in the work entitled *Christ with Saint Joseph in the*

G ⓖ **J** ⓙ

Carpenter's Shop, the child Jesus holds a candle while Joseph works. The Le Nain brothers painted peasants in their homes (see the painting called *Peasant Family)*. The clothes and background are rustic but are contrasted by an elegant stemmed glass.

Retrace your steps, turn left into room 19, go straight ahead and take the elevator in room A or the staircase just beyond and go down to the Entresol level.

❿ CHARDIN, HIS STILL LIFES AND GENRE SCENES

To reach the rooms where these works are to be found, go through seven rooms before reaching room 39. The painter showed everyday scenes of children and also specialized in still-life subjects.

ENTRESOL
THE MEDIEVAL LOUVRE

The tour ends with a visit to the medieval Louvre.

.Turn right at the bottom, and go between the two staircases.

The Château du Louvre dates back eight hundred years. Philippe Auguste had it built to defend Paris. Visit the ❾ MOATS – ditches which were formerly filled with water – between the château itself on the right (which had been built outside Paris) and the city walls on the left which protected the

capital. A passage on the right at the end of the moats leads to the ⓛ DONJON or keep, the best preserved part of the fortress where food and arms were stored. Do not forget to visit the room called ⓜ SAINT LOUIS before leaving this section.

Go through the door between the showcases, down the staircase then straight ahead to reach the exit by the Pyramide.

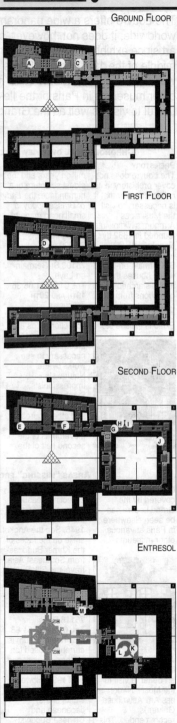

GROUND FLOOR

FIRST FLOOR

SECOND FLOOR

ENTRESOL

CHILDREN'S STUDIOS

To familiarize children with the museum's collections and the various artistic techniques, the Louvre has opened studios where talks are given by lecturers from national museums and artists
◆ A 1½, 2 or 2½ hour session costs 28F. The price for the subscription scheme is 95F for a course of four sessions.
◆ Tickets can be

bought at the group welcome desk in the Hall Napoléon under the Pyramide.
◆ Reservations are made in the morning for that afternoon: Tel. 01 40 20 52 63
◆ Studio activities are also open to school groups. Tel. 01 40 20 51 77 For more detailed information, you can obtain a copy of the *Calendar of Studio Activities* from the museum. (See ◆ 318.)

The Louvre offers a wide panorama of every form of artistic creation worldwide; it does not, however, cover every aspect in the history of art since exhibits only date from three thousand years ago until the middle of the 19th century. Some civilizations or schools are less well represented than others. To make up for these gaps, there are other museums in Paris or the Île-de-France region which would be useful to visit as well as the Grand Louvre.

CHRONOLOGICAL OVERVIEW: "BEFORE" AND "AFTER" THE LOUVRE

PREHISTORY

The Louvre does not cover prehistory in its collections. For that it is necessary to visit the MUSÉE DES ANTIQUITÉS NATIONALES, founded in 1862 by Napoleon III, in the royal château at St-Germain-en-Laye, which houses the nation's archeological collections from the origins of mankind to Charlemagne. Exhibits include stone tools going back one million years and the oldest sculpture of a human face, the *Lady of Brassempouy*, a small head made of mammoth ivory dating from 22,000 BC.

◆ Place du Château 78103 St-Germain-en-Laye
Tel. 01 34 31 65 36

19TH AND 20TH CENTURIES

The Louvre's collection stops at 1848 and a visit to the MUSÉE D'ORSAY is necessary to see works by the Naturalists, Impressionists, Symbolists, some revolutionary artists and other figures from the artistic movements of the second half of the 19th century and early 20th century (from 1848 to 1914). Techniques cover photography, painting, sculpture, architecture, town planning and the decorative arts.

◆ 1, rue de Bellechasse 75007 Paris
Tel. 01 40 49 48 14

This journey through the late 19th century can be continued at the MUSÉE DE L'ORANGERIE DES TUILERIES with its Walter-Guillaume collection which includes paintings by Cézanne, Renoir, Matisse, Picasso, Rousseau, Derain . . . and in a room built during the painter's lifetime, the famous *Water Lilies* by Monet.

◆ Jardin des Tuileries 75001 Paris
Tel. 01 42 97 48 16

All the excitement of the plastic arts throughout the 20th century, both from France and abroad, can be seen on the 3rd and 4th floors of the MUSÉE D'ART MODERNE DU CENTRE GEORGES-POMPIDOU.

◆ 75191 Paris Cedex 04
Tel. 01 42 77 12 33

The 20th century is also the focal period of the MUSÉE D'ART MODERNE DE LA VILLE-DE-PARIS with its collection of contemporary paintings.

◆ 11, av. du Pdt-Wilson 75016 Paris
Tel. 01 40 70 11 10 and 01 47 23 61 27

AREAS "MISSING" FROM THE GRAND LOUVRE

Certain areas not covered by the Grand Louvre can be seen elsewhere in Paris at various other museums.

ASIAN WORLD

To get to know Asian art better, a visit to the MUSÉE NATIONAL DES ART ASIATIQUES-GUIMET is recommended. This

museum has been collecting treasures from central Asia to the Far East since 1945. See the Angkor smile on the faces of the Khmer Buddhas from Southeast Asia, travel the Silk Route and admire the gods and demons from Nepal and Tibet.

◆ 6, place d'Iéna 75116 Paris
Tel. 01 47 23 61 65

NB: This museum is currently closed for restoration work and is not due to reopen until 1999. However, you can see the works of the Japanese and Chinese Buddhist pantheon on display at the new galleries, added to the Guimet in 1991 and which are installed close by at the Hôtel Heidelbach.

◆ 19, av. d'Iéna 75116 Paris
Tel. 01 47 23 61 65

AFRICAN WORLD

The visitor's rendezvous with Africa is at the MUSÉE DES ARTS AFRICAINS ET OCÉANIENS. This old colonial museum with its 1930's architecture presents collections from black Africa and Australasia. Included are masks, small statues, arms, jewels and fabrics. The basement houses an aquarium.

◆ 293, av. Daumesnil 75012 Paris
Tel. 01 44 74 34 30

ISLAMIC WORLD

To supplement the Islamic collection at the Louvre, a visit should be made to the INSTITUT DU MONDE ARABE (IMA) whose museum has exhibits of Arab-Islamic art, culture and civilization from the earliest times to contemporary objets d'arts.

◆ 1, rue des Fossés-St-Bernard 75005 Paris
Tel. 01 40 51 38 38

PARIS AND ITS HISTORY
Since the history of the Louvre cannot be separated from that of Paris, a visit should be made to the MUSÉE CARNAVALET dedicated to the capital's history from its beginnings right to the present day.
♦ 23, rue de Sévigné
75003 Paris
Tel. 01 42 72 21 13
Historic Paris can also be seen at the MUSÉE NATIONAL DU MOYEN ÂGE –

THERMES DE CLUNY which shows Paris in the days of antiquity in the Lutèce thermal baths dating from the 2nd to 3rd centuries. The museum also houses the 15th-century Cluny monastery, one of the world's most interesting medieval collections which it would be worthwhile seeing in addition to the collection from the same period at the Louvre. The collection's masterpiece is the famous tapestry *Lady with the Unicorn*.
♦ 6, place Paul-Painlevé
75005 Paris
Tel. 01 43 25 62 00
As an adjunct to the Louvre's collection, a visit should also be made to the DÉPARTEMENT DES MONNAIES, MÉDAILLES ET ANTIQUES DE LA BIBLIOTHÈQUE NATIONALE which has a large collection of antique Greek, Roman and oriental coins.

♦ 58, rue de Richelieu
75002 Paris
Tel. 01 47 03 81 26
The MUSÉE DU PETIT-PALAIS built for the 1900 Universal Exhibition, is another must for anyone wanting to extend a visit to the Louvre. It houses a treasury of old art including French and Flemish primitives, Renaissance works from the Italian and Northern Schools, Flemish and Dutch painting from the 17th century as well as *objets d'art* and paintings from the 18th century which complement the collections both at the Louvre and the Musée d'Orsay.
♦ 1, av. Dutuit
75008 Paris
Tel. 01 42 65 12 73
THE MUSÉE DES ARTS DÉCORATIFS has French decorative works of art from the Middle Ages to contemporary pieces.
♦ Palais du Louvre
107, rue de Rivoli
75001 Paris
Tel. 01 44 55 57 50
THE ÎLE-DE-FRANCE
Slaves by Michelangelo, now in the Louvre, was originally in the Château d'Écouen. The work of art had been presented by Henri II to the local landowner, Anne de Montmorency. Today, the Château d'Écouen, one of the major Renaissance buildings in France, houses the MUSÉE NATIONAL DE LA RENAISSANCE set up in 1969 by André Malraux. It offers a wonderful opportunity to see French and European 16th-century works of art.
♦ 95440 Écouen
Tel. 01 39 90 04 04
In the MUSÉE DU CHÂTEAU DE

FONTAINEBLEAU, another jewel of Renaissance architecture, visit the François I gallery decorated by Rosso Fiorentino and Primaticcio, Tuscan artists invited to the French court. Some of their work is in the Louvre.
♦ 77300 Fontainebleau
Tel. 01 60 71 50 70
The MUSÉE DES CHÂTEAUX DE VERSAILLES ET DE TRIANON has opened the apartments of the king, queen and both the Grand and Petit Trianon, which reflect the spirit of 17th-century France. The Galerie des Glaces has a ceiling painted by Charles Lebrun, whose paintings and drawings can also be seen at the Louvre.
♦ 78000 Versailles
Tel. 01 30 84 74 00
The CHÂTEAU DE CHANTILLY houses the apartments of the Condé princes (17th and 18th centuries), and the MUSÉE CONDÉ with its large French collection (from Clouet to Delacroix), Italian and northern European paintings and the manuscript of the *Très Riches Heures du duc de Berry* (15th century).
♦ 60631 Chantilly
Tel. 01 44 54 04 02
At Sèvres the MUSÉE NATIONAL DE CÉRAMIQUE shows amongst its 50,000 pieces of ceramic art from around the world, a superb collection of 5,000 pieces of Sèvres china. The Louvre also has some pieces of the same china in its *objets d'art* section.
♦ 92310 Sèvres
Tel. 01 41 14 04 20
The Louvre has the

Coronation of Napoleon I painted by David, the official painter during the Empire. Relive the Napoleonic era at the MUSÉE NATIONAL DES CHÂTEAUX DE MALMAISON ET BOIS-BRÉAU dedicated to Napoleon and Josephine.
♦ 92500 Rueil-Malmaison
Tel. 01 47 49 48 15

FRENCH MONUMENTS
All the principal pieces of French monumental art from the Romanesque to the 19th century are faithfully reproduced to scale at the MUSÉE DES MONUMENTS FRANÇAIS housed within the Palais de Chaillot. The visitor will learn about France and its history. There are 6,000 pieces of sculpture, chosen as being the masterpieces by French masters, copies of wall paintings and around 200,000 old photographs.
♦ Palais de Chaillot
1, place du Trocadéro
75116 Paris
Tel. 01 44 05 39 10

ORIENTAL ANTIQUITIES

MESOPOTAMIA	IRAN	LEVANT	ISLAM
◆ **EARLY MESOPOTAMIA:** Sumer and Akkad 4000–2400	◆ **SUSE**, period of Uruk c. 3200	◆ **CHALCOLITHIC PERIOD,** Negev (Palestine) 3500–3000	
◆ **MARI** 2400–2000	◆ **SUSE,** period of the archaic dynasties c. 2400		
◆ **NEO-SUMERIAN** 1st half of 18th century	◆ **SUSE,** Elamite Empire c. 2100		
		◆ **ANCIENT HITTITE EMPIRE** 1600–1400 ◆ **UGARIT** 14th –13th century	
◆ **KHORSABAD,** Assyria end of 8th–7th century	◆ **SASSANIAN EMPIRE** 7th–3rd century ◆ **SUSE,** c. 500		
		◆ **PALMYRIA** 2nd–3rd century	
			◆ **MESOPOTAMIA** 9th century ◆ **CALIPHATE OF CORDOBA** ◆ **KHURASSAN** (western Iran) mid 10th century ◆ **IRAN** end 12th–beginning 13th century ◆ **SYRIA OR EGYPT** end 13th century
			◆ **TURKEY,** Iznik 16th century ◆ **ISPAHAN** 17th century ◆ **MOGHUL INDIA** 16th–19th century

BC

0

AD

EGYPTIAN ANTIQUITIES	GREEK, ESTRUSCAN AND ROMAN ANTIQUITIES	
	GREECE	ITALY

♦ ANCIENT KINGDOM
2700–2200

♦ PRE-HELLENIC AGE
2700–2400

♦ MIDDLE KINGDOM
2060–1785

♦ NEW KINGDOM
1555–1080

♦ ARCHAIC GREECE

♦ LATE PERIOD
664–332

♦ CRETE
Archaic period

♦ ETRUSCANS
end 6th–1st century

♦ GREECE MAJOR
2nd half 5th century

♦ ROMAN REPUBLIC
5th century–27 BC

♦ PTOLEMAIC PERIOD
332–30

♦ HELLENIC PERIOD
3rd–1st century

♦ ROMAN EGYPT
30–392 AD

♦ ROMAN EMPIRE
27 BC–235 AD

♦ LATE EMPIRE
235–410

♦ COPTIC
392–641

EUROPEAN PAINTING						
PERIODS	FRANCE	ITALY	SPAIN	NORTHERN SCHOOLS		GREAT BRITAIN
				GERMANY	FLANDERS/ HOLLAND	
C. XIII		◆ Cimabue (1240–1302) ◆ Giotto (1267–1337)				
C. XIV International Gothic	◆ Portrait of Jean II le Bon, King of France (c. 1350, anon.)					
C. XV	◆ Jean Fouquet (1420–77/81) ◆ Enguerrand Quarton (known in Provence from 1444–66)	◆ Fra Angelico (1417–55) ◆ Piero della Francesca (1422–92) ◆ Paolo Uccello (1397–1475) ◆ Leonardo da Vinci (1452–1519) ◆ Raphael (1483–1520)	◆ Bernardo Martorell (1427–52)	◆ Maître de la Sainte Parenté (1470/80–1515) ◆ Albrecht Dürer (1471–1528)	◆ Jan van Eyck (?–1441) ◆ Roger van der Weyden (1390/1400–64) ◆ Quentin Metsys (1465/6–1530)	
C. XVI	◆ Fontaine-bleau School	◆ Titian (1488/9–1576) ◆ Veronese (1528–88) ◆ Tintoretto (1518–94)	◆ El Greco (1541–1614)	◆ Lucas Cranach the Elder (1472–1553) ◆ Hans Holbein the Younger (1497/98–1543)	◆ Pieter I Bruegel the Elder (1525–69) ◆ Peter Paul Rubens (1577–1640)	
C. XVII	◆ Georges de La Tour (1593–1652) ◆ Le Nain brothers (1600/10–48) ◆ Nicolas Poussin (1594–1665) ◆ Charles Lebrun (1619–90) ◆ J.-Antoine Watteau (1684–1721)	◆ Caravaggio (1571–1610)	◆ Francisco de Zurbarán (1598–1664) ◆ Jusepe de Ribera (1591–1652) ◆ Bartholomé Esteban Murillo (1618–82)		◆ Frans Hals (1581/85–1666) ◆ Rembrandt (1606–69) ◆ Johannes Vermeer (1632–75)	
C. XVIII	◆ F. Boucher (1703–70) ◆ J.-Honoré Fragonard (1732–1806) ◆ Jacques-Louis David (1748–1825) ◆ Théodore Géricault (1791–1824)	◆ Francesco Guardi (1712–93)	◆ Francisco José de Goya y Lucientes (1746–1828)			◆Thomas Gainsborough (1727–88) ◆ Sir Joshua Reynolds (1723–92)
C. XIX	◆ Eugène Delacroix (1798–1863) ◆ J.-A.-D. Ingres (1780–1867) ◆ J.-B.-C. Corot (1796–1875)			◆ Caspar David Friedrich 1784–1840)		◆ Joseph Mallord William Turner (1775–1851)

PRACTICAL
INFORMATION

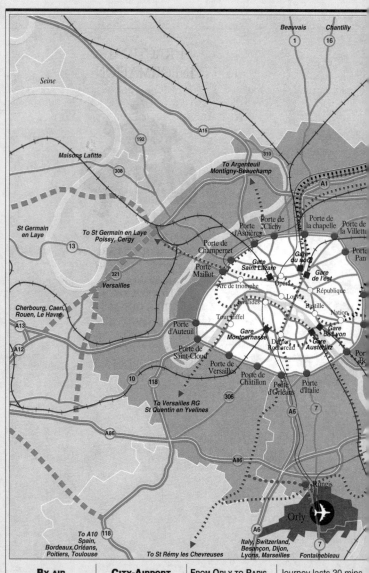

BY AIR

Paris is linked to major cities in France and throughout the world by various airlines.

◆ Domestic air services are handled by Air Inter and certain tour operators offering reduced air fares. However, since 1995 the French market has also been open to other companies.

CITY-AIRPORT CONNECTIONS

USEFUL PHONE NUMBERS

◆ Roissy (Charles de Gaulle) Airport: Tel. 01 48 62 22 80 or 01 48 62 12 12
◆ Orly Airport: Tel. 01 49 75 15 15
◆ Minitel 36 15 HORAV serves Paris airports. Information is given in French and English.

FROM ORLY TO PARIS

◆ Taxi: 150– 200F with an additional charge of 6F per piece of luggage.
◆ To hire a chaffeured car, contact Aéroports Limousine Service, Tel. 01 40 71 84 62.
◆ Cars Air France buses leave from Orly-Ouest (Gate E, Arrivals) and Orly-Sud (Gates C or D) for Les Invalides.

Journey lasts 30 mins (depending on traffic), with a stop at Montparnasse station, every 12 mins 5.30am–11.10pm (40F).

◆ Orlybus leaves from the same terminals, Gate J (Arrivals) and Gate H, platform 4, for place Denfert-Rochereau, every 12 mins 6.30am–11pm.At a fare of 30F, it is the

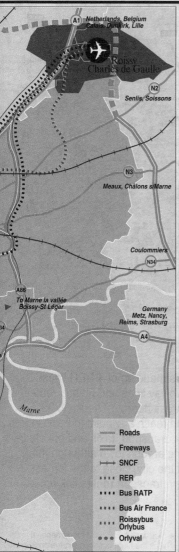

Map labels: Roissy Charles de Gaulle; Netherlands, Belgium, Calais, Dunkirk, Lille (A1); Senlis, Soissons (N2); Meaux, Châlons s/Marne (N3); Coulommiers (N34); To Marne la vallée Boissy-St Léger (A86); Germany, Metz, Nancy, Reims, Strasburg (A4); Marne

Key:
- Roads
- Freeways
- SNCF
- RER
- Bus RATP
- Bus Air France
- Roissybus Orlybus
- Orlyval

less expensive option.
♦ Orlyval: this automated overground train takes passengers to Antony station (RER line B) every 8 mins, 6am–10.30pm, Mon–Sat and 7am–11pm Sun. Fare 52F, including RER.
♦ Orlyrail: this train runs from Gate F at Orly-Ouest to the SNCF Orly station,

where passengers can transfer to line C of the RER. The shuttle runs every 15 mins from 5.30am to midnight (11F).
♦ Bus Jet runs from the airport to the subway station Villejuif-Louis-Aragon.The service is free of charge.

FROM ROISSY TO PARIS
♦ Taxi:180–230F.
♦ Cars Air France buses leavefor the

porte Maillot and the Charles-de-Gaulle-Étoile every 12 mins between 5.40am and 11pm. The journey takes 40 mins (depending on traffic), fare 55F. Air France buses are free for under-four year olds.
♦ Also, a Cars Air France bus goes to Montparnasse station every hour on the hour 7am–9pm,
♦ The free ADP shuttle runs between terminals 1 and 2 and the Roissy Aéroport Charles-de-Gaulle station, connecting with RER line B to Châtelet-des-Halles.
♦ Roissybus runs between Roissy and the Opéra. Buses run every 15 mins from 5.45am to 11pm. Journey time around 45 mins, fare 40F.
♦ Two RATP buses connect Roissy-Gare RER station with the city. The journey takes between 45 mins and 1 hour.
♦ Bus line 350 runs to the Gare du Nord and the Gare de l'Est. It leaves every 15 mins (30 mins weekends and public

holidays) 6am–11.51pm.
Fare: 6 tickets.
♦ Bus line 351 goes to the place de la Nation every 30 mins (40 mins weekends and public holidays) 5.30am–9.30pm.
Fare: 6 tickets.

BY TRAIN
Paris has six main-line stations all linking with bus and subway services:
♦ Gare du Nord for the north, Belgium and the United Kingdom.
♦ Gare de l'Est for the east and Germany, Austria and Switzerland.
♦ Gare de Lyon for the southeast, Switzerland and Italy.
♦ Gare d'Austerlitz for central and southwest France, Spain and Portugal.
♦ Gare Montparnasse for the west and TGV services to the west and Spain.
♦ Gare St-Lazare for Normandy and the UK, via Dieppe and Le Havre.

◆ GETTING AROUND PARIS

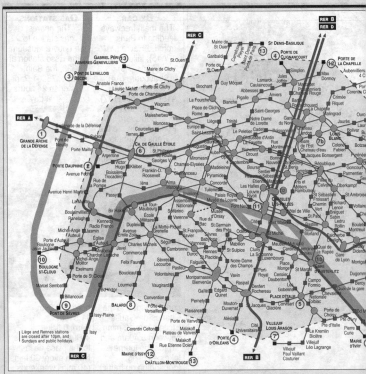

The Paris public transport system is made up of 4 RER lines (suburban commuter trains), 15 subway lines and 58 bus routes which criss-cross the capital and areas nearby. Thanks to its interchange facilities, the visitor can reach any point in Paris in less than half-an-hour. Apart from public transport, taxis and private cars provide an alternative way of getting around town although they usually take longer. At the heart of the city, close to the largest museum in the world, the city's main transport routes link up.

PUBLIC TRANSPORT

MÉTRO (SUBWAY)
The metro operates between 5.30am and 1.15am and its multiple interchange systems make it possible to change lines (a journey has no maximum time limit).

BUS
Bus timetables and routes are posted at the bus stops. They cross all over Paris from 5.30am to 8.30pm. Lines 21,

26, 27, 31, 38, 52, 62, 63, 72, 74, 80, 85, 91, 92, 95, 96 and the PC (*Petite Ceinture* – Inner Circle) operate till 12.30am. On Sundays and public holidays, there is a reduced service and certain lines do not operate at all.

◆ **NOCTAMBUS**
This is the night bus service. The terminus is Châtelet, Avenue Victoria. The route Châtelet–Pont-de-Neuilly takes in the Louvre, Concorde and the Champs-Élysées. Departures are hourly on the half-hour from 1.30am to 5.30am.
Fare 16,50F.

◆ **BALABUS**
The Paris transport authority (RATP) has set up a service linking the city's main

monuments. It operates on Sundays and public holidays from 12 noon to 8pm, April through September, between the Gare de Lyon railroad station and La Défense. Its route includes Notre-Dame, Pont-du-Carrousel (Quai du Louvre), Musée d'Orsay, Concorde and Champs-Élysées. The whole trip lasts 50 minutes and the stops are indicated by a Bb sign.

RER

This quick, efficient express rail network links Paris to the suburbs. Four lines (A, B, C and D) are in operation and these split into several branches to cover as wide an area as possible.

◆ Fares within the Paris city boundaries are the same as the subway.

◆ Beyond that, the fare varies according to destination. Through tickets can be bought at RER stations connected to the subway system.

◆ Line A leaves from Cergy, Poissy, St-Germain-en-Laye and ends at either Marne-la-Vallée (Disneyland Paris) or Boissy-Saint-Léger.

◆ Line B goes from Roissy-Aéroport Charles-de-Gaulle or Mitry-Claye to Robinson or Saint-Rémy-lès-Chevreuses.

◆ Line C connects Montigny-Beauchamps, Argenteuil, Versailles-Rive Gauche or St-Quentin-en-Yvelines to Massy-Palaiseau, Dourdan or St-Martin-d'Étampes.

◆ Line D goes from d'Orry-la-Ville to Châtelet.

◆ All these lines (except C) stop at Châtelet-les-Halles, to connect with subway line 1 (Château-de-Vincennes – La Défense) which stops at the Palais-Royal – Musée du Louvre.

MÉTÉOR

The Météor (Rapid East-West Métro) will come into service in 1997. The automated system will have 18 stations with 13 in Paris itself; 8 of these will connect at 11 metro stations and the main-line railroad stations of Lyon and St-Lazare (with a stop at the Pyramides station). A first phase of the project will link Tolbiac-Masséna to Châtelet, via the Gare-de-Lyon.

FARES

Depending on length and type of stay in Paris, the visitor has a choice of fare structures for traveling.

◆ If you stay in the area close to the Louvre, the cheapest means of travel apart from walking is to buy a carnet of 10 tickets valid on both buses and subway trains (44F). One ticket on its own costs 7.50F.

◆ Children up to the age of 4 travel free and at half-fare up to the age of 10.

◆ On buses the fare is 1 ticket regardless

of the length of the journey on that line. If you need to transfer to a different line, you will have to use another ticket.

◆ Tickets need to be punched (composté) on buses and metro trains, there are machines to do this as you get on the bus, and by the entrance gates inside the métro stations. make sure to keep your ticket until the end of your journey.

ALTERNATIVE WAYS TO BUY TICKETS

◆ If you intend to make many journeys over several days, it is better to buy a personalized card with coupons.

◆ The length of validity, weekly or monthly, and number of zones must be chosen. If staying in Paris, 2 zones are sufficient.

◆ Card Formule 1 (1 day, 3 zones 40F; 5 zones 100F), Paris Visite (2, 3 or 5 days, 3 zones 70F, 105F, 165F. 5 zones 170F, 230F and 315F); Orange card, 5 zones, can also be used for travel to the suburbs and includes the use of Orlybus, Roissybus,

Orly-Rail and Roissy-Rail.

◆ Paris Visite offers reductions on certain journeys.

◆ These personalized cards allow unlimited travel. The ticket is not punched on the bus but is simply shown to the driver.

◆ Information: Minitel 36 15 RATP or Tel. 01 43 46 14 14 from 6am to 9pm.

◆ Museums and Monuments card (1 day: 70F, 3 days: 140F, 5 days: 200F) is on sale in museums and at monuments, at RATP, the Tourist Office, SNCF and airports. It allows unlimited access to over sixty sites and monuments in the Paris area.

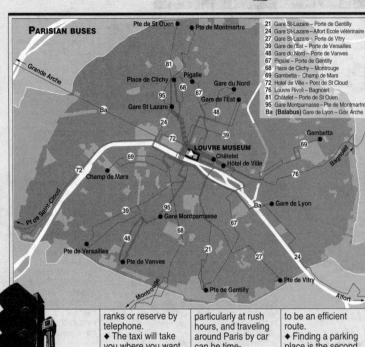

PARISIAN BUSES

Grande Arche

Pte de St Ouen ● ● Pte de Montmartre

81

Place de Clichy ● Pigalle
68 67
95 Gare du Nord
Gare St Lazare ● Gare de l'Est
48
Ba 24
39

72
Gambetta
69
LOUVRE MUSEUM
69 Châtelet
72 Champ de Mars Hôtel de Ville 76
Pt de Saint-Cloud
Ba ● Gare de Lyon
39 95
Pte de Saint-Cloud Gare Montparnasse
68 67
48
Pte de Versailles ● 21
● Pte de Vanves 27 24
Montrouge
● Pte de Gentilly ● Pte de Vitry
Alfort

21	Gare St-Lazare – Porte de Gentilly
24	Gare St-Lazare – Alfort Ecole vétérinaire
27	Gare St-Lazare – Porte de Vitry
39	Gare de l'Est – Porte de Versailles
48	Gare du Nord – Porte de Vanves
67	Pigalle – Porte de Gentilly
68	Place de Clichy – Montrouge
69	Gambetta – Champ de Mars
72	Hotel de Ville – Pont de St Cloud
76	Louvre Rivoli – Bagnolet
81	Châtelet – Porte de St Ouen
95	Gare Montparnasse – Pte de Montmartre
Ba	**(Balabus)** Gare de Lyon – Gde Arche

TAXIS

Taxis are an ideal, practical and fast way of getting around town, particularly at the quieter moments of the day and night. The price of a taxi ride is reasonable and within the city boundaries varies between 50F and 100F at most (including pick-up). Although there are more than 13,000 taxis in Paris, there are not as many taxis in the streets as in New York or London, so the best way to find a cab is to go to one of the taxi

ranks or reserve by telephone.
◆ The taxi will take you where you want to go.
◆ They can be hailed on the street or reserved by telephone.
◆ There are many taxi ranks spread all over town, especially in tourist areas, stations and airports.

TAXI COMPANIES
◆ Alpha Taxis
Tel. 01 45 85 85 85
◆ Taxis Bleus
Tel. 01 49 36 10 10
◆ Taxis G7
Tel. 01 47 39 47 39
or 01 47 39 32 51

PRIVATE VEHICLES
Using a private vehicle is not recommended in Paris. Traffic conditions are extremely difficult,

particularly at rush hours, and traveling around Paris by car can be time-consuming and expensive.
◆ The Louvre is situated in the axis which links the center of town to the city boundaries. The riverside quay roads and the Rue de Rivoli which border the museum are important east–west throughroads connecting with equally important north–south roads (from the Place de la Concorde to the west to the Place du Châtelet to the east). Although in theory the Louvre museum is easily accessible from these approach roads they are usually too congested

to be an efficient route.
◆ Finding a parking place is the second major problem for the driver in Paris. Parking bays in nearby streets are snapped up and most make a charge (15F per hour). Parking inspectors circulate constantly to check that payment has been made and are ruthless if the ticket is not on the car or the time paid for has overrun.
◆ Another solution is the parking lots. These can be paid by the hour or half-day. There is one under the Carrousel gardens (◆ 314).
◆ It is generally advisable to use public transport.

Paris is a cosmopolitan city. At its center, the area bounded by the Place de la Concorde, the Place de l'Opéra, the banks of the Seine, les Halles and the Rue de Réaumur, is the most popular part of the capital for tourists. It brings together all the amenities to help the visitor during his stay in the city: multilingual staff in stores, a host of banks and bureaux de change, foreign bookstores and the 24-hour post office on the Rue du Louvre.

USEFUL INFORMATION

PHOTOGRAPHY

◆ If possible, take a camera without automatic flash since this is forbidden for certain works of art.

◆ For indoor shots, film with sensitivity over or equal to 400 ASA will generally allow photos to be taken without a flash.

A NIGHT OUT

Always book in advance for theaters and concerts either by mail or telephone. Even shows and plays without famous stars or concerts not just featuring popular classics are often sold out.

HOTELS

The same applies to hotels. Always reserve, particularly during school holidays.

STUDENT CARD

This card entitles the holder to reductions in certain museums, sites, theaters and movie theaters.

YOUTH HOSTELS CARD

This card and the list of appropriate accommodation can be obtained from the United Federation of Youth Hostels (FUAJ), 27, rue Pajol 75018 Paris. Tel. 01 44 89 87 27.

ESSENTIAL

A city plan with an index of streets, subway and bus routes is very useful for finding your way round the capital.

BEST TIME TO VISIT THE CITY

It is pleasant to visit Paris at all times of the year, although July and August should be avoided because of the huge influx of tourists.

TOURS IN PARIS

Tour companies arrange trips to the places of interest such as the Georges-Pompidou Center, the Eiffel Tower, the Science and Industry Development, the château at Versailles and both the Louvre and Orsay museums. Nights out in Paris include the Lido, the Moulin-Rouge or the Folies-Bergère. An evening trip by bus or river boat (bateau-mouche) is a must in both summer and winter.

EVENTS IN PARIS

◆ "Journées du patrimoine": this takes place in September – generally over the third weekend of the month. More than sixty sites can be visited either free or at reduced cost, and there are concerts and guided tours. Buildings such as ministries, prefectures, public and private buildings and some churches open specially for the public.

◆ Information: Caisse Nationale des Monuments

Historiques et des Sites, Hôtel de Sully, 62, rue St-Antoine 75004 Paris. Tel. 01 44 61 21 69 and 01 44 61 21 70

◆ Science Fair: science museums and research laboratories open to the public over a weekend in June.

◆ Fête du Cinéma (Movie Fair): In June

over one, two or three days, depending on the year.

◆ Music Fair: June 21

◆ "Le Temps des Livres" – Book fair mid to end October.

◆ "Ciné-mémoire": screening of rediscovered or restored movies (end October–mid November).

USEFUL ADDRESSES

◆ Tourist and Congress Office of Paris, 127, avenue des Champs-Élysées 75008 Tel. 01 49 52 53 54 Open daily from 9am to 8pm. Branch offices (open from 8am to 9pm) are to be found in all rail stations in the city. What's on in Paris (24-hour recorded information in English): Tel. 01 49 52 53 56.

◆ French Museums Head Office, 6, rue des Pyramides 75001 Tel. 01 40 15 73 00

◆ Police Prefecture 7, bd. du Palais 75004 Tel. 01 53 71 53 71 or 01 53 73 53 73

FAVORITE PASTIMES

◆ The Big Wheel in the Tuileries fairground. From the top there is a splendid view of the Louvre Pyramid and the banks of the Seine (in June).

◆ A concert in the Tuileries Gardens (in June).

◆ The Rue de Rivoli and the windows in the Samaritaine are all lit and decorated for Christmas.

MAIL

◆ Post offices are open Monday to Friday from 8am to 7pm and Saturday from 8am to noon. Remember to use the self-service machines – in five languages, French, English, German, Italian and Spanish – to frank your mail.

◆ For a letter weighing less than 20g, the 3F rate applies to France and the European Union and for the US it costs 4.30F.

◆ The main post office is open all year 24 hours a day.
52, rue du Louvre
75001 Paris
Tel. 01 40 28 20 00.

BUDGET

Plan for spending in one week:

◆ a couple in top-range luxury hotel including dinner: 25,000F

◆ a family of four in a one-star hotel and bistro meals: 8,000F

◆ economy stay full-board at a youth hostel: 1,600F per person

USEFUL MINITEL SERVICES

Minitel is a terminal linked to the telephone and provides directory and practical information services. These have to be paid for and are accessible through a system of codes.

◆ 36 15 MICHELIN or ITI or ROUTE: itineraries and tourist information.

◆ 36 15 FUAJ: everything on Youth Hostels.

◆ 36 15 CULTURE: Ministry of Culture service for program information on festivals, museums, exhibitions, shows and "Heritage Days" and ordering reproductions of museum exhibits.

◆ 36 15 LOUVRE: full information on the museum and its events.

HEALTH

Pharmacies are usually open from 8am to 8pm except Sunday and Monday morning. When closed, the address of the nearest pharmacy on duty is displayed.

◆ 24-hour pharmacy: Pharmacie Dhery 84, avenue des Champs-Élysées 75008
Tel. 01 45 62 02 41

◆ American Hospital 63 blvd Victor Hugo 92202 Neuilly
Tel. 01 46 41 25 25

◆ British Hospital 3 rue Barbès 92300 Levallois
Tel. 01 47 58 13 12

◆ English Pharmacy 62, avenue des Champs-Élysées 75008
Tel. 01 43 59 22 52 Open daily 8am to midnight

◆ British and American Pharmacy 1, rue Auber 75009
Tel. 01 42 65 29 42 Open Mon.– Fri., 8.30am to 8pm and Sat. 10am to 8pm

PRESS

◆ The main international newspapers are on sale in Paris.

◆ *Time Out* is a free English-language brochure listing venues and events for entertainment. It is available in main hotels, car rental offices, Paris Tourist Office, Virgin Megastore in the Carrousel, and in the following English-language bookstores:
Brentano's
37, avenue de l'Opéra
75002 Paris.
Tel. 01 42 60 52 50 and W.H. Smith 248, rue de Rivoli 75001 Paris.
Tel. 01 44 77 88 99.

◆ *Pariscope*, a guide to shows in Paris, comes out on Wednesday and includes a *Time Out* section in English.

◆ Japanese tourists will find their monthly *Paris–Tokyo* at the office of Voyageurs au Japon 30, rue Ste-Anne 75001 Paris.
Tel. 01 42 61 60 83. The monthly *Paris Dayori* is distributed free in the main hotels and duty-free stores. For Japanese magazines, books, records and videos go to the Book Forum Junku 18, rue des Pyramides 75001 Paris.
Tel. 01 42 60 89 12.

TELEPHONE

international code (00 from the UK, 011 from the US), then the country code for France (33), followed by the area code (1 for Paris or 2/3/4/5 for other areas of France) and then the 8-digit-number you require.

TELEPHONING PARIS FROM ANYWHERE IN FRANCE

From October 18, 1996, a new dialing code system has been in operation and is as follows:
Dial the code for Paris (01) followed by the 8-digit number. 01 also has to be dialed when both caller and receiver are within the 01 Paris area.

USEFUL NUMBERS

SAMU (Medical emergencies): 15
Police: 17
Fire department: 18
SOS Help (English language crisis line) Tel. 01 47 23 80 80 3–11pm daily.

◆ Charges vary according to time of day. Weekday rates drop considerably after 6pm and even more after 9.30pm and at weekends and public holidays.

◆ Payphones can now take smart cards, phonecards of 50 (40.60F) or 120 units (97.50F). These can be purchased from tobacco stores (*bureaux de tabac*), post offices, airports and subway stations.

INTERNATIONAL TELEPHONE CALLS

◆ To call the UK or the US from France dial the international code (00) followed by the country code (44 for the UK, 1 for the US).

◆ To call France from abroad, dial the

PUBLIC HOLIDAYS

- January 1
- Easter Monday
- May 1
- May 8
- Ascension Day (a Thursday in May or June)
- Whit Monday
- July 14 – National Day
- August 15
- November 1
- November 11
- December 25

MONEY

The French franc (F) is divided into 100 centimes (c).
- Notes: 500F, 200F, 100F, 50F and 20F.
- Coins: 20F, 10F, 5F, 2F, 1F and 50c, 20c, 10c, 5c.
- Post offices generally have a bureau de change service available.
- The post office at the Louvre has an automatic machine for changing foreign currency.
- The following cards allow cash withdrawals from cash machines in all banks: Visa, Eurocard/ Master Card, American Express.
- Otherwise there are several bureaux de change in the Rue de Rivoli.

PAYMENT FACILITIES

International bank cards are accepted in hotels, restaurants and stores. Usually a sign in the window shows which credit cards and travelers' checks are accepted as payment. Apart from cash, stores will also accept French checks and credit cards for amounts in excess of 100F. Luxury stores accept foreign currency but not usually Eurocheques.

LOSS OR THEFT

- BANKERS CARDS AND VISA:
Tel. 01 42 77 11 90
- EUROCARD/MASTER CARD and customers of the CRÉDIT AGRICOLE and the CRÉDIT MUTUEL:
Tel. 01 45 67 84 84
- American Express:
Tel. 01 47 77 72 00
- Diner's Club
Tel. 01 47 62 75 00
- IDENTITY PAPERS AND PASSPORTS:
Advise the nearest "commissariat de police" as soon as possible and your consulate if you are a foreigner.

◆ EMBASSIES AND CONSULATES:
US Embassy
2 Ave Gabriel
75008 Paris
Tel. 01 42 96 12 02
UK Embassy
35 rue du Faubourg St-Honoré
75008 Paris
Tel. 01 42 66 92 41
UK CONSULATE
16 rue d'Anjou
75008 Paris
Tel. 01 42 66 91 42

PURCHASES

- Since the opening of the single market, EU citizens can purchase any quantity of goods with no restriction on value. Purchases are subject to the regulations of the internal market, in other words they include taxes. Duty-free stores do not, therefore, concern EU citizens any more, but they are still worthwhile for the international visitor.
- Stores usually open from 9.30am to 6.30pm or 7pm. They close on Sunday and sometimes Monday.

morning except stores catering specifically for tourists, particularly around the Rue de Rivoli.
◆ Some stores close at lunchtime.

Galerie Véro-Dodat. _À La Civette._

Jewelers on the Place Vendôme, luxury boutiques on the Rue St-Honoré, Rue Royale and Rue Cambon, duty-free stores on the Rue de Rivoli, antique and fine art dealers are all side-by-side in this area which was once inhabited by farmers, butchers, journalists, seed merchants and stockbrokers. This intermingling of peoples is still evident today in the store signs which can be seen around the center of town.

BELLES LETTRES AND FINE BOOKS

Strolling along the river banks past the open-air bookstores run by the _bouquinistes_, there is always the hope that the green boxes fixed to the top of the riverbank walls will throw up some rare publication. The age of making a real find, however, has passed. Founded in 1802, under the arcades in the Rue de Rivoli, the bookstore Galignani, has three departments: a general French book section, an anglo-

American section and an international section dealing with fine arts.
GALIGNANI
224, rue de Rivoli, 75001.
Opposite the Palais-Royal, this long-established bookstore sells magnificent old books as well as the most recent publications.
LIBRAIRIE DELAMAIN
155, rue St-Honoré, 75001. For rare editions and old prints browse round the **LIBRAIRIE ANCIENNE ET MODERNE**
45, galerie Vivienne, 75002. Book lovers will also want to visit another venerable institution at
LES ARCADES
8, rue de Castiglione, 75001.

ITINERARY FOR AN ANTIQUE-HUNTER

The Louvre des Antiquaires, one of the world's largest markets for objets d'art, consists of 250 art and antique stores, a bar, restaurant, bureau de change, transport company and an office which carries out expert valuations. Styles and periods are mingled together and regardless of whether your interest is in archeology or Art Deco, all tastes are catered for.
LE LOUVRE DES ANTIQUAIRES
2, place du Palais-Royal, 75001.
Between the Louvre and les Halles, the St-Honoré village, with its fifteen or so antique dealers and picture restorers, is a charming, hidden-away spot. Its setting is a small area of greenery which in summer has all the

charm of a miniature patio.
VILLAGE ST-HONORÉ
91, rue St-Honoré, 75001.
The Galerie Véro-Dodat, opened in 1826 and listed in 1965, retains the essence of its luxurious decoration thanks to its ceilings painted with allegories, its mirrors, its windows with their brass frames surrounded by small imitation marble columns and its black and white tiles. At certain times of the day, it is deserted and time seems to stand still. Collectors will enjoy browsing around these especially the one belonging to Robert Capia, expert restorer of antique dolls.
GALERIE VÉRO-DODAT
2, rue du Bouloi, 75001.

FOR GOURMETS

◆ The coffee merchants, Verlet, turn the choosing and savoring of coffee into a gourmet experience. Some of the world's finest brands are available. Verlet also stocks

an excellent range of teas.
VERLET
256, rue St-Honoré, 75001.

◆ Stohrer, the pastry specialist since 1730, is well worth a visit if

only for its listed shop front. However, its pastries and sweets, some of the best in Paris, are highly recommended.
STOHRER
51, rue Montorgueil, 75002.

◆ Legrand the wine merchants sells a marvelous selection of French wines at all prices. Some can be tasted on the spot.
LEGRAND FILLES ET FILS
1, rue de la Banque, 75002.

Between the Louvre and the Place du Châtelet, the Quai de la Mégisserie is one of the oddest markets in Paris. It specializes in selling animals – from banal poultry to exotic birds, from mice to pythons – and provides an ideal opportunity to add to one's menagerie.

Chantal Thomass boutique.

La Samaritaine.

THE ART OF LIVING
Smokers will marvel at the vast array of pipes and lighters from all round the world available here.
LA CIVETTE
157, rue St-Honoré 75001.
The Rue Royale is the place to find high-class tableware: Christofle, Bernardaud, Baccarat crystal, Lalique and Saint Louis. The grand tradition of French tableware.

Since the late 1800's some of the most prestigious names in Paris have been based in and around Place Vendôme.
VAN CLEEF AND ARPELS (no. 22). This celebrated jeweler, founded in 1906 by Alfred Van Cleef and Charles Arpels, has numbered among its clientele maharajas, movie stars, princesses and divas.
CARTIER (nos. 7 & 23). At the end of the 19th century, Cartier supplied royalty and imperials. Today it draws a varied clientele with its traditional and

PLACE VENDÔME
innovative designs.
BOUCHERON (no. 26). Boucheron opened here in 1883.
GUERLAIN (no. 2). The perfume house of Guerlain (Samsara, Shalimar, Vétiver, l'Heure Bleue, Chamade) has been synonymous with French luxury for over a century.
CHANEL (no. 7). The handbag with the crossover "C"'s, Chanel's no. 5 perfume and fashion collections became symbols of French elegance throughout the world. Coco Chanel worked here and lived at the Ritz

which has a entrance on rue Cambon. In 1993 Chanel opened a jewelry store at no. 29, rue Cambon.
CHARVET (no. 28, rue Cambon 75001). Founded in 1838 at the height of dandy fashion, Charvet was the first shirtmaker to provide bespoke items. Official supplier to the Jockey Club, he dressed Edward VII, Marcel Proust and General de Gaulle, whose measurements are kept in the store's records. Shirts (ready-to-wear or made-to-measure), bow ties, ties and handkerchiefs.

FASHION
RUE DU JOUR
The major names in ready-to-wear seem to have decided to meet up here.
AGNÈS B combines the classic with the audacious in her four boutiques, men, women, Lolita and children. JEAN-PAUL GAULTIER JUNIOR has a line of clothing for young people. CLAUDIE PIERLOT and UN APRES-MIDI DE

CHIEN both sell the smart, sexy clothes liked so much by trendy young girls.
RUE ETIENNE-MARCEL
Designers here tend to be Japanese: COMME DES GARÇONS, the line by Irei Kawakubo; YOHJI YAMAMOTO for sober and up-to-the-minute wear favored by movie director Wim Wenders; JUNKO SHIMADA with various

lines for men, women and children. There is also JOSEPH, offering English knitwear and collections by designers such as Azzedine Alaïa, John Galliano, Helmut Lang . . .
PLACE DES VICTOIRES
The VICTOIRE boutique sells top designer labels for men and women and was the first in the 1960's to prosper.

KENZO, THIERRY MUGLER and, at the edge of the Place des Victoires, JEAN-CHARLES DE CASTELBALJAC are at the luxury end of the ready-to-wear market. Finally CHANTAL THOMASS, the designer who revolutionized lingerie, offers the most elegant underwear to be found anywhere.

SHOPPING MALLS
Those wishing to spend a minimum amount of time shopping do not need to look far. Everything Paris can offer is focused there.
FORUM DES HALLES
The mall attracts 30 million visitors a year, drawn in by the concentration of 260

stores over 4 levels in one vast commercial complex. There are clothes stores (DANIEL HECHTER), gourmet food stores (COMPAGNIE ANGLAISE DES THÉS, DUBERNET), restaurants, various gadget stores and a multimedia store.
The RER Châtelet-les-Halles station is

also in the mall. A direction finder is situated at the reception booth, porte Lescot, level 3.
LA SAMARITAINE
Its slogan "You find everything at the Samaritaine" is not a lie. Sports gear, perfumes and luxury items, the formal and informal all happily

jostle together in the huge premises overlooking the Seine. Its ceramic direction table, on the roof of store 2 (9th floor), takes in the riverside roads and offers a splendid view over the Louvre and surrounding area (Quai de la Mégisserie 75001).

Hotels in Paris, whether luxurious or simply quaint, are frequently veritable museum pieces themselves: red carpets, paintings by masters, liveried footmen, listed buildings. The visitors' books and accounts ledgers read like pages from literature and historical archives, the salons and apartments like chunks of history. Choose between a comfortable place of refuge, a stopover place to spoil yourself, an ivory tower or simply a place to relax. Here is a selection of favorites.

PALACES

The center of Paris has always attracted famous travelers. Three of the most beautiful hotels will give you a warm welcome but at a price. A room for two will cost a minimum 2500F a night.

◆ THE RITZ ◆ *359*
15, Pl. Vendôme, 75001.
More than a luxury hotel, the Ritz is a legend and a flagship for hotels around the world. At the end of the 19th century, César Ritz, an apprentice sommelier from Switzerland, learned his trade in the grand hotels of old Europe. He ended up buying the 18th-century mansion which had belonged to the Duc de Lauzun. He achieved

his dream in 1898 which was to offer "all the refinements a prince could wish for in his own home". Among famous regulars, let us mention the writer Ernest Hemingway, Coco Chanel who lived there for over forty years, and Marcel Proust who dined there several times a week.

◆ HÔTEL DE CRILLON ◆ *358*
10, place de la Concorde, 75008.
In 1758 Louis XV entrusted the architect Jacques-Ange Gabriel with the building of the two façades on Place de la Concorde. Behind one of these grew the Crillon mansion. This became a luxury hotel in 1909 and everyone of note coming to Paris has stayed there including Theodore Roosevelt, King George V, Emperor

The Meurice from the Tuileries Gardens.

Hirohito, Charlie Chaplin, Sophia Loren and Orson Welles. The presidential suites, recently redecorated by Sonia Rykiel, open onto the most beautiful square in the world. It has restaurants, bar, winter garden and boutiques.

◆ LE MEURICE ◆ *359*
228, rue de Rivoli, 75001.
For almost two hundred years, this hotel stayed true to its founders' motto: "No detail too small, no effort too great." Built in 1817 by a postmaster to enchant British high

society, it was nicknamed the Hotel of Kings. In the 1950's the rich heiress Florence Gould had the idea of opening the doors of the Meurice, where she lived, to a galaxy of writers including Gide, Mauriac, Léautaud and Cocteau. She also created the Max Jacob and Roger Nimier awards there. Today the discussions to decide on the Prix Novembre are held at the hotel.

Also the HÔTEL INTERCONTINENTAL, ◆ *358*
3, rue de Castiglione, 75001.

LUXURY HOTELS

Starting at 1500F for a double room, these hotels offer guests complete comfort in historical settings.

◆ HÔTEL LOTTI ◆ *359*
7–9, rue de Castiglione, 75001.
The Lotti opened in 1910 under the influence of the Duke of Westminster who, whenever he was in Paris, wanted a more intimate place to stay with all the comforts

of a luxury hotel. The main salon is hung with old masters while the bedrooms have Louis XV and XVI furniture. Breakfast is a sumptuous occasion.

◆ GRAND HÔTEL INTERCONTINENTAL ◆ *358*
2, rue Scribe, 75009.
The Grand Hôtel Intercontinental was built near the Opéra for the 1867 Universal Exhibition

by the architect Armand. At its opening in May 1862, the Empress Eugénie declared, "It's exactly like home. I thought I was at Compiègne or Fontainebleau."

◆ HÔTEL DU LOUVRE ◆ *358*
Place André-Malraux, 75001
The hotel nearest the museum, opposite the Comédie-Française, the Hôtel

du Louvre has recently been restored. Its large elevators lead to many salons and give access to the suite from which Pissarro, the Impressionist painter, did his scene of the Avenue de l'Opéra in 1898.

◆ Near to the Louvre, is the prestigious NORMANDY HÔTEL ◆ *359*
7, rue de l'Échelle, 75001

> "WHEN I DREAM OF THE LAND BEYOND PARADISE,
> I AM ALWAYS AT THE RITZ IN PARIS"
>
> ERNEST HEMINGWAY

The Intercontinental.

The Ritz.

SIMPLER HOTELS

These offer charm at reasonable prices.

◆ **HÔTEL RICHELIEU MAZARIN** ◆ *360*
51, rue de Richelieu
75001
Between the Palais-Royal, the Bibliothèque Nationale and the Louvre.

◆ **HÔTEL DU PALAIS** ◆ *359*
2, quai de la Mégisserie
75001
Small hotel with 14 rooms in the historic center offers tranquility and a friendly welcome.

◆ **HÔTEL DE LILLE** ◆ *359*
8, rue du Pélican
75001
This small hotel is part of the Théâtre du Châtelet building. The rooms have an unrestricted view over the Seine, the Conciergerie and Notre-Dame.

CHARMING HOTELS

Apart from the great hotels, there are hotels which are full of charm and offer a high level of comfort. Allow 700F to 2000F for a double room. ◆ **HÔTEL BRIGHTON** ◆ *359*
218, rue de Rivoli
75001
This hotel is housed in a Second Empire arcaded building on the Rue de Rivoli. The rooms on the 4th and 5th floors have balconies with superb views over the Tuileries Gardens, the Louvre, the Musée d'Orsay, the Invalides and the Eiffel Tower.
◆ **HÔTEL CASTILLE** ◆ *358*
37, rue Cambon
75001
Painted walls and rich fabrics contribute to the exquisite Venetian-style décor.
◆ **HÔTEL RÉGINA** ◆ *359*
2, pl. des Pyramides
75001
Opened in 1900, the Régina keeps alive the tradition of French luxury. The rooms are decorated with either Louis XVI or Directoire furniture and antique tapestries. The entrance lobby itself is worth the trip.
◆ **LE RELAIS DU LOUVRE** ◆ *359*
19, rue des Prêtres-St-Germain-l'Auxerrois, 75001
This elegantly furnished 18th-century house is now one of the Relais du Silence in Paris.
◆ **HÔTEL DES TUILERIES** ◆ *359*
10, rue Saint Hyacinthe, 75001
In the shadow of St-Germain-l'Auxerrois, the old parish of the kings of France, this charming hotel with its Directoire and English decoration is a step away from the Louvre. There are only 20 rooms and it is quiet and intimate.

COMFORTABLE HOTELS

These two-star and three-star hotels offer a good standard of comfort. Prices from 450F.
◆ **HÔTEL GAILLON OPÉRA** ◆ *359*
9, rue Gaillon
75002.
Situated between the Louvre and the Opéra, this attractive hotel has antique furniture and exposed beams. Each room has its own character.
◆ **HÔTEL DE LONDRES ET DE STOCKHOLM** ◆ *359*
300, rue St-Honoré (entrance at 13, rue St-Roch)
75001.
An old bourgeois house turned into a hotel, near the Tuileries Gardens and the Louvre.
◆ **HÔTEL MOLIÈRE** ◆ *359*
21, rue Molière
75001.
In a quiet street between the Louvre and the Bibliothèque Nationale.
◆ **HÔTEL DE LA PLACE DU LOUVRE** ◆ *359*
21, rue des Prêtres-St-Germain-l'Auxerrois
75001
Looking out onto the church of St-Germain-l'Auxerrois, this hotel enjoys a wonderful situation very close to the Louvre.
◆ **HÔTEL ST-ROCH** ◆ *359*
25, rue St-Roch
75001.
Very close to the Rue St-Honoré, the Louvre and the Tuileries.

Régina Hotel.

BREAKFAST IN A LUXURY HOTEL
If your budget does not stretch to staying in a luxury hotel, you can still enjoy the luxury and refinement of breakfast at the Ritz or Crillon. Allow 150F to 250F per person. Booking is advisable.

Angelina.

The Grand Véfour.

The Grand Colbert.

The area round the Louvre offers a wide choice of restaurants, from the most luxurious to the simplest tea rooms with brasseries, foreign restaurants, summer terraces and old bistros in between. So many places and so many different aspects of Paris are all close at hand.

IN THE GARDENS OF THE PALAIS-ROYAL

After a visit to the Louvre, what could be more enjoyable than a stroll round the hidden gardens of the Palais-Royal?
Take the vaulted passage between the Conseil d'État and the Comédie-Française. Since the 18th century, these arcades have been the setting for elegant late-evening dining.

★ LA GAUDRIOLE
◆ 367
30, rue de Montpensier
75001.
Specialties from southwest France simmered gently by René Tramont; also La Muscade.

COURTYARDS AND PATIOS

Oases of tranquility in the heart of the capital or places to see or be seen. It is always pleasant to lunch or dine there in summer.

★ ROSE THÉ ◆ 368
91, rue St-Honoré
75001.
Enchanting tea room in the St-Honoré village where everything is homemade: salads, savory and sweet tarts, fruit cocktails and fresh vegetables – in summer tables are laid in the flower-covered courtyard surrounded by antique stores.
Also Le Pluvinel (Hôtel Régina), Il Cortile (Hôtel El Castille), the Bar Vendôme,

La Terrasse Fleurie (Intercontinental), and L'Espadon (Ritz).

TEA ROOMS

All tea rooms open at lunchtime serve light meals such as savory tarts, salads and hot vegetable dishes in winter.

★ ANGELINA ◆ 368
226, rue de Rivoli
75001.
The old Rumpelmeyer establishment, with its fin-de-siècle décor, is something of an institution. Can be a long wait before being served.
Also Muscade and A Priori Thé.

Lucas Carton.

GOURMET RESTAURANTS

★ LE GRAND VÉFOUR
◆ 365
17, rue de Beaujolais
75001.
This listed restaurant, marvelously situated in a gallery of the Palais-Royal, is unique in Paris for its Directoire décor. The young chef Guy Martin cooks dishes which combine classic principles and inventive ideas.

★ LUCAS CARTON
◆ 365
9, pl. de la Madeleine
75008.
Alain Senderens reigns supreme in this Parisian temple to the gastronomic arts . Specialties: duck Apicius, lobster with vanilla and chicken with crayfish and asparagus.

★ CARRÉ DES FEUILLANTS ◆ 365
14, rue de Castiglione
75001.
Chef Alain Dutournier cooks dishes from Gascony which he has adapted for today. Specialties: venison terrine with foie gras, hare à la royale.
Also: L'Espadon (Ritz), the Meurice (Hôtel Meurice) and Maxim's.

The Véro-Dodat.

L'Incroyable.

OTHER GRAND TABLES

A little less expensive or more simple than the more prestigious establishments, these restaurants maintain the grand tradition of French cooking.

★ **DROUANT** ♦ *365*
18, rue Gaillon 75002.
In this Parisian institution, home of the Prix Goncourt, whose décor has been renovated, the classic cooking of Pierre Grondard continues to attract a gourmet clientele.
Also:
Le Mercure Galant, Chez la Vieille, Chez Pauline, Chez Georges and L'Ostréa.

BRASSERIES

They usually stay open late and offer a non-stop service with a range of simple dishes like quiches, sandwiches and salads, traditional specialties and the dish of the day.

★ **LE GRAND COLBERT** ♦ *366*
2, rue Vivienne 75002.
It is in this very attractive and recently restored Galerie Colbert, a genuine 1830's setting with mosaics and frescos on the walls, that the best brasserie cooking in the area is to be found.
Also the Brasserie du Louvre, the Nemours and the Café de l'Époque.

BISTROS

In Paris the word "bistro" has many meanings: from the luxury canteens used by politicians or celebrities looking for genuine Parisian atmosphere down to the restaurants frequented by the populace at large.

★ **LE VÉRO-DODAT** ♦ *366*
19, galerie Véro-Dodat 75001.
Situated in the famous Galerie, this restaurant offers good fresh food in an atmosphere which is highly suitable for intimate dinners.
Also: Petit Mâchon.

OPEN LATE

After a visit to a movie theater or a discothèque, these late-night spots will satisfy even the most voracious of appetites.

★ **CHEZ DENISE "LA TOUR DE MONTHLÉRY"** ♦ *367*
5, rue des Prouvaires 75001.

A real Paris night-time institution with a lively atmosphere and filling dishes of pork and mutton, steaks, fish stews, tripe with calvados and bœuf bourguignon.
Also: La Poule au Pot, Au Pied de Cochon ♦ *367.*

FOREIGN RESTAURANTS

Paris is a cosmopolitan city and foreign restaurants abound. Around the Louvre and Opéra are numerous Japanese restaurants offering specialties from the Land of the Rising Sun. The food of other countries is also available.

★ **SAUDADE** ♦ *368*
34, rue des Boudonnais, 75001.
A refined setting to enjoy carefully prepared Portuguese dishes along with a choice of Portuguese wines. About 250F per person.
Also: Issé, Le Maroc, Fellini.

From Diderot to Antoine Blondin to Ernest Hemingway, philosophers, writers, poets, French or not French, have sung the praises of French cafés, a must for anybody who wants to experience the real Paris. There are popular cafés, wine bars, pubs, beer halls, bars whose very atmosphere inspires intimate conversations, and bars that enjoy a certain vogue for a time and then disappear. Muffled or noisy, smart or informal, Parisian or foreign, they all have one thing in common: as soon as you are inside, you feel at home.

FOR THAT FIRST COFFEE IN THE MORNING OR A DRINK AT THE BAR

This is the Paris of Doisneau and Prévert; a timeless way for people to meet and enjoy themselves.

LE NEMOURS ◆ *366*
2, galerie de Nemours
Place Colette
75001.
Genuine and popular, this café-brasserie is an ideal stopping-place for a quick sandwich or a salad and a good glass of draft beer.
Also: Café de l'Époque and A. Gutenberg.

PUBS

Belgium's flatness and Ireland's green are recalled in some pubs in the center of town with their songs and friendly atmosphere.

FLANN O'BRIEN ◆ *369*
6, rue Bailleul
75001.
Open till 1am, this pub is Irish-run and one of the most lively in Paris. A good Guinness, perhaps the best in town, can be drunk here to the strains of folk tunes or rock bands from the British Isles. Around 10pm, the owner switches on the Skynews channel on TV to listen to the latest news on the political situation in Ireland.
Also: Sous-Bock Tavern, the Mannekin-Pis, Quigley's Bar and the Bow Bell.

CAFÉS AND BARS WITH ENTERTAINMENT

A last drink before turning in or even a little alcove to while away the rest of the night.

LE PRESSING ◆ *369*
20, rue du Louvre
75002.
Disc jockey on Saturday night until 4am, playing funk, soul, acid jazz and rhythm and blues. Cocktails in the basement. Live bands on Thursday nights.
LILLIPUT ◆ *369*
55, rue d'Argout
75002.
This café is so crowded that the few tables are not enough for all the customers who throng around on the pavement outside. It is popular with

young people. Even the waiters dance behind the counter to soul and rock music. Drinks are very reasonably priced, so take care not to overdo it.
Also: Banana Café, Le Comptoir and the Bar de l'Entracte.

Bar in the Ritz.

Café du Louvre.

WINE BARS

Wine bars are always pleasant places to meet. Since the main purpose is tasting, wine is served by the glass and depending on the place, this can be accompanied by a sandwich, cheese, a dish of the day or even a full meal.

WILLY'S WINE BAR ♦ *368*
13, rue des Petits-Champs 75001
With the wide choice of wines by the glass on offer (these change every month) Willy's is one of the main tasting haunts for beginners and old-hands. There is a good menu which changes daily according to market availability of produce. Standard

dishes are well-prepared.
AUX BONS CRUS ♦ *368*
7, rue des Petits-Champs 75001
The new owners have wisely decided not to change the décor, which has been the same since 1905: the hand-operated lift for loading the wine racks is on the point of becoming a collector's item. Food is simple: salt pork with lentils, salt beef, cheeses, salamis, spicy steak tartare, cheese fondue, omelets. Good selection of wines by the glass.
LE RUBIS ♦ *368*
10, rue du Marché–St-Honoré 75001
Barrels set the scene and when the place gets

too crowded, customers move out onto the street. This is one of the last down-to-earth wine bars in Paris where the décor has not changed, prices are reasonable and the welcome warm. There are excellent salami sandwiches made with Poilâne bread; dish of the day 40–50F.
LE BAR DE L'ENTRACTE ♦ *368*
47, rue Montpensier 75001
There are very few tables outside and at sunset, the very beautiful theater of the Palais-Royal looks like a paddle steamer on the Mississippi. Marcel Duveau's son is gradually starting up this

establishment again and his wife Babette is turning out some good food (salmon en papillote, andouillette with white wine). A little hideaway for a drink either before or after the theater.
Also: Juvenile's, the Cloche des Halles and the Taverne Henri IV.

GRANDER BARS

Some of the bars made famous by celebrities are worth visiting. In spite of their great age, these bars can sometimes seen intimidating, but they should not be missed.

HARRY'S BAR ♦ *369*
5, rue Daunou 75002
In this legendary bar opened in 1911, everything (with the exception of the red imitation-leather banquettes) is made of wood, from the large polished counter up to the ceiling. The walls are covered in pictures, armor and star-studded flags. The most famous English-speaking writers have left mementos, ordered one of those mythical hot dogs,

scribbled a few lines in the alcove on the ground floor and listened to the pianist playing blues in the basement. Whether you go there to retrace the steps of Ernest Hemingway, or to pay homage to the place where the "Bloody Mary" was created, or just to spend a pleasant evening tête-à-tête, Harry's Bar is worth a round-trip ticket from Manhattan. There is

a gentle reminder to "dress correctly".
BAR HEMINGWAY ♦ *369*
RITZ HOTEL
15, place Vendôme 75001
After being closed for some years, the Hemingway Bar reopened on August 26, 1994. A war correspondent in Paris in 1944, the great author is alleged to have stood at the head of an American contingent liberating the city.

Decorated in green velvet and oakwood, the bar is ideal for literary daydreaming with its well-stocked library and walls covered in photographs of great writers. There is a wide selection of foreign beers, vintage ports and cocktails.
LE RÉGINA ♦ *369*
1, place des Pyramides 75001
Space and discretion are the keynotes to the first floor of the hotel where people from the world of fashion and the arts congregate for a chat. The barman has twenty years' experience and can make you a delicious cocktail to suit your taste.
Also: the St-James bar and the Normandy (in the Hôtel Normandy).

◆ PARIS ON FOOT

Bateaux-mouches at Vert-Galant square.

The Bank of France.

The area around the Louvre has a wealth of old churches, mansions, monuments and museums. Whether you are a music lover, antique hunter or a lover of gardens, the variety of activities in the center of Paris will overwhelm you. Do not miss a trip on the Seine which will offer you one of the most magical views of the capital.

WALKS

PASSAGES AND GALLERIES

The area surrounding the Louvre is crammed with passages: Passage du Grand-Cerf, Passage Choiseul, Passage du Perron at the Palais-Royal, Passage des Pavillons; and galleries: the Galeries Vivienne, Colbert, Véro-Dodat and the galeries de Chartres and de Valois in the Palais-Royal. These covered walkways were highly prized by the Surrealists who saw them as fantastical places. They offer the visitor the triple advantage of being havens of peace cut off from the traffic, historic sites, often listed, whose architecture is worth the trip, and finally as places with a choice of restaurants, tea rooms and various boutiques. In other words, elegant settings for walking about or shopping.

BIBLIOTHÈQUE NATIONALE ◆ 361

This huge national library which houses one of the world's largest collections,

has a long history dating back to Mazarin. The entire building is not open to the public, but many parts are. Opposite the entrance is the famous reading room built by Labrouste in 1868 which is visible through a two-way mirror. The Mansart gallery built in 1645 is almost always open. The room containing medals and antiques (open every day from 1pm to 5pm) houses a magnificent collection of objects including the famous large cameo of the Ste-Chapelle and the Cup of Chosroës. On Tuesdays, the Office for Historic Monuments organizes a visit to the library at 3pm (price: 25–35F).
58, rue Richelieu
75002

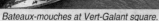

1er Arrt
RUE CROIX
DES PETITS CHAMPS

OPÉRA GARNIER (L'OPÉRA DE PARIS)
◆ 360
As Charles Garnier's masterpiece of Second Empire architecture (1860–75), the Opéra stands out through its sheer magnificence, fashionable in the 1860's. Since 1996, performances have been held in the beautifully restored auditorium. It is also possible to visit the library-museum and the theater (the entrance ticket covers all parts) open daily from 11am to 5pm. Visit the auditorium, the magnificent main staircase, the front foyer, the Salons de la Lune and du Soleil, the gallery of the Grand Foyer and the mirrored Rotunda. The library-museum has a permanent exhibition laid out in three rooms on the history of opera,

ballet and staging.
Place de l'Opéra
75002
(main entrance).

BANQUE DE FRANCE (BANK OF FRANCE)
◆ 360
Since 1811 the bank has had its headquarters in the old Hôtel de Toulouse where the famous Galerie Dorée, one of the most magnificent 17th-century galleries, is still in existence. It can only be visited through a lecture organized by the Office for Historic Monuments.
39, rue Croix-des-Petits-Champs
75001

BOURSE DE PARIS (STOCK EXCHANGE)
◆ 360
The Brongniart Palace, built between 1808 and 1826, remains one of Europe's top financial centers. The stockbrokers' central enclosure (Corbeille room), decorated with paintings in grisaille by Meynier and Pujo,l can be visited from Monday to Friday from 1pm to 3pm.
Place de la Bourse
75002

354

St-Germain-l'Auxerrois.

Tuileries Gardens.

INFORMATION

◆ There are two pocket-sized rival weekly publications on sale at newsstands. They are *Pariscope* (3F) and the *Officiel des Spectacles* (2F), both giving listings of the week's cultural events: museums, theaters, exhibitions, movies, café-theaters with opening and booking times and telephone numbers.

◆ The National Office for Historic Sites and Monuments organizes lecture-tours and issues any necessary passes.

The price is 37F (30F reduced).
For all information:
Tel. 01 44 61 21 69 or 01 44 61 21 70

Cultural and sports programs can also be obtained from local town halls.

TOWN HALL IN ARRONDISSEMENT 1
4, place du Louvre
Tel. 01 44 50 75 01

TOWN HALL IN ARRONDISSEMENT 2
8, rue de la Banque
Tel. 01 42 61 55 02

FORUM DES HALLES

Opened in 1979, the Forum is a vast four-sided building on the site of the old market (les Halles), surrounded by several levels of galleries with shops. It offers a wide variety of leisure activity: the FNAC-Forum meetings area, the Auditorium of the Halles, the House of the Conservatoires, the children's garden, a swimming pool and the Suzanne Berlioux gymnasium and of course the gardens which cover it. Entrances: rues Pierre-Lescot (main), Berger, Rambuteau, Coquillière, and the Pont-Neuf gate.

CONCERTS IN CHURCHES ◆ 360

CHURCH OF ST-GERMAIN-L'AUXERROIS
Old royal parish where there are free bell-ringing concerts from 5pm to 5.30pm in summer and 1pm to 1.30pm in winter.
2, pl. du Louvre 75001

CHURCH OF NOTRE-DAME-DES-VICTOIRES
This church which became the seat of an archbishop in 1740, is the headquarters of the Arch-confraternity of the Virgin and remains a major place of pilgrimage in Paris.
Place des Petits-Pères 75002

CHURCH OF ST-ROCH
The church contains numerous excellent works of art and an organ which, in the 18th century, was considered to be one of the finest in France. Regular concerts, especially on Sundays at 5pm.
Rue St-Honoré/Rue Saint-Roch 75001

CHURCH OF ST-EUSTACHE
The main organ, recently restored, keeps alive the musical tradition of this church which was consecrated in 1637. Its choir is world-famous and every Sunday at the 11am high mass there is some very fine music.
2, rue du Jour, 75001.

CHURCH OF THE MADELEINE
This church which has no belfry, has magnificent front pillars and looks more like a pagan temple of ancient Greece. There are regular concerts of classical music there.
Place de la Madeleine 75008

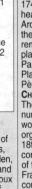

WALKS IN THE GARDENS

GARDENS IN THE PALAIS-ROYAL
Surrounded by three elegant shopping galleries with several attractive boutiques and restaurants, it is one of the most beautiful secluded gardens in Paris. Open till sunset. Entrance: Place Colette, 75001

TUILERIES GARDENS
Open from 7.30am to 7.30pm from end September to end March and from 7am to 9pm in summer. In July and August, the gardens close at 11.45pm (12.45am on Saturday). As part of the work being carried out on the Grand Louvre, the gardens are undergoing alterations (due for completion in spring 1997). This magnificent French garden offers a lovely walk and an exceptional view between the Louvre and the Concorde. Art for Children organizes walks and visits for children aged 3 to 12.
For information:
Tel. 01 46 08 50 88
Games, merry-go-rounds, pony rides and puppet theaters at 3.30pm and 4.30pm on Wednesdays and weekends and all week during school holidays.

After a day spent going round the museums, monuments and stores, a break is essential. Let yourself unwind. Paris is a non-stop festival of fun. Between movies and theaters (the Comédie-Française is a mere step away), the choice is limitless. Begin the evening with a concert or a visit to the theater and round it off in a jazz club.

RESERVATIONS

These can be made in advance by telephone, mail or in person. Theaters always keep some last-minute seats available. Fnac-Forum and Virgin Megastore (open on Sunday) in the Carrousel du Louvre act as ticket agencies for all types of shows. Two theater booths, one on the Place de la Madeleine and the other in the RER Châtelet-les-Halles rail station sell tickets for that evening at half-price. There is a surcharge of 16F per ticket but it is still cheap. The booth at the Madeleine is open from 12.30pm to 8pm from Tuesday to Saturday, and the one at les Halles closes at 4.30pm. Obviously tickets are much in demand and are snapped up as soon as the booths open. You can also dial Minitel 36 15 THEATEL or SPECTAMATIC. 36 15 CULTURE allows you to find the show which interests you through the name of the organizer, the venue, the theme, the date and time or title, and makes your reservation.
NB: Theaters are nearly all closed on Monday. Tips are only accepted in private theaters.

COMÉDIE-FRANÇAISE
◆ *360*

The "Français", as Parisians have nicknamed it, is a venerable old lady indeed. The house is not only the temple of the classical repertoire where Molière played. Ever since Antoine Vitez and then Jacques Lassalle were presidents, it has opened its doors to movie directors and foreign producers and now puts on plays which would formerly have been banned, such as comedies by Feydeau or modern foreign drama. 45 minutes before the start, the box office on rue Montpensier offers 112 gallery seats (maximum of four per person) at 25F.
1, place Colette
75001
For information:
Tel. 01 44 58 14 00

OPERAS

OPÉRA BASTILLE
Place de la Bastille
75012
Tel. 01 44 73 13 00
OPÉRA-COMIQUE
5, rue Favart
75002
Tel. 01 42 44 45 46

PRIVATE THEATERS
Except the Daunou theater which specializes in contemporary pieces, these theaters put on mainly boulevard comedies. Reservations are recommended but you can always try your luck at the Madeleine booth or go straight to the theater box office before the start of the performance.
THÉÂTRE DU PALAIS-ROYAL ◆ *360*
38, rue de Montpensier
75001.
THÉÂTRE DAUNOU ◆ *360*
9, rue Daunou
75002.
THÉÂTRE DE LA POTINIÈRE ◆ *360*
7, rue Louis-le-Grand
75002
THÉÂTRE DE LA MICHODIÈRE ◆ *360*
4 bis, rue de la Michodière
75002
THÉÂTRE DES BOUFFES PARISIENS ◆ *360*
4, rue Monsigny
75002

CLASSICAL CONCERTS
THÉÂTRE DE LA VILLE
2, place du Châtelet
75004
Music from around the world, theater and contemporary dance are all on the bill at this theater where excellence is guaranteed. Artists appearing there include Jean-Claude Gallotta, Pina Bausch, Karine Saporta, Philippe Decouflé.
Information on Minitel:
36 15 THEAVILLE
THÉÂTRE MUSICAL DE PARIS-CHÂTELET
2, rue Édouard-Colonne
75001
Chamber and symphonic music, contemporary dance, opera on one of Europe's biggest stages.
For reservations:
Tel. 01 40 28 28 40
or 36 15 CHÂTELET

Duc des Lombards.

ROCK, VARIETY, JAZZ
The area's nicest and most fun piano bars are all concentrated around the Halles, in the Rue des Lombards. From top jazz through to strict tempo tango, interpreted by the best bands and dancers around, even the most hard to please enthusiast will be

Ticket office at la Madeleine.

The Comédie-Française.

Théâtre de la Ville.

happy there. The Gambrinus (rock and country), the Sunset (jazz, jazz-rock), the Baiser salé (jazz), the Duc des Lombards (jazz and Latin American) are, respectively, at nos. 62, 60, 58 and 42. Concerts usually begin at 10pm. The Petit Opportun is a great address for jazz lovers.
15, rue des Lavandières-Ste-Opportune 75001

OLYMPIA
The oldest concert hall in Paris is the ultimate attainment for the greatest French singers. To perform there is tantamount to consecration.The hall's proportions are particularly suitable for live concerts and the programs put on there are often wonderfully varied.
Reservations essential:
Tel. 01 47 42 25 49
28, bd des Capucines 75009

L'Officiel des Spectacles and Pariscope give details of the week's films and publish cinema details by arrondissement.
◆ The Forum des Halles has several movie theaters (reduced admission charges on Monday and Wednesday).
◆The Vidéothèque de Paris is a filmed souvenir of Paris

There are discos for all tastes: from the famous – and very un-Parisian – Scala, to the very exclusive Ritz Club. Funky atmosphere guaranteed till dawn.
LA SCALA
188 bis, rue de Rivoli 7500.
From 10.30pm to dawn, this disco with eight bars and three floors caters mainly for tourists.
BLACK AND WHITE
31 bis, rue des Lombards 75001
From 11pm to dawn.Smart African night spot.

(documentaries of feature movies with some connection with the city). The admission charge (subscriptions are available) allows the visitor to see the movies on automatic viewing units or in larger theaters when there are themed series of movies or retrospectives.

LA PLANTATION
45, rue de Montpensier 75001
From 11pm to dawn. The other and older Afro disco in the area. Ray Sugar and Claude Nougaro have often danced the night away doing sambas and salsa.
RITZ CLUB
38, rue Cambon 75001
From 8.30pm to dawn. To be admitted, you have to be taken by a member, a guest of the hotel or someone famous. In this intimate club with Napoleon III style décor, elegant food

FORUM DES HALLES
porte St-Eustache, 2, Grande-Galerie, 75002
Tel. 01 40 26 34 30

is available and dancing is not quite so wild. Admission is by sponsorship and is 3,000F; annual subscription is 2,800F.
LE BALISIER
47, rue Berger 75001
From 11pm to dawn. Caribbean music and atmosphere.

DRINKING AND DANCING
Halfway between the classic nightclub and a bar, these places allow for dancing as well as having conversations. The idea works well and you might have a hard time making your way through to the floor. Snacks are always available. These new-style bars are mainly in the area round the Halles.
LE COMPTOIR
14, rue Vauvilliers 75001
LE PRESSING
20, rue du Louvre 75001
LES BOUCHONS
19, rue des Halles, 75001

Olympia.

GENERAL

STORES
Stores are usually open from 10am to 7pm. Be warned: some close for lunch between 1pm and 2pm. Department stores such as Printemps, Galeries Lafayettes, Bon Marché, La Samaritaine and Les Trois-Quartiers are open throughout the day and some are even open on public holidays and Saturdays and Sundays leading up to Christmas.

SHOWS
Shows normally begin around 8.30pm and are usually finished by midnight in plenty of time for the last métro (1am). Most shows have matinées during the week and also Sunday performances at either 3pm or 5pm. Ask at the theater box office for details.

DISCOTHEQUES AND NIGHTCLUBS
Nightclubs open around 10pm and close at dawn (5am or 6am).

RESTAURANTS
Many restaurants close one day a week although the day varies from restaurant to restaurant.

WINE BARS
Many wine bars also serve food such as plates of cold meats and cheeses. They close on Sundays.

SERVICES

TOURIST INFORMATION

TOURIST & CONGRESS OFFICE OF PARIS
127, av. des Champs-Elysées 75008
Tel. 01 49 52 53 54

Open daily 9am–8pm. Answerphone giving program of events:
Tel. 01 49 52 53 55

LA MAISON DE LA FRANCE
8, av. de l'Opéra 75001
Tel. 01 42 96 10 23

LEISURE

VEDETTES DU PONT-NEUF
Square du Vert-Galant, Île de la Cité 75001
Tel. 01 46 33 98 38
Daily at 10am, 1.30pm and 9pm.
Half-hour boat trips along the Seine with commentaries.

SUZANNE-BERLIOUX GYMNASIUM
Forum des Halles (entrance at porte du Jour)
4, pl. de la Rotonde 75001
Tel. 01 42 61 51 75
*Courses on offer include martial arts, dance, trampolining and acrobatics.
Swimming pool at 10, pl. de la Rotonde 75001
Tel. 01 42 36 98 44*

PRACTICAL INFORMATION

TOWN HALL (MAIRIE) 1ST ARRONDISSEMENT
4, pl. du Louvre 75001
Tel. 01 44 50 75 01

TOWN HALL (MAIRIE) 2ND ARRONDISSEMENT
8, rue de la Banque 75002
Tel. 01 42 61 55 02

LOUVRE MUSEUM POST OFFICE
Carrousel du Louvre 75001
Tel. 01 42 61 41 51
Open Mon. and Wed. 9.30am–9.30pm, Thur.–Sat 9.30am–6pm, Sun. 10.30am–6pm.

MAIN POST OFFICE
52, rue du Louvre 75001
Tel. 01 40 28 20 00

Open 24 hours.

EMERGENCIES

SAMU
(medical emergencies)
15
POLICE
17
FIRE BRIGADE
18

ACCOMMODATION

YOUTH HOSTELS

CENTRE INTERNATIONAL DE PARIS-LOUVRE (YOUTH HOSTEL HEAD OFFICE)
20, rue Jean-Jacques Rousseau 75001
Tel. 01 42 36 88 18
Open daily all year round.
*Travel agency for young people. This is a private organization which runs several accommodation centers in Paris for people aged between 18 and 35.
Cost: 120F per person per night (including breakfast). Rooms of 2, 4, 6, 8 and 10 beds. Reservations can only be made on the actual day from 9am to 2am.*

CENTRE INTERNATIONAL DE PARIS-OPÉRA (B.V.J)
11, rue Thérèse 75001
Tel. 01 42 60 77 23
Closed Nov., Dec. and Jan.

CENTRE INTERNATIONAL DE PARIS-LES HALLES (B.V.J)
5, rue du Pélican, 75001
Tel. 01 40 26 92 45
Closed Nov., Dec. and Jan.

HOTELS – 4 STAR

GRAND HÔTEL INTER-CONTINENTAL★★★★
2, rue Scribe 75009
Tel. 01 40 07 32 32
Fax 01 42 66 12 51
Double rooms from 2,100F. Lounges, two restaurants, l'Opéra

and la Verrière, le Café de la Paix, two bars, winter garden, boutiques.
◆ 348

HÔTEL CASTILLE★★★★
37, rue Cambon 75001
Tel. 01 44 58 44 58
Fax 01 44 58 44 00
Double rooms from 1,990F. Il Cortile restaurant is laid out around a small Italian courtyard. Florentine-style décor.
◆ 349

HÔTEL DE CRILLON ★★★★
10, pl. de la Concorde 75008
Tel. 01 44 71 15 00
Fax 01 44 71 15 02
Double rooms from

3,200F, suites from 4,900F. Les Ambassadeurs restaurant, Crillon bar, winter garden, hotel lounges.
◆ 348

HÔTEL ÉDOUARD VII ★★★★
39, av. de l'Opéra 75002
Tel. 01 42 61 56 90
Fax 01 42 61 47 73
Double rooms at 1,300F. View of the Opéra Garnier. Rooms in English and Oriental styles.

HÔTEL INTER-CONTINENTAL ★★★★
3, rue de Castiglione 75001
Tel. 01 44 77 11 11
Fax 01 44 77 14 60
Double rooms from 2,200F to 2,700F. Two restaurants, the Café Tuileries and La Terrasse Fleurie.
◆ 348

HÔTEL DU LOUVRE ★★★★
Pl. André Malraux 75001

Tel. 01 44 58 38 38
Fax 01 44 58 38 01
*Double rooms from
1,350F. The Louvre
brasserie, "The
Defender" bar, winter
garden.*
◆ *348*

HÔTEL LOTTI ★★★★
7, rue de Castiglione
75001
Tel. 01 42 60 37 34
Fax 01 40 15 93 56
*Double rooms from
1,920F. Gourmet
restaurant, bar.*
◆ *348*

HÔTEL MEURICE ★★★★
228, rue de Rivoli
75001
Tel. 01 44 58 10 10
Fax 01 44 58 10 15
*Double rooms from
2,600F, suites from
5,500F. Le Meurice
restaurant, Pompadour
bar, business center,
shops, reception halls.*
◆ *348*

NORMANDY HÔTEL ★★★★
7, rue de l'Échelle
75001
Tel. 01 42 60 30 21
Fax 01 42 60 45 81
*Rooms: 1,375–1,580F
Suites: 1,875–2,780F*
◆ *348*

HÔTEL RÉGINA ★★★★
2, pl. des Pyramides
75001
Tel. 01 42 60 31 10
Fax 01 40 15 95 16
*Double rooms from
1,520F. Le Pluvinel
restaurant, English-style
bar, interior garden,
lounges.*
◆ *349*

LE RITZ ★★★★
15, pl. Vendôme
75001
Tel. 01 43 16 30 30
Fax 01 43 16 31 78
*Double rooms from
3,200F, suites from
5,500F. Bar Hemingway,
Ritz Club, Espadon
restaurant, interior
garden, lounges,
swimming pool, gym,
squash, sauna.*
◆ *348*

**HÔTEL ROYAL
ST-HONORÉ ★★★★**
221, rue St-Honoré
75001
Tel. 01 42 60 32 79
Fax 01 42 60 47 44
*Double rooms: 1,550F.
This hotel underwent a*

*complete renovation. It
reopened in June 1993.*

HÔTEL SCRIBE ★★★★
1, rue Scribe
75009
Tel. 01 44 71 24 24
Fax 01 44 71 24 42
*Double rooms from
2,200F. Headquarters
of the Jockey Club since
1926.*

**HÔTEL ST-JAMES AND
ALBANY ★★★★**
202, rue de Rivoli
75001
Tel. 01 44 58 43 21
Fax 01 44 58 43 11
*Double rooms 950F,
suites 1,700F, duplex
2,700F. Le Noailles
restaurant, interior
garden, English-style
bar St James, private
garage.*

**HÔTEL
WESTMINSTER ★★★★**
13, rue de la Paix
75002
Tel. 01 42 61 57 46
Fax 01 42 60 33 66
*Double rooms from
1,250 to 1,450F.
Charming old rooms.*

HOTELS – 3 STAR

**GRAND HÔTEL
DE MALTE ★★★**
63, rue de Richelieu
75002
Tel. 01 42 96 58 06
Fax 01 42 86 88 19
*Double rooms at 780F.
This mansion once
belongied to the knights
of the Order of Malta
and was turned into a
hotel during the French
Revolution.*

HÔTEL BRIGHTON ★★★
218, rue de Rivoli
75001
Tel. 01 47 03 61 61
Fax 01 42 60 41 78
*Double rooms from
690F to 900F, breakfast
included.*
◆ *349*

**HÔTEL DUMINY
VENDÔME ★★★**
3, rue du Mont-Thabor
75001

Tel. 01 42 60 32 80
Fax 01 42 96 07 83
*Double rooms at
800F.*

**HÔTEL GAILLON
OPÉRA ★★★**
9, rue Gaillon
75002
Tel. 01 47 42 47 74
Fax 01 47 42 01 23
*Double rooms from
600F to 800F.*
◆ *349*

HÔTEL MOLIÈRE ★★★
21, rue Molière
75001
Tel. 01 42 96 22 01
Fax 01 42 60 48 68
*Double rooms from
580F to 720F.*
◆ *349*

**HÔTEL DE LA PLACE
DU LOUVRE ★★★**
21, rue des Prêtres-
St-Germain-l'Auxerrois
75001
Tel. 01 42 33 78 68
Fax 01 42 33 09 95
*Double rooms from
612F to 812F.*
◆ *349*

**HÔTEL DES
TUILERIES ★★★**
10, rue St-Hyacinthe
75001
Tel. 01 42 61 04 17
Fax 01 49 27 91 56
*Double rooms: 790F,
990F and 1,200F.
Mansion house dating
from the 18th century.
Member of Relais du
Silence.*
◆ *349*

**LE RELAIS
DU LOUVRE ★★★**
19, rue des Prêtres-
St-Germain-l'Auxerrois
75001
Tel. 01 40 41 96 42
Fax 01 40 41 96 44
*Double rooms from
820F.*
◆ *349*

HOTELS – 2 STAR

**GRAND HÔTEL
DES DUCS
DE BOURGOGNE ★★**
19, rue du Pont-Neuf
75001

Tel. 01 42 33 95 64
Fax 01 40 39 01 25
*Double rooms: 540F
with shower, 590F with
bath. In one of the old
districts of Paris.*

**GRAND HÔTEL
DU PALAIS-ROYAL ★★**
4, rue de Valois
75001
Tel. 01 42 96 15 35
Fax 01 40 15 97 81
*Double rooms from
500F to 560F.
This hotel was
constructed in the early
19th-century, at the
same time as the Rue
de Valois.*

**HÔTEL DES
DUCS D'ANJOU ★★**
1, pl. Ste-Opportune
75001
Tel. 01 42 36 92 24
Fax 01 42 36 16 63
*Double rooms from
592F. This hotel is
conveniently situated in
Les Halles.*

**HÔTEL DE LONDRES
ET DE STOCKOLM ★★**
300, rue St-Honoré
(entrance at 13, rue
St-Roch)
75001
Tel. 01 42 60 15 62
Fax 01 42 60 16 00
*Double rooms from
450F to 550F.*
◆ *349*

HÔTEL ST-ROCH ★★
25, rue St-Roch
75001
Tel. 01 42 60 17 91
Fax 01 42 61 34 06
*Double rooms from
400F to 550F.*
◆ *349*

HOTELS – 1 STAR

HÔTEL DE LILLE ★
8, rue du Pélican
75001
Tel. 01 42 33 33 42
*Double rooms with
washbasin 220F, with
shower 270F.*
◆ *349*

**HÔTEL DU
PALAIS ★**
2, quai de la Mégisserie
75001
Tel. 01 42 36 98 25
Fax 01 42 21 41 67
*Double rooms
with washbasin from
230F to 320F, with
shower from 350F to
380F.*
◆ *349*

HÔTEL RICHELIEU MAZARIN *
51, rue de Richelieu
75001
Tel. 01 42 97 46 20
Fax 01 47 03 94 13
Double rooms at 330F.
◆ *349*

THEATER

COMÉDIE-FRANÇAISE
1, pl. Colette
75001
Tel. 01 44 58 14 00
Reservations:
Tel. 01 45 15 00 15
The place to see plays of the classical repertory (including Molière, Racine and Corneille).

MAISON DE LA POÉSIE
161, rue Saint-Martin
75003
Tel. 01 44 54 53 00
Poetry readings, talks and lectures.

THÉÂTRE DES BOUFFES-PARISIENS
4, rue de Monsigny
75002
Tel. 01 42 96 60 24
French farce.

THÉÂTRE DAUNOU
7, rue Daunou
75002
Tel. 01 42 61 69 14
Contemporary plays.
◆ *356*

THÉÂTRE DE LA MICHODIÈRE
4 bis, rue de la Michodière
75002
Tel. 01 47 42 95 22
Vaudeville, tragi-comedies.

THÉÂTRE DU PALAIS-ROYAL
38, rue de Montpensier
75001
Tel. 01 42 97 59 81
French farce ◆ *356.*

THÉÂTRE DE LA POTINIÈRE
7, rue Louis-le-Grand
75002
Tel. 01 42 61 44 16
French farce.

RESERVATIONS

AGENCE DE THÉÂTRE PERROSSIER
6, pl. de la Madeleine
75008
Tel. 01 42 60 58 31
Theater bookings.

MUSIC

AUDITORIUM DES HALLES
Forum des Halles
5, porte St-Eustache
(level 2)
75001
Tel. 01 42 36 14 09
Concerts, chamber music, symphony orchestras.
◆ *355*

OLYMPIA
28, bd des Capucines
75009
Tel. 01 47 42 25 49
The Olympia offers a varied repertoire of French and international music.
◆ *357*

OPÉRA BASTILLE
120, rue de Lyon
75012
For reservations:
Tel. 01 44 73 13 00
Opera, lyric opera, concerts. This is the new Paris temple of lyric opera.

OPÉRA-COMIQUE
Salle Favart
5, rue Favart
75002
Tel. 01 42 44 45 46
Operas, concerts and plays.

OPÉRA GARNIER
8, rue Scribe
75009
For reservations:
Tel. 01 44 73 13 00
Classical and contemporary ballet and dance, opera.
◆ *354*

THÉÂTRE DE LA VILLE
2, pl. du Châtelet
75004
For reservations:
Tel. 01 42 74 22 77
International styles of music, a range of singers, contemporary dance and theater.
◆ *356*

THÉÂTRE MUSICAL DE PARIS-CHÂTELET
1, pl. du Châtelet,
75001
For reservations:
Tel. 01 40 28 28 40.
Minitel 36 15 CHATELET.
Chamber music, symphonies, opera and contemporary dance.
◆ *356*

CONCERTS IN CHURCHES

ÉGLISE DE LA MADELEINE
Pl. de la Madeleine
75008
14, rue Surène
Tel. 01 40 07 03 91
Classical concerts.
◆ *355*

ÉGLISE NOTRE-DAME-DES-VICTOIRES
6, rue Notre-Dame-des-Victoires
Tel. 01 42 60 90 47
Place of pilgrimage.

ÉGLISE RÉFORMÉE DE L'ORATOIRE
4, rue de l'Oratoire
75001

Tel. 01 42 60 21 64
Concerts.

ÉGLISE ST-EUSTACHE
75001
Tel. 01 42 36 31 05
Organ concerts.
◆ *355*

ÉGLISE ST-GERMAIN L'AUXERROIS
2, pl. du Louvre
75001
Tel. 01 42 60 13 96
Concerts and bell-ringing daily.

ÉGLISE ST-ROCH
24, rue St-Roch
75001
Tel. 01 42 60 81 69
Concerts. Remarkable décor.
◆ *355*

PLACES TO VISIT

BANQUE DE FRANCE
39, rue Croix-des-Petits-Champs
75001
Tel. 01 42 92 42 92
Tours of the Grande gallery as part of the Caisse des Monuments Histoires lectures only.
◆ *354*

BOURSE DE PARIS
Palais de la Bourse
75002
Tel. 01 40 41 62 20
Tours Mon.–Fri., 1pm–3pm.
◆ *354*

CAISSE NATIONALE DES MONUMENTS HISTORIQUES
Hôtel de Sully
62, rue St-Antoine
75004
Tel. 01 44 61 20 00
Tours and lectures at the Hôtel de Sully as well as day trips to Île-de-France and other areas and daily guided tours of Paris. Registration:
Tel. 01 44 61 21 69 or 01 44 61 21 70
◆ *355*

LA MAISON DE LA CHINE AND DE L'EXTRÊME-ORIENT
36, rue des Bourdonnais
75001
Tel. 01 40 26 21 95
Much more than a tour operator, also puts on exhibitions.

LA VIDÉOTHÈQUE DE PARIS
Forum des Halles
porte Ste-Eustache
2, Grande Galerie
(level 3)
75001
Tel. 01 44 76 62 00
Open 1pm–9pm (10pm
Thur.). Closed Mon.
*Movies of Paris and on
other themes.*
◆ 357

MUSEUMS

PARIS

BIBLIOTHÈQUE NATIONALE
58, rue de Richelieu
75002
Tel. 01 47 03 81 26
Open daily 1pm–5pm.
*Display of medals and
antiques. Temporary
exhibitions.*
◆ 333, 354

GALERIE NATIONALE DU JEU DE PAUME
1, pl. de la Concorde
75001
Tel. 01 47 03 12 50
Opening hours:
Wed.–Fri. noon–7pm,
Sat.–Sun. 10am–7pm,
Tue. evening
noon–9.30pm.
Closed Mon.
*Contemporary art
exhibitions. Bookstore
and cafétéria.*

INSTITUT DU MONDE ARABE
1, rue des Fossés-
St-Bernard
75005
Tel. 01 40 51 38 38
Open daily 10am–6pm
except Mon.
◆ 332

MANUFACTURE ROYALE DES GOBELINS
42, av. des Gobelins
75013
Tel. 01 44 08 52 00
Two afternoon tours,
2 pm and 2.45pm on
Tue., Wed., Thur.

MUSÉE D'ART MODERNE, CENTRE NATIONAL GEORGES-POMPIDOU
19, rue Beaubourg
75004
Tel. 01 44 78 12 33
Open Mon.–Fri.
noon–10pm, Sat.–Sun.
10am–10pm. Closed
Tue.
◆ 332

MUSÉE D'ART MODERNE DE LA VILLE DE PARIS (MAM)
11, av. du Président-
Wilson
75016
Tel. 01 53 67 40 00
Open Tue.–Fri.
10am–5.30pm,
Sat.–Sun.10am–7pm.

MUSÉE NATIONAL DES ARTS AFRICAINS ET OCÉANIENS
293, av. Daumesnil
75012
Tel. 01 43 46 51 61
Open Mon.–Fri.
10am–5.30pm,
Sat.–Sun. 10am–6pm
◆ 332

MUSÉE DES ARTS ASIATIQUES-GUIMET
6, pl. d'Iéna
and Galeries du
Panthéon bouddhique
19, av. d'Iéna 75116
Tel. 01 47 23 61 65
The museum is closed
for restoration works until
1999. However, you can
visit the Buddhist
pantheon (open daily
9.45am–5.15pm.
Closed Tuesday) .
◆ 332

MUSÉE DES ARTS DÉCORATIFS
Palais du Louvre
107, rue de Rivoli
75001
Tel. 01 44 55 57 50
Open Wed.–Sat.
12.30–6pm, Sun.
noon–6pm. Closed Mon.
and Tue.
◆ 333

MUSÉE CARNAVALET
23–29, rue de Sévigné
75003
Tel. 01 42 72 21 13
Open daily except Mon.
10am–5.40pm.
◆ 333

MUSÉE GRÉVIN
Forum des Halles
55, Grand Balcon
(level 1) 75001
Tel. 01 40 26 28 50
Open Mon.–Sat.
2pm–6pm
*Annex to the main
museum, located at
10, bd Montmartre.*

MUSÉE DE L'HOLOGRAPHIE
Forum des Halles,
15–21, Grand Balcon
(level 1) 75001
Tel. 01 40 39 96 83
Open Mon.–Sat. 10am–

7pm, Sun.
and public
holidays
1pm–7pm.

MUSÉE DU LOUVRE
34–36, quai
du Louvre
75001
Tel. 01 40 20 50 50
Open daily except Tue.
9am–6pm. Evenings
until 9.45pm: Mon. (part
of the museum) and
Wed. (whole museum).

MUSÉE DES MONUMENTS FRANÇAIS
Palais de Chaillot
1, pl. de Trocadéro
and du Onze-Novembre
75116
Tel. 01 44 05 39 10
Open daily except Tue.
10am–6pm.
◆ 333

MUSÉE NATIONAL DU MOYEN-ÂGE – THERMES DE CLUNY
6, pl. Paul-Painlevé
75005
Tel. 01 43 25 62 00
Open daily except Tue.
9.15am–5.45pm.
◆ 333

MUSÉE D'ORSAY
1, rue de Bellechasse
75007
Tel. 01 40 49 48 14
Open daily except Mon.
Hours: Tue., Wed., Fri.,
Sat. 10am–6pm,
Thur. 10am–9.45pm,
Sun. 9am–6pm.
◆ 332

MUSÉE DU PETIT-PALAIS
1, av. Dutuit
75008
Tel. 01 42 65 12 73
Open daily except Mon.
and public holidays
10am–5.40pm.
◆ 333

ORANGERIE DES TUILERIES
Pl. de la Concorde
75001
Tel. 01 42 97 48 16
Open 9.45am– 5.15pm
except Tue.
◆ 332

PAVILLON DES ARTS
Forum des
Halles
Terrasse
Lautréamont
101, rue
Rambuteau
75001
Tel. 01 42 33
82 50
Temporary exhibitions.

AROUND PARIS

◆ 332–3

CHÂTEAU DE CHANTILLY
60500 Chantilly
Tel. 01 44 54 04 02
Train: Gare du Nord to
Chantilly
Open Mar 1–Oct. 31
10am–6pm.
Open Nov. 1–Feb. 28
10.30am–12.45pm and
2pm–5pm. Closed Tue.

CHÂTEAU D'ÉCOUEN/ MUSÉE DE LA RENAISSANCE
95440 Écouen
Tel. 01 39 90 04 04
Train: Gare du Nord, to
Écouen-Ezanville.
Open daily except Tue.
9.45am–12.30pm and
2pm–5.15pm.

CHÂTEAU/MUSÉE DE FONTAINEBLEAU
77300 Fontainebleau
Tel. 01 60 71 50 70
Train: Gare de Lyon
(direction Montereau-
Sens) to Fontainebleau.
Open daily except Tue.
9.30am–12.30pm and
2–5pm.

CHÂTEAUX DE MALMAISON AND DE BOIS-PRÉAU
15, av. du Château
92500 Rueil-Malmaison
Tel. 01 47 49 48 15
Line: RER A
(direction

St-Germain-en-Laye) to
Granche Arche. Bus 258
will take you right up to
the château.
Opening times:
April 1–Sep. 30
10am–noon and
1.30–5pm.
Oct. 1–Mar. 31
10am–noon and
1.30–4.30pm.
Closed Tue.

**CHÂTEAU DE
ST-GERMAIN-EN-LAYE/
MUSÉE DES
ANTIQUITÉS
NATIONALES**
Pl. du Château
78103 St-Germain-en-
Laye
Tel. 01 34 51 53 65
Line: RER A to
St-Germain-en-Laye.
Open daily
9am–5.15pm.

**CHÂTEAU DE
VERSAILLES/MUSÉE
NATIONAL D'HISTOIRE**
78000 Versailles
Tel. 01 30 84 74 00
Train: Gare St-Lazare to
Versailles
Open Tue.–Sun.
9am–6pm.

**MUSÉE NATIONAL
DE LA CÉRAMIQUE**
Pl. de la Manufacture
92310 Sèvres
Tel. 01 41 14 04 20
Métro: Porte de
St-Cloud.
Open daily except Tue.
10am–5pm.

**BOOKSTORES/
MUSEUM STORES**

**BOUTIQUE DU MUSÉE
DES ARTS DÉCORATIFS**
107, rue de Rivoli, 75001
Tel. 01 42 61 04 02
Open Wed.–Sun.
12.30–6pm.
*Design items and
reproductions of
museum pieces.*

**BOUTIQUE MUSÉE ET
COMPAGNIE (RMN)**
49, rue Étienne-Marcel
75001
Tel. 01 40 13 49 12
*Jewelry, models,
playing cards, diaries,
posters and various
reproductions of*

*museum pieces from
the Louvre.*
◆ 323

**CHALCOGRAPHIE DU
MUSÉE DU LOUVRE
(RMN)**
Galerie du Carrousel
Allée de France
Tel. 01 40 20 59 35
*Brass rubbings and
reproductions of works
of art from the Louvre.*
◆ 322

LIBRAIRIE COLBERT
2, rue Vivienne
(Colbert Gallery)
75002
Tel. 01 47 03 85 71
*National Library
bookstore. Art books.*

**LIBRAIRIE DU MUSÉE
DES ARTS DÉCORATIFS**
107, rue de Rivoli
75001
Tel. 01 42 96 21 31
Open daily 10am–7pm.

**LIBRAIRIE DU MUSÉE
DU LOUVRE (RMN)**
Hall Napoléon
Tel. 01 40 20 53 53
*Museum store on two
floors with art books on
one and items from the
RMN (casts, jewelry,
scarves) on the other.*
◆ 322

MUSÉE HALLES (RMN)
Forum des Halles
75001
Porte Berger, level 2
Tel. 01 40 39 92 21
*Reproductions, casts,
jewelry, works from the
Louvre.*
◆ 323

PARIS MUSÉES
1, rue Pierre Lescot
75001
Tel. 01 40 26 56 65

*Catalogs, art books,
scarves with artists,
designs, contemporary
jewelry.*

**BOOKSTORES
(NEW AND
SECONDHAND)**

GALIGNANI
224, rue de Rivoli
75001
Tel. 01 42 60 76 07
*Art books in English
and French.*
◆ 346

**LIBRAIRIE
ANCIENNE ET
MODERNE**
DF Jousseaume 45–46
and 47, galerie Vivienne
75002
Tel. 01 42 96 06 24
*Three bookstores
each specializing in a
particular subject:
plastic arts, fine art and
literature and history.*
◆ 346

**LIBRAIRIE
DES ARCADES**
Antoine Grandmaison
et compagnie
8, rue de Castiglione
75001
Tel. 01 42 60 62 96
Antique bookstore.
◆ 346

LIBRAIRIE DELAMAIN
155, rue St-Honoré
75001
Tel. 01 42 61 48 78
*New and secondhand
books.*
◆ 346

LIBRAIRIE F.M.R
15, galerie Véro-Dodat
75001
Tel. 01 40 41 02 02
*High-quality art books
by the publisher Franco
Maria Ricci.*

LIBRAIRIE GAUGUAIN
13, passage Véro-Dodat
75001
Tel. 01 45 08 96 89
*Rare and antique
books.*

LIBRAIRIE PARALLÈLES
36, rue des Bourdonnais
75001
Tel. 01 42 33 60 00

*This bookstore
specializes in books on
jazz, movies, rock
music and science
fiction.*

W.H. SMITH
248, rue de Rivoli
75001
Tel. 01 44 77 88 99
*English language
bookstore. Newspapers,
magazines, novels and
specialist books.*

**ANTIQUES
AND ART**

ANNE JOLIET
9, rue de Beaujolais
(passage du Perron)
75002
Tel. 01 42 96 55 13
Music boxes.

**BOUTIQUE
DU PALAIS-ROYAL**
9, rue de Beaujolais
(passage du Perron)
75002
Tel. 01 42 60 08 22
*Antique wooden
toys.*

CASA LOPEZ
34, galerie Vivienne
75002
Tel. 01 42 60 46 85
*Showroom and
boutique. Famous for its
wool rugs and
tapestries.*

**EN ATTENDANT
LES BARBARES**
50, rue Étienne-Marcel
75002
Tel. 01 42 33 37 87
*Contemporary design
with primitive influences.
The furniture on display
blends natural elements
(wood, leather) with
modern materials (steel,
composite materials).*

LOUVRE DES ANTIQUAIRES
2, pl. du Palais-Royal
75001
Tel. 01 42 97 27 00
Minitel 3615 LDA
Open Tue.–Sun.
11am–7pm.
*250 antiques displayed
over three floors.*
◆ *346*

MICHEL BOYER
7, rue de la Banque
75002
Tel. 01 42 96 62 31
*Modern furniture made
from exotic woods and
glass and wood.*

MIDORI'S, GALERIE D'ART JAPONAIS
13, rue Villedo
75001
Tel. 01 47 03 33 03
*Classes in ikebana
(Japanese floral art).*

ROBERT CAPIA
26, galerie Véro-Dodat
75001
Tel. 01 42 36 25 94
*Antique 19th- and 20th-
century dolls.*
◆ *346*

LE VILLAGE SAINT-HONORÉ
91, rue Saint-Honoré
75001
*Tucked away in this
quiet and charming
corner of Paris are
fifteen antique stores
and furniture restorers,
grouped together
around a small patch of
greenery.*
◆ *346*

TABLEWARE AND TABLE DECORATION

BACCARAT
11, pl. de la Madeleine
75008
Tel. 01 42 65 36 26
Crystal glassware.

BERNARDAUD
11, rue Royale 75008
Tel. 01 47 42 82 66
Limoges porcelain.

CRISTALLERIES DE SAINT-LOUIS
La Maison Royale
13, rue Royale
75008
Tel. 01 40 17 01 74
*Established in 1586.
China and Saint-Louis
crystal.*

GALERIES DU PALAIS-ROYAL
Three galleries (Valois,
Montpensier, de
Beaujolais) opening
onto the Palais-Royal,
75001
*Several tableware stores
with everything you
could possibly
need for table
decoration.*

LALIQUE
11, rue Royale
75008
Tel. 01 42 65 33 70
*Decorative items,
vases, Lalique
glassware.
There is also an outlet
at Carrousel du Louvre:
99, rue de Rivoli 75001.*

PAVILLON CHRISTOFLE
9, rue Royale
75008
Tel. 01 49 33 43 00
*First opened in 1830.
General tableware and
silverware.*

ODIOT ORFÈVRE
7, pl. de la Madeleine
75008
Tel. 01 42 65 00 95
*Suppliers of silverware
since 1690. Offers
quality cutlery,
reproductions of
collectors' pieces.*

VILLAGE ROYAL
Rue Royale
75008
*Elegant shopping arcade
containing several stores
selling tableware as well
as fashion accessories
and jewelry.*

FLORISTS

LACHAUME
10, rue Royale
75008
Tel. 01 42 60 57 26
*Master florist since
1845. Bouquets from
800F. Flower
arrangements.*

MAXIM'S FLEURS
5, rue Royale
75008
Tel. 01 47 42 88 46
*Small bouquets from
300F, Arrangements
from 700F.*

MISCELLANEOUS

LA CIVETTE
157, rue St-Honoré
75001
Tel. 01 42 96 04 99
*Tobacco store selling
quality cigars and
tobacco, referred to by
Casanova in his
"Memoirs".*
◆ *347*

LA DROGUERIE
9-11, rue du Jour
75001
Tel. 01 45 08 93 27
*Old-fashioned
haberdashers: buttons
in every color, zippers,
thread.*

GALERIE LAGUIOLE
1, pl. Ste-Opportune
75001
Tel. 01 40 28 09 42
*Major stockist of French
cutlery presented in a*

*sober setting of
shades of gray.*

MOBUKA FRANCE
18, rue Montmartre
75001
Tel. 01 45 08 80 02
Ribbon specialist.

LE FORUM DES HALLES
Espace Expansion
1, rue Pierre-Lescot
75001
Tel. 01 44 76 96 56
*Located on the site of
the former Halles, there
are now several levels
of shopping galleries
with 260 stores.*
◆ *347, 355*

LA SAMARITAINE
19, rue de la Monnaie
and quai de la
Mégisserie
75001
Tel. 01 40 41 20 20
*Four large stores
where "you can find
everything!". Stunning
Art Deco façade.*
◆ *347*

LES TROIS-QUARTIERS
23, bd de la Madeleine
75001
Tel. 01 42 97 80 12
*A complex of 75
boutiques, spread over
three floors.*

ANNICK GOUTAL
14, rue de Castiglione
75001
Tel. 01 42 60 52 82
*Famous for its scents
which have won Annick
Goutal a worldwide
reputation.*

GUERLAIN
2, pl. Vendôme
75001
Tel. 01 42 60 68 61
*One of the major
brands of French
perfume: Samsara,
Shalimar, Vetiver,
l'Heure bleue,
Chamade.*
◆ *347*

LES SALONS DU PALAIS ROYAL SHISEIDO
142, galerie de Valois
75001
Tel. 01 49 27 09 09
*Beauty products by the
Japanese company
Shiseido.*

JEWELRY

ALFRED DUNHILL
15, rue de la Paix
75002
Tel. 01 42 61 57 58
Jewelry, precious
stones and watches.

**BOUCHERON
JOAILLERIE**
26, pl. Vendôme
75001
Tel. 01 42 61 58 16
High-quality jewelry.
◆ 347

CARTIER
7 and 23, pl. Vendôme
75001
Tel. 01 40 15 03 51
Internationally famed for
its "must" collections.
◆ 347

CHANEL
7, pl. Vendôme
75001
Tel. 01 42 86 29 87
Clocks, watches, jewelry.
◆ 347

CHAUMET
12, pl. Vendôme
75001
Tel. 01 44 77 24 00
Chaumet is renowned
for its gold rings.

JEAN DINH VAN
7, rue de la Paix
75002
Tel. 01 42 61 66 21
Contemporary jewelry
by the Vietnamese
jeweler Jean Dinh Van.

POIRAY
1, rue de la Paix
75002
Tel. 01 42 61 70 58
Cabochon rings with
colored precious and
semi-precious stones.
Famous for its Poiray
watches with a choice
of straps in 450 different
colors (leather or fabric).
Pendants on ribbons.

**VAN CLEEF
AND ARPELS**
22, pl. Vendôme
75001
Tel. 01 42 61 58 58
Top of the range
jeweler.
◆ 347

FASHION

ABSINTHE
74–76, rue Jean-
Jacques Rousseau
75001
Tel. 01 42 33 54 44

Designer-label clothing
including Dries Van
Noten and Paz y Fé.

AGNÈS B
2–3–6–10, rue du Jour
75001
Tel. 01 45 08 56 56
Four different stores:
men, women, Lolita and
children.
◆ 347

BARBARA BUI
23, rue Étienne-Marcel
75001
Tel. 01 42 36 47 14
Collections inspired by
ethnic designs from all
over the world.

CERRUTI 1881
27, rue Royale
75008
Tel. 01 53 30 18 81
Men's clothes.
Also at:
15, pl. de la Madeleine
Tel. 01 47 42 10 78
Women's clothes.

CHANEL
29, rue Cambon
75001
Tel. 01 42 86 28 00
Haute couture and
accessories for women.
◆ 347

CHANTAL THOMASS
1, rue Vivienne
75001
Tel. 01 40 15 02 36
In a converted 18th-
century building, close
to the Bibliothèque
Nationale and the
Palais-Royal (large
salon, blue room,
vestibule, library at one
end and elegant fitting
rooms at the other).
◆ 347

CHARVET
28, pl. Vendôme
75001
Tel. 01 42 60 30 70
Shirts (ready-to-wear
and tailored), ties,
handkerchiefs.
◆ 347

CLAUDIE PIERLOT
1, rue Montmartre
75001
Tel. 01 42 21 38 38
Chic and simple, well-
cut clothing in quality
fabrics.
◆ 347

**COMME DES
GARÇONS**
40-42, rue Étienne-
Marcel
75001
Tel. 01 42 36 91 54
Clothing by Japanese
designer Rei Kawakubo.
◆ 347

**JEAN-CHARLES
DE CASTELBALJAC**
5, rue des Petits-
Champs 75001
Tel. 01 42 60 37 33
Colorful clothing with
plastic art influence.
◆ 347

JEAN-PAUL GAULTIER
6, rue Vivienne
75002
Tel. 01 42 86 05 05
Gaultier's baroque and
modern designs are
beautifully displayed in
this store covered by a
glass roof.
◆ 347

JOSEPH
44, rue Étienne-Marcel
75002
Tel. 01 42 36 87 83
Knitwear by the
celebrated English
designer Joseph.
◆ 347

**JUNKO SHIMADA
DESIGN**
54, rue Étienne Marcel
75002
Tel. 01 42 36 36 97
Women's clothing,
sportswear and
children's wear by
this Japanese
designer.
◆ 347

KENZO
3, pl. des Victoires
75001
Tel. 01 40 39 72 03
Top-quality ready-to-
wear clothing by the
Japanese designer
Kenzo. Colorful
flowered fabrics.
◆ 347

LOUIS FÉRAUD
265, rue St-Honoré
75001
Tel. 01 42 60 08 08
Menswear.

RENATA
17, rue St-Florentin
75008
Tel. 01 42 60 11 69
This French label has
been producing
designer clothing for
twenty years. A range of
women's clothing. Suits
and sweaters in silk,
cashmere and wool.
Hand-embroidered
blouses.

STÉPHANE KÉLIAN
6, pl. des Victoires
75001
Tel. 01 42 61 60 74
High-quality shoes.
Specialty: braided
leather.

THIERRY MUGLER
12, pl. des Victoires
75001
Tel. 01 42 60 06 37
Extraordinary designs.
◆ 347

**UN APRÈS-MIDI
DE CHIEN**
4, rue du Jour, 75001
Tel. 01 40 26 92 78
Trendy, stylish clothing.
◆ 347

VENTILO
27 bis, rue du Louvre
75002
Tel. 01 42 33 18 67
Boutique with a tea
room on the top floor.

VICTOIRE
12, pl. des Victoires
75001
Tel. 01 42 61 09 02
Also at: 10–12, rue du
Colonel-Driant 75001
Tel. 01 42 97 44 87
Designer-label clothing
for men and women.
◆ 347

YOHJI YAMAMOTO
47, rue Étienne-Marcel
75001
Tel. 01 45 08 82 45
and 25, rue du Louvre
Tel. 01 42 21 42 93

Ready-to-wear, simple-cut Zen-style clothing for men, made famous by Wim Wenders in his film "A Notebook on Clothes and Cities".

◆ 347

RESTAURANTS

HAUTE CUISINE

LES AMBASSADEURS
Hôtel de Crillon
Pl. de la Concorde
75008
Tel. 01 44 71 16 16
Open daily, lunchtime and evening

Business lunches at 330F during the week, evening menus from 590F. Sumptuous décor: long mirrors, polished crystal, marble floor and attractive molded ceiling.

LE CARRÉ DES FEUILLANTS
14, rue de Castiglione
75001
Tel. 01 42 86 82 82
Closed Sat. lunchtime and all day Sun.
Lunch menu from 260F.
Specialties: chestnut and pheasant bouillon, oysters with coarsely grated foie gras. Good quality food.

◆ 350

L'ESPADON
Hôtel Ritz
15, pl. Vendôme
75001
Tel. 01 43 16 30 80
Lunchtime menu: 370F, evening menu: 590F.
Delicate food and excellent wines in a sumptous setting.

LE GRAND VÉFOUR
17, rue de Beaujolais
75001
Tel. 01 42 96 56 27
Closed Sat. lunchtime and Sun.
Menus: business lunches at 305F; dinner at 750F or à la carte 700–800F.
Stunning décor in this choice setting in one of the Palais-Royal galleries; the menu was designed by Jean Cocteau. This is one of the classiest restaurants in Paris, and once numbered Napoleon, Victor Hugo and Voltaire among its patrons. These days guests include heads of state.

◆ 350

LUCAS CARTON
9, pl. de la Madeleine
75008
Tel. 01 42 65 22 90
Closed Sat. lunchtime and Sun.
Menu 375F (lunch).
Expect to pay 580–1,030F for the à la carte menu.
Famous restaurant in a listed building (Art Nouveau woodwork in maple and sycamore by Planel). Particularly recommended: duck-liver pâté with cabbage, coquilles St-Jacques (scallops), lobster with vanilla, grilled pigeon or rabbit à la royale (stuffed with foie gras and truffles).

◆ 350

MAXIM'S
3, rue Royale
75002
Tel. 01 42 65 27 94
Closed Sun.
À la carte: 800–900F.
This world-famous restaurant with its Belle Époque décor has become an institution.

Specialties: œuf de caille au caviar, noisette d'agneau Edouard VII.

LE MEURICE
Hôtel Meurice
228, rue de Rivoli
75001
Tel. 01 44 58 10 50
Set menu 320F.
À la carte: 265–370F.
Simple but refined food.

GOURMET

CHEZ GEORGES
1, rue du Mail
75002
Tel. 01 42 60 07 11
Closed Sun. and public holidays.
Menu: 200–300F. The archetypal good Parisian restaurant.

CHEZ PAULINE
5, rue Villedo
75001
Tel. 01 42 96 20 70
Closed Sat. lunchtime and Sun.
Menu from 220F.
Fashionable bistro with molded ceiling and large mirror-walls.
Offers traditional Burgundy cuisine.

CHEZ LA VIEILLE
1, rue Bailleul
75001
Tel. 01 42 60 15 78
À la carte : 250F.
Tucked away at the end of an entrance hall, this is incontestably one of the best bistros in Paris. Popular with politicians and business people.

DROUANT
18, rue Gaillon, 75002
Tel. 01 42 65 15 16
Open 7pm–midnight
Menus start at 300F but expect to pay around 500F if you are planning to try the oysters, coquilles St-Jacques (scallops) and the house desserts of this renowned restaurant.

◆ 351

LE MERCURE-GALANT
15, rue des Petits-Champs
75001
Tel. 01 42 97 53 85
Closed Sat. lunchtime and Sun.
Menus: 210F at lunchtime, 280F and 400F in the evening.
Classic French décor and cuisine.

L'OSTRÉA
4, rue Sauval
75001
Tel. 01 40 26 08 07
Closed Sat. lunchtime and Sun.
À la carte 100–150F.
Specialty: fish and seafood.

TRADITIONAL CUISINE

AU CHIEN QUI FUME
33, rue du Pont-Neuf
75001
Tel. 01 42 36 07 42
Open daily noon–2am.
Menus: 188F including drinks. Oysters, fish and traditional cuisine. Large terrace. Established 1740.

AUX CRUS DE BOURGOGNE
3, rue Bachaumont
75002
Tel. 01 42 33 48 24
Closed Sat. and Sun.
À la carte 155–285F
The atmosphere of Les Halles in surroundings that have remained unchanged since 1900. Traditional French cuisine.

L'ESCARGOT-MONTORGUEIL
38, rue Montorgueil
75001
Tel. 01 42 36 83 51
Open daily until 11pm.
Menus: 180F lunchtime, 190F and 250F evenings. This historic restaurant, with its stunning décor and the gold sign depicting a gastropod, has served snails and oysters since 1874.

LE PAVILLON BALTARD
9, rue Coquillière
75001
Tel. 01 42 36 22 00
Open daily lunchtime and evening.
Menus: 130F and 138F.

Former butcher's in les
Halles offering a wide
variety of dishes:
seafood, oysters,
sauerkraut.

PHARAMOND
24, rue de la Grande-
Truanderie 75001
Tel. 01 42 33 06 72
Closed Sun. and Mon.
lunchtime.
Menu at 250F.
This restaurant dating
from 1900 serves the
best andouillettes and
tripe in Paris. The décor
– decorative glass and
long mirrors – is typical
of the early 20th
century.

BRASSERIES

A. GUTENBERG
29, rue Coquillière
75001
Tel. 01 45 08 11 11
Closed Sun.
À la carte: 80–100F.
Art Nouveau décor
dating from 1913 using
a technique of blowing
gold dust into the glass.
Dish of the day, grills,
beers.

BRASSERIE
ÉLISÉE LOUVRE
Galerie du Carrousel
75002
Tel. 01 40 20 96 06
Closed Sun. evening
À la carte 150–200F.

LA BRASSERIE
DU LOUVRE
Pl. du Palais-Royal
75001
Tel. 01 42 96 27 98
Open daily until
11.30pm.
Menu 170F. Terrace.

CAFÉ DE L'ÉPOQUE
2, rue du Bouloi
75001
Tel. 01 42 33 40 70
Closed Sun.
À la carte 100–150F.
A fish and a meat dish
of the day, terrines,

pots-au-feu. Friendly
atmosphere.

CAFÉ RICHELIEU
Musée du Louvre,
Richelieu Wing,
2nd floor
Tel. 01 47 03 99 68
Closed Tue.
Set lunch for 69F.
Choice of sandwiches
from 23F.
◆ 324

LE GRAND COLBERT
Galerie Colbert
4, rue Vivienne 75002
Tel. 01 42 86 87 88
Open daily lunchtime
and evening.
Menu: 155F.
Brasserie with an
enormous copper bar.
Excellent food.
◆ 351

LE NEMOURS
2, galerie de Nemours
Pl. Colette
75001
Tel. 01 42 61 34 14
Open daily until 1am.
À la carte: 60–80 F.
Terrace.
◆ 352

TAVERNE DES HALLES
12, rue de la
Cossonnerie
75001
Tel. 01 42 36 26 44
Open daily 8am–2am.
Menu: 65F. À la carte:
80–100F. Eighteen
different draft beers,
moules-frites (mussels
with french fries).

LE VAUDEVILLE
29, rue Vivienne
75002
Tel. 01 40 20 04 62
Open daily until 4am.
Menus: 112F and
189F.
This brasserie,
dating from 1827,
patronized by
stockbrokers,
theatergoers
and journalists,
serves
traditional
dishes and
good seafood platters.

BISTROS

BISTROT VIVIENNE
4, rue des Petits-
Champs
75002
Tel. 01 42 60 04 60
Closed Mon. and Sat.
evenings, Sun.
Daily specials: 60–80F.

LE BRIN DE ZINC
50, rue Montorgueil
75002
Tel. 01 42 21 10 80
Dish of the day 60F,
lunchtime.
Before the relocation of
les Halles, this
renowned bistro was
called La Grille. It is a
true bistro with its
period bar and a
basement with original
decoration. Generous
portions: black pudding
and rib steak.

CHEZ PIERROT
18, rue Étienne-Marcel
75002
Tel. 01 45 08 05 48
Closed Sun.
Menu: 195F.
Quaint old bistro serving
traditional cuisine.
Dishes on offer include:
andouillette grillée, filet
d'agneau provençal.

LE PETIT MÂCHON
158, rue St-Honoré
75001
Tel. 0142 60 08 06
Closed Mon.
Menus: 150F and 180F.
Lyonnais cuisine.

LE VÉRO-DODAT
19, galerie Véro-Dodat
75001
Tel. 01 45 08 92 06
Closed Sun.
Menu: 138F.
Located at the heart of
the Véro-Dodat gallery,
good food at reasonable
prices.
◆ 351

ECONOMY

BATIFOL
12, place du Marché-
St-Honoré
75002
Tel. 01 42 60 47 21
Closed Sun.
Menu: 80F.
A Parisian chain,
serving
traditional
local food:
potée
(boiled meat
with cabbage), pot-au-
feu, tête de veau
(calves' head).

L'INCROYABLE
26, rue de Richelieu
75001
Tel. 01 42 96 24 64
Open daily to 9pm
except Sat. evening and
Sun.
Menus: 70–80F.

In an alley leading from
the Palais-Royal.
Decorated like an inn
with check tablecloths.
◆ 351

LESCURE
7, rue de Mondovi,
75001
Tel. 01 42 60 18 91
Closed Sat. pm.and Sun.
Menu: 100F.
Good-quality basic food
(haddock, bœuf
bourguignon, pâté en
croûte, chicken with
rice) in friendly
atmosphere.

LE PALET
8, rue du Beaujolais
75001
Tel. 01 42 60 99 59
Closed Sat. lunchtime
and Sun.
Menus: 80F and 98F.
Specialties include: fillet
steak St Pierre with
camembert, duck with
honey.

GARDEN, TERRACE
AND PATIO CAFÉS

CAFÉ MARLY
93, rue de Rivoli
75001
Tel. 01 49 26 06 60
À la carte: 150–300F.
Located in the Grand
Louvre. Entrance via the
arcades of the Cour
Napoléon. Magnificent
view of the Pyramide
and the Cour Marly.
Terrace open in good
weather.
◆ 324

IL CORTILE
Hôtel Castille
75001
37, rue Cambon
Tel. 01 44 58 45 67
Menu: 195F lunchtime
and evening. Opened
in 1993, this restaurant
greets customers in
an interior courtyard.
The cuisine and the
décor are both Italian
in style.

LA GAUDRIOLE

30, rue de Montpensier
75001
Tel. 01 42 97 55 49
*Menu: 160F. In the
gardens of the Palais-
Royal. This restaurant
has all the charm of a
rustic bar with tables in
the open air. There is
the added attraction of
a small theater with its
trompe l'œil drapes.
The carefully chosen
menu offers dishes
such as fresh foie gras
and bream feuillantine.*
◆ 350

PIERRE, À LA FONTAINE GAILLON

1, pl. Gaillon
75002
Tel. 01 42 65 87 04
Closed Sat. lunchtime
and Sun.
*Menu from 165F. This
former 17th-century
mansion house was
built by Hardouin-
Mansart and has been
converted into an eating
place. Attractive terrace
overlooking a small
square. Specialties :
smoked salmon,
shellfish, seafood,
pigeon terrine.*

LE PLUVINEL

Hôtel Régina
2, pl. des Pyramides
75001
Tel. 01 42 60 31 10
Closed Sun.
*Menu: 160F lunchtime.
A la carte, evening:
250–300F. A delightful
haven, with tables
surrounded by flowers.
In winter, food is served
in a paneled dining
room.*

LA TERRASSE FLEURIE

Hôtel Inter-Continental
3, rue de Castiglione
75001
Tel. 01 44 77 10 44
Closed Sat. and Sun.
*Menus: 250–450F.
Tables are set in an
interior courtyard of the
palace. The terrace is
heated and protected
by a large canopy from
October to May.*

LE TOUPARY

Magasin 2 de la
Samaritaine (5th floor)
Quai du Louvre
75001
Tel. 01 40 41 29 29
Closed Sun.

*Menus: 90F and 130F
lunchtime, 180F
evening. Brasserie and
restaurant opened in
1994 on the top floor of
La Samaritaine. Not
only does this offer
designer decoration,
guests can also enjoy a
view over Pont-Neuf.*

LATE OPENING

L'ALSACE AUX HALLES

16, rue Coquillière
75001
Tel. 01 42 36 74 24
Open all night.
*Menu: 167F.
Shellfish, seafood,
sauerkraut and grills.*

AU PIED DE COCHON

6, rue Coquillière
75001
Tel. 01 42 36 11 75
Open all night.
*Menus: 123F and 189F.
This establishment had
its golden age during
the time that les Halles
was in this area. On
offer are platters of
seafood, oysters and
the famous pigs' trotters
which gave this bar its
name.*

CAFÉ DE LA PAIX

12, bd des Capucines
75009
Tel. 01 40 07 30 20
Open daily until 1am.
*Superb Second Empire-
style décor.*

CHEZ DENISE, LA TOUR DE MONTLHÉRY

5, rue des Prouvaires
75001
Tel. 01 42 36 21 82
Open 24hrs Mon.–Fri.
*À la carte: 210–270F.
Specialties: stuffed
cabbage, calves
kidneys, meat and fish*

*served on dishes
designed by Moretti.*
◆ 351

HOLLYWOOD SAVOY

44, rue Notre-Dame-
des-Victoires
75002
Tel. 01 42 36 16 73
Closed Sat. and Sun.
lunchtime.
À la carte, 300–350F.

*French cuisine.
Restaurant with live
music – rock, country,
jazz and blues. Open
until 2am.*

LA POULE AU POT

9, rue Vauvilliers
75001
Tel. 01 42 36 32 96
Open from 7pm until
dawn, closed Mon.
*Menu from 160F. This
restaurant is a veritable
institution of les Halles,
serving chicken in every
possible form.*

BUSINESS RESTAURANTS

LE GRAND LOUVRE

Hall Napoléon,
musée du Louvre
Tel. 01 40 20 53 63
*Menu: 178F lunchtime
and evening. Expect to
pay around 250F à la
carte. Set beneath the
Pyramide. Serves foie
gras and haddock.*
◆ 324

POQUELIN

17, rue Molière
75001
Tel. 01 42 96 22 19
Closed Sat. lunchtime
and Sun.
*Menu: 189F lunchtime
and evening. Located
beneath the sign
depicting Molière.
Specialties: breast of
duck with honey and
lemon, roasted fish.*

FOREIGN CUISINE

BRASSERIE MUNICHOISE

5, rue Danielle
Casanova
75001
Tel. 01 42 61 47 16
Closed Sat. lunchtime,
Sun. and Aug.
*À la carte: 200F.
Its Bavarian-style
atmosphere, cuisine
and beers are typical of
establishments found in
the Rhine region.*

CHEZ VONG

10, rue de la Grande-
Truanderie
75001
Tel. 01 40 39 99 89
Closed Sun.
*Menu: 150F lunchtime.
À la carte, evening:
250–350F. Chinese-
Vietnamese restaurant.
Steamed and spicy
food, shellfish, poultry in
the best Asian tradition.*

LE FELLINI

147, rue de l'Arbre Sec
75001
Tel. 01 42 60 90 66
Open daily lunchtime
and evening.
*Menu: 110F.
À la carte in the
evening. Situated in a
quiet, historic street.
Serves good Italian
specialties.*

ISSÉ

56, rue Ste-Anne
75001
Tel. 01 42 96 67 76
Closed Sat. lunchtime,
Sun. and Mon.
lunchtime.
*Menus: lunch 110F and
150 F; dinner 150F and
200F. Excellent sushi
and sashimi.*

KINUGAWA

9 rue du Mont-Thabor
75001
Tel. 01 42 60 65 07
Closed Sun. and
Dec. 25–Jan. 7
*Menu: 150F lunchtime.
One of the best
Japanese restaurants in
Paris.*

LE MAROC

9, rue Danielle-
Casanova
75001
Tel. 01 42 61 38 83
Open daily lunchtime
and evening.

*À la carte: 250F and
300F.
Picturesque dining
rooms with mosaics.
and oriental lanterns.*

Le Moï
5, rue Daunou
75002
Tel. 01 47 03 92 05
Closed Sat. lunchtime
and Sun.
*Á la carte 130–200F.
Quality Vietnamese
restaurant. Specialties:
Tonkinese soup, spring
rolls, chicken saté and
coconut milk.*

Saudade
34, rue des Bourdonnais
75001
Tel. 01 42 36 03 65
Closed Sun.
*Menu: 129F lunchtime.
À la carte, evening:
190–230F. Portuguese
specialties including
cod (grilled, flaked,
baked, with garlic) and
excellent port wines.*
◆ 351

Universal Resto
Galerie du Carrousel
99, rue de Rivoli, 75001
Tel. 01 46 92 47 47
*Under 100F for lunch
(main course, dessert
and a beverage).
A group of restaurants of
different nationalities
(Italian, Mexican,
Lebanese, Asian,
French).*
◆ 324

Aux Bons Crus
7, rue des Petits-Champs
75001
Tel. 01 42 60 06 45
*The delightful décor of
this cheerful bar is very
Parisian.*
◆ 353

**Aux Tonneaux
des Halles**
28, rue Montorgueil
75001
Tel. 01 42 33 36 19
*Beaujolais and Touraine
wines.*

Le Bar de l'Entracte
47, rue de Montpensier
75001
Tel. 01 42 97 57 76

*Plates of cheese or cold
meats or the house dish
of the day served with a
glass of wine from the
Touraine (Bourgueil).*
◆ 353

**La Cloche
des Halles**
28, rue Coquillière
75001
Tel. 01 42 36 93 89
*Beaujolais, Bourgogne,
Loire and Rhône valley
wines served with a
plate of charcuterie
(45F) or cheese (50F).*

Juvénile's
47, rue de Richelieu
75001
Tel. 01 47 97 46 49
*Popular with local
residents. Depending
on the time of day, the
chef-sommelier
recommends a glass of
fino, manzanilla, oloroso
or sherry to go with the
tapas served.*

**Relais
Chablisien**
4, rue Bertin Poirée
75001
Tel. 01 45 08 53 73
*Chablis is favored here,
but not to the point of
neglecting other
varieties of French wine.
Quaint and friendly
setting.*

Le Rubis
10, rue du Marché-St-
Honoré
75001
Tel. 01 42 61 03 34
*Popular and
quintessentially Parisian
wine bar.
Traditional décor.*
◆ 353

Taverne Henri IV
13, pl. du Pont-Neuf
75001
Tel. 01 43 54 27 90
*Good wines with
charcuterie and
cheese.*

Willy's Wine Bar
13, rue des Petits-
Champs
75001
Tel. 01 42 61 05 09
*Famous venue for wine
tasting.*
◆ 353

**Tea Rooms
and Pâtisseries**

Angelina
226, rue de Rivoli
75001
Tel. 01 42 60 82 00
Open Mon.-Fri.
9.30am–7pm, Sat.–Sun.
9.30am–7.30pm
*Perfect for a delicious
cup of hot chocolate.*
◆ 350

À Priori Thé
35–37, galerie Vivienne
75002
Tel. 01 42 97 48 75
Open Mon.–Sat. noon–
6pm; Sun. 1–6pm
Tea rooms.

Cador
2, rue de l'Amiral-
de Coligny
75001
Tel. 01 45 08 19 18
Pâtisserie and tea room.

Ladurée
16, rue Royale, 75008
Tel. 01 42 60 21 79
*Tea room and
confectioners.*

La Muscade
36, rue Montpensier
75001
Tel. 01 42 97 51 36
Tea room, lunches.

Pandora
24, passage Choiseul
75002
Tel. 01 42 97 56 01
Closed Sat. and Sun.
*Brunches, light lunches,
tea room in a rococo-
style setting.*

Rose Thé
91, rue St-Honoré, 75001
Tel. 01 42 36 97 18
Closed Sun.
Tea room.
◆ 350

Pâtisserie Stohrer
51, rue Montorgueil
75002
Tel. 01 42 33 38 20
◆ 346

**Coffee and
Chocolate**

**À la Marquise
de Sévigné**
32, pl. de la Madeleine
75008
Tel. 01 42 65 19 47
Excellent chocolate.

Café Verlet
256, rue St-Honoré
75001
Tel. 01 42 60 67 39
*Coffee beans and
ground coffee from
around the world.*
◆ 350

**La Fontaine
au Chocolat**
201, rue St-Honoré
75001
Tel. 01 42 44 11 66
*High quality chocolate
in small imitation
elmwood boxes.
Specialties: flavored
chocolate and
chocolate-covered
roasted almonds.*

Godiva
237, rue St-Honoré
75001
Tel. 01 42 60 44 64
*Eighty different types
of Belgian chocolate.
Specialty: dark
chocolate praline.*

Toraya
10, rue St-Florentin
75001
Tel. 01 42 60 13 00
*Japanese confectionery,
"sasagomoro" and
"yukimachi".*

Fauchon
26, pl. de la Madeleine
75008
Tel. 01 47 42 60 11
*This delicatessen is the
perfect place for luxury
foods (fresh produce,
wines, teas,
chocolates). There is
also a brasserie, a
trattoria and a
restaurant.*

Foie Gras Import
34, rue Montmartre
75001
Tel. 01 42 33 31 32
*Foie gras of duck from
the southwest of
France.*

Hédiard
21, pl. de la Madeleine
75008
Tel. 01 42 66 26 58
*Delicatessen.
Restaurant upstairs.*

Labeyrie
6, rue Montmartre 75001
Tel. 01 45 08 95 26
*Foie gras from the
southwest of France
from about 170F per
pound.*

LEGRAND FILLES ET FILS

1, rue de la Banque
75002
Tel. 01 42 60 07 12
Delicatessen. Wines and spirits.
◆ 346

LA MAISON DE LA TRUFFE

19, pl. de la Madeleine
75008
Tel. 01 42 65 53 22
Truffles in every form.

PUBS

BOW BELL

33, bis, rue des Bourdonnais
75001
Tel. 01 45 08 55 99
A rather quaint English pub. French and foreign rock bands Sat. eve.

FLANN O'BRIEN

6, rue Bailleul
75001
Tel. 01 42 60 13 58

Irish owner. Excellent Guinness.
◆ 352

KITTY O'SHEA'S

10, rue des Capucines
75001
Tel. 01 40 15 08 08
Open daily noon–2am. Irish pub. Guinness and Smithwicks. Specialties: smoked salmon, Irish stew.

MANNEKEN PIS

4, rue Daunou, 75002
Tel. 01 47 42 85 03
Serves moules-frites until 2am. Bar until 5am. Wide range of draft beers.

QUIGLEY'S BAR

5, rue du Jour
75001
Tel. 01 45 08 17 04
Serves beer. Formerly called James Joyce Pub. Cozy.

SOUS-BOCK TAVERN

49, rue St-Honoré
75001
Tel. 01 40 26 46 61

Four hundred types of beer.

TIGH JOHNNY'S THE IRISH PUB

55, rue Montmartre
75002
Tel. 01 42 33 91 33

BARS WITH CHARACTER

HARRY'S BAR

5, rue Daunou
75002
Tel. 01 42 61 71 14
Open daily 10am–4am. Cabaret "Ivories" (piano-bar) 10pm–2am. Cocktails, aperitifs, liqueurs and spirits.
◆ 353

BAR HEMINGWAY

Hôtel Ritz
15, pl. Vendôme
75001
Tel. 01 42 60 23 71
Several portraits of writers on the walls.
◆ 353

LE RÉGINA

Bar de l'hôtel Régina
1, pl. des Pyramides
75001
Tel. 01 42 60 31 10
Cocktails – anything you care to ask for!
◆ 353

BAR ST-JAMES

6, rue du 29 juillet 75001
Tel. 01 44 58 43 21
English-style bar.

DANCE BARS

LE COMPTOIR

37, rue Berger
75001
Tel. 01 40 26 26 66
Very trendy. Terrace with a view of St Eustache church.

LILLIPUT

55, rue d'Argout
75002
Tel. 01 45 08 10 17
Soul and rock music.
◆ 352

LE PRESSING

20, rue du Louvre
75001
Tel. 01 40 20 00 14
Funk, soul, acid jazz . . .
◆ 352

LES TROTTOIRS DE BUENOS-AIRES

37, rue des Lombards
75001
Tel. 01 40 26 29 30
Dancing on Sunday from 8pm. Live tango music.

DISCOTHEQUES

LE BALISIER

47, rue Berger
75001
Tel. 01 42 33 74 26
Open 11pm until dawn. Island music.
◆ 357

BLACK AND WHITE

31 bis, rue des Lombards 75001
Tel. 01 42 21 14 92
African nights.
◆ 357

NÉO-JAPONESQUE

21, rue Montorgueil
75001
Tel. 01 42 36 87 87
Eclectic music, dance floor.

LA PLANTATION

45, rue de Montpensier
75001
Tel. 01 49 27 06 21
African discotheque.
◆ 357

RITZ CLUB

38, rue Cambon
75001
Tel. 01 42 60 38 30
◆ 357

LA SCALA

188 bis, rue de Rivoli
75001
Tel. 01 42 61 64 00
Young people's nightclub.
◆ 357

PIANO BARS

AU DUC DES LOMBARDS

42, rue des Lombards
75001
Tel. 01 42 33 22 88
Restaurant Tue.–Sat. Live music nightly at 10.30pm: jazz, latin.

BAISER SALÉ

58, rue des Lombards
75001
Tel. 01 42 33 37 71
Live jazz bands at 10pm.

LE BARAGOUIN

17, rue Tiquetonne
75002
Tel. 01 42 36 18 93
Beer, wine and spirits. Rock, pop and jazz music.

LE DIEU GAMBRINUS

62, rue des Lombards
75001
Tel. 01 42 21 10 30
Closed Sun., Mon., Tue. Rock and country music from 10pm until dawn.

LE PETIT OPPORTUN

15, rue des Lavandières Ste-Opportune
75001
Tel. 01 42 36 01 36
Jazz .

SUNSET

60, rue des Lombards
75001
Tel. 01 40 26 46 60
Jazz from 10pm each evening.

APPENDICES

◆ BIBLIOGRAPHY

◆ GENERAL READING ◆

◆ Françoise BROYELLE, Michel LACLOTTE, *The Louvre*, Réunion des Musées nationaux / Scala Books, London 1993.

◆ *Le Louvre, 7 visages d'un musée*, Réunion des Musées nationaux, Paris, 1986.

◆ Geneviève BRESC, *Mémoires du Louvre*, Découvertes Gallimard / Réunion des Musées nationaux, Gallimard, Paris, 1993.

◆ *Le Louvre, trésors du plus grand musée du monde*, Sélection du Reader's Digest, Paris, 1991.

◆ *Autour du Grand Louvre: le musée, l'art, la ville*, "*Le Débat*", n°82, Gallimard, Paris, 1994.

◆ Violaine BOUVET-LANSELLE, Marie-Thérèse Genin, *Destination Louvre, côté Denon*, Réunion des Musées nationaux, Paris, 1990.

◆ Françoise BROYELLE, Jean-Marie TROLLO, Daniel SOULIE, *Destination Louvre, côté Sully*, Réunion des Musées nationaux, Paris, 1990.

◆ Annette ROBINSON, *Le Louvre*, Scala, Paris, 1994.

◆ Jean-Pierre CUZIN and Michel LACLOTTE, *The Louvre: Paintings*, Scala Books, London, 1993.

◆ Frédéric VITOUX, *Paris vu du Louvre* A. Biro, Paris, 1993.

◆ Jean-Baptiste LEBRUN, *Réflexions sur le Muséum* Réunion des Musées nationaux, Paris, 1992.

◆ *Grand Louvre, le musée, les collections, les nouveaux espaces*, Réunion des Musées nationaux / Connaissance des Arts, special edition, 1993.

◆ *L'ouverture de l'aile Richelieu*, Bicentenaire du Louvre, Réunion des Musées nationaux, Revue du Louvre, 5/6 Dec. 1993.

◆ GUIDES ◆

◆ Pierre QUONIAM, *Louvre, La visite*, Réunion des Musées nationaux, Paris, 1993.

◆ *Louvre, Les collections*, Réunion des Musées nationaux, Paris, new edition, 1993.

◆ *Les Antiquités orientales, guide du visiteur*, Réunion des Musées nationaux, Paris, 1993.

◆ *Les Arts de l'islam, guide du visiteur*, Réunion des Musées nationaux, Paris, 1993.

◆ *Les Objets d'art. Moyen Âge et Renaissance, guide du visiteur*, Réunion des Musées nationaux, Paris, 1993.

◆ Jean GALARD, *Visiteurs du Louvre. Un florilège*, Réunion des Musées nationaux, Paris, 1993.

◆ Catherine RAGER, *Pikto-Louvre*, A. Biro, Paris, 1991.

◆ Marie-Thérèse GENIN, *Le Louvre, guide du visiteur pressé*, Réunions des Musées Nationaux, Paris, 1993.

◆ *Le Peinture française, guide du visiteur*, Réunion des Musées nationaux, Paris, 1993.

◆ *Les Peintures flamande, hollandaise et allemande, guide du visiteur*, Réunion des Musées nationaux, Paris, 1994.

◆ Jean-René GABORIT, *La Sculpture française, guide du visiteur*, Réunion des Musées nationaux, Paris, 1993.

◆ COLLECTIONS ◆

◆ Michel LACLOTTE and Jean-Pierre CUZIN, *The Louvre: European Paintings*, Réunion des Musées nationaux / Scala Books, London, 1993.

◆ *La Peinture au Louvre, 100 chefs d'oeuvre*, Réunion des Musées nationaux / Hazan, Paris, 1992.

◆ Alain MADELEINE-PERDRILLAT, *Un dimanche au Louvre* Skira, 1994.

◆ Lawrence GOWING, *Les Peintures du Louvre*, Édition de la Martinière, Paris, 1994.

◆ Stéphane LOIRE, *La Peinture au Louvre* F. Hazan, Paris, 1992.

◆ Arnauld BREJON DE LAVERGNÉE, *Ecoles flamande et hollandaise*, Réunion des Musées nationaux, Paris, 1900.

◆ Alain PASQUIER, *The Louvre: Greek, Etruscan and Roman Antiquities*, Réunion des Musées nationaux / Scala Books, London, 1991.

◆ Annie CAUBET, Marthe BERNUS-TAYLOR, *The Louvre: Near Eastern Antiquities*, Réunion des Musées nationaux / Scala Books, London, 1991.

◆ Christiane ZIEGLER, *The Louvre: Egyptian Antiquities*, Réunion des Musées nationaux / Scala Books, London, 1990.

◆ Jean René GABORIT, *The Louvre: European Sculpture*, coed. Réunion des Musées nationaux / Scala Books, London, Paris, 1994.

◆ HISTORY ◆

◆ Christiane AULANIER, *Histoire du palais et du musée du Louvre*, 10 vol., Réunion des Musées nationaux, Paris, 1948–1971.

◆ Germain BAZIN, *Souvenirs de l'exode du Louvre,*

1940–1945, Somogy, Paris, 1992.

◆ Jean-Marc LERI, Alfred FIERRO, *Le Louvre, 1180–1989*, Guide Historia-Tallendier, Paris, 1989.

◆ Claude DAUFRESNE, *Louvre et Tuileries, Architecture de papier*, Pierre Mardaga editor, Liège, 1987.

◆ ARCHITECTURE ◆

◆ Emile BIASINI, Dominique BEZOMBES, Jean LEBRAT, Jean-Michel VINCENT, *Le Grand Louvre*, Electa Moniteur, Paris, 1989.

◆ IEOH MING PEI, Emile BIASINI, *Les Grands Dessins du Louvre*, Hermann., Paris, 1989.

◆ Catherine CHAINE, Jean-Pierre VERDET, *Le Grand Louvre, Du donjon à la pyramide* Hatier, Paris, 1989.

◆ Christian DARDENNES, *Le Grand Louvre, dessins et chantier, 1991–1993*, Ser, Paris, 1993.

◆ Guy NICOT, *Au Louvre. La Cour Napoléon transfiguée*, Réunion des Musées nationaux, Paris, 1993.

◆ VIDEO ◆

◆ Richard COPANS, *Au Louvre avec les maîtres*, Réunion des Musées nationaux / Editions Montparnasse, 1993.

◆ Stan NEUMANN, *Louvre, le temps d'un musée*, Réunion des Musées nationaux / Editions Montparnasse, 1993.

◆ Alain FLEISCHER, *Louvre, le grand musée*, Réunion des Musées nationaux / Editions Montparnasse, 1993.

◆ Nicolas PHILIBERT, *La Ville Louvre*, Editions Montparnasse, 1990.

◆ Alain Jaubert, *Palettes*, various titles, Editions Montparnasse, 1989–1994.

◆ LIST OF ILLUSTRATIONS

Illustrators :
Cover and fold out: Philippe Biard, Jean-Michel Kacédan.
Maps: Dominique Duplantier.
Nature : Anne Bodin, Frédéric Bony, Jean Chevallier, François Desbordes, Claire Felloni, Gilbert Houbre, Jean-Michel Kacédan, Catherine Lachaud, Pascal Robin, John Wilkinson.
Practical information: Maurice Pommier.
Computer graphics: Service de la signalétique du Musée du Louvre.

Acknowledgements:
We would like to give special thanks to: Dominique Camus (practical information), Clio Karageorghis, Guy Nicot, Marie-Claude Parisis, Béatrice Tambafandouno, and the team of Nino and Salvo Pecora.

INDEX

Page numbers in bold refer to the Practical information section.

◆ **WORKS OF ART** ◆